ISBN 978-0-483-12068-6
PIBN 10467943

FB &c Ltd, Dalton House, 60 Windsor Avenue, London, SW19 2RR.
Company number 08720141. Registered in England and Wales.

For support please visit www.forgottenbooks.com

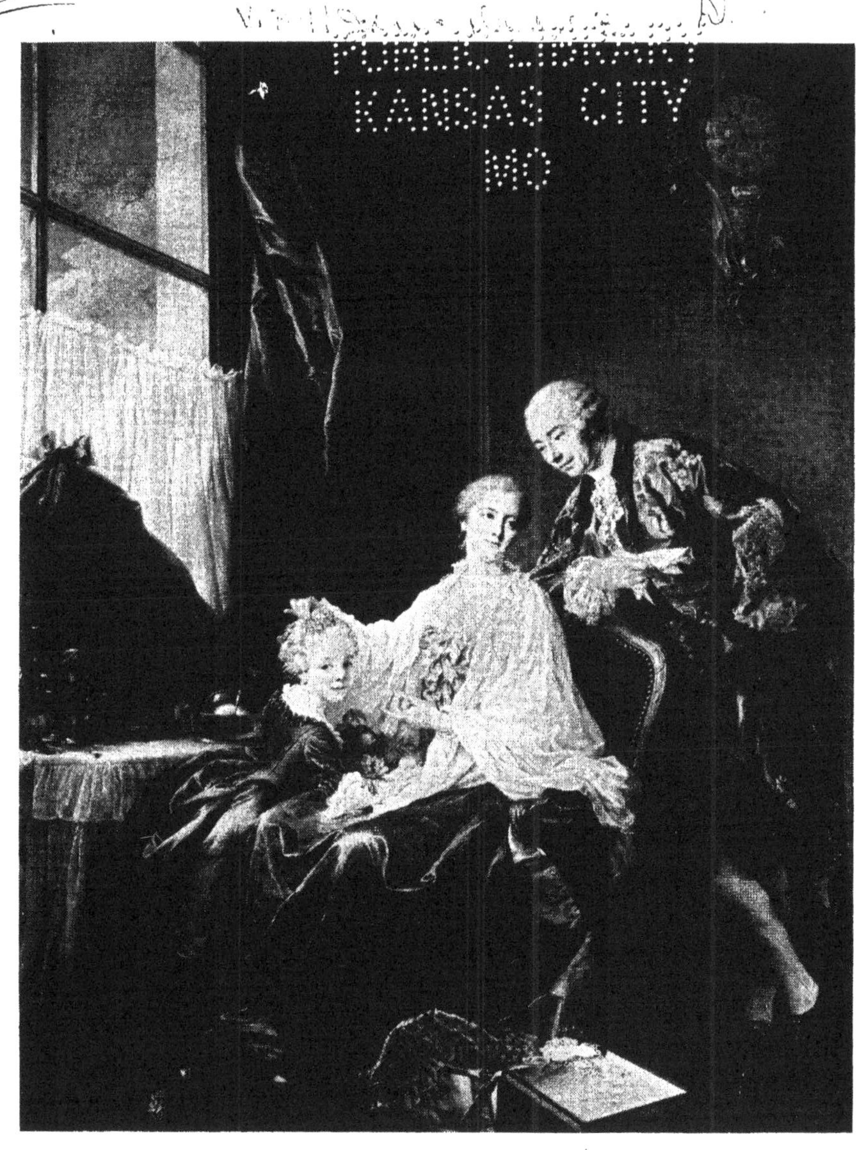

journal of SOCIAL HYGIENE

vol. 39 january 1953 no. 1

JANUARY 1953

About our cover . . .

Group portrait by Francois-Hubert Drouais. Nineteenth of a series of Journal covers on family life . . . photograph courtesy of the National Gallery of Art (Kress Collection).

Harriett Scantland, Editor
Elizabeth McQuaid, Assistant Editor

Eleanor Shenehon, Editorial Consultant

THE JOURNAL OF SOCIAL HYGIENE

official periodical of the American Social Hygiene Association, published monthly except July, August and September at the Boyd Printing Company, Inc., 374 Broadway, Albany 7, N. Y. Acceptance for mailing at the special rate of postage provided for in Section 1103, Act of October 3, 1917. Entered as second-class matter at the Post Office at Albany, N. Y., March 23, 1922.

The JOURNAL does not necessarily endorse or assume responsibility for opinions expressed in articles, nor does the reviewing of a book imply its recommendation by the American Social Hygiene Association. Subscription price: $3.00 per year. Single copy: 35¢.

Introducing ASHA's new executive director . . .

Appointment of Conrad Van Hyning as executive director of the American Social Hygiene Association was announced December 1 at a meeting of the association's board by Philip R. Mather, of Boston, president.

Mr. Van Hyning, who has had long experience in various health and welfare agencies, was formerly general director of the National Travelers Aid Association. In his new post he succeeds Dr. Walter Clarke, who retired last June after almost 40 years with the American Social Hygiene Association.

During extensive service in the welfare field Mr. Van Hyning was director of public welfare for the District of Columbia and was assistant executive director of New York State's Emergency Relief Administration and New York City's Welfare Council. He has taught public welfare and community organization courses at both City College of New York and the New York School of Social Work.

(please turn to page 48)

Formerly director of Bellevue Hospital's division of psychiatry. Now professor of psychiatry at the University of California Medical School. Medical superintendent of the Langley Porter Clinic. Consultant to the Surgeon General, U. S. Army.

Karl M. Bowman, M.D.

The Problem of Homosexuality

by Karl M. Bowman, M.D., and Bernice Engle

Since the term homosexuality has many different meanings, it is necessary to describe the various ways it is used in the literature. We speak of two types of homosexuals—the overt and the latent, each subject to further classification.

Overt homosexuals

We think of the overt homosexual as a person who carries out a sexual act with a person of the same sex.

However, as Kinsey has pointed out, we do not have two clear-cut groups with homosexuals as one distinct class and heterosexuals as another. In between the extremes of exclusively homo- or heterosexual behavior lie a number of gradations, based on the relative amounts of such experience or response in each man's history. Midway on a seven-point scale is the group whose overt sexual experience and reactions are about equally divided between homo- and heterosexual behavior. The Kinsey calculation is that four percent of white males are "exclusively homosexual throughout their lives," after the onset of puberty.

It is of some interest that Kinsey reports homosexual relations in the active male population of single, postmarital and married men to be of much lower frequency than is heterosexual intercourse in these same three groups . . . and "long-time relationships between two males are notably few."

The legal misnomer

From the legal standpoint, any person convicted of carrying out a sexual act with a person of the same sex would be convicted of homosexual activity and classified as a homosexual. Some individuals so convicted may be completely homosexual in their attitude and behavior and have no interest whatever in heterosexuality.

However, other individuals so convicted by the courts may not have really desired such a homosexual experience, may have felt disgusted at having yielded to the approaches of the other individual, may have in the past led an active heterosexual life, and may lead an exclusively heterosexual life in the future. Calling such persons homosexuals is comparable to calling a person with one-sixteenth Chinese blood and fifteen-sixteenths white blood an Oriental and not a Caucasian.

Latent homosexuals

The second group are those individuals who are called latent homosexuals—individuals who have never had overt homosexual experiences.

This group has two subgroups:

- Those who consciously desire homosexual relationships but carefully control these impulses in the same way that many persons who desire heterosexual relationships carefully control such desires. There are, for example, a great many young women with normal heterosexual drives and feelings who are virgins.
- Those who, at a conscious level, have no interest in homosexual relations and even react with disgust to such an idea. However, they do have strong homosexual drives at an unconscious level, and their behavior is often motivated by these drives which come out in some disguised fashion.

It will be seen, therefore, that when we speak of homosexuality we are not talking of simple homogeneous groups, but are describing a number of groups which in many ways differ from each other.

A social problem

Society is interested mainly in the overt homosexual who leads a fairly active homosexual life and who may be responsible for initiating others into homosexual activities. The latent homosexual is ordinarily no legal or sociological problem, although his latent homosexuality may result in all sorts of neurotic behavior which makes him a problem to the psychiatrist.

This article deals primarily with the overt homosexual and will discuss something about the incidence of overt homosexuality, its causes, its treatment and possible ways of prevention. First it will review historically the occurrence and incidence of homosexual behavior in human beings, and then will discuss studies of homosexual behavior in vertebrates and particularly in mammals.

In Greece, the Orient and Israel

Homosexual relationships have been common in many cultures at all periods. Certain societies—for example, the upper classes of classical Greece—have considered male and to some extent female homosexual relationships as ideal, superior to heterosexual unions.

Nine years old—
*mean age**
for the first
homosexual contact.

Such Oriental religions as the Hindu, Buddhist and Mohammedan have not discriminated against homosexuality.

A study of sex customs sponsored by Kinsey traces our stigma on homosexuality to the strong rise of nationalism in the Jewish tribes which after their return from Babylon banned all social customs, including sexual ones, that smacked of foreign influence. Christianity, the child of Judaism, continued these bans as she spread her influence over the western world.

Kinsey statistics

The famous Kinsey studies give much definite information—based on personal histories of more than 5,000 male interviewees—about the prevalence of homosexuality in our country.

- At least 37% of the total male population has had "some overt homosexual experience to the point of orgasm between adolescence and old age."
- Half of all men single until age 35 have had such overt experience after the onset of adolescence.
- The largest amount of overt homosexual activity occurs in men who go to high school but not beyond.
- In preadolescent histories homosexual play occurs more frequently than does heterosexual play, and the mean age for the first homosexual contact is about nine years.
- Among preadolescent boys the most common homosexual activities are exhibitionism and mutual manipulation of the genitalia.
- About a third of adult males attain orgasm at least once through another male's oral stimulation of the penis.

Kinsey finds that a high percentage of imprisoned men become involved in homosexual activity after some length of incarceration, although in short-term institutions perhaps half the men engage in no homosexual activity during their stay. In Kinsey's opinion, the fact that male juvenile offenders are often segregated for some years in correctional institutions and that boys in private boarding schools or even in day schools see mostly their own sex also affects the problem of homosexuality.

The Kinsey studies on women have not yet been published. However, partial studies by other investigators indicate that overt, active homosexuality is less frequent among girls and women than among boys and men.

Primitive societies

The homosexual factors observed in primitive man and in animals form an important background for man's homosexual activities. In *Patterns of Sexual Behavior,* Ford and Beach trace the biologic tendency for inversion of sexual behavior throughout the mammals, including human beings.

Although never the predominant sexual activity in any society or animal species, homosexuality occurs to some extent among adults of almost all cultures so far observed or studied, including those which ban it most severely. Again, it is more common among males than females in both human beings and animals, especially the primates.

In 28 of the 76 primitive societies for which Ford and Beach found first-hand data, homosexual relations were reported to be absent, rare or highly secret. All 28 societies used specific social pressures and punishments ranging from ridicule to threat of death. In the one exception—a South American tribe without sanctions on homosexuality and with extremely permissive codes regarding sexual relations—homosexuality was rare, but the major preoccupation centered about food, not sex.

In the 49 societies in which some type of homosexuality was considered normal, many tribes looked upon preadolescence as a time for experimentation in various sexual practices, heterosexual and homosexual.

Most overt homosexuals do not attend college.

In her work with seven South Seas peoples Mead noted a widespread worry that boys might not grow up to be men, without any corresponding anxiety that girls would have trouble becoming women. Mead relates this worry to the more common occurrence of homosexuality in men.

Animals

Ford and Beach's review of zoologic evidence shows the occurrence of inversion of sexual behavior in all mammals, but much more common in male than in female animals. The authors admit the difficulty of defining homosexual behavior in animals, since the expression of climax (the Kinsey criterion for human outlets) is hard to detect in animals. Homosexual-like relationships often precede sexual maturity in male monkeys and apes, but occur less frequently in maturity and accompany rather than substitute for heterosexual unions.

From their cross-cultural and cross-species comparisons Ford and Beach conclude that the cerebral cortex more and more controls sexual behavior, especially in males, as mammals go up the evolutionary scale . . . and hormonal control becomes less and less important. Females, both animals and human beings, continue to depend more on sex hormones for reaction to sexual stimuli. Both sexes have many sexual mechanisms in common. The authors conclude that tendencies leading to homosexual relations are probably less strong than are those leading to heterosexuality.

The foregoing discussion indicates that investigators into the causes of male homosexuality must tackle such problems as possible physical or hereditary abnormalities in sex organs and glands, and psychologic and social influences on the development of sexuality.

Hormones and sex

The whole subject of sex hormones and their relation to other glandular secretions is a most complex one and needs careful, extensive investigation. Considerable animal experimentation and human studies show quantitative rather than qualitative differences in hormonal balances.

For example, a male animal given large amounts of androgen (the so-called male hormone) will attempt to mate with almost any animal of proper size. Glass et al., Hoskins and Pincus, Perloff and others have investigated whether ratios between androgen and estrogen (the female

Latent homosexuals may not recognize their inclination.

hormone) differ in normal and in homosexual males. Results have been most inconclusive. Samples have been small and controls often lacking.

Kinsey has pointed out that these studies fail to take into account such known facts as the wide variations of hormonal content in urine samples from the same individual, combinations of both heterosexual and homosexual experience at every possible gradation between the two extremes, and changes at later ages from exclusively homo- or heterosexual patterns to the opposite. Biologic factors would have to correlate with the degree of heterosexual-homosexual balance in each male's history. He cites the example of two males who had indulged for respectively 15 and 17 years in almost exclusively homosexual behavior and then began at ages 30 and 28 to have frequent heterosexual relations.

Cases of hermaphroditism throw some light on the question of homosexuality. Capon, reviewing 40 previous authenticated cases, reported a patient, aged 29, with ovotestis on the right and ovary on the left, who had been reared as a male and regarded his marriage as satisfactory. Capon agrees with other writers that in most cases of true hermaphroditism the individual's libido and object of sexual desire depend on his upbringing rather than on his chemical quantification.

Physical appearance and homosexuality

Sheldon's studies of constitutional structure, continued in his survey of 200 delinquent youths, have correlated anthropometric analyses with various types of delinquency.

In homosexual males pronounced structural types were rare, nor did the youths have grossly feminine arm-leg proportions, feminine pubic hair pattern or fat distribution. Rather, what appeared were a feminine character of face, hands and skin, characteristic gestures and coordination and type of voice or facial expression. In no case could a known male homosexual be picked out from his somatotype picture.

Sheldon recommends careful studies and comparisons of non-delinquent and delinquent homosexuals.

Inherited or constitutional factors

An older theory traced the cause of overt male homosexuality to an inherited constitutional base. A few contemporary studies have investigated the incidence of homosexuality in families, especially the proportion of male to female siblings of male homosexuals, in order to show an abnormal chromosomal inheritance. Kallmann in 1947 began a carefully planned twin and sibship study of overt male adult homosexuals.

Recently Kallmann reported on the genetic aspects in a series of 85 adult male twin subjects rated by the Kinsey scale as exclusively or predominantly homosexual.

Of the 85 men, 45 were co-twins of two-egg, and 40 of one-egg, pairs. He included both siblings and offspring of the male homosexuals, to see whether in number and sex they conformed to the averages for the population, since if they did not, this might indicate some genetic factors as being present. He found no statistically significant differences.

The comparative data about the twin partners of the 85 homosexual subjects were more explicit.

The co-twins of the 45 men in the two-egg pairs had a moderately increased tendency to overt homosexuality, when compared with Kinsey ratios for the total male population.

Far more striking were the figures for the 37 co-twins available for study of the 40 men in the one-egg group. Not one could be classified as entirely heterosexual, and 33 were wholly or mainly homosexual. The majority agreed with their homosexual co-twins both in overt practice

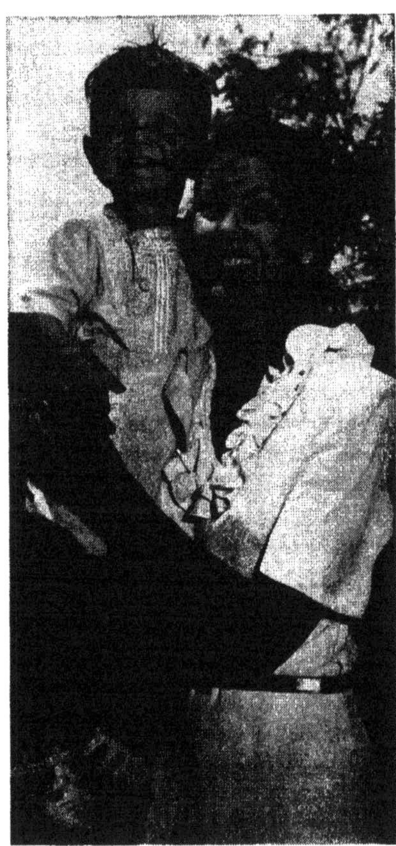

His father takes an important part in his training . . his mother offers warm care and affection.

and in degree of homosexuality, even tending to very similar sex activities and in some cases to feminized appearance and behavior. Yet many pairs claimed to have developed the sexual pattern independently and far apart from each other.

No single cause

Kallmann concludes that these data are not yet extensive enough to fully support a genetic theory of male homosexuality. They do show a multiple causation. Apparently, biologic components and factors of personality development are so closely interrelated that a variety of mechanisms at different developmental stages may disturb the individual's attainment of sexual maturity. Kallmann compares the range of causes, from a genetic standpoint, to the extent of developmental possibilities in left-handedness. He urges more basic research in the biologic components of male homosexuality, an abnormality which he has found to be the source of much unhappiness and discontent.

Its roots in childhood

Psychologic views about homosexuality are also varied. According to Fenichel, a young man has attained normal genital maturity when his object choice "becomes more or less limited to the opposite sex . . ." and he achieves full orgasm. A further psychoanalytic view which has attained fairly general acceptance is the idea that homosexuality stems from a fixation during early childhood sexual development or a regression to infantile sexuality, and is aggravated if the boy has a weak father (or none) in his upbringing.

All observers agree that overt homosexuality is less common in women, probably less intense and meets with less social disapproval than in men. Perhaps there is less censure because of the greater demonstrativeness socially allowed to women and the fact that their relations more often than men's approximate a mother-child relationship.

Observers also agree that under certain conditions normal men substitute homosexual for heterosexual relations and thus make the best of necessity. Another group seems to have little preference and depends on whichever relations are more readily available.

The masculine or feminine role

In the exclusively homosexual group, attempts have been made to classify individuals as active or passive in sexual activity. This classification is not clear-cut, since many men assume either the masculine or feminine role without much choice.

However, a small number of exclusively homosexual men regard themselves as women, adopt occupations usually held by women, try to dress

in feminine attire and often ask for castrative surgery. I have records of two such men who requested amputation of penis and testicles, construction of an artificial vagina and suitable hormonal administration. (In contrast, two women asked for hysterectomy and amputation of breasts, with endocrine therapy, in the hope that the clitoris could be elongated into a penis.) Male homosexuals of this type are colloquially called "queens," often have effeminate looks and behavior and apparently differ from the main group of homosexuals, who are like average men. This group offers an extremely interesting field for study.

It should be noted here that the large group of homosexuals contains many men of a particularly virile, masculine type, a number of whom go in for active sports and become noted athletes. Intensive study of a group of these men would also be desirable.

Treatment

The problem of treatment is one of the most thorny in medical therapies. A number of methods have been reported, only to be discarded later as ineffective.

- Glass and coworkers found uneven results in hormonal therapy of male homosexuals.
- Lurie reported benefit in four boys treated by androgen therapy.
- In Perloff's cases, administration of androgen increased sexual activity or working capacity of homosexual men without changing at all their choice of sexual object.
- Freed also reported failure of androgen therapy in male homosexuality.
- Owensby claimed success in freeing psychosexual energy by metrazol convulsions in six cases, but these results have not been confirmed.
- Thompson later reported failure with electroconvulsive shock therapy in six cases of homosexuality.

Castration here and abroad

Surgical methods have also been applied to treatment of homosexuality. Several European countries, notably Denmark, have used castration as therapy for sexual criminals, including homosexuals who attacked young males. According to reports, the rather extensive experience in countries like Denmark, other Scandinavian countries, Switzerland and Holland has resulted in fairly strong though not uncritical support. Danish therapists have found a distinct reduction of desire, so that castrates have been able to avoid further sexual crimes.

One or two reports in this country advocate the treatment, but the medical attitude is, in general, adverse. However, there has been no really serious investigation here of the actual results of castration nor of its therapeutic aspects. Therapeutic castration therefore seems to be a valid subject for research, under carefully controlled scientific study.

A very few reports have concerned use of lobotomy in cases of sexual psychopathy. In one case lobotomy apparently relieved the increasing homosexual drive in a man of 52 who had been sexually involved with two small boys . . . but later investigation showed that the operation had not actually improved the fundamental sexual abnormality.

A long-term study of the effects of lobotomy upon various sexual activities is in progress, but results have not yet been reported.

Psychiatric treatment

Reports on individual and group psychotherapy of homosexuals in cases followed for considerable periods are discouraging. Many psychiatrists state that treatment does not influence the homosexuality but may help in the patient's better adjustment. This opinion was expressed by the founder of psychoanalysis in his letter to an American mother. Freud declared that homosexuality is "nothing to be ashamed of, no vice, no degradation," and it is a "great injustice to persecute (it) as a crime and cruelty too."

Although cure is usually no longer possible, analytic treatment may perhaps bring harmony, peace of mind and full efficiency to the unhappy neurotic patient . . . and sometimes it succeeds in "developing the blighted germs of heterosexual tendencies" present in every homosexual.

Recently a patient of 30 applied for treatment in order to make a heterosexual adjustment and to be at ease with people. He had suffered in puberty a double tragedy of which his family never spoke. At 13 his twin sister died of an abortion procured because she was pregnant by him, and his favorite older married sister became ill while caring for her and also died suddenly. When he later resumed sexual intercourse he noted intense anxiety and thereupon began homosexual relations.

In the five years prior to applying for treatment he had been gravely dissatisfied with his poor work adjustment and with several homosexual relationships. Treatment of more than a year resulted in some improvement in his work and social adjustments. There was a decrease in amount of homosexual activity and an increased interest in young women, although no overt heterosexual activity occurred.

The patient believed that he would eventually be able to marry. However, he recognized that many problems still prevented his making an even halfway normal adjustment. This case illustrates one of the many complex aspects of homosexuality.

Active homosexuality has less attraction for women.

Conflict

In April of 1950 Anna Freud presented at a New York meeting four dissimilar cases of manifest male homosexuality~~, which~~ have been briefly reported. An active conflict in these patients between their masculine and feminine tendencies had prevented full identification with their father. Miss Freud found that when the patients appreciated this conflict between desires for both active and passive roles, when they became aware of their unconscious fantasy about their changing role in the homosexual relationship, they understood their problem and could discuss it. The full resolution of these conflicts and accompanying fantasies resulted in the patients' achieving sexual normality.

These cases should be reported in much fuller detail and followed carefully over a long period before valid conclusions can be drawn.

University students

B. H. Glover states that cases of homosexuality and other socially offending sex problems seen in a university department of student health have increased since the war. Using direct psychotherapy, he enlisted each patient's cooperation in a complete program of reconditioning and reeducation. With the aim of modifying their whole ecology, Glover urged the patients to drop as fast as possible all suspect marks of homosexuality and all homosexual connections, and to form new interests and activities.

He hoped that the patients would gradually learn to develop masculine mannerisms and interests, and thereby gain confidence. He warned them to consider treatment a lifelong self-help project, without guarantee of success. After a year only one of 12 patients had significantly improved.

Laws

Throughout history society has imposed legal penalties for sexual conduct regarded as harmful to individuals and the group. Laws regarding homosexuality vary even more than do medical and anthropologic views.

In 46 states statutes specify sodomy (defined usually according to common law as sexual intercourse per anum between two males) as illegal, and in the other two states (New Hampshire and Vermont) more general laws cover the subject of sodomy. Four states prohibit sexual intercourse per os or per anum between man and man, man and woman, or human being and animal or corpse.

The California law (Penal Code, Title 9, Chapter 5, 286–287) penalizes by not less than one year's imprisonment "every person who is guilty of the infamous crime against nature, committed with mankind or with any animal," and the slightest penetration is enough "to complete the crime against nature."

Ploscowe points out that despite the legal coverage arrests and prosecutions for sodomy between adults are rare. For example, arrests in New York City for the 10-year period from 1930 to 1939 averaged 140 a year, and the majority involved juveniles and adolescents. In Ploscowe's opinion the Kinsey studies rightly question the value of statutes regarding sodomy and emphasize the reasonableness of limiting those provisions to protection of children and adolescents.

Any causal connection between homosexuality and criminality is not at all clear. Homosexuals as a group are unhappy and discontented, but most of them control their social conduct within the same legal bounds as do others.

In California

Recently the California legislature appropriated money for beginning long-time research on the problem of sex behavior and for working out better ways to deal with the problem of sex offenses. Under terms of the law the State Department of Mental Hygiene, acting through the medical superintendent of Langley Porter Clinic, plans and conducts scientific research into the "causes and cures of sexual deviation, including deviations conducive to sex crimes against children, and the causes and cures of homosexuality, and into methods of identifying potential sex offenders."

Thus it is apparent that California legislators are troubled mainly about sex crimes against young children and sex crimes of violence, although homosexuality is also a matter of concern.

A community survey of one California county has been made, with surveys planned for other representative counties, as to what practices govern detection, prosecution, conviction and punishment or rehabilitation of sex offenders, including homosexuals. Many experienced psychiatrists believe that homosexuality is no offense unless young children or violence or public indecencies are involved. Implementation of this belief would mean the changing of certain laws about the culpability of adult homosexuals and their acts.

Also being carried out in the California project are biochemical and endocrine studies of certain steroid sex hormones and antienzymes in the urine and blood of homosexuals committed to two state hospitals near Los Angeles. This piece of research aims to determine possible endocrine or other biochemical imbalances in these patients and any correlation with emotional and mental factors. So far the investigation has succeeded in refining methods and more accurate measurements, and it is hoped that conclusive evidence may soon result.

A plan to compare an adequate number of homosexuals with a control group in all phases of diagnosis and treatment has been outlined. Collection of such data and their analysis would require at least a three-year study, but would provide useful facts applying to a large number of homosexuals.

What about prevention?

The problem of prevention has not been too well explored and doubtless awaits more valid evidence of the causes of homosexuality and of successful treatments. At the present state of knowledge there seems to be no genetic approach which can be advocated. While Kallmann's studies of heredity are suggestive, we are not justified in advocating mass sterilization of homosexuals as a solution to this problem.

Some observers argue that social factors and cultural attitudes in this country oppose the extension of heterosexuality and thus indirectly encourage the formation of homosexual ties. Parents and educators are always afraid that boys and girls will get into trouble if they see too much of each other or indulge in heavy petting. Many young people have limited opportunities to make contacts with the opposite sex.

Kinsey has stated that the individual's sexual pattern depends in part upon the circumstances of his early history and his conditioning to various sexual experiences. His data indicate that long-time institutionalization of male adolescents, whether correctional or educational, tends to induce a homosexual pattern.

Father plus mother

This means that methods of child-rearing, the question of coeducational training and cultural attitudes toward early heterosexual activities should be scrutinized carefully, if homosexual patterns are to be avoided.

Knowledge of psychosexual development suggests that the father should take an important part in training the boy and restraining his instinctual

---

Former instructor in the department of classics, University of Kansas. Now research assistant in sexual deviation at the Langley Porter Clinic, San Francisco. Co-author of psychiatric articles and books, including Psychiatry in World War II.

Bernice Engle

Mother and father, too, for good sexual adjustment.

drives, while the mother should offer warm care and affection. The boy thus has a man to identify with and a beloved mother-figure to possess as an ideal.

Boys and girls should have many opportunities to mix with each other and to form early attachments, but sexual interests should not be stimulated until adolescence has begun.

Taboos

Society at the present time does not seem prepared to relax its prohibitions on extramarital heterosexual intimacies. The influence of most religious organizations would be against any such modification of conventions regarding sex behavior. The fear of pregnancy (since no completely effective contraceptive device exists at the present time) further influences sexual behavior and indirectly favors discreet homosexual relationships.

American sex laws also reflect the present social attitude toward heterosexuality outside marriage and toward known homosexual relations. Many written codes heavily penalize premarital or extramarital intercourse and homosexual experiences. Whether society is ready to modify current sex laws in order to make them closer to actual practices among the different groups is not clear at this time.

References

1. Kinsey, Alfred C., Pomeroy, W. B. and Martin, C. E. Sexual Behavior in the Human Male. Philadelphia, W. B. Saunders Co., 1948.
2. Ford, Clellan S. and Beach, Frank A. Patterns of Sexual Behavior. New York, Harper and Brothers, 1951.
3. Mead, Margaret. Male and Female. New York, William Morrow, 1949.
4. Glass, S. J. and Johnson, R. H. Limitations and complications of organotherapy in male homosexuality. Journal of Clinical Endocrinology. 4:540–44 (Nov.) 1944.
5. Hoskins, R. G. and Pincus, G. Sex-hormone relationships in schizophrenic men. Psychosomatic Medicine. 11:102–12 (Mar.) 1949.
6. Perloff, W. H. Role of the hormones in human sexuality. Psychosomatic Medicine. 11:133–39 (May) 1949.
7. Kinsey, Alfred C. Homosexuality. Criteria for a hormonal explanation of the homosexual. Journal of Clinical Endocrinology. 1:424–28 (May) 1941.
8. Capon, A. W. A case of true hermaphroditism. Lancet. 1:563–65 (Mar. 10) 1951.
9. Sheldon, W. H. Varieties of Delinquent Youth. New York, Harper and Brothers, 1949.
10. Kallmann, Franz. Comparative twin study on the genetic aspects of male homosexuality. Journal of Nervous and Mental Disease. 115:283–98 (Apr.) 1952.
11. Fenichel, Otto. The Psychoanalytic Theory of Neurosis. New York, Norton, 1945.
12. Lurie, L. A. The endocrine factor in homosexuality. American Journal of Medical Sciences. 208:176–86 (Aug.) 1941.
13. Freed, S. C. Estrogens and androgens. American Journal of Medical Sciences. 205: 735–47 (May) 1943.
14. Owensby, N. M. Homosexuality and lesbianism treated with metrazol. Journal of Nervous and Mental Disease. 92:65–66 (July) 1940.
15. Thompson, George N. Electroshock and other therapeutic considerations in sexual psychopathy. Journal of Nervous and Mental Disease. 109:531–39 (June) 1949.
16. Tappan, Paul. Treatment of the sex offender in Denmark. American Journal of Psychiatry. 108:241–49 (Oct.) 1951.
17. A letter from Freud. American Journal of Psychiatry. 107:786–87 (Apr.) 1951.
18. Waldhorn, H. W. Clinical observations on the treatment of manifest male homosexuality. Psychoanalytic Quarterly. 20:337–38 (Apr.) 1951.
19. Glover, Benjamin H. Observations on homosexuality among university students. Journal of Nervous and Mental Disease. 113:377–87 (May) 1951.
20. Bensing, R. C. A comparative study of American sex statutes. Journal of Criminal Law and Criminology. 42:57–72 (May) 1951.
21. Ploscowe, Morris. Sex and the Law. New York, Prentice-Hall, 1951.
22. Sex Deviation Research, March 1952. Sacramento Assembly, State of California.
23. Bowman, Claude C. Social factors opposed to the extension of heterosexuality. American Journal of Psychiatry. 106:441–47 (Dec.) 1949.

CREDITS

Photo courtesy Australian News and Information Bureau, pp. 8, 15.

Scriptural, sexual, spiritual

Sex in the Old Testament

by Rabbi Stanley R. Brav

Religion, any schoolchild will assert, is what you find in the Bible. Holy Writ is essentially the textbook of faith. Many know the Bible is this . . . plus.

But the suggestion that it is one of man's oldest primers of sex behavior almost smacks of blasphemy . . . until one realizes how rare is such a primer in world literature and how eminently qualified is the Book of Books to play such a role. Particularly is this true of the Hebrew Scriptures or Old Testament, sacred alike to Jews, Christians and Mohammedans by the hundreds of millions. Can the juxtaposition of the sexual and the spiritual in mankind's most hallowed pages be an accident, something of chance or "happenstance"?

It is instructive to survey the range of Biblical treatment of sexual behavior, quite aside from general references to family relationships and such tangential data as the genealogical "begats." There is the brilliantly-limned illustrative narrative, the specific legislative injunction, the didactic moral counsel and the colorful, erotic poetry. Each serves its own function, multiple and diverse yet transparently of a particular pattern.

No one chapter or book is devoted to the subject. It is staggered throughout and interwoven with many others, as in life generally. Nor is there overbalance. Sex is obviously important, yet never is it made to appear preeminent or central among life's values. It is given its place, its due place, never more . . . but never less!

No "birds, bees and flowers" approach sullies Scriptural directness with artificial circumlocution. Characteristically, "Adam knew Eve his woman and she conceived and bore Cain . . . and again his brother Abel" (Genesis 4:1, 2). The niceness of "knowing" to describe intercourse is self-evident. Is is only equaled in its common Biblical synonym, so well instanced when the mythical "sons of God came in unto the daughters of men and they bore (giants in the earth in those days)" (Genesis 6:4).

Yet again we can read, without verbal camouflage, "My well-beloved . . . shall lie all night betwixt my breasts" (Song of Solomon 1:13).

They censored the Bible

There is a recognition of facts here and a candor that matches the naturalness of saying, "They shall be one flesh. And they were both naked, the man and his woman, and were not ashamed." One blushes for the prudery of yesteryear that bowdlerized such passages. *Honi soit qui mal y pense.* "The imagination of man's heart" may be "evil from his youth," but nonetheless "seedtime and harvest, cold and heat, summer and winter, and day and night" need not cease therefore (Genesis 8:21, 22).

There is no denying that even to heavenly creatures the daughters of men can appear more than passing fair (Genesis 6:2). Abram feared for his life because of Sarai's beauty, and he did not hesitate to tell her (Genesis 12:11). Very lovely, indeed, the Egyptians found her (Genesis 12:14).

The candor of Solomon

Other women, including Rebekah (Genesis 24:16; 26:7), Rachel (Genesis 29:17), Esther (2:7), and Bathsheba (II Samuel 11:2) are similarly described. In fact, Rachel—and later Esther—were not only well-favored but "beautifully formed." And there can be no question as to the pulchritude of the Shulamite, or whatever damsel is envisioned in the Song of Songs:

> "How beautiful are thy sandaled feet, O princess!
> . . . Thy thighs like jewels, set by the skilled craftsman;
> Thy navel like a round goblet. . . .
> Thy belly a heap of wheat set about with lilies;
> Thy two breasts like twin roes. . . .
> Thy neck . . . of ivory, thine eyes as pools of water. . . .
> How fair and pleasant art thou, O love, for delights!
> Straight as a palm, breasts as clusters of grapes."
> (Song of Solomon 7:1–8)

Reticence and excessive delicacy would seem to be later products than Holy Writ. Which is not to suggest that standards of sexual morality are less than sharply defined. Somewhere—early—a man's woman became his wife, and two or more types of marriage are delineated, as well as concubinage and other domestic relationships. One might desire more specific reference to wedding ceremonies proper, but one can find reference to cognate customs and practices. That polygamy does not pay seems to be one of the minor but undeniable verities of Scripture.

The norm is established in Proverbs (18:22), "Whoso findeth a wife findeth a good thing, and obtaineth favor of the Lord." But it had

A wife is a good thing.

better not be an odious shrew (Proverbs 30:23). It had better be someone approximating the priceless woman of virtue whose works praise her in the gates (Proverbs 31:10–31).

Deviations from the norm are more in point here.

And harlots there were

The wayward woman, in a Book given us by men, comes in for particularly scathing denunciation. It is not enough to legislate, "Thou shalt not commit adultery" (Exodus 20:14; Leviticus 18:20; 20:10, Deuteronomy 5:18; 22:22, etc.)—even in quadruplicate—making it altogether clear that the male is equally obligated. It is not enough to devise a bitter-water ordeal for the wife suspected of adultery (Numbers 5:11f). We have to be informed that "an adulterous woman . . . eateth, and wipeth her mouth, and saith, I have done no wickedness" (Proverbs 30:20). She is on the hunt for precious life itself (Proverbs 6:26).

She may be "attired as a prostitute, and subtle of heart . . . loud and stubborn, lying in wait at any street-corner, to catch and kiss a man, and to importune him with impudent face: 'I have been looking all over for you and I have found you; I have decked my bed with tapestry coverings and fine linen . . . I have perfumed it with myrrh, aloes and cinnamon. Come, let us take our fill of love until the morning; let us comfort ourselves with amorous adventure. For my husband is not at home, he is off on a long journey . . .'" (Proverbs 7:10f).

In adultery—dishonor

The youngster, "void of understanding," who is caused by her to yield, who is forced by the flattery of her lips, "goeth after her straightway as an ox goeth to the slaughter . . . till a dart strike through his liver; as a bird hasteth to the snare, knowing not that it is his very life he is surrendering . . . for she hath cast down many wounded: yea, many strong men have been slain by her" (Proverbs 7:21–23, 26).

It stands to reason: "By means of a whorish woman one is reduced to a crust of bread. . . . Can a man take fire in his bosom, and his clothes not be burned? Can one walk on hot coals and his feet not be charred? So he that goeth in to his neighbor's wife; whosoever toucheth her shall not be innocent. Men do not despise a thief, if he steal to satisfy his soul when he is hungry. . . . But whoso committeth adultery with a woman lacketh understanding; he destroyeth his own soul. A wound and dishonor shall he get; and his reproach shall not be wiped away. . . ." (Proverbs 6:25f).

Pharaoh had to guard lest he be adulterous unawares (Genesis 12:11f), and Abimelech, also, on an occasion or two (Genesis 20:1f and 26:6f). David's paramount sin—for which he suffered painful punishment—was adultery with Bathsheba (II Samuel 11:2–5).

Potiphar schemes in vain

To be sure, there is a way of dealing with the scheming adulteress—even at a risk. Potiphar's wife "cast her eyes upon Joseph and said, 'Lie with me,' but he refused, and said, 'My master has trusted me utterly with everything that is his . . . how then can I do this great wickedness, and sin against God?' And it came to pass that though she spoke to Joseph day after day, he paid her no heed to lie with her nor to be with her. And shortly thereafter, when they were in the house, and none others were within, that she caught him by his garment, saying, 'Lie with me,' and he left his garment in her hand, and fled . . . (Genesis 39:7–12).

"Give not thy strength to women" (Proverbs 31:3) is a general counsel, so vividly personalized in the stories (Judges 14; 15; 16) of Samson, blind in this respect long before the Philistines gouged out his eyes. But it would seem to refer particularly to the prohibition of promiscuity among the unmarried, no less than to philandering among the married.

Unmistakable is the contrast between marital felicity as early as possible, and dealings with strange women:

> "Drink waters out of thine own cistern,
> And running waters out of thine own well . . .
> Let them be only thine own and not strangers' with thee . . .
> Rejoice with the wife of thy youth.
> Let her be as the loving hind and pleasant roe;
> Let her breasts satisfy thee at all times;
> And be thou ravished always with her love.
> And why wilt thou . . . embrace the bosom of a stranger?"
> (Proverbs 5:15, 17–20)

As bitter as wormwood—her end

"The lips of a strange woman drop honey and her mouth seems smoother than oil, but her end is bitter as wormwood, sharp as a two-edged sword. Her feet go down to death, her steps take hold on hell. . . . Remove thy way from her, and approach not nigh the door of her house, lest thou give thine honor unto others . . . lest strangers be filled with thy wealth . . . and thou mourn at last, when thy flesh and thy body are consumed" (Proverbs 5:3–11).

The way of a man with a maid.

Yes, the foolish, predatory woman of vice is not far afield. "She is sitting at the door of her house—often in the 'best places'—clamoring for custom: 'If you are stupid and ignorant, come in,' she says. 'Stolen waters are sweet, and bread eaten in secret is pleasant.' But he knoweth not that the dead are there, and that her guests are in the depths of the netherworld" (Proverbs 9:13–18).

Violation of virgins

The Law proclaimed that a man discovered to have raped an unbetrothed virgin is required to bear full responsibility for her future (Exodus 22:16, 17; Deuteronomy 22:28, 29). Parents are sternly forbidden to make prostitutes of their daughters "lest the land fall to whoredom and . . . be full of wickedness" (Leviticus 19:29).

Judah was ready to burn Tamar for her harlotry until, realizing his own unwitting incest and his neglect to provide for his daughter-in-law's future, he was compelled to confess, "She hath been more righteous than I" (Genesis 38:6f).

Simeon and Levi refused to accept the good faith of Shechem, after he had "taken Dinah, and lain with her, and defiled her." His offer of marriage was met with ugly revenge. When Father Jacob protested his sons' wholesale violence, they justified themselves, "Should he deal with our sister as with a harlot?" (Genesis 34:1–31).

No less dramatic is the imbroglio of David's children. Amnon plots a liaison with his half-sister, Tamar. She begs for mercy, " 'Nay, my brother, do not force me; for no such thing ought to be done in Israel: do not thou this folly! And I, whither shall I carry my shame? And as for thee, thou shalt be one of the fools in Israel. Now, therefore, I pray thee, speak unto the king; for he will not withhold me from thee.' Howbeit he would not hearken unto her voice; but being stronger than she, forced her, and lay with her" (II Samuel 13:12–14). Absalom, Tamar's true brother, shortly disposed of his sister's seducer.

Ph.D., Webster University.
Graduate of Hebrew Union College.
Former chairman, religious section,
National Council on Family Relations.
Author, father of four children.
Rabbi of Rockdale Avenue Temple, Cincinnati.

Rabbi Stanley R. Brav

All this is strong brew. But it is not out of proportion in a society that condemned to death the adulterer and the adulteress, the homosexual and the sodomite . . . that defined incest meticulously (Leviticus 18:20; cf. Deuteronomy 27:20–23; Genesis 38:8f) . . . that sought to provide the childless widow with a new husband (Deuteronomy 25: 5f, cf Ruth) . . . that gave the groom the right to expect virginity in his bride, yet protected the newly-married from slander and the betrothed from attack (Deuteronomy 22:13–21, 23–28). Divorce was both permitted and restricted (Deuteronomy 24:1–4; 22:19, 29), and something resembling sexual hygiene was rather specifically prescribed (Leviticus 15:16f).

Sexual extremes

Primitive passions were not confined to prehistoric legend. Euphemism veils the sin of Ham (Genesis 9:22; cf. Leviticus 18:7, etc.) that merits a father's curse, and the pagan denizens of Sodom (Genesis 19:1f) only make their infamous threats. But history reveals the ravages of sexual brutality in a corner of Israel itself, bringing about bitter internecine warfare and resulting in the decimation of the guilty Benjamites (Judges 19–21).

Sex ethics men had to learn the hard way, on the road up from the primeval jungle. The twentieth century has no monopoly on human bestiality.

From shadow into light

So much that is negative—the "abomination before the Lord"—is only the dark and deep shadow that throws into high relief the essential rightness of sexual morality loftily conceived . . . the tenderness that finds passing wonderful "the way of a man with a maid," (Proverbs 31:19) . . . and the infinite beauty of "love strong as death . . . which many waters cannot quench, nor floods drown" (Song of Solomon 8:6–7).

At the summit of sublimity is Hosea (3:1), "Then said the Lord unto me, 'Go yet, love a woman dear to her paramour, even an adulteress, even as the love of the Lord . . .' " and "I will betroth thee unto me for ever; yea, I will betroth thee unto me in righteousness, and in justice, and in loving kindness and in mercy. I will betroth thee unto me in faithfulness: and thou shalt truly know the Lord" (Hosea 2:19).

Not far removed from these heights is the more earthy "I will go up to the palm tree, I will take hold of the boughs thereof . . . I am my beloved and my beloved is mine" (Song of Solomon 7:8, 10).

The sexual is not to be ignored, neither is it to be repressed nor even sublimated, Sacred Scripture seems to tell us. It is to be accepted as a divine blessing, to be refined and disciplined and consecrated. It is to be made spiritual . . . to the greater glory of a loving Creator.

(Most of the translations are from the King James version, with occasional free rendering by the author.)

COLLIER'S

"What I don't like about boys is, they're so darn necessary!"

WILLIAM VON RIEGEN

Marriage and the law

Medico-legal requirements in Massachusetts

by Nicholas J. Fiumara, M.D., and Arthur J. Hassett

One of a man's fundamental rights is his right to marry. This right is based on the natural law. To achieve the ends of marriage (*proles et fides*), nature has imposed certain conditions under which a marriage may take place . . . physical maturity, capacity to give consent, etc. While the right to marry is inherent in the individual, the exercise of that right demands that he be willing and able to assume marital duties and responsibilities.

Marriage is also a social institution. The state, representing society, is an interested third party to every marriage. It has the right and obligation to regulate the conditions of marriage so far as these clearly concern the interests of society . . . for example, to require the marriage license and waiting period. It determines the rights and duties of a husband and wife so far as these rights have social consequences, especially those concerning the care of their children or the economic position of the members of the family . . . for instance, their position as heirs.

Consequently, a good part of the law relates to the problems of marriage and to the reciprocal rights, obligations and duties of each member of the family.

Here we're concerned with marriage as a social institution, with our states' medical and legal requirements for marriage. Our aim: to supply the answers to questions asked of busy physicians by patients planning to be married. We selected the questions from the letters and telephone inquiries of physicians to the Division of Venereal Diseases.

First, it might be well to clarify a few fundamental concepts. Under Massachusetts law, one files a notice of intention of marriage. After a waiting period, one receives a certificate of notice of intention of marriage. This certificate—when properly signed following the marriage ceremony—becomes a marriage certificate. The certificate of notice of intention of marriage is commonly known as the marriage license—though not legally so designated.

Age

To obtain a marriage license without parental consent, a male must be 21 years old and a female 18 (General Laws, Chapter 207, Section 33). These ages are commonly referred to as the legal age for marriage.

America's maze of premarital laws confuses couples trying to get married, frustrates public health people trying to control syphilis. To focus attention on the need for greater uniformity, the Journal features Massachusetts' premarital medico-legal requirements, invites VD control officers of other states to discuss the problem.

Males not less than 18 but not yet 21 and females not less than 16 but not yet 18 may obtain a marriage license provided the clerk or registrar has received in writing the consent of the father or guardian of each of the minors (General Laws, Chapter 207, Section 33) and provided also that they furnish documentary proof of age (General Laws, Chapter 207, Section 33A).

If the marriage clerk or registrar has reason to believe that the applicants are below the legal age for marriage, he must receive documentary proof of age before issuing the marriage license (General Laws, Chapter 207, Section 33A).

A license may be granted to a boy under 18 or a girl under 16 only after a hearing and order by the probate court for the county or the district court in the judicial district where the minor lives, provided both parents or guardians of the minors have given their consent to the court (General Laws, Chapter 207, Section 25).

Application for marriage license

The details of applying for and obtaining a marriage license vary depending on whether . . .

- Both applicants live in Massachusetts
- Both live in the same city or in different cities of the state
- One of them is a member of the Armed Forces
- One or both are residents of another state
- The couple plan to marry in Massachusetts or outside the state.

Marriage in Massachusetts

Both Massachusetts residents

- If both candidates reside in the same city or town they may apply for the marriage license at the office of the clerk or registrar of their city or town. Both must apply in person. They may apply together or singly, but both must file their intentions to marry.

• If the candidates reside in a different city or town each must file a marriage intention with the clerk or registrar of his or her residence.

• If one or both candidates are members of the Armed Forces, only one needs to appear and file marriage intentions for both, provided one lives in Massachusetts. If both reside in the same city or town, the marriage intention is filed at the office of the city or town clerk or registrar. If they come from different communities, the person making the application files intentions in both places.

One a Massachusetts resident

• The Massachusetts resident may file marriage intentions for both in his city or town. This applies both to civilians and members of the Armed Forces.

Both non-residents

• Both must appear and file intentions at the clerk's or registrar's office of the city or town where the marriage is to take place.

Out-of-state marriage

Rules vary from state to state and depend on whether or not one of the partners is a member of the Armed Forces. The general requirement is that both candidates appear and file intentions at the city or town of the state where the marriage is to take place. They will be wise to take along documentary proof of identity and age . . . birth certificate, auto license, etc. If a couple plans to be married in another state, they do not apply for a license in Massachusetts.

Applications of divorced persons in Massachusetts

• If one or both applicants have been divorced, the divorced person must file with the clerk or registrar a certificate or certified copy of the divorce record obtained from the clerk or corresponding official of the court which granted the divorce. This certificate must contain the title and location of the court, the names of the parties to the divorce proceedings, the name of the party who obtained the divorce, the cause of divorce, and the date the decree became absolute (General Laws, Chapter 207, Section 21).

• If there has been more than one divorce, a certificate for every divorce must be filed with the marriage intention. A person from whom a divorce has been granted who files a notice of intention to marry within two years after the divorce decree becomes absolute must—if his divorced partner has died—also file with the marriage intention a certified copy of the death certificate (General Laws, Chapter 207, Section 21).

• If for any reason the person making the marriage application cannot obtain a certificate of the facts relating to his divorce, he may state under oath—before a probate judge in the county where the marriage intention is to be filed—the facts required in a certificate and explain why he could not get this certificate. If the applicant can satisfy the judge that he is telling the truth, the judge can issue a certificate with the necessary facts, and this may be filed with the notice of intention to marry.

When to apply—the waiting period

Since there is a five-day waiting period (counting Saturdays, Sundays and holidays) between application for and issuance of the license, and since city and town clerk's offices are generally closed Saturdays, Sundays and holidays, applicants are advised to apply early. The license is valid for 60 days from the date one has filed intentions. If a person does not marry within this period, he must return the license to the clerk or registrar who issued it (General Laws, Chapter 207, Section 28).

Waiver of waiting period

The five-day waiting period between the application and issuance of the license may be dispensed with for good and sufficient reasons. Waivers may be obtained under these conditions (General Laws, Chapter 207, Section 30, as amended):

Judicial process

When a prospective couple feels it expedient and necessary to have the marriage take place before the five days required by law from the date of their application, they may petition for a waiver of the waiting period from a judge of a probate court, a justice of a district court, a special judge of probate and insolvency or a special justice of a district court.

After hearing the evidence, the judge may grant a certificate stating that in his opinion the intended marriage should be solemnized without delay. On receipt of this waiver the clerk or registrar will issue at once the certificate of notice of intention to marry.

If both applicants are Massachusetts residents or if both are not residents of this state, both must appear before the judge as well as the marriage

---

M.D., Boston University's School of Medicine. Master of Public Health, Harvard University. Director of the Massachusetts Department of Public Health's division of venereal diseases.

Nicholas J. Fiumara, M.D.

A court hearing and order for the 15-year-old.

clerk or registrar. But if just one is a Massachusetts resident, only the resident need appear before the judge or justice for the waiver.

If the male applicant is under 18 or the female under 16, their parents must accompany them in their appearance before the judge and give their consent.

Imminent death of either party

In extraordinary or emergency cases when the death of either person is imminent, the clerk or registrar issues a marriage license at once on receipt of a request from a minister, priest, rabbi, chairman of an incorporated local spiritual assembly of Baha'is, or attending physician.

Pregnancy

If a woman is near the termination of her pregnancy, and if a minister, clergyman, priest, rabbi or attending physician requests it, the clerk or registrar may issue a marriage license at once. The premarital medical certificate would not be required in this case (General Laws, Chapter 207, Section 28A). If pregnancy is not far advanced, a waiver may be obtained from a judge or justice.

Fee for marriage license

A fee of $2.00 is charged for filing the notice of intention of marriage.

Medical certificate

A premarital examination law has been in effect in Massachusetts since 1941. It has been amended twice, the last time on February 20, 1950. Its objectives:

- To find cases of syphilis.
- To prevent the spread of syphilis.

In examining a patient planning to marry, the doctor keeps in mind two questions:

- Does the patient have syphilis?
- If so, is the disease in a stage or form that is infectious or potentially so?

To obtain the answers to these two questions, the physician tests the patient's blood. Questions have been asked on how thorough should the physical examination be, particularly in the case of female applicants. And how advisable is a pelvic premarital examination?

In most instances the patient's history will determine the extent of the examination. For example, if a patient has no history of promiscuity, a negative blood test for syphilis would be sufficient evidence that the patient in all probability does not have syphilis.

However, if the patient has a history of promiscuity—particularly of recent sexual exposures—a physical examination will determine whether or not the patient has a primary lesion, a lesion of secondary syphilis, or healed scars of these lesions.

Whereas a patient with secondary syphilis invariably shows a positive reaction, only 25% of the patients have a positive reaction when syphilis first appears (although by the end of the third week of primary syphilis most patients will develop a positive blood test).

As a consequence, many physicians perform a blood test for syphilis on the prospective couple during their first visit. If the blood test reports are

Not yet 21, he must have his father's consent.

negative and if there is no history of promiscuity, the physician signs the certificates and gives them to the couple. But if there is a history of recent sexual exposures (within three months)—and even if the blood test is negative—the doctor examines the patient to determine whether or not he may have sero-negative primary syphilis.

The thorough physical examination

While the premarital law does not require an examination except for syphilis, more and more patients are asking their doctors for a thorough physical examination before their wedding. These patients want to know their physical status before their marriage and to have any defects corrected. It is hoped that more physicians will encourage their patients to obtain a more thorough physical examination than that required by the premarital examination law.

In Massachusetts 39 laboratories as well as the State Wassermann Laboratory have been approved by the State Department of Public Health this year for performing serologic tests for syphilis. In addition, the state health department has agreed to accept the report of any standard blood test for syphilis performed by laboratories operated by or for any state health department, District of Columbia, New York City, territory of the United States, laboratories of the Armed Forces, U. S. Public Health Service, and provincial health departments of Canada.

The blood test for syphilis is valid for 30 days prior to the issuance of the marriage license. The 30 days are counted from the date the blood was drawn from the patient. Persons may visit their doctor to apply for a medical certificate as long as 85 days prior to the wedding.

Procedure on discovering syphilis

Should the doctor discover that his patient has syphilis, he determines the stage of the disease and then decides whether or not the disease is in a communicable or potentially communicable form.

A certified copy of the divorce record if they remarry.

Born and educated in Boston. Lecturer at Boston College's School of Nursing and Wesson Maternity Hospital. Massachusetts state registrar of vital statistics and deputy secretary of state.

Arthur J. Hassett

After this, he has to inform the couple of the disease in one partner. He must also explain the nature of the disease, whether or not it is in an infectious stage, and the chances of transmitting it to the non-infected partner and to their children.

If the disease is in a non-infectious stage, the patient is not required by law to receive treatment before the physician signs the premarital certificate. But for the sake of the infected patient and the future spouse, the physician should recommend treatment to prevent the development of late syphilis.

Infectious syphilis

A patient with infectious syphilis requires different handling from one with the disease in a non-infectious stage. The doctor is forbidden to sign the medical certificate until the patient with infectious syphilis has received adequate therapy.

By regulation, infectious or potentially infectious syphilis is the primary, secondary and early latent stages of syphilis.

Early latent syphilis has been defined as the presence of a symptomless infection characterized by a repeatedly positive standard blood test for syphilis with negative spinal-fluid serologic findings and with a history of a primary lesion within four years, or in the absence of an initial lesion, when the patient is less than 30 years old. Although *late latent syphilis* in women of child-bearing age is potentially communicable to the fetus during pregnancy, it is not a bar to marriage. However, these women should receive treatment at the earliest opportunity.

The need for follow-up

Would a patient with infectious syphilis be prevented from marrying? The answer is no, provided he has received (in the opinion of his physician) adequate treatment before the wedding.

What is adequate treatment? Ideally, adequate treatment for infectious syphilis is six million units of penicillin distributed over a 10-day period, and two years of satisfactory post-treatment observation. The latter indicates that at the end of two years the patient has a negative blood and spinal fluid serology . . . or less desirable, but acceptable, a negative spinal fluid serology and a blood reagin fastness of low titre. Thus, ade-

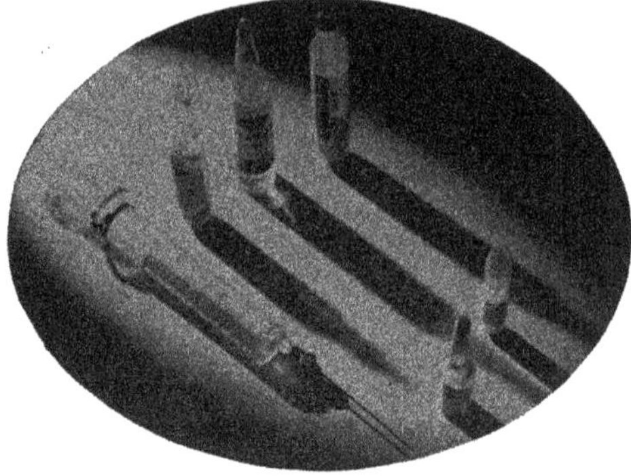

The premarital examination law requires a blood test for syphilis.

quate treatment ideally requires the marriage to be postponed for at least two years.

However, when the candidates for marriage are unwilling to delay their wedding, the physician is permitted to sign the certificate provided the infected partner has received minimum adequate therapy. In our opinion, minimum adequate therapy is 2,400,000 units of penicillin distributed over a four-day period.

When discussing the disease with both partners, the physician should stress the necessity for faithful post-treatment observation of the patient in order to discover or prevent an infectious relapse.

Massachusetts residents marrying in another state

There have always been a number of Massachusetts residents who have married in another state because the future spouse was an out-of-state resident or, for instance, because of employment. During World War II, the number of out-of-state marriages for Massachusetts residents increased. Because of the amount of interstate civilian travel at the present time, and the Korean war, the physician sees more and more applicants for examination and a medical certificate for use in another state.

That these medical certificates are not acceptable in some states is only too evident from the anguished long-distance telephone calls we receive in the Division of Venereal Diseases.

Therefore, in talking to patients who want to be married in another state, the physician must keep in mind three important questions:

- Will the other state or territory accept the signature of a physician licensed and registered to practice in Massachusetts?
- Will the other state accept the blood test report of the Massachusetts State Wassermann Laboratory? (The other laboratories are not considered because so few states accept the reports of laboratories approved by a state health department.)

• Will the other state accept the Massachusetts certificate if the blood sample is examined at the State Laboratory?

These questions are fundamentally important because their answers determine whether a physician signs the Massachusetts certificate or a certificate of the state where the patient will marry, or sends the patient to a physician in the other state for a blood test and certificate.

To help the physician

The following comments and accompanying tables will help the physician in reaching the correct decision.

At the present time (September 1, 1952), 39 states, three territories and four Canadian provinces have premarital examination laws. Of them, 19 states and two territories will accept the Massachusetts medical certificate when signed by a Massachusetts physician and the blood test performed at the State Wassermann Laboratory.

Eleven states will accept the report of the Massachusetts State Wassermann Laboratory and the signature of a Massachusetts physician but require that the Bay State physician sign the out-of-state form. To expedite matters, it is suggested that for marriages in these states, physicians write across the laboratory slip the name of the state. When the blood test has been completed at the State Wassermann Laboratory, the clerk will insert the premarital form of the appropriate state together with the laboratory report. If the particular state requires that the pertinent part of the form be completed by the laboratory director—and some do—that will be done.

If physicians have questions as to the requirements of Massachusetts or of other states or territories, they are cordially invited to telephone or write to the Massachusetts State Division of Venereal Diseases for a prompt answer. District health offices, local boards of health, and city and town clerks or registrars also supply information on these requirements.

A person with infectious syphilis must have treatment before marriage.

TABLE I

LABORATORIES APPROVED IN MASSACHUSETTS FOR THE PERFORMANCE OF SEROLOGIC TESTS FOR SYPHILIS

Location	Laboratory
Boston	Boston Dispensary
	Boston Health Department
	Commonwealth Clinical Laboratory
	Leary Laboratory
	Massachusetts General Hospital
	Massachusetts Memorial Hospitals, Genito-Infectious Disease Clinic
Brockton	Brockton Health Department Laboratory
Brookline	Sias Laboratories
Cambridge	Mount Auburn Hospital
Clinton	Clinton Hospital
Fall River	St. Anne's Hospital
	Union Hospital
Fitchburg	Burbank Hospital
Great Barrington	Fairview Hospital
Greenfield	Franklin County Public Hospital
Haverhill	Hale Hospital
Holyoke	Holyoke Hospital
	Providence Hospital
Lawrence	Lawrence General Hospital
Lowell	Lowell General Hospital
Montague	Farren Memorial Hospital
New Bedford	Burt Clinical Laboratory
	St. Luke's Hospital
Newton	Newton-Wellesley Hospital
North Adams	North Adams Hospital
Norwood	Norwood Clinical Laboratory
Pittsfield	Hillcrest Hospital
	Pittsfield General Hospital
	St. Luke's Hospital
Quincy	Quincy City Hospital
Salem	Salem Hospital
Springfield	Mercy Hospital
	Springfield Hospital
Tewksbury	Tewksbury State Infirmary
Waltham	Waltham Hospital
Worcester	St. Vincent Hospital
	Worcester Health Department Laboratory
	Worcester City Hospital
	Worcester Hahnemann Hospital

Note: These laboratories are in addition to the State Wassermann Laboratory, at 281 South Street, Jamaica Plain.

TABLE II

PREMARITAL LAWS IN THE UNITED STATES AND CANADA

Reciprocity between Massachusetts and Individual States, Territories, New York City, and Canadian Provinces

State, Territory or Province	Massachusetts Certificate Acceptable	Out-of-State Certificate Acceptable in Massachusetts	Waiting Period in Days between Application for and Issuance of License	Number of Days Blood Test Valid
Alabama	Yes	Yes	0	30
Alaska	Yes	Yes	3	30
Arizona	NO LAW		0	
Arkansas	NO LAW		0	
California	Yes	Yes	0	30
Colorado	Yes	Yes	0	30
Connecticut	Yes	Yes	5	35
Delaware	Yes	Yes	24 hrs., residents 4 days, non-res.	30
District of Columbia	NO LAW		5	
Florida	No	Yes	3	30
Georgia	Yes	Yes	0	30
Hawaii **	Yes	Yes	3	30
Idaho	Yes	Yes	0	30
Illinois	No	Yes	1	15
Indiana	No	Yes	0	30
Iowa	Yes	Yes	0	20
Kansas	Yes	Yes	3	30 resident 20 non-res.
Kentucky	No	Yes	3	15
Louisiana	Yes	No *	3	15
Maine	Yes	Yes	5	30
Maryland	NO LAW		2	
Michigan	No	Yes	5	30
Minnesota	NO LAW		5	
Mississippi	NO LAW		0	
Missouri	Yes **	Yes	3	15
Montana	Yes	No	0	20
Nebraska	No	Yes	0	30
Nevada	NO LAW		0	
New Hampshire	Yes	Yes	5	30
New Jersey	Yes	Yes	3	30
New Mexico	NO LAW		0	
New York State	Yes	Yes	0	30
New York City	Yes	Yes	3	30
North Carolina	No	Yes	3	30
North Dakota	No	Yes	0	30
Ohio	No	Yes	5	30
Oklahoma	No	Yes	0	30
Oregon	No	Yes	3	10
Pennsylvania	No	Yes	3	30
Puerto Rico	No	No		10

State, Territory or Province	Massachusetts Certificate Acceptable	Out-of-State Certificate Acceptable in Massachusetts	Waiting Period in Days between Application for and Issuance of License	Number of Days Blood Test Valid
Rhode Island	Yes	Yes	0 residents and male non-res. 5 non-res. females	40
South Carolina	NO LAW		24 hours *	
South Dakota	Yes	Yes	0	20
Tennessee	No	Yes	3	30
Texas	No	Yes	0	15
Utah	No	Yes	0	30
Vermont	Yes	Yes	5	30
Virginia	No	No	0	30
Virgin Islands	NO LAW			
Washington	NO LAW			
West Virginia	No	Yes		30
Wisconsin	No	No		15
Wyoming	No	Yes		30

CANADA

State, Territory or Province	Massachusetts Certificate Acceptable	Out-of-State Certificate Acceptable in Massachusetts	Waiting Period	Number of Days Blood Test Valid
Alberta	No	No		14
British Columbia	Law never put into effect			
Manitoba	Yes	No	0 ***	30
New Brunswick	NO LAW			
Newfoundland	NO LAW			
Nova Scotia	NO LAW			
Ontario	NO LAW			
Prince Edward Island	No	No		30
Quebec	NO LAW			
Saskatchewan	No	Yes		30

* No official certificate prescribed.

** Massachusetts premarital form to be accompanied by the Wassermann Laboratory slip.

*** Special authorization required for out-of-state residents.

Note: An out-of-state premarital examination certificate acceptable in Massachusetts must be signed by a physician licensed to practice in any of the states, District of Columbia and territories of the United States or a medical officer of the U.S. Armed Forces or Public Health Service. The blood test for syphilis must have been performed at a laboratory operated by or for a State Department of Public Health, the District of Columbia, New York City, a Territorial Health Department, the Armed Forces or Public Health Service of the United States or a Provincial Health Department of Canada.

TABLE III

STATES, TERRITORIES AND CANADIAN PROVINCES REQUIRING OWN PREMARITAL CERTIFICATE BUT ACCEPTING THE LABORATORY REPORT OF STATE WASSERMANN LABORATORY AND PHYSICAL EXAMINATION OF MASSACHUSETTS PHYSICIAN

(December 1, 1950)

State	Massachusetts State Wassermann Laboratory Report Acceptable	Massachusetts Physician's Physical Examination Report Acceptable
Florida	Yes	Yes
Illinois	Yes	Yes
Indiana	Yes	Yes
Kentucky	Yes	No
Michigan	Yes	Yes
Nebraska	Yes	Yes
North Carolina	Yes	No
North Dakota	Yes	Yes
Ohio	Yes	No
Oklahoma	No	No
Oregon	Yes	No
Pennsylvania	Yes	No
Puerto Rico	Blood test not required	No
Tennessee	Yes	Yes
Texas	Yes	Yes
Utah	Yes	Yes
Virginia	Yes	Yes
West Virginia	Yes	No
Wisconsin	Yes	Yes
Wyoming	Yes	No
	CANADA	
Alberta	No	No
Prince Edward Island	No	No
Saskatchewan	Yes	No

HAVE YOU . . .

Renewed your ASHA membership for 1953?

Mailed your 1953 subscription to the JOURNAL OF SOCIAL HYGIENE?

Motivation of the volunteer venereal disease patient

by John A. Morsell

The importance of getting the venereally infected person to come in voluntarily for diagnosis and treatment is evident in the great diversity of educational activities designed to increase the number of these volunteers.

A Brief Presentation of the Venereal Disease Control Plan in the USA, published by the U. S. Public Health Service's venereal disease division, succinctly states these goals: "To raise the level of personal suspicion, activities in this field are directed toward the public generally and toward specific groups, toward patients during treatment and toward the medical profession. The approach varies, but the message is constant: it tells when to suspect venereal disease and what to do about it; it offers the assurance that nearly all acquired venereal disease can be cured quickly and efficiently."

To achieve these goals, however, has required increasing understanding of the factors which either aid or hinder the infected person in reaching his decision to volunteer. VD educators have come to realize that they must often overcome basic resistances, and that their assurances of simple and effective treatment may not always dispel these resistances. Furthermore, even when educators bring a person to the point of suspecting infection, he may not act promptly. And a few days' delay is of great consequence.

What made them volunteer?

The study discussed here was the second of two conducted cooperatively by the Ohio Department of Health, the Columbus health department, the U. S. Public Health Service's venereal disease division and Columbia University's Bureau of Applied Social Research. By studying individuals diagnosed or treated by public facilities, we hoped to trace the influences responsible for their being either volunteers or non-volunteers.

A detailed questionnaire was administered to 1,000 persons, 400 of them patients in the central Ohio rapid treatment center, the remainder interviewed in the Columbus health department's clinic. Although we tried to include as many early syphilis cases as possible, the sampling was by no means restricted to these patients. It was, rather, representative of the varied types of cases (including some non-infected persons) with which the public VD facility deals on a day-to-day basis.

The interviews

The information obtained in the interviews covered these matters:

- The individual's social characteristics (age, race, sex).
- His knowledge and opinions about venereal disease.
- The symptoms, if any, he had noticed before coming in.
- The length of time it had taken him to decide to come in.
- The extent to which VD educational material had reached him.
- His current diagnosis and the number and type of his sex contacts, if any (where required).

Interviewers paid particular attention to determining whether, and at what point, each respondent had had any suspicion that he might have contracted a venereal disease.

Factors influencing suspicion

To say that venereal disease education seeks to "raise the level of personal suspicion" implies that suspecting venereal infection is equivalent to volunteering for diagnosis—the primary educational objective. The Columbus data confirm this judgment . . . in four-fifths of the cases the association between suspicion and volunteering was perfect. Those with suspicions volunteered and those without suspicions did not volunteer. Detailed analysis showed that the exceptions to this rule were, for the most part, only apparent exceptions.

In view of this correlation and the simplicity it allows in handling data, we shall deal here with the factors influencing suspicion of infection. But it should be clear that for all practical purposes we are concerned with volunteering as the end result of the suspicion.

Three very broad factors were found to be related to the development of suspicion of infection:

- The presence and nature of signs or symptoms of disease.
- The extent and quality of knowledge about the signs or symptoms.
- The degree to which venereal disease was taken as a matter of ordinary personal concern.

A fourth factor—attitudes toward sex—had only an indirect association.

Influence of symptoms

Noticeable signs or symptoms were characteristic of most of the Columbus patients whose suspicions led them to volunteer for diagnosis. This was true of both sexes, although the relationship between symptoms and suspicion was stronger among men than among women. It would be easy to conclude that noticeable symptoms are tremendously significant in getting people to suspect infection. This is obviously the case in the sense that no other experience is so likely to be the foundation for suspicion.

Results were tabulated according to age, sex, race.

But it is not the whole story. *Of itself,* the symptom is neither necessary nor sufficient to cause suspicion of venereal disease . . . 15% of the volunteers said they had not been aware of any symptom, and 29% of the non-volunteers said that they *had* observed symptoms.

Not only is it apparent, therefore, that other factors operate in conjunction with symptoms to produce varied results, but differences in the number and character of symptoms lead to different outcomes. As with the group of Mississippi syphilis patients reported on by Gray, Usilton and Carlson in the June, 1951, issue of the *Journal of Venereal Disease Information,* the appearance of more than one symptom coincided with a greater likelihood of suspicion. At the same time, it usually meant that the patient was slower to arrive at his suspicion. Plural symptoms do not ordinarily appear at the same time, and those for whom the first one was not conclusive evidence needed more time and additional symptoms for confirmation.

Location of symptoms

A more significant distinction was found when symptoms were classified according to their nature and location. Those reported by the Columbus patients were first divided according to whether they had been noticed on or around the genitals or elsewhere on the body. The "genital" symptoms were again divided into:

- Those of urethral or vaginal origin—drip, discharge—more characteristic of gonorrhea.

- The more visible, external sores or rashes generally associated with early syphilis.

A very definite sex difference was observed with this classification . . . genital symptoms predominated among men but were reported by only a little more than half the women.

The division between the urethra-vaginal type and the other genital symptoms was about even in both sexes.

Although fewer women than men had suspected VD, both showed the same kind of association between type of symptom and suspicion. Suspicion was most frequent in the case of urethral-vaginal symptoms, with other genital and non-genital symptoms following in that order.

Furthermore, the same degree of relationship prevailed between the type of symptom reported and the accuracy of the patients' "self-diagnosis"—the kind of disease they thought they might have. Those with genital symptoms were more likely than the others to suspect the same disease which they were later diagnosed as having.

To know, to act

The study of community opinion in Columbus (reported in the December, 1952, issue of the JOURNAL OF SOCIAL HYGIENE) indicated that differences in the amount of information which people possessed about VD bore little or no relation to their attitudes about VD. Since their attitudes are presumably linked up with their behavior, this suggests that knowledge may play a less important immediate role—whatever its long-term role—in leading to action.

On the other hand, the person who is infected with syphilis obviously requires a certain minimum of information if he is to come to any conclusion at all about what ails him. Of all the items that might make up this minimum, certainly the central one would be a knowledge of the symptoms of syphilis. In the absence of this knowledge, a person experiencing symptoms but not identifying them as possibly syphilitic might or might not get to proper medical attention, and if he did it would tend to be after some delay.

The members of our sample were divided into two classes according to whether their knowledge of the symptoms of syphilis was rated high or low on a scale of correctness. In general, these respondents possessed a level of knowledge considerably higher than that found among the respondents chosen from the population at large for the community study. Probably for this reason the differences between sub-groups in the clinical sample were insignificant: much the same percentages of men and women, of Negroes and whites, were on both levels of symptoms-knowledge.

When respondents on the two levels were compared with respect to whether or not they had had suspicions of infection, those on the high level turned out to have been somewhat more likely to have such suspicions.

No symptoms

Another important facet of knowledge about syphilis is that its symptoms are sometimes slight, unobtrusive or transient. Consequently, there is need for more than customary alertness to the possibility of catching it.

Respondents were asked whether they thought it is possible to have syphilis without having any signs or symptoms of it. A majority were aware of this possibility. And regardless of the type of symptoms they had experienced themselves, they were more likely to become suspicious than were those who did not know that syphilis can be asymptomatic.

Interestingly enough, this knowledge appeared to be most clearly associated with suspicion in the case of those respondents who reported no symptoms of their own . . . those who were, on that account, most in need of this information. It is clearly important to stress the need to be alert to the possibility of infection.

Sources of VD knowledge

While the members of the clinical sample were better informed about syphilis than were those questioned in the community-wide survey, our attempt to trace the principal sources of their knowledge was equally unsuccessful, probably for the same reasons. No one source of knowledge stands out as contributing the most to their current knowledge.

The two groups are alike also in that those whose earliest knowledge was acquired when they were under 20 were better informed than those who first learned at later ages. Furthermore, persons who had learned before they were 20 were more likely to have added to their knowledge afterward.

We cannot be sure of the reason why the age of introduction to venereal disease information should make such a difference, but its importance for the VD educator is apparent. He should stress that it is important for parents to tell their children early the facts they need to know about VD.

Effect of being "VD conscious"

The clinical respondents, like those interviewed in the community-wide study, differed in the extent to which they were ready to think of venereal disease as a matter of possible concern to themselves personally. This does not mean that any of them were in a state of continual suspicion that they might have caught VD . . . it means simply that they did not need a unique circumstance to convince them of the possibility of their own infection. For these respondents, catching a venereal disease was not unthinkable. The question asked was: "Did you ever think it (VD) just couldn't happen to you?" Those who answered "No" were called "VD conscious."

About three-fifths of the members of the clinical sample were thus classified as "VD conscious." They were considerably more likely to have suspected infection than were those not so classified . . . in fact, no other attribute seems to have had quite so strong an association with suspicion of infection.

Differences within the sample were of much interest. Negroes were slightly more "VD conscious" than whites, veterans more so than non-veterans, men very much more so than women. The sex difference is especially worth noting, since it is so often taken for granted that men's greater tendency to volunteer for diagnosis can be explained simply on the basis that their symptoms are different.

It is evident from this finding that psychological differences must also be given their proportional weight.

Response to educational materials

As one would expect, differences in "VD consciousness" led to different reactions to educational material. They are so similar to the reactions encountered among the respondents of the Columbus community study that we seem justified in regarding "VD consciousness" as the practical equivalent of the "psychological readiness" discussed in the other study.

Clinical respondents who were "VD conscious"—like community respondents with "psychological readiness"—reacted to what they read or heard by thinking about their own health or about getting a medical check-up. And this response in turn was positively related to suspecting venereal infection.

Clinical patients knew more about VD than other people.

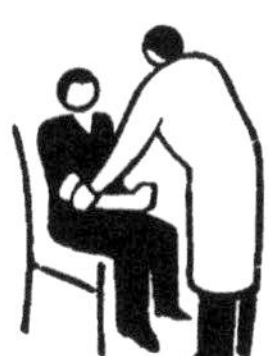

Influence of attitudes toward sex

Since people interpret the acquisition of venereal disease as evidence of sexual transgression, the interview inquired into the way people felt about extramarital sex relations . . . on the hypothesis that those who approved or were indifferent would be more disposed to suspicion than those who disapproved.

These questions asked whether respondents approved, disapproved or were neutral toward premarital sex relations and asked for their estimates of the extent to which people generally indulge in them. The same questions were used in interviewing the community-wide sample, and the differences between the two groups are clear-cut . . . over half (52%) of the community respondents—but barely a third (32%) of the clinical respondents—said they disapproved of sexual relations before marriage.

There was no *direct* association between these opinions and the likelihood that infection would be suspected. But persons who disapproved and at the same time believed that most other people *do not have* such relations were less likely than others to report suspicion. Disapproval, when accompanied by a *high* estimate of the extent of premarital sex relations, did not not seem to affect the development of suspicion.

The most significant aspect of the moral issue among these respondents appears to have been whether or not they would feel themselves singled out for disapproval by the kind of behavior which venereal infection implies.

Factors influencing prompt volunteering

Prompt volunteering is important because it reduces the possibility of the spread of infection and improves the patient's chance of cure. Our study was concerned, therefore, with what might be learned of the factors which tend to hasten or retard the infected individual in making up his mind to get medical attention and in carrying out his decision.

We classified volunteer respondents as "delayers" or "non-delayers" according to the number of days they said had elapsed between the appearance of a symptom and their visit to the clinic. The half that came in most quickly were "non-delayers" and the other half "delayers." Depending on whether or not symptoms had been noted, the median time interval ranged from six to 15 days for the sample as a whole.

Influence of symptoms

As in the case of suspicion of infection, differences in type of symptoms led to differences in the time interval. Persons with genital symptoms naturally came sooner than those whose symptoms were elsewhere.

Interestingly enough, however, patients who became suspicious in the absence of symptoms were, by that token, so alert to the possibility of VD that they were the quickest of all to volunteer. This is in line with the fact that "VD conscious" respondents as a group were likely to have had generally shorter time intervals than those who were not "VD conscious."

Influence of knowledge

Differences in a knowledge score (based on knowledge both of syphilis symptoms and of the possibility of their absence) were reflected in differenees in delay, although the degree of association was not high. Among

Young men lack urgency in seeking treatment.

women, high-level knowledge led to prompter volunteering, but among men there was either no relationship or the relationship was reversed.

Particularly among the younger men, a high level of syphilis knowledge appeared to be associated with tendencies to delay. Perhaps the kind of knowledge these men have makes them feel they are "in control of the situation," with the result that they are deliberate rather than hasty in what they do when they suspect infection. At any rate, their knowledge seems lacking in the elements that give a sense of urgency toward action.

An illustration of this is that respondents on a high knowledge level were more likely than the rest to have made a "self-diagnosis" of syphilis. Yet those who thought they had syphilis did not come to diagnosis any sooner than those who thought they had gonorrhea or some unspecified venereal disease.

Knowledge that included information about the much more serious consequences of untreated syphilis would presumably have aided in more prompt appearance for diagnosis. Evidently VD material must refer continually to the physical consequences of untreated syphilis.

Influences of attitudes toward VD

Answers to a series of attitude questions reflected the influence of sentiments and opinions about venereal disease *per se* on speed in seeking diagnosis. Although most respondents indicated that the idea of having syphilis worried them in some way or other, this did not seem to be related to delay.

Fears about treatment, however, were so related . . . among men, those who said they were afraid of the pain attendant upon the use of "needles" tended to be later in coming to diagnosis. For reasons we cannot explain, women appeared to react to fear of pain in exactly the opposite manner.

About half the respondents said that to be infected with syphilis would (or did) make them feel guilty, as if they had done something wrong. In some instances this was guilt because of moral violation, in others because of failure to "be careful." The former was considerably more frequent among women, the latter more frequent among men.

The relationship between feelings of guilt and differences in the time interval was slight and confined to the white respondents. Again the sexes differed, with women being deterred by feelings of moral guilt.

Fear of disclosure

This seems related to the fact that women are much more fearful than men of the results for themselves if their infection should become known to others. In general, women who expressed this fear of disclosure were much more likely to delay than were those without such fear. Among men there appeared no relationship of this sort.

When the "others" to whom disclosure is feared are one's own friends, there seems to be less association with delay, even among women. This probably arises from the fact that moral issues were not so plainly involved where friends are concerned . . . the principal concern of both men and women, in this connection, was the possibility of transmitting the disease to their friends.

In every instance in which respondents indicated some kind of worry or fear in connection with the idea of syphilis, they were asked whether this would (or did) cause them to wait before coming to diagnosis. Those who showed a tendency to be "hesitators" by answering "yes" were found to be delayers in two-thirds of the cases . . . among the non-hesitators, almost the same proportion were found to be non-delayers.

Conclusions

Volunteering for diagnosis stems from a suspicion of infection, which should then be acted upon promptly. Raising the level of suspicion and encouraging promptness are twin objectives of VD education.

The results of the study discussed in this paper were consistent with other findings which indicate that the presence of symptoms—especially the more obtrusive kind located on or near the genitals—is basic to most suspicion of infection.

It confirmed the importance of knowing the nature of the symptoms of syphilis and of knowing that these symptoms may sometimes be lacking.

It gave evidence that if people are convinced that venereal disease is a possibility for themselves—if they are "VD conscious"—they are more

Women usually don't want their infection known to others.

likely to become suspicious when given cause. They are also more receptive and responsive to VD messages contained in educational materials.

It revealed that if people think they will be classed with a minority of sexual wrongdoers, they will be reluctant to admit the possibility of infection, even to themselves.

Promptness in volunteering depends also on the symptoms people have. Genital symptoms lead to quicker action, but people who are sufficiently alert to the possibility of VD to volunteer in the absence of symptoms come in soonest of all.

Most other factors which are associated with volunteer delay operated differently for men and women . . . greater knowledge about syphilis hastened the volunteering of women but not that of men; fear of pain retarded men but not women; feelings of guilt and fears of disclosure delayed women but not men. There was an indication that many men—especially those otherwise well-informed—lacked a sense of urgency which they might develop if they thoroughly realized the serious consequences of delay in the treatment of syphilis.

Summary

This paper reviews some of the findings of a study of 1,000 persons who came to medical attention as venereally infected or possibly infected in Columbus, Ohio, between September, 1948 and April, 1949. The data were analyzed for what they could show about the factors which influence volunteering for diagnosis and which on that account have significance for venereal disease education.

HAVE YOU . . .

Introducing ASHA's new executive director . . .

(continued from page 1)

As director during World War II of Community War Services in the Caribbean area Mr. Van Hyning negotiated with foreign governments and island possessions of the United States to assure satisfactory protection of the health of American service personnel stationed in Puerto Rico, the Virgin Islands and South America. He also worked with military and civil officials to provide adequate recreation for servicemen and to prevent the spread of venereal disease.

After the war Mr. Van Hyning headed UNRRA's welfare division both here and in Europe. Later he reorganized the displaced persons program, directed repatriation and consolidated UNRRA's activities with voluntary and other international agencies.

The new social hygiene director is married and has three children. His home is in Greenwich, Conn.

Miss Eleanor Shenehon, who has been acting director of the American Social Hygiene Association since June, will return to her post as director of the association's liaison office in Washington, D. C.

journal of SOCIAL HYGIENE

vol. 39 february 1953 no. 2

IN THIS ISSUE

FEBRUARY 1953

About our cover . . .

Linda rushes to greet the daddy she has never before seen, an English able-seaman returned home after two years in Korean waters. Twentieth of a series of Journal covers on family life . . . United Press photo courtesy the London Daily Graphic, United Press Associations and Planet News, Ltd.

THE JOURNAL OF SOCIAL HYGIENE

official periodical of the American Social Hygiene Association, published monthly except July, August and September at the Boyd Printing Company, Inc., 374 Broadway, Albany 7, N. Y. Acceptance for mailing at the special rate of postage provided for in Section 1103, Act of October 3, 1917. Entered as second-class matter at the Post Office at Albany, N. Y., March 23, 1922.

Recreation— for body, brain and soul

Recreation has been viewed from various perspectives throughout the history of our country. Our Puritan ancestors looked upon it as a reward for work . . . no work, no play. A little later a somewhat more liberal point of view (but one that still tied work and play together) began to prevail and was more or less summed up in the phrase "All work and no play make Jack a dull boy." This concept of recreation as a kind of antidote to work still failed to recognize recreation as a basic human need for man's fulfillment of himself.

More recently we have grown in our realization that recreation is good for man . . . good for his body, good for his brain, good for his soul. We no longer view physical recreation—active sports—as merely a reward for work nor as a way of working off energies that might be directed into unworthy channels. We see it as a means of developing coordination between mind and body, as a psychologically healthy form of competition and as a means of developing one of mankind's higher spiritual aspirations . . . cooperation.

We see other forms of recreation, especially those which summon the individual's inventive and creative powers, as a way of self-fulfillment to which every human being has a right . . . a right inherent in his *being* a human being. We view the social intercourse of home hospitality as offering the young person who is away from his own community and his normal circle of friends some of the finest human experiences of which men and women are capable.

As a totality, as a body, a brain and a soul, man has an inalienable right to the self-development and social development of sound recreation. We owe a particular recognition of this fact to young men and women in the Armed Forces and to other young people—and their families—who are today moving about the country to serve the nation's production needs. Through the UDF and its member agencies—UCDS, USO, NRA and ASHA—America can assure its military personnel and defense workers of pleasant recreation in wholesome surroundings.

by
members of a committee of the NY TB & Health Association's social hygiene division . . .

Myron Blanchard
National Jewish Welfare Board

Beatrice Carreau
University Settlement

John A. Ledlie
National Council, YMCA

Monte Melamed
Grand Street Settlement

Edward W. Pastore
Boys' Clubs of America

Douglas M. Kahn
NY TB & Health Association

Social hygiene in group work agencies

From 12 to 18, boys and girls live through a period of change. During these years they face a number of adjustment problems that are in part an outgrowth of their developing glandular system. These problems also involve the working out of satisfactory relationships with their parents, brothers and sisters, and friends. In addition, they are striving for status in the community, while learning new habits and attitudes acceptable to the adult world.

The difficulties met by many youngsters in this period have led to its description as a time of great stress and strain. Although this may not be true for some, many find that growing up and becoming psychologically stable and mature is a process that involves various difficult personal and social adjustments.

Group work agencies are concerned with providing the youngsters they serve with knowledge and experiences that will facilitate these adjustments.

Methods and programs used by group workers to meet various needs of adolescents are intrinsically related to the objectives of social hygiene and mental hygiene. Group workers should give attention to such specifics as adolescent social life, family influences, and the psychological and educational values inherent in discussions, programming and the effect of the leader's personality on members of the group.

Group workers interested in clarifying and improving the methods they use with teen-agers should find this article helpful for it is concerned with these matters. It provides a list of books and other publications for those who wish to explore the field more thoroughly. It also lists suitable visual aids.

Social Life of the Adolescent

The most significant time for the development of friendships is the period of adolescence. During one's childhood, parents, brothers and sisters are dominant influences. In adulthood, one's work, life philosophy and family are major concerns. But in adolescence, friendship is relatively more important.

The teen-ager sometimes feels he is not understood by his elders. Whether or not this is true, his friends may give him the acceptance and encouragement he needs. His companions may also offer an opportunity for learning-experiences outside the home and school, in this way stimulating self-reliance and adequate social adjustment. If the adolescent lacks friends, his emotional and social growth may be hampered.

Boy-Girl Relationships

Perhaps the most profound change young people experience is the sudden appearance of sexual impulses and characteristics. These markedly influence their relationships with members of the opposite sex.

At this time boys and girls begin to take more interest in each other. They start learning how to get along socially and to understand each other's expectations, customs and habits. They begin to appreciate differences determined by sex.

Friendship then becomes more complex and possibly more difficult. There are new attitudes and new meanings that require tactful clarification and interpretation. In this the informed group worker can be most helpful.

Like co-education, joint programs in group work and recreation agencies have opened up many opportunities for normal social activities for adolescents.

- They make it possible for boys and girls to learn to understand and get along with each other . . . and in this way to become more adequately prepared for adulthood.

- They offer increased opportunities for a fuller life.

Nevertheless, the relationship between the sexes and the meaning of sex in our society are subject to much confusion and misinterpretation. A sense of guilt, shame and immature attitudes—fostered by misinformation—contribute to many psychological problems. The few who are "sex deviates" or who are indifferent to the sex aspect of their lives may have experienced either distortion or neglect in the educational process relating to this phase of their development.

Because social contacts with members of the opposite sex influence one's adjustment in adolescence to some extent, some of the problems that arise in these contacts require consideration.

Necking and Petting

These much-debated patterns of behavior present no new problems . . . they have persisted for a long time.

Necking and petting are common experiences among boys and girls, and in marriage usually precede intimate relationships. But necking and petting may lead to serious problems for adolescents.

If necking and petting become the end-all of social activities, they may result in fewer opportunities for learning to adjust maturely to the opposite sex. Boys out for what they can get and girls reputed to be easy-going and permissive on dates and at parties miss out on more meaningful experiences. Their friendships are apt to suffer distortion and narrow the possibility of healthy and fruitful relationships.

Some adolescents may be confused in their standards and feelings, and experience mental conflicts. In their necking and petting they may become extremely affectionate, or angry, or feel guilty, or decide there isn't much to it. Since many married couples face emotional difficulties, it is reasonable to believe that adolescents who pet are not free from them.

If handled properly, some discussion of the confusion, ambivalence, guilt or shame, hostility or detachment that accompanies necking and petting is advisable in the group, for boys and girls who understand the relationship between their emotions (confusion, shame, guilt, etc.) and their social activities will achieve more stable and satisfying adjustments.

It is important for them to understand, for example, the question of possible pregnancy. Intensive necking and petting may easily develop into intimacies that bring on conception. For young unmarried people such a situation presents most serious consequences. It often produces a crisis for some adolescents who are somewhat unstable in the natural course of their development.

Adolescents are not practically or emotionally prepared for the responsibilities of parenthood. If they become involved in such a situation and are financially and otherwise able to meet it, there still may not be the

Adolescent friendships lead to adult friendships.

genuine love needed for a mature family relationship. In other instances, they may share mutuality of feeling but lack social and economic preparedness.

Such problems as premarital pregnancy and forced marriage lead to the conclusion that in our society the adolescent has to learn how to postpone expression of biological urges until marriage, when he is more readily able to accept their consequences. He needs to learn that postponement rewards him in the future for he is then able to live more fully and accept his responsibilities.

If necking or petting is apt to lead to intimate embraces, adolescents should take steps to avoid this possibility. Their elders and leaders likewise have a responsibility.

Crushes

While some adolescents need help *in making friends,* others need help *in achieving a balance in their friendships.* To avoid serious crushes, it is essential to maintain an interest in many people, instead of centering all one's attention on a single person, whether that individual is of the same or opposite sex, of the same age, younger or older.

Crushes represent a fleeting though normal and common phase of development. But if they become serious, group workers have to be careful in their approach to the subject.

A fair father allows a fair measure of freedom.

Since crushes may lead to later maladjustments, the group worker should guide the adolescent toward an appreciation of the values inherent in a wide social outlook and many friendships. He might even take the lead in introducing other young people into the adolescent's life, without giving the impression that the adolescent is being criticized or rejected, or that his crush is silly and childish.

Total Personality

Since one's total personality determines one's reactions, necking, petting and crushes, and attitudes towards the opposite sex result from more than the sex drive. For example, a girl involved in an intensive crush may find this experience the only way she can compensate for rejection by her parents, low self-esteem or other personality problems. A boy preoccupied with dating may be reacting to competition within his group.

Relation of the Adolescent to His Family

Emancipation

A recognized characteristic of most teen-agers is their natural striving for emancipation from the control of their family. To understand the adolescent is to appreciate this process and the varied parental pressures and peer-group expectations related to it.

Among some parents it is traditional to use authoritarian methods in rearing their youngsters. They set strict rules of conduct in accord with their customs, ideals, beliefs and values. To a great extent, they make decisions for the adolescent . . . in education, choice of friends, vocation, or other aspects of his life. He may have little choice in matters directly affecting him.

But in many homes youngsters would consider it strange if they were not allowed a fair measure of freedom in deciding about matters important to them. Our democratic way of life and the number and variety of interests outside the home provide young people with the chance to learn and adjust under their own power, with but limited direction from their parents.

Whatever the attitudes of their parents (democratic, authoritarian, etc.), present-day youngsters are less dependent on them than formerly and sometimes question their ideas and attitudes. Many parents are no longer looked up to as all-knowing, all-wise and all-powerful by their adolescent sons and daughters. Boys and girls often turn to friends, teachers, organizations and clubs for *additional* help in their development.

Conflict

Much conflict between parents and their adolescent sons and daughters stems from a clash of demands between the two groups. This is a natural development of the emancipation period. How much and what kind of freedom shall the adolescent have? That is the basic question in the conflict.

To the dismay of many parents, adolescents may want to decide how late to stay out at night, and want to choose their school, friends, vocation, etc. Their parents' reaction to their desires will influence them in the way they learn to get along in the world.

To complicate matters, adolescents are often confused by contradictions in what adults expect of them. As young children they are usually told what to do. Then suddenly as they reach the teens they may be beset with requests to act independently and self-sufficiently.

Along with this conflict, some young people find themselves in situations where parents are at odds as to what they want from their children.

Slowly and surely, sustained by Dad, she's assured.

One parent may expect thoroughgoing assertiveness, the other complete submissiveness.

Furthermore, when children reach adolescence they often become extremely sensitive to the pressures of their environment. Sometimes this situation may produce a great deal of tension, as when boys and girls of foreign-born parents or of minority groups become embarrassed by the behavior and ideas of their families.

On the other hand, parents may find such an attitude very hard to understand. By their standards, they have tried to train their children to be responsible individuals. Suddenly the adolescents rebel . . . and begin to criticize parents for not following their own more recently acquired standards.

Young people who are involved in these various conflicts may feel a great strain. They may be helped by parents who are flexible and understanding, who can to some extent clarify the situation, compromise or reach middle-of-the-road agreements, and who, most of all, continuously give them support and love.

In developing programs and discussions, group workers can be most helpful if they will lead boys and girls to recognize that . . .

- Parents have their rights, needs and normal worries.
- There are at least two sides to each issue.
- Family conflicts should be resolved by democratic means.

You can help adolescents who lack confidence in their parents by leading them to see that neither their elders nor other persons are perfect and that all people differ in various ways. Some of these differences (in ideas, customs, demands, etc.) between people are natural and to be expected.

Group work agencies may be of additional help by providing parent groups with educational discussions on problems in the parent-adolescent relationship.

Indulgent Parents

Some adolescents are faced with the problem of indulgent parents who want to be close and intimate companions and friends to their children and are disappointed if their efforts do not bring the desired response. They frighten their children away by their over-identification with the youngsters.

Adolescents really prefer to live their own lives, even though they may enjoy intimacy with their parents. Boys and girls want to communicate and be friendly with their elders, but do not wish them to over-emphasize their relationship. Furthermore, they want their parents to act like adults,

His dad with his mother,
now he with his girl—
how far-reaching is example!

with the reserve and dignity usually associated with well-mannered older people.

Parental Attitudes

During a boy's early years it is important that his mother accept him emotionally and be responsive to him. If she makes him feel that his affection is not acceptable to her, she may handicap his later relationships with the opposite sex. A boy also bases some of his attitudes toward girls on what he observes of his father's relationship with his mother.

How a girl will respond to members of the opposite sex will likewise be determined by the way her father treats her, and the relationship existing between her parents. The more affection, love and consideration in the family, the better the chance for a happy girlhood.

Understanding and Working with the Group

Effective group leadership requires adequate appreciation of how individuals function in the group, as well as an understanding of the relationships of adolescents to their friends and families. Appreciation of the individual's relationship to the group is of specific importance if the group worker is to be helpful in influencing participation of the adolescent in group activities. He needs to know the teen-ager's personality, abilities, capacities, religion, cultural background, aims and needs.

Personality

It is clear that a group worker needs to understand basic personality processes in order to interpret interpersonal relationships correctly and to help the group become productive. To a certain extent, this understanding of personality depends on a knowledge of the factors that have shaped an individual. In addition to his family, he has felt the influence of other relatives, adults and friends, of his school—with all its efforts to educate and socialize—and of many communal institutions.

The group is composed of many different kinds of personalities. Some youngsters are shy and over-reserved, others dominating and aggressive. There are the umpire types, the humorous, the sad, the doers, the thinkers, the talkers, the cooperators, etc., each relating to the others in his or her own unique way.

The group's atmosphere and movement will be determined by the continuous interaction of these different members. It is during this interaction that the alert group leader may help members to mature in their social relationships.

What are the mechanisms and reactions used by the members of the group toward each other, and the purpose for which they are used? Do members express considerable aggression toward one another? Is somebody always being blamed for something? Who is compensating and for what reasons? Is the group prone to making excuses? Are some members extra-shy?

What is the psychological relationship between the leader and the members of the group? Is it mutually satisfying, positive, infantile or strained?

In the answers to these questions lie clues to effective leadership. For a more elaborate treatment of interpersonal relationships, see the bibliography on group work at the back of this article.

Ability and Capacity

The abilities and capacities of its members in part determine the nature of a group's activities and growth. The ability of an individual is the way he functions in various situations . . . social activities, sports, arts and crafts, etc. His capacity is the extent to which he is able to develop his ability.

Your understanding of the ability and capacity of members of a group can contribute to your orientation to the group. Your choice of suggestions for activities—social or folk dancing, hikes, projects, discussions—and your guidance of the group's functions should be determined by what the group can do and what its potential may be.

It is important to remember that there are individual differences in the group. The rate of learning, ability and capacity vary with each person . . . the same standard of performance cannot be expected for all. There will be as many standards as there are youngsters in the group. Oversimplified or too-complicated tasks, and extremes in one's expectations of their achievement may leave members of the group with negative attitudes toward group relationships.

Religion and Culture

A leader's work is made easier if he knows something about the religious and cultural backgrounds of the group's members.

Is the group heterogeneous or homogeneous? Are all its members Protestant, Jewish, Catholic or of some other faith, or is the group mixed, with a varied distribution of the different religious faiths? Knowledge of their faiths will be of value when you are conducting a discussion on boy-girl relations, dating, engagement or marriage. With this knowledge you can help the adolescent to clarify his ideas and feelings within the tenets of his own religion.

What are the cultural backgrounds of a group . . . Italian, Polish, Irish, Jewish, second- or third-generation American, Negro, Chinese, or a mixture? Different customs, standards and points of view expressed in a group toward the opposite sex and toward each other are determined in part by the cultural experiences of its members. Your understanding of them depends upon your knowing as much as possible about the cultural influences in their lives.

Aims

Some aims of a group are obvious and easily stated. Others are unconscious. The primary purpose of members of a discussion group may seem to be an interest in the topics they discuss. But some, without realizing it, may like this group because it happens to be the only co-ed group open to them.

There are aims which may develop as a group or club goes along. One club started on the basis of a common interest in basketball. Through the years the members took on other sports and parties, participated in the community center's councils, and finally worked on community and family projects.

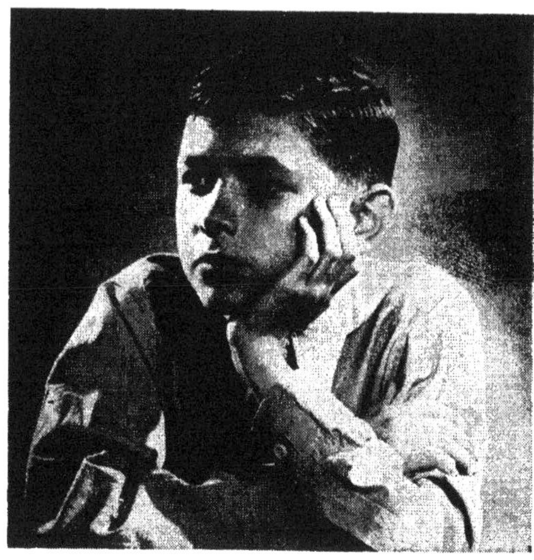

The thinker too contributes to the group.

If the group is ready, then dancing by all means.

A distinct function of the group worker is to help clarify the group's aims. The clearer they are to the members, the easier it is for the group to make plans to achieve them.

Needs

With the modern emphasis on psychological development, a pertinent question often asked is: What are the needs and desires of the interlocking and constantly changing motives and wishes of all the group's members?

For Activity

Adolescents have a marked need for active experience. It is related to their need to learn about getting along with members of the opposite sex.

The need for active experience is also indicated by new tensions that are related to changes in the physical development of adolescents.

Co-ed parties, hikes, sports and active welfare projects give adolescents a chance to mobilize their energies and reduce tensions in a constructive way. At the same time they offer new learning experiences with each other. In working together on projects, boys and girls get good experience for some of the responsibilities of family life and citizenship.

Activities and experiences that can be employed constructively in an integrated series of meetings are . . .

- The arranging of hikes, trips, co-ed camping, etc., in which the major responsibility for planning and carrying through the activities is placed on the group.

- The developing of party committees to arrange a series of home parties that will help boys and girls in their social development, especially those least active socially.

- Dancing . . . beginning with dance games, square-dancing and other group dancing, and gradually progressing to social dancing.

- Lectures, discussions, films, forums, radio talks, and television programs that develop an appreciation of the value of happy and stable friendships, courtships and family relationships.

For Information

Somewhere along the way in the group's progress, there may arise the need for facts and figures to help clarify selected notions of its members. If the group is concerned about boy-girl relationships and a number of members evidence ignorance or misconceptions about the subject, the leader may find it necessary and appropriate to call upon an expert for help. If sufficiently capable, he himself may provide some of the basic facts.

With older adolescents interested in marriage, discussions and publications on courtship, engagement, marriage and home economics may serve a useful purpose.

For Discussion

Sometimes a group may desire to discuss a subject, rather than have a formal lecture. Since questions involving necking, petting and late hours do not always have definite and fixed answers, the group needs a chance to explore these problems verbally at its own pace and in its own way.

For Expression

Members of a group don't always want answers or corrective and well-intentioned interpretations. Many times they just want to talk, voice their feelings and opinions, even contribute a little nonsense . . . because these acts, when they are accepted, build up a sense of belonging. Freedom to vent their ideas—as well as irrelevancies—help them establish their identity as accepted members of a recognized community group.

For Acceptance

A person feels accepted not only when he is given an opportunity for relatively free discussion, but when he is respected and appreciated as an individual as well.

His need for acceptance is especially important during adolescence. This is a time of transition, when a young person needs to be a member of a group in which he achieves standing, and where he feels he is accepted as worthy and valuable in himself.

But there are times when it is difficult to accept some of the group's members, especially if the values of the leader and the members cross paths. For example, if a member uses vulgar language, it may not be wise for the leader to censor such talk each time it occurs. It may be best to accept it as part of the group's standard, perhaps as a test of the leader and an attempt to discover if he is a regular guy. Perhaps not making an issue of it will contribute to a sense of acceptance in the adolescents, and make easier for both leader and members their future and more encompassing club relationships.

The Value of Discussion

Among the many valuable opportunities for growth open to a group are educational discussions. No matter what the topic—petting or friendship or romantic love—good group discussion is one (certainly not the only one) of the most effective ways for developing clear ideas and healthy attitudes.

The following factors are significant in successful discussion experiences . . .

A relaxed group with a leader not too silent nor too vocal.

Informality

Many leaders believe desirable discussion develops more quickly in an informal atmosphere. The experience of sitting in a semi-circle or full circle in a well-lighted and nicely furnished room and of contributing to a discussion with questions and pertinent comments is more desirable and effective than sitting in regimented rows in a room that has little warmth and listening to a didactic talk, followed by the usual 10 minutes for questions.

Informality usually insures that the group's leaders and members find it pleasant and easy to communicate with one another in a relaxed atmosphere, on subjects that satisfy the group's overall needs.

Leader's Role

There are many opinions as to the role of the leader in a discussion. How much and what he should say depends on his knowledge of a specific topic, the group's information and needs, and the kind of responses the leader feels he ought to make to help the group's members develop.

Certainly, the leader should not do most of the talking, nor should he refrain from participation. There are times when he may take 30 minutes of an hour session to present some social hygiene information or other information the group lacks or wants. In other situations he may start the discussion with a few comments, and say only what is necessary to guide and stimulate discussion during the remainder of the session. He may call upon a capable member to make the summary.

Some leaders prefer to direct discussions solely along lines suggested by the group's questions and opinions, and do not stimulate the discussion with any of their own ideas. They feel it is their function to guide and clarify the group's discussion and to interpret where they can help the group develop insight into a particular situation.

Catharsis

Certain psychological experiences the leader should help the group obtain are of considerable importance because they enable the members to increase their sense of well-being and understanding.

Earlier we noted that individuals derive a sense of identity and belongingness when they are permitted and encouraged to express their opinions and feelings in a group. In the center of this experience is the process of relieving oneself of hidden or repressed emotions and ideas.

Especially in a group's first few meetings this release of repressions, known psychologically as catharsis, also provides a general sense of satisfaction and comfort. It clears the way for the further growth of unity in the group, leads to attachments that give strength to the group.

There are two dangers to recognize—the creation of anxiety and the development of hostility:

- When the group's members express themselves about some possibly anxiety-provoking subject—such as boy-girl relationships, sexual development, etc.—the discussion may drive some who are not sufficiently mature to tolerate the situation out of the group.
- Some members may feel no limits on the expression of hostility. This may occur with young adolescents who start arguments and are insulting or use name-calling.

If uncontrolled, these negative emotions may prevent growth in the group. A leader needs to understand the concept of limits in order to help a group function in terms of the growth possibilities of its members.

Emotional Support

Another experience adolescents need is the feeling of being supported by their group leader and by their fellow members.

Without playing favorites, the leader should encourage and show appreciation of the members' participation, however meager and naive it might be. Inspired by the leader's strength and hearty recognition, the weaker members of the group may reach a point where they can function with self-confidence. The stronger members who identify themselves with the leader may absorb this approach, and use it to strengthen the group almost unwittingly.

Reality-Testing

When encouraged, the expression of differences in a group permits a real testing of one's ideas. This is especially true if conflicting points of view are verbalized. Ideas that are unrealistic and false stand a chance of being modified and corrected. Discussion can help adolescents to develop valid ideas of the world in which they live.

The Leader's Knowledge of Himself

It is a psychological principle that his own conflicts or immaturity may prevent the leader of a group from providing opportunities for growth to the members of that group. If a group worker is embarrassed by questions about necking, petting and related conduct because of his own unresolved conflicts or anxieties, it is not easy or even possible for him to clarify the subject in a way beneficial to the group. If he transmits his anxiety or confusion to the adolescents, he perpetuates the problem for them, instead of clarifying it.

A leader will be limited to the extent that he has not resolved his own personality problems in areas connected with his work. He may obtain help from a competent supervisor if he is willing to face his difficulties. When his personal problems are very involved, he should seek professional counsel.

It is important for a leader to be clear about his own values, attitudes and feelings, and the ways in which he may express them in a group. A truly democratic process neither excludes the leader's concepts nor warrants an imposition of his ideas. When he contributes his opinions, he should not lay them down categorically. Instead, it is important for him to make it clear to the group that his reactions represent another approach to consider along with their own contributions.

The leader of a group is fundamentally a guide and inspiration to each member of that group. Democratically he helps members to develop their potentialities and to grow toward mature social and personal adjustments.

Reading List

On the Adolescent

Adolescence, Part 1, 43rd Year Book of the National Society for the Study of Education. University of Chicago Press, Chicago, Ill., 1944. *See especially:*

(1) *Adolescence as a Period of Transition,* by L. K. Frank.

(2) *Physiological Changes in Adolescence,* by Nathan W. Shock.

(3) *Adolescent and the Family,* by L. K. Frank.

Adolescent Personality, A Study of Individual Behavior, by Peter Blos, Appleton-Century Co., New York, 1941.

Dating Days, by L. A. Kirkendall and R. F. Osborne. Science Research Associates, Chicago, Ill., 1949.

Emotion and Conduct in Adolescence, by Caroline Zachry. Appleton-Century-Crofts, New York, 1940.

Guiding the Adolescent, by D. A. Thom, M.D. U. S. Children's Bureau, Washington, D. C. Rev. 1946.

Teen Time, Guideposts to Mental Health, No. 3. New York State Department of Mental Hygiene, Albany, N. Y., 1951.

The Dynamics of Human Adjustment, by Percival Symonds. Appleton-Century Co., New York, 1946.

Understanding Sex, by L. A. Kirkendall. Science Research Associates, Chicago, Ill., 1947.

Understanding Yourself, by W. L. Menninger, M.D. Science Research Associates, Chicago, Ill., 1948.

On Group Work

Group Work With American Youth, by G. L. Coyle. Harper and Brothers, New York, 1948.

Mental Hygiene in Teaching, by F. Redl and W. W. Wattenberg. Harcourt, Brace & Co., New York, 1951.

So You Want to Help People, by Rudolph M. Wittenberg. Association Press, New York, 1947.

Social Group Work Practice, by G. Wilson and G. Ryland. Houghton Mifflin, New York, 1949.

The Art of Group Discipline, by Rudolph M. Wittenberg. Association Press, New York, 1951.

For Adolescents

So Youth May Know, by Roy E. Dickerson. New York, Association Press, 1948.

Planning Your Life for School and Society, by L. A. Eastburn, V. H. Kelly and C. J. Falk. New York, Charles Scribner's Sons, 1948.

Your Own Story, by Marion Faegre. Minneapolis, University of Minnesota Press, 1943.

A Girl Grows Up, by Ruth Fedder. New York, McGraw-Hill Book Co., 1948. 2nd ed.

Youth Grows into Adulthood, by Morey R. Fields, Jacob A. Goldberg and Holger F. Kilander. New York, Chartwell House, 1950.

Looking Ahead, ed. by Ethel R. Forbes. New York, Horizon House, 1946.

How to Chart Your Own Career, by Grenville Kleiser. Los Angeles, Willing Publishing Co., 1945.

Adolescence and Youth, by Paul H. Landis. New York, McGraw-Hill Book Co., 1945.

Coming of Age, by Esther Lloyd-Jones and Ruth Fedder. New York, McGraw-Hill Book Co., 1941.

Making the Most of Your Life, by Douglas Lurton. New York, McGraw-Hill Book Co., 1945.

A Boy Grows Up, by Harry C. McKown. New York, McGraw-Hill Book Co., 1949.

Making the Most of Your Personality, by Winifred V. Richmond. New York, Farrar & Rinehart, 1942.

A Doctor Talks to Teen-Agers, by William S. Sadler. St. Louis, C. V. Mosby Co., 1948.

Visual Aids

Are You Popular?

A portrayal of a teen-age boy and girl who are friendly, considerate and interested in others, and therefore popular. 16 mm, 10 minutes, sound, color, 1948. Coronet Films, Chicago, Ill.

Choosing for Happiness.

A dramatization of the problems of selecting a mate. 16 mm, sound, 1949. McGraw-Hill Book Co., New York, N. Y.

How Do You Know It's Love?

Portrays the nature, development and maturity of love. Contrasts experience of younger and older couples. Dr. Reuben Hill is the educational consultant. Audience: young people and adults. 16 mm, 13 minutes, sound, black and white, and color. A Coronet Instructional Film. Coronet Films, Chicago, Ill.

How to Say No.

Deals with such teen-age behavior problems as smoking, drinking and lovemaking. Discusses ways of saying no in such situations, and still maintaining status and keeping friends. Evelyn Duvall, Ph.D., is the educational consultant. 16 mm, 10 minutes, sound, black and white. A Coronet Instructional Film. Coronet Films, Chicago, Ill.

It Takes All Kinds.

A portrayal of specific personality patterns and the importance of understanding and evaluating them in the behavior of a prospective marriage partner. 16 mm, sound, 1949. McGraw-Hill Book Co., New York, N. Y.

Marriage for Moderns.

Ideals and goals of adult love and their relationship to a satisfactory and happy marital relationship. 16 mm, sound, 1949. McGraw-Hill Book Co., New York, N. Y.

Marriage Is a Partnership.

Struggle of a newly-married couple to complete the weaning-from-parents process and attain closer marital relationships. Dr. Lemo D. Rockwood is the educational consultant. Audience: young people and adults. 16 mm, 16 minutes, sound, black and white. A Coronet Instructional Film. Coronet Films, Chicago, Ill.

Shy Guy.

A shy adolescent boy in a strange town is started on the road to friendly relationships with other high school youth by practicing some of the principles he observes among other well-adjusted youth. Some oversimplification, but a good device to stimulate discussion. 16 mm, 12 minutes, sound, color, 1948. Coronet Films, Chicago, Ill.

The Meaning of Engagement.

Explains the meaning and function of the engagement period in preparing for a successful marriage. Dr. Reuben Hill is the educational consultant. For late teen-agers and adults. 16 mm, 12 minutes, sound, black and white. A Coronet Instructional Film. Coronet Films, Chicago, Ill.

The Other Fellow's Feelings.

Typical problems of young adolescents, teasing and ridicule. Avoids categoric solutions. Stimulates discussion and judgment. Audience: young adolescents and teachers. 16 mm, 8 minutes, sound, black and white. Part of a series on Discussion Problems in Group Living by Young America Films, New York, N. Y.

This Charming Couple.

A study of the false ideas and goals engendered by romantic love. 16 mm, sound, 1949. McGraw-Hill Book Co., New York, N. Y.

Understanding Your Emotions.

A general understanding of emotions, what they are, what they do, where they come from, and how they are changed. Dr. A. R. Lauer is the educational consultant. Audience: young people and adults. 16 mm, 13½ minutes, sound, black and white, and color. A Coronet Instructional Film. Coronet Films, Chicago, Ill.

Who's Boss?

The problems which a couple experience in adjusting to married life. 16 mm, sound, 1949. McGraw-Hill Book Co., New York, N. Y.

You and Your Family.

The film features three situations: (a) the family refuses Mary permission for a date, (b) family members shirk their household chores, and (c) Bill and his father disagree upon a time for coming home. These scenes are dramatized and summarized, and the audience is then invited to discuss how each situation could be met satisfactorily. 16 mm, 8 minutes, sound, 1946. Association Films, New York, N. Y.

You and Your Friends.

A teen-age party is shown. The audience is asked to evaluate different types of behavior portrayed by those at the party. Self-centeredness, lying, behind-the-back criticism, and breaking a promise are contrasted with better qualities of behavior. To be used in stimulating discussion. 16 mm, 7 minutes, sound, 1941. Association Films, New York, N. Y.

M.A. in guidance, Northwestern University. Former teacher, counselor and psychiatric social worker. Now editor of guidance publications for Science Research Associates.

Nancy C. Wimmer

Trends in family life education in schools

by Nancy C. Wimmer

Grandmother and Grandfather would be shocked were they to walk in on some of our high schools today and find groups of boys and girls conducting panels on such topics as "Should high school students go steady?" "What causes problems in marriage?" "How should we tell our children about sex?" They would undoubtedly be fearful that the good old *fundamentals* of education had been replaced by *fun.*

They might join in the barrage of criticism schools have faced in recent years. Probably the major criticism is that they've been neglecting the 3 R's for frills. (In Los Angeles, a parent writing to the school board to protest the poor education his children were getting, misspelled nine words in one short letter!)

Actually, though evidence is somewhat fragmentary, it appears that children today are as well grounded in readin', ritin', 'n' 'rithmetic as children at any time in our history. And what the critics overlook is the fact that many, many more students are going to school than have ever gone before—not just the "cream of the crop." In the last 50 years our secondary school population has grown 20-fold, while our population has only doubled. That means that vast numbers of young people of all kinds of abilities and learning aptitudes are in school.

And schools have been facing this challenge under major handicaps. At the same time that our school enrollments have increased, public expenditure per pupil for education has decreased in relation to national income. In 1930 it was 3.3% of the national income . . . in 1950 it was down to 1.8%,

It's costing less to send a pupil to school today.

Despite obstacles

Though classrooms are crowded, salaries often low, added duties numerous, support inadequate, schools have been doing a rather astounding job of introducing family living education. And though Grandmother might be shocked by a visit to the panel discussion on dating and marriage, she would, I am sure, agree that schools could take on no more important job than helping young people *build happy families.* There is probably no job in which all of us have such a stake as helping young people with this task.

The need and the demand for education for family living

One and a half to two million children under 18 live in homes broken by divorce. Almost 400,000 divorces and annulments are granted every year. If the trend continues, somewhat less than one out of every three marriages started in the last decade will end in divorce.

This picture is not a very pretty one. Nor is the picture of the many young people that are growing up with serious problems of maladjustment.

- Juveniles account for 60% of all the crimes committed in the United States. They commit 1½ million major crimes a year.
- Estimates indicate that over 100,000 high school students will become alcoholics.
- Mental health statistics indicate one child in eight is so emotionally maladjusted as to need professional help.

To improve mental health

We do not have any evidence that family living education is—or can be—a panacea for all these ills. But we do know that emotional immaturity is the major cause of most divorces and that it is the chief cause of tension and instability in the home and a major contributor to delinquency.

We know too that neuroses beget neuroses. The child from the unstable, unhealthful environment builds his own home on an equally shaky foundation unless he is given help in learning to build a more solid one. Family living education, with its emphasis on mental health, is a major step in providing the help young people need if they are to build happy, healthy homes.

Pressure from below

High school students, especially, want help. A recent poll of 3,000 youngsters conducted by the Purdue Youth Opinion Panel disclosed that 51% of these students wanted their schools to offer more courses on family life education. Sixty percent of the seniors said they weren't getting enough help with their problems of family life.

Many of us forget that most boys and girls do not go to college. (Only 10% of our young people today graduate from college.) So most children, if they have not been given family living education in elementary or high school, are unlikely to get it.

Aware of both the need and the demand for helping young people, schools throughout the country are starting programs where there are none and improving those that have already been launched.

What schools are doing

How they're getting programs started

Getting the family living education program started—whether in the school or community—is about as tough as any part of the job. But there is indication that community acceptance of and demand for it is increasing.

Those who have learned the hard way say there are several rules to follow:

Leave sex out of it! The community is still reluctant to support sex education—at least when it's blatantly labeled sex education. And educators in this field agree, too, that sex education is but a part of family living education.

Community support

Let the whole community in on it! Time and time again it has been demonstrated that where the entire community has been brought in on the program from the very beginning success is more likely to be assured. There are in every community those who resist innovations . . . both within the school and outside of it. If community support is obtained first, teachers especially feel more secure about their role in the program.

Such a step often results, too, in the planning of a community-wide program.

For instance, in one school in California the students petitioned for the course. Their petition was referred to the PTA, which voted for the course and presented a series of programs on the idea to the community. Unanimously, the board of education voted to support the program. Then representatives of the churches, social agencies and business were called together to help launch family living in this community. Out of a high school students' petition a whole community program got started.

In Asheville, a city-wide Family Council helps plan and carry out the school program, coordinates it with study courses for adults in the PTA, churches and clubs, and cooperates in an annual family life institute for studying family life problems. In short, it is a program with something for the entire family—parents and children. And that is actually the ideal type of program. Members of this community are indeed working out their problems together.

Social agencies have a major contribution to make to the school where family living education may be very new. They have experience and a knowledge of family problems that it is impossible for most school people to have.

Teacher-parent-pupil

The best family living courses are teacher-parent-pupil planned. Parents who know what family living is all about—what its goals are—are its ardent supporters. Schools have proved this. Parents are leery of programs they know nothing about.

Juveniles commit more than a million major crimes a year.

One Chicago mother who found out her child was taking a family living course—the class was spending some time on a unit on personal appearance, personal daintiness and hygiene—stormed into the school and said to the principal, "My daughter comes to school to be learned—not smelled." Had that mother been informed of the goals of the course, that wouldn't have happened. So rule no. 3 is: *Broadcast it!*

Broadcasting the program

Lester Kirkendall, of Oregon State College, an authority in this field, has demonstrated the need for working closely with local newspapers. When schools have the newspapers' support, a great deal of the job of selling the community is accomplished. On the other hand, in one middlewest community the newspaper report of the school's sex education program—in reality a family living course not at all concerned primarily with sex education—brought the community rafters down.

But your local paper can be your best promotion device if you ask for its support.

What schools are teaching

In spite of an already overcrowded curriculum—each year some new subject seems to deserve a spot in the school program—schools have found some ingenious ways of introducing family life education. They have added units to regular courses, have added separate courses, have developed integrated programs with all teachers participating.

Of major importance is the job they are doing in offering parents a part in family living education. In Highland Park, Mich., for instance,

Neurotic parents—
neurotic children.

parents literally enter school when their children start. And parents of various age groups can take child-study courses.

Who teaches?

Because family living education is comparatively new, we do not really have teachers who are trained in this field. So schools are finding that they must plan their program around those faculty members who by training and—more important—by virtue of their personalities and maturity—seem best suited to carry on the program. Teachers with the right personal qualifications have wonderful opportunities to obtain the necessary training in some of the workshops conducted throughout the country. In two well-known school systems—Hinsdale, Ill., and Highland Park—science teachers with skill in working closely with youngsters and with a genuine interest in the field developed outstanding programs.

But whether the program is integrated into many courses, whether it is a unit added to such already established courses as social studies, home economics or biology, the goal is the same and it determines the content. The goal is to help young people become more adequate, mature, stable individuals who are capable of making harmonious and happy marriages.

Pupils' worries

For that reason, topics like self-understanding, emotional maturity and principles of mental health are stressed. Devices such as the Science Research Associates' *Youth Inventory*—which reveals the problems children feel are bothering them most—help schools plan course content.

Seniors wanted help with family problems.

From such checklists they learn the kinds of problems the children in *their* school worry about. They learn that high school students worry about problems of getting along with their own families, being popular, dating. They worry about how to select a mate, how to run a home, how to raise a family.

What we do in family living education varies from age group to age group. Elementary school children are concerned about getting along with their parents and their brothers and sisters. They are worried about having friends, about losing their tempers.

High school students become each year more concerned about dating and marriage. For that reason, family living courses that include units on preparation for marriage and parenthood are usually not held until the junior or senior year. The early high school courses emphasize personal guidance and social and personal adjustment.

In California and Illinois

For example, a school system in California offers a 9th-grade family living unit that covers emotional maturity, family relationships, health, boy-girl relations. And then 10th-grade biology has a unit on growing up physically.

In the 12th grade a required class called human relationships is offered to boys and girls separately. In this course students discuss the physical, psychological and cultural factors affecting the two sexes. They discuss the problems of boy-girl relations, courtship and marriage, parenthood and the more mundane problems—but real ones—of finances and home management.

The programs are as varied as our American school systems. In some towns in Illinois, family living education for 7th graders includes units on being friends, sharing home duties, caring for children. There is no single pattern. Each school works out the program that best suits the needs of its group.

Techniques

How do teachers of family living courses run their classes? Certainly it isn't like teaching algebra or American history. There are no final facts to memorize. The discussion method—seldom the lecture method—is used most frequently. If you stopped in a typical class you might see them dealing with a parent-child problem by role-playing. Johnny, playing the role of father, gets new insight into the problems his father faces.

Question boxes in which students drop questions anonymously are popular.

The football player in the nursery

In many schools, children learn about child behavior by spending time in the school nursery. I saw a delightful school scene at the Highland Park nursery school—part of the public school system—where students in the family living course all have a chance to work with nursery school students. I was watching a massive Highland Park football player take a group of pre-schoolers outside for play. After he had their play underway he moved over to the fence where two of his team pals were looking in from the outside. I thought their conversation would run to next Saturday's game, but instead I heard the "temporary" nursery teacher say to his friends, "Gee, there's one little kid I'm having a lot of trouble with. He just doesn't get along with anyone. Wonder what his home environment's like?"

Other schools, where class activities must be kept within the class, call in outside experts . . . social workers, child psychologists, physicians, psychiatrists, clergymen, parents.

Students publicize a course

In Hinsdale, students have formed a panel in their classes to go out to community organizations—the PTA, Kiwanis and Rotary—and tell them about the course. They discuss with the organizations the problems that they feel they, as teen-agers, have in dealing with adults . . . the problems they want help with.

Films are frequently used. There are some very fine ones available.

How to be popular? Many don't know.

At this age they worry about getting along with their family and friends.

Parents are invited to classes frequently—and not just mothers. Real efforts are made to get fathers to participate in the courses.

Counseling

In many schools, counseling services are also available. Schools realize that the group cannot by any means handle all its problems. As a matter of fact, it takes a very skillful teacher to recognize when children are getting beyond their depth and into areas too difficult to cope with. When children are deeply disturbed by certain problems, they should see a competent counselor.

Skits, dramatizations, buzz sessions . . . these too are used frequently in the family living class. Many schools have bookshelves for parents as well as for students. These contain books and pamphlets dealing with the whole area of family living.

Booklets have special merits

For some time now we at Science Research Associates have been working with leaders in the field of mental health to develop booklets that would fit easily into the family living program in schools and in the community. The flexibility of booklets makes it possible for a teacher to tailor-make her course.

They are particularly valuable in short courses where a textbook really covers too much territory. Mrs. Marjorie Cosgrove, head of family living education for the Highland Park schools, and Mary Josey, head of family living education in the Berkley, Mich., schools, have worked with Science Research Associates to develop a combination work-textbook that provides not only the content for a course but also activities, quizzes, thought-provoking questions and suggested readings.

The problems ahead

- *Community acceptance.* Although a recent study of trends in family living education indicated that community acceptance is increasing, we still have a long way to go. One of the major problems schools face is developing skills in selling communities on the need for such programs. By combining their forces with those of other community agencies and by working closely with such groups they can accomplish a great deal.

- *Lack of trained personnel.* It will be some time before there will be trained personnel for family living education. In the meantime, both the school and community have ample resources—good teachers, good specialists in the community. Where schools have selected teachers who, though lacking in specific training in the field, are mature, responsible and interested in helping young people with their problems of family living, the programs have succeeded.

- *Lack of research and experience.* Family living courses are still too new for us to really know whether we have found the best patterns for what we're trying to do. We will need to keep an experimental attitude toward our problems. What techniques are best? Where do we start—first grade, junior high, high school? What do we cover? In the near future we must be able to find the answer to questions like "Are we meeting the needs of our pupils?"

  We know, for instance, that the family living patterns of lower-class children are very different from those of middle- and upper-class children. We are not meeting the needs of the lower-class child if we are teaching only middle-class standards. For instance, middle-class practices of child-rearing are frequently too rigid, lower-class practices too permissive. We can help youngsters best if we are aware of these differences.

- *Establishing a continuous program.* When a group of 68 specialists in family living education, representing 19 states, were asked about family life education in elementary schools, three-fourths of them said that in the schools with which they worked such programs were getting underway. The goal, of course, is to provide meaningful programs throughout the child's school experience . . . and also to provide parents and adults with the help they need. In short, our goal is a school and community program.

We have a long way to go yet . . . but the signs are encouraging. Some ingenious programs have appeared, and despite handicaps many communities are providing their children and adults with major help in building happy families.

Graduate of Jefferson Medical College of Philadelphia. Associate in ophthalmology, University of Pennsylvania graduate school. Special consultant, USPHS, VD Division. Member of American Academy of Ophthalmology and Oto-Laryngology.

George P. Meyer, M.D.

Syphilis of the eye

by George P. Meyer, M.D.

The seriousness of syphilis lies in the widespread harm that follows the appearance of the initial sore, the chancre. The devastating effects of the infection may manifest themselves not only in the eyes but in the skin, bones, circulatory system, brain and spinal cord . . . in fact, in any part of the body.

In many instances the condition complained of is obviously syphilitic. But there are so many other obscure complaints whose causes must be diligently investigated because they may stem from syphilis that this disease is aptly called "The Great Masquerader." Its manifestations are Protean.

Frequency and importance

Disease of the eye is but one of many evils that follow the development of syphilis. Ophthalmologists have long appreciated the importance of this etiologic factor in widespread ocular disability and blindness. A few figures concerning blindness might serve to illustrate this point.

Because statistics have no value unless there is some uniformity in nomenclature, it is important to define blindness. There are several definitions. Blindness may be:

- Total loss of light perception in one eye only.
- Total loss of light perception in both eyes.
- Loss of visual acuity to below 20/200 in the better eye. This is called industrial blindness and is the criterion of blindness being more widely adopted. It is of this type we speak.

It has been estimated that there are 250,000 industrially blind in this country. Of these 10% to 15%—25,000 to 35,000—are blind because of syphilis.

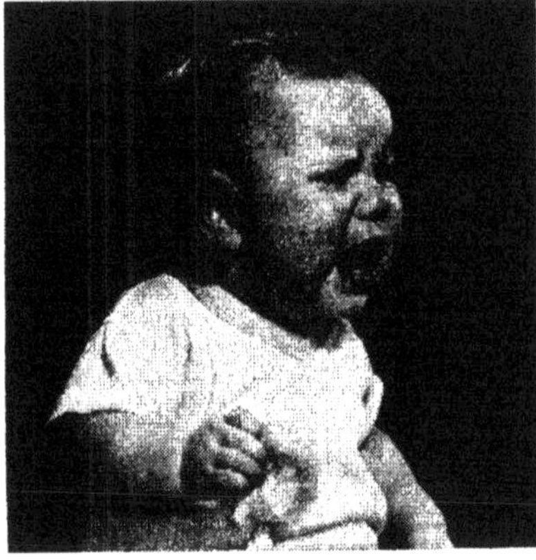

Prenatal care prevents congenital syphilis.

There are, of course, a much greater number of individuals with partial blindness resulting from syphilis who do not lend themselves to statistical analysis, but who nevertheless suffer from a disability which is largely preventable.

Clinical considerations

Syphilis may be transmitted in several ways. While sexual intercourse is the most common method for spreading the disease, infections do occur very infrequently through handling of infected towels, surgical instruments or kissing. Babies are infected by syphilitic mothers.

The manner of transmission of the causative organism, the spirochete, may be unusual and bizarre. There are cases on record where a person's eye was infected by a well-intentioned but syphilitic individual who sought to remove with his tongue a foreign body from the eye of his unsuspecting victim.

Syphilis may be congenital or acquired.

Congenital syphilis is transmitted to a baby born of an untreated syphilitic mother.

Acquired syphilis is first manifested by the presence of a firm or indurated painless round ulcer, the so-called primary lesion or chancre. This is followed in most untreated cases by secondary eruptions and inflammations, and late or tertiary manifestations in the bone, circulatory, nervous or other systems.

Clinical manifestations

The eye may become involved in either congenital or acquired syphilis. There is no structure of the eye or its adnexa which may not be affected by syphilis. Among the more common manifestations . . .

How people become blind . . . infectious diseases cause 14% of the blindness in children. Syphilis is the most serious of these diseases. An estimated 100,000 babies face blindness because of syphilis.

How people become blind . . . infectious diseases cause 23% of the blindness in adults. Syphilis is the most frequent of these diseases. But the new "miracle drugs" now make it possible to cure cases in a short time. If treatment is adequate and started early, blindness may be averted.

- Acute or chronic dacryocystitis is an inflammatory affection of the tear drainage system.
- The lids or conjunctiva may be the site of the primary lesion, the chancre.
- The cornea may be inflamed by a congenitally acquired syphilitic infection, which causes interstitial keratitis.
- The iris and ciliary body may be acutely diseased, typically in the secondary stage of an acquired syphilitic infection.
- The retina and choroid among the deeper structures of the eye may be diseased in both the congenital and acquired forms of syphilis.
- The optic nerve in both congenital and acquired syphilis may become so involved that serious impairment of vision or even blindness may result.

All these and other conditions may cause some loss of vision, but the conditions which are the most frequent cause of syphilitic blindness are interstitial keratitis and optic atrophy.

Interstitial keratitis is an inflammation of the cornea, the clear portion of the anterior coat of the eye through which light passes to the retina. It results from congenital syphilis and occurs chiefly in early life but may first appear in middle age. This inflammation is often followed by scarring, which interferes with the transparency of the cornea. The extent of the loss of transparency determines the amount of visual damage.

Optic atrophy following involvement of the optic nerve may occur either in congenital or acquired syphilis and is the most frequent cause of syphilitic blindness.

Treatment

The best treatment for syphilis of the eye is prevention.

ASHA helps to fight syphilitic blindness.

Much progress has been made in the prevention of congenital syphilis by adequate prenatal care of expectant mothers in detecting and eradicating hidden or obvious infection, and in the more general use of premarital Wassermann tests. A great amount of good, too, has been accomplished in the prevention of acquired syphilis by intelligent prophylactic measures and the laudable work of the medical profession in cooperation with agencies like the American Social Hygiene Association, the United States Public Health Service, the Society for the Prevention of Blindness, and many others.

Once syphilis has been acquired, the chief hope for the avoidance of disastrous eye complications lies in the early detection and treatment of the infection in its early stages before visual damage can occur. Early treatment is relatively easy and usually completely successful, thanks to the gratifying effectiveness of the newer medicines such as penicillin. If syphilis has affected the central nervous system or the eye directly, vigorous medical measures—such as the use of penicillin and fever-inducing agents such as malaria, typhoid or other inoculations—can do much to prevent loss of vision.

If blindness has ensued, treatment is of little avail in restoring sight.

It can be seen, therefore, that the earlier treatment is instituted the better the outlook. To this end there must be continued effort to educate the public to the dangers of syphilis, and there must be continued cooperation between the medical profession and its allied groups to detect and treat this condition early.

Optic atrophy of congenital neurosyphilis

R. D. (3081), a white man of 26, first complained of impaired vision two years prior to the time he came to the clinic. At the onset of impaired vision he obtained glasses from an optometrist. For about a year he thought they improved his vision. He then visited a physician who gave him injections in the arm and buttocks for about a year.

Corrected vision in the right eye was 10/200, in the left eye 20/200. Both optic nerves showed evidence of irreversible atrophy with marked loss of the normal wide field of vision. A physical examination revealed the presence of congenital syphilis with involvement of the nervous system. Serologic and spinal fluid tests for syphilis were positive. Treatment did not restore any vision.

Comment: Treatment might have been of some value if the case had been treated medically earlier. Thirty-one percent of our patients with optic atrophy consulted an optometrist first. In many cases this may be the cause of unwarranted delay in adequate therapy.

Sixty-one percent of the cases when first seen by us are industrially blind. This is true of the case just cited and emphasizes the need for early diagnosis.

Rapidly progressive optic atrophy

In the case of M. L. (2999), a white woman of 49, vision became blurred four months prior to the time she came to the hospital for glasses. The patient, who worked as a dress operator, was separated from her husband. She had no knowledge of being infected with syphilis . . . she had never had any tests or treatment for syphilis. She had no other complaints except occasional shooting pains in the legs of about two years' duration (a symptom of locomotor ataxia or tabes, a syphilitic disease of the central nervous system).

Corrected visual acuity in her right eye was 20/50, in the left 20/50. Her optic nerves seemed already pale in spite of the short history of her symptoms. Her field of vision was markedly reduced.

Studies proved the presence of neurosyphilis of the tabetic type with optic atrophy. Despite vigorous treatment and the full cooperation of the patient she was blind within two years.

Comment: There are cases in which the syphilitic damage inexorably progresses to total blindness in spite of all we can do.

Slowly progressive optic atrophy

S. S. (3546), a white man of 56, a pushcart vendor, had had impaired vision for 10 years. Thirty years before he had a chancre for which he had no treatment. Five years before we saw him he was treated inadequately at another hospital for syphilitic optic atrophy. His vision at that time was 20/200 in each eye. No further treatment had been given. When we saw him the vision in the right eye was 10/200 and in the left 7/200. There was marked contraction of the visual field. Studies proved the presence of syphilis, tabes and optic atrophy.

Comment: There are instances where the progress in the disease is exceedingly slow. We can conclude that adequate therapy fails to help

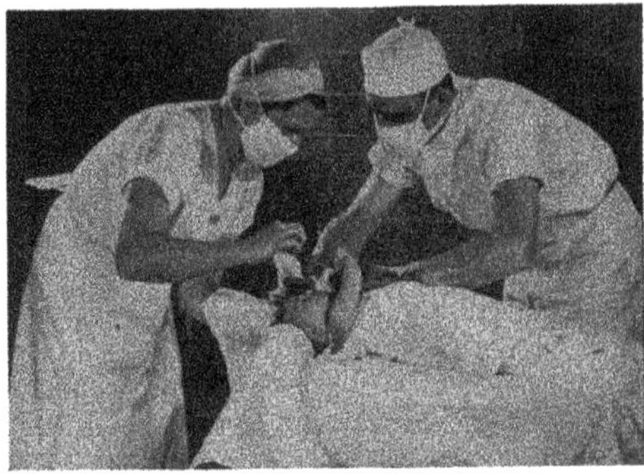

The best treatment is . . . prevention.

some cases, and that inadequate therapy does not accelerate a very leisurely progress in the course of the disease in other cases.

Pre-atrophic stage of optic nerve involvement

G. F., a white woman of 51, was first seen in May of 1946. Because of a positive Wassermann reaction she had received injections in the arms and buttocks at irregular intervals for "many years." She desired a change in her glasses. Other than the visual impairment and occasional lancinating leg pains of several years' duration, she had no complaint.

Examination revealed positive serologic tests for syphilis and neurologic evidence of tabes. Her vision was normal. The perimetric study of her fields of vision showed a definite cut indicating some functional loss in the optic nerve.

Vigorous treatment with penicillin was given and the visual fields returned to normal.

Comment: This case illustrates the happy result obtainable when the diagnosis of optic nerve damage is made in its earliest stage. It is in this stage only that the process is revocable. Should the pathologic process proceed to the stage of optic atrophy—the death of some or all of the fibres in the optic nerve—the condition is irrevocable and the most that we can hope for is to prevent further progress in the destruction of the nerve.

The outlook

For a long time it was assumed that optic nerve damage as a result of syphilis was inevitably followed, sooner or later, by blindness. Our observation and study of many hundreds of these cases at the Wills Hospital in Philadelphia has convinced us that this gloomy outlook is wholly unwarranted. Vigorous and adequate treatment gives happy results . . . moderately advanced cases are arrested and early cases may even have a restoration of normal function. True, a few cases are uncontrollable, but they are now fortunately the exception.

Other syphilitic eye disorders are amenable to treatment. Since in the main they are less dangerous than optic atrophy, the outlook for them is more cheerful . . . especially with the development and use of antibiotics.

However, syphilis of the eye is preventable and should never occur if diagnosis and treatment are carried out in the early stages of the disease before eye complications develop.

As a matter of fact, syphilis itself is preventable, and the decreasing incidence of syphilis—both congenital and acquired—is the happy result of the untiring efforts of the medical profession in cooperation with its friendly allies, the Public Health Service, the Society for the Prevention of Blindness, the American Social Hygiene Association and many others, through their educational programs and treatment facilities. May their work with an enlightened public rid us soon of this dread disease and save the sight of countless thousands.

CREDITS

Photo courtesy U.S. Army, p. 49.

Photo courtesy National Girl Scout News Bureau, from the film, *The Growing Years*, p. 53.

Photo courtesy National Recreation Association (C. S. Barrett), p. 60.

Photo courtesy National Recreation Association (Paul Parker), p. 62.

Photo courtesy McGraw-Hill Text-Films, p. 77.

Data on blindness courtesy National Society for the Prevention of Blindness, p. 81.

Photos and text courtesy of WHO Newsletter, June, 1952, pp. 86–91.

The Happy Ending

Her story began when health workers in an Egyptian village visited her during her pregnancy and persuaded her to have a medical examination.

At the clinic she learned that the infection of syphilis was in her blood and she was told how dangerous this was for her unborn baby.

But she was told, too, that her case had been discovered in time and that modern medicine could almost certainly prevent her child from being born with the disease. She agreed to take the penicillin treatment.

Here you see the result—a healthy child, in the arms of a proud mother. The photograph was taken at the clinic, which she still attends for a regular check-up.

Shielding the Unborn from Sickness

Today it is possible to safeguard the newborn against congenital syphilis with almost 100% certainty, provided the expectant mother is given penicillin treatment during pregnancy. The problem is how to find the expectant mothers suffering from syphilis and treat them in time.

In Egypt this question is being tackled in a joint effort by the Egyptian government and the World Health Organization. WHO provided a team of international experts, including a venereologist, a serologist, a public health educator and a public health nurse.

A campaign against congenital syphilis is launched in the province of Gabiah, Egypt. Robert Bogue, WHO public health educator, holds a conference of social workers. Facing Mr. Bogue, Aziz Habashy explains case-finding technique in Arabic.

One of the villages included in the campaign is Birma.

The Egyptian Ministry of Health established this international team in a clinic at Tanta, the most populous city in the fertile Delta region between Cairo and Alexandria. They attached Egyptian experts to the team to match the WHO experts, as well as a number of laboratory workers and nurses for training.

But first, support of village headmen must be obtained—the political leader in tarbush and the religious leaders in white headdress. With their approval plans then go to the village health committee, which begins a case-finding campaign.

Throughout this Delta region, of which Tanta is the natural center, the Ministry of Social Affairs has established social centers in the numerous and crowded villages, some of which have as many as 10,000 people. It is through these social centers that the first—and important—step is taken to use the safeguards of modern science to protect the unborn generation.

A survey in Tanta itself showed that about 10% of pregnant women are syphilitic. In the villages the percentage is probably higher. By comparison, in Sweden the incidence is less than one percent.

The hakimah (public health nurse and midwife), attached to Birma's social center, finds a suspect. In the courtyard of a mud-walled house she persuades a young married woman to go to the Tanta clinic to be examined.

are there, the woman head of the is a little knows that ion is not own interest of the baby ing.

After an interview with the doctors she must have a blood test. The sample is taken by Egyptian nurses, Shafica H. Fahmy and Naffussa A. K. Labib, and is then sent to the laboratory.

While she waits, her blood sample will be examined by a WHO serologist, Dr. H. G. S. Ruge, of Kiel. On his left is his Egyptian teammate, Dr. Ahmed Montassar. On his right is an Egyptian laboratory assistant who is being trained in modern blood-test techniques.

She goes back to the doctors. She has the infection, but they tell her that if she will accept penicillin treatment her baby will almost certainly be born healthy.

es and comes for examina- e result? Her s born free of

by Carl C. Bare, Deputy Inspector

Cleveland Police Department

A clean slate for Cleveland

Where big-city prostitution is held to a minimum

Cleveland enjoys the reputation of being one of the cleanest cities in the United States. The Kefauver committee's investigations and the American Social Hygiene Association's surveys attest to that.

In 1952 one of ASHA's investigators reported that in Cleveland he found only seven brothels operating in a very limited way. In only a few bars could he find a prostitute and in just one hotel would bellboys call a girl to his room. Not one taxi driver could take him to a place of prostitution.

Once upon a time

Not always has Cleveland enjoyed an enviable reputation. Some years ago prostitutes were easily available in Cleveland. An influential press and an aroused public demanded a change. When the citizens indicated that they wanted and were willing to support strict enforcement, that's what they got.

For several years a vice bureau spread its net over the whole city, which is divided into six districts each under the command of a deputy inspector.

To keep prostitution permanently at a minimum — that is the crux of the enforcement problem. Spurts of frenzied police activity followed by periods of complacency serve only to impress upon racketeers the need for intensified corruption of officials. In Cleveland, informed citizens, sincere public officials and honest police through unremitting effort show racketeers that prostitution is not profitable.

In recent years a civilian-dress detail in each district has been able to handle the problem of detecting and apprehending violators of vice, gambling and related regulations, and the vice bureau has been discontinued. How successful they have been is evident from Cleveland's present record.

A record well earned

It is a remarkable record for a city of over a million and a half people . . . a record that could not be achieved without the support of three groups:

- The people. They wanted their prostitution laws enforced and were willing to support enforcement. The most efficient police department can't enforce laws if the people are antagonistic to enforcement.
- The elected public officials. They took their official duties seriously and did not interfere with the enforcement activities of the police department. Furthermore, they were willing to support the police against criticism from the racketeers or those who unwittingly supported the racketeers.
- The police department. Honest, efficient men, they wanted to be proud of their town.

The job is never done

Clean though Cleveland now may be, only continued intensive enforcement will keep it so. In 1951, 645 women and 196 men were arrested in connection with prostitution. Of these, 199 women and 42 men were sentenced severely enough by cooperative judges to discourage further violations. The others were released on waivers for lack of sufficient evidence . . . after they had been given VD tests.

If Cleveland's people, her press and her elected officials continue to cooperate, the police department will see to it that the city is known as an unprofitable place for prostitutes and their exploiters.

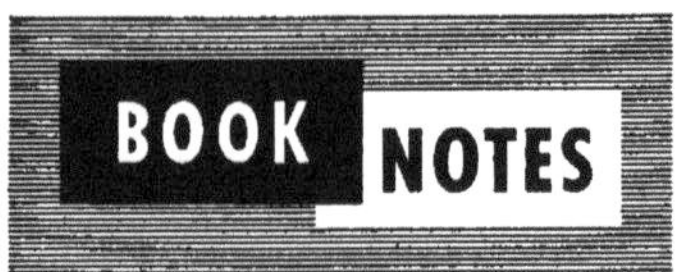

by *Elizabeth B. McQuaid*

Sex-Character Education, by John A. O'Brien. New York, Macmillan, 1952. 220p. $2.75.

This is a useful book for parents and those who work with parents in church, school or community programs. At points, however, it seems unjustly critical of both parents and schools. The point of view throughout is reverent, practical and constructive in dealing with the subject and method of teaching sex to children and young people in the home.

A valuable part of *Sex-Character Education* is the resource material for parents including reprints and excerpts from earlier pamphlets and articles by Esther Emerson Sweeney, Paul Popenoe, Daniel A. Lord, S.J., Edward B. Lyman and others.

John A. O'Brien, professor of philosophy of religion at the University of Notre Dame and widely known author of a dozen other books, has written the first six and last chapters of *Sex-Character Education*. They are strongly motivational and a wholesome antidote to the purely physical interpretations of sexual life. Some readers, however, may think them slightly sentimental.

Rev. Richard E. Lentz
National Council of the Churches of Christ in the United States of America

---

Toward Manhood, by Herman N. Bundesen, M.D. Philadelphia, Lippincott, 1951. 175p. $2.95.

Toward Manhood, for teen-age boys, discusses the reproductive anatomy of both sexes, treats briefly such common concerns as nocturnal emissions and erotic interests and desires, and in more detail discusses premarital sex standards, venereal diseases, prostitution, sexual aberrations and marriage readiness. The book has no index.

Dr. Bundesen incorporates views gained from medical practice and service as a public health officer. His attitude is sympathetic and liberal. For example, he gives strong support to the idea of earlier marriages for mature couples.

In its treatment of sex, however, the book is traditional and somber. The detailed discussions of aberrations and possible "perils" of misconduct overshadow a too-vague and over-generalized positive treatment. Sex is made unreservedly too much a burdensome, oppressive thing. Sex, the boy is told, is a "terrific drive" (p. 57), and he may sometimes feel "obsessed by lewd devils which he cannot fight off no matter how hard he tries" (p. 69).

The adolescent boy "is entitled to know all we can tell him" (p. 10). Yet the discussion points up questions which are left untreated, e.g., the effectiveness of contraceptive methods, prediction of marital sex adjustments, and newer methods of treating venereal disease. The treatment of masturbation is brief and unrealistic. These omissions prevent the realization of this laudable objective.

Lester A. Kirkendall
Associate Professor of Family Life
Oregon State College

A Healthy Personality for Your Child, by James L. Hymes, Jr., M.D. Washington, D. C., Children's Bureau, U. S. Government Printing Office, 1952. 23p. 15¢.

This 23-page illustrated pamphlet by Dr. Hymes, professor of education at George Peabody College for Teachers, Nashville, Tenn., is designed to aid parents in helping their children achieve emotional and social health.

It outlines in understandable fashion the various stages of personality development of a child from infancy through adolescence. It is illustrated with line-drawings and arresting headings.

Dr. Hymes clearly outlines the important steps through which all children go in establishing their own individuality. He stresses the parents' need for understanding, and the various problems arising in the child's struggle for independence and identity plus his need for recognition. He cites the common concerns of parents as they see the child emancipating himself from complete dependence in infancy and expressing his sense of values and his own identity in adolescence.

This booklet should be of value both to parents and educators since it is simply and practically written. It is crisp and to the point in a difficult field—personality development and the struggle of children for emancipation from parental over-control and over-concern.

Josephine Abbott Sever, Public Relations Director
Children's Medical Center, Boston

Memo to Members

The American Social Hygiene Association will hold its annual business meeting in New York City, March 6, 1953, in the Keystone Room of the Hotel Statler, 7th Avenue and 33rd Street. There will be two sessions:

3:30 p.m. Annual business meeting of members, with reports of committees, election of officers and presentation of the executive director's annual report.

5:00 p.m. First meeting of the members of the 1953 Board of Directors.

Members may submit suggestions and proposals regarding program, selection of officers and administration of the Association's affairs for referral to the appropriate standing committees and the Board of Directors for study and action.

WINIFRED N. PRINCE, *Secretary*
American Social Hygiene Association

journal of SOCIAL HYGIENE

vol. 39 march 1953 no. 3

IN THIS ISSUE

MARCH 1953

About our cover . . .

A Dutch Family, by Frans Hals. Twenty-first of a series of Journal covers on family life . . . photograph courtesy of the Cincinnati Art Museum (Mary Emery Collection).

Harriett Scantland, Editor
Elizabeth McQuaid, Assistant Editor

Eleanor Shenehon, Editorial Consultant

THE JOURNAL OF SOCIAL HYGIENE

official periodical of the American Social Hygiene Association, published monthly except July, August and September at the Boyd Printing Company, Inc., 374 Broadway, Albany 7, N. Y. Acceptance for mailing at the special rate of postage provided for in Section 1103, Act of October 3, 1917. Entered as second-class matter at the Post Office at Albany, N. Y., March 23, 1922.

The JOURNAL does not necessarily endorse or assume responsibility for opinions expressed in articles, nor does the reviewing of a book imply its recommendation by the American Social Hygiene Association. Subscription price: $3.00 per year. Single copy: 35¢.

Preinduction Health and Human Relations

None of us stands still. Both our environment and experience demand constant adjustments if we are to grow and develop towards emotional maturity. Today America's young people must cope with the normally difficult problems of adolescence, intensified by the demands of a complex culture and a long-term national emergency.

Youth-serving agencies and schools and colleges will find the American Social Hygiene Association's latest book, *Preinduction Health and Human Relations,* a stimulating resource in their efforts to help young people meet the problems of the day:

- Changes in family situations as fathers—and mothers, too—move into defense industry, often in distant communities.
- Uncertainties about dating, courtship and marriage in these unpeaceful times.
- Newly encountered influences on personal morality.
- Pressures of promoters of prostitution and allied vice, always intensified during critical periods.
- Postponement of education and vocational plans.
- And in many instances temporary frustration of the normal desire to marry and raise a family.

Many must postpone marriage and parenthood.*

The book is based on classroom-tested materials used by schools and colleges that pioneered in preinduction education in its broadest sense. Principles formulated by the American Association for Health, Physical Education and Recreation and by the National Education Association and the American Association of School Administrators have been valuable guides for the editors, Roy E. Dickerson, executive secretary of the Cincinnati Social Hygiene Society, and Mrs. Esther Emerson Sweeney, director of community service for the American Social Hygiene Association.

Preinduction Health and Human Relations—not a course of study—is a curriculum resource which brings together ideas and information usually scattered through various courses and several grades. Here are broad concepts, not methods. Here are new materials for strengthening courses, for integration into many courses, for a special course or for part of a course. Here are ideas to help teachers, clergymen and group workers to plan units and group discussions . . . that young people may grow physically, emotionally, socially and spiritually.

The editors of *Preinduction Health and Human Relations* are indebted to Cincinnati's public schools and to other schools and colleges for permission to use and modify curricular outlines, and to many busy authorities who gave valuable advice and criticisms for developing the book.

Effective Living in the National Emergency is the first of a series of chapters from Preinduction Health and Human Relations *which the* Journal *plans to publish in successive issues.*

Effective Living in the National Emergency

For the Instructor

This chapter provides instructors and group leaders with material for one or two introductory sessions with young people. Although the general aim of this book is the preparation of young people for healthful living in the present national emergency and the development of healthy attitudes towards playing their part in the nation's defense, it is essential to clarify certain basic and specific points at the outset:

- Healthful, effective living is a personal and social responsibility at all times and a mode of life that will facilitate youth's achieving its goals.
- The national emergency (and the demands it makes on individuals and on the country generally) needs to be faced calmly as a reality in the lives of all Americans, probably for a long time to come.
- To meet constructively any emergency, short or protracted, one needs to exercise appraisal, intelligent planning and maximum effort in integrating that emergency into one's total scheme of living.

Adults may need to guard against undue concern that discussion of the national emergency may be alarming to young people. Youth's capacity to face and deal with reality, when its terms are understood, ought not to be underestimated. Indeed, evasive silence regarding the national emergency is apt to cause youth far more uneasiness than a candid and calm appraisal of it or an opportunity to analyze it and relate it to both their day-by-day living and to their plans for their own lives.

For Use with Students

At all times—in war or peace, in national emergencies or in times when the country is secure and unthreatened—people want to get the most from life and to bring to the job of living the best possible equipment. In its broadest terms health—physical, intellectual, emotional and spiritual—is basic equipment for full, productive, satisfying and effective living.

Preinduction health education is not limited to preparing young men and women for service in the Armed Forces, since practically everyone will have some part to play in the nation's defense and security for an indefinite time to come. If not actually in the Armed Forces or defense work, young men and women may find themselves being, in a sense, inducted into jobs and responsibilities related to the national emergency. In one way or another, housewives and mothers, college students, businessmen and women are affected also.

In short, development of the best health in outlook, attitudes and physical and spiritual fitness is essential to all living as well as to making one's maximum contribution to national needs.

What Can Be Anticipated?

The national emergency may continue for many years. It is not of this country's making, yet it must be met with every resource we possess.

Most young men and many young women will enter the Armed Forces for a period of their lives, gaining much by the experience and giving much to the country's protection.

Requirements of defense industry are expected to grow heavier, not lighter. Calls for manpower will increase. Young men and women will play their part by turning out the thousands of products needed to equip the Armed Forces, as their older brothers and sisters did in World War II.

Many of America's homes will undergo change as fathers (and mothers too) enter defense industry either in their own community or in other parts of the country.

Today's young people are in many ways better prepared right now to take these changes and concomitant adjustments in stride than were young people before World War I, for example. Boys and girls now in high school have already demonstrated their adaptability to rapidly changing circumstances. They adjusted successfully to the problems of World War II, many of which were far graver than those anticipated in the present national emergency.

But now they will have new roles to play, roles played previously by older brothers and sisters, by fathers and mothers. Being able to look ahead a little and to foresee and plan around the national emergency is to their advantage.

Many boys and girls going into the services will never have been away from home before. Many will enter defense industries in communities at a distance from home. Undoubtedly many will have far more freedom than ever before.

Being away from home will present some new problems and will require the best and most mature use of this new freedom. This may be difficult for some. Parents, clergymen and teachers who have been good friends and advisers—the people to whom youth has normally turned for help in making decisions—will not be right at hand. Young people will, of course, find new counselors in the Armed Forces and in their new communities, though not immediately. Meanwhile, they will have to depend upon their own experience in decision-making, upon their own standards, inner resources and convictions.

*On leave—
dissipation
or clean fun?*

High school boys and girls are eager to stand on their own feet . . . and rightly so. They want to meet and solve their own problems and to face life as young adults. To accomplish this without the people to whom they normally turn when problems seem a little too big to tackle alone, boys and girls need to think out a good many issues right now.

Many problems young people face in the national emergency would have to be faced sometime, in any event. Others have their roots in the emergency itself and either would not exist at all or would exist to only a limited degree but for the emergency.

Everyone's Everyday Job of Development

Whether the emergency had arisen or not, all young people would have to learn how to deal with friendship, love, marriage and family life to their own and society's best advantage.

- Everyone must learn how to understand and manage emotions and how to make them serve him constructively. Learning this is a normal, fundamental job.

- Another everyday job is to find ways to keep fit and to prevent the fatigue and tension that may affect one's ability to control emotions.

- All human beings have to learn how to appraise their actions against permanent values and how to live, grow and develop along lines of good moral and spiritual health.

- Learning to use one's intellect, learning to *learn,* to plan, to organize work or study, to bring reason and judgment into situations where emotion may move one to act impulsively, even wrongly . . . these are all part of living and growing.

Mind, body, emotions, spirit require maximum development in war or peace if human beings are to enjoy and get the most out of the experience of living.

Young men and women want to get on with the job of living and to fulfill their own hopes, ambitions and goals. The everyday job of personal development need not be hindered by the emergency . . . with good planning and forethought it can be accelerated in the process of making one's contribution to the emergency.

There are things to learn in practically any new situation, people to meet and work with, opportunities to make decisions on important issues, acquaintances to make that may lead to lifelong friendships and to lasting, happy marriage and family life. Business, industry, the Armed Forces . . . all offer the young man and woman innumerable opportunities for realizing the best in themselves.

Special Problems of the National Emergency

War, the threat of war or a long period of national defense brings some problems into sharp focus, creates some difficulties that must be met and solved, sets up certain tensions in everyday life that need to be alleviated in sound and constructive ways.

Sudden changes in one's way of living—induction into the Armed Forces, transfers from one location to another within the service, movement about the country to work in defense industry—may create feelings of anxiety and fear. In such circumstances many young people become lonely, homesick and discouraged.

There are ways of meeting these problems. The important first steps are:

- To anticipate what these potentially upsetting conditions may be.
- To foresee what they may mean to oneself.
- To plan how best to meet them.

For many young men and women the emergency involves long periods of living and working almost entirely with people of their own sex. Normal day-to-day relations with young people of both sexes are curtailed. Such a circumstance calls for reserves of good mental health with which to meet the strain of this particular mode of life. After a long time at sea or at a remote military post a young man on leave may decide to abandon his usual moral and social standards when he meets girls. Or he may—if he brings mature judgment and reason and sound personal values to bear on his impulses and emotions—behave with maturity and decency and seek good times that harm neither himself nor another.

Stepping up of industrial production may from time to time make inroads on the physical and nervous energies of young people. There are ways to offset the effects of fatigue. To achieve their value as habits rather than just as remedies, they need to be known and thought about and practiced now.

There will be other advisers after induction.

Life in the Armed Forces entails living within a framework of discipline. Young men and women who have never learned to live comfortably within the normal demands of the discipline of civilian living may find this somewhat of a hardship. Individual wishes and whims cannot be countenanced in the Armed Forces (any more than they can be, actually, in civilian life).

Young people need to think about discipline now, to weigh what discipline really involves and to recognize how great a part it plays in their day-to-day living . . . even though it may not be labeled "discipline."

Acceptance of discipline is not just meaningless submission. It is positive cooperation for the attainment of a goal. It is teamwork, with each individual pulling his own weight. Whether in the Armed Forces or on a football team, discipline requires prompt, willing obedience to commands. The best discipline in military or civilian life is, of course, self-discipline . . . the individual's doing what is right because he knows it is right and because he wants to do what is right. Willingness, cooperation and enthusiasm are the key words in discipline.

Young people, reflecting on how they now live in matter-of-fact, pleasant cooperation with classmates, teammates and family, will realize that discipline is not the formidable word it seems to be. But in any group of young people there are usually a few who do not offer ready, enthusiastic and willing cooperation. They probably need some special help, counseling or guidance in this aspect of living.

Boy-Girl Relationships

Relations between boys and girls are also likely to present some problems during war or emergency. Boys and girls frequently act on impulse and emotion in wartime or other times of crisis. Sometimes they marry hastily, without regard for the fact that marriage is not a temporary relationship and that it requires a great deal of advance thinking and planning. Such marriages are usually entered into with good will on both sides but, especially where there has been little time for deep roots to be developed in the relationship, due weight is not given to what long separations may do to a marriage. Nor is there understanding, perhaps, of how hard it may be for a girl to set up and maintain a home in community after community when her husband is transferred to various military installations.

Many young girls—during both World War I and World War II—lowered their standards of personal behavior in their relationships with boys. Sometimes, feeling that dates were becoming hard to get, they resorted to what amounted to "buying" a date at the price of their own self-respect. Mistaken notions of patriotism—completely out of perspective—led some girls into feeling that they "owed" boys in the Armed Forces a "debt," one they paid at the expense of their own self-esteem.

Boys, too, rationalized promiscuous sexual behavior as "a last fling." Or they accepted the standards of some of their buddies and tried to convince themselves that promiscuous sexual relations with pick-ups, prostitutes or even young women of their acquaintance were evidence of being "manly" and "grown up."

Mature people work for distant goals, not immediate satisfactions. Mature people see rationalizations for what they are . . . ways of justifying to oneself what one wants to do, whether right or wrong.

Mature people realize that in many aspects of life one must defer immediate satisfactions for long-term goals. Carefully supervised dieting means saying "no" to chocolates, potatoes or ice cream sodas today for a trim figure and healthy body tomorrow. A sound plan of study, aimed at specific scholastic achievements, may mean "no" to movies or dancing when they interfere with the job at hand.

Similarly, the achievement of mature, lasting love and a happy marriage requires that one defer many immediate gratifications for a goal that is real, even though not immediately within reach.

In wartime, or in a national emergency, certain problems of physical health and well-being demand awareness, wise planning and sensible health-consciousness. The special conditions of life in the Armed Forces and in crowded industrial areas call for special safeguards against such diseases as influenza, common colds, malaria and dysentery. Such communicable diseases as syphilis and gonorrhea usually increase in both civilian and military populations because of lowered barriers against sexual promiscuity.

The preservation of physical health and fitness and especially the avoidance of communicable diseases—saboteurs of national defense—are responsibilities

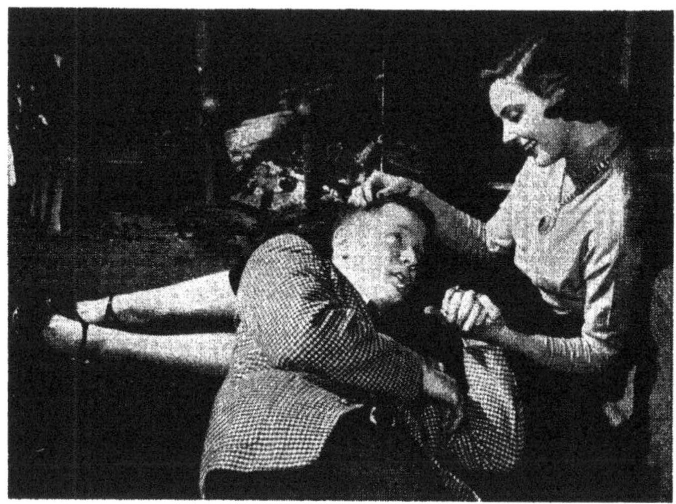

How to deal with love? One of their most stirring problems.

youth can meet by anticipating them, by planning to meet them and by maintaining good health habits.

Foreseeing, Understanding, Planning—Everybody's Job

All these problems created or intensified by the national emergency can be intelligently and rationally resolved. Primarily, they require an understanding of oneself. They demand thinking and planning in terms of a philosophy of life and of human relations. How each individual meets them will affect his entire life.

All the years spent in school would be meaningless if they failed to help boys and girls to anticipate, understand, meet and solve genuine life problems. The last years in high school are a time when all young men and women can bring together all they have learned in school, at home, in church and in their experience of life up to now . . . and use it to meet the future competently and confidently.

Class Activity

- Ask each student to write (unsigned) five questions he would like to to have answered during forthcoming sessions. Have them tabulated by one or two students. Supply each student with a copy of the results. Throughout the course he can see whether or not the questions have been answered or require further discussion.

Class Discussion

- Why should the individual concern himself with physical health and fitness in view of the fact that the Armed Forces have such excellent health programs?
- Why does discipline depend upon cooperation? Couldn't discipline be established successfully under a system of orders and punishments?
- Why should boys and girls understand the nature and meaning of the national emergency? Why should they understand what the country is fighting for in time of war?
- Is world communism "a real and present danger" to world peace? To the security of the United States?

BOB BARNES
"Boy! Guess what I learned at recess today!"
THE SATURDAY EVENING POST

Reprinted by special permission of the Saturday Evening Post

Sex Education in Pennsylvania's Public Secondary Schools

by John W. Masley and Arthur F. Davis

One of many problems confronting school administrators today is the question of public education's responsibility for a child's social hygiene or sex education. Many feel that sex education, one phase of family life education, is a responsibility of the child's parents . . . others say the schools should play an active role in this field. If the schools assume this responsibility, these questions then arise:

What should they teach?

Whom should they teach?

Who should teach?

When should they begin?

These are the questions school administrators must answer . . . and they're questions not in many cases easily solved.

To see how some schools have handled sex education, we took a look at the present practices in the public secondary schools of Pennsylvania.

Procedure

In our survey we used two research techniques, the questionnaire and the interview. With a carefully constructed questionnaire we hoped on the one hand to obtain information on a school's sex education program and on the other to give to school administrators who answered our questions sound ideas about the scope of a well-rounded program.

Several recognized leaders in the field reviewed and criticized our preliminary questionnaire and helped us make it as effective a tool as possible.

During the school year of 1950–51 we mailed our questions to the principals of all the public secondary schools in Pennsylvania. We received 777 replies (75.4% of the schools) . . . from all types and sizes of schools in all parts of the state.

To reinforce the results of the questionnaire, we visited 15% of the schools which indicated they had a planned program of sex education, and interviewed school administrators and teachers. These schools, too, varied in size, type and location.

Types of programs

From our questionnaire-survey and interviews we learned that Pennsylvania's public secondary schools offered many varieties of sex education programs. About 80% provided sex instruction in some form; only 20% had none at all. Among the schools offering sex education, a third planned the program and the others provided it informally or incidentally.

We learned that most of the schools which provided no sex instruction at all were small schools, and that most of those which had planned programs were large. While a larger percentage of junior high schools had no sex education programs, senior highs and combination junior-senior highs had the greatest number of planned courses.

Reasons for lack of program

To find out why some schools did not offer planned sex education, we asked the administrators what prevented the development of a program. Two out of five replied: "Lack of trained teachers." One out of five said the deterrent was parental objection or curriculum tradition.

Only 15% said they did not feel the need for sex instruction in the schools. About the same number said objection by religious groups hindered the development of sex education in the schools, which might mean that the church felt it was assuming adequately the responsibility of providing sex education. Or it might mean that the school and church were cooperating closely, each assuming a specified part of the job.

First steps

How should a school administrator go about developing a sex education program?

To get a comprehensive picture of how the programs got started in Pennsylvania, we asked the principals whose schools had planned programs, to tell us what they had done.

We asked, "Who were among the first in your community to recognize the need for and take positive action in the development of the sex education program in your high school?" Four out of five administrators replied, "The teachers." One out of four said the students were among the first to see the need, and one out of 10 said parents, parent-teacher groups or school boards. Few mentioned the clergy or civic organizations.

Apparently the schools, especially the teachers, first recognized the responsibility of public education in this field.

The administrators pointed out also that in the actual planning of sex

They need more teachers with more special training.

instruction, they got more help from the teachers and students than from any other source. While the administrators themselves were not among the first to see the need for sex education, at the planning stage half of them played an important role.

About one school in four had help from public health nurses in instituting a sex education program, and about one in seven had help from physicians. Few had help from parents as such.

Clearly, the teachers and administrators carried the greatest share of the responsibility in planning the sex education programs of their schools. Why? Because of lack of cooperation on the part of other groups? Because the schools took on the responsibility? Our study does not answer these questions. It does show that the schools took the lead in planning.

Resources

We obtained a slightly different picture when we asked the principals to name the more helpful resources they used in developing their sex education programs. Most frequently they mentioned teachers of health education, biology and home economics, but a sizable percentage also mentioned outside groups—physicians, public health nurses, social hygiene lecturers and ministers.

Instructional units in the programs

Analysis of the programs themselves reveals a complex picture of practices. The replies to our questionnaire (and our interviews) show that very few schools follow a pattern in presenting various units in their program. The

Public health nurses help to develop school programs.

schools which had planned programs of sex education taught well-defined units in well-defined courses . . . while those which provided informal or incidental sex instruction depended largely upon students' questions or other demands to introduce a specific topic.

The course in which a unit was taught varied from school to school, as did the grade level at which it was introduced. Some schools separated the boys and girls for sex instruction; other didn't.

When we analyzed separately each of the units on the questionnaire, we made several observations on the handling of specific topics:

Anatomy of the generative organs

This subject was taught in two-thirds of the planned programs but in only a fourth of the informal programs. Most of the planned programs allotted the topic to health classes, with boys and girls separated. Where taught incidentally, it appeared most often in biology, with girls and boys together.

Senior high schools usually carried this unit in the 10th grade. Combination junior-senior high schools—the 7th grade through the 12th—most often put it in the 12th grade if in a planned program, otherwise in the 10th grade. In junior high schools—the 7th grade to the 9th—it was taught in the 9th grade . . . and 12% of the schools introduced it as early as the 7th grade.

Reproduction

The teaching of animal reproduction followed a similar pattern in both the planned and informal programs. About half the schools included it in a mixed biology class in the 10th grade. But the junior high schools most often taught it in health classes, with boys and girls separated.

In planned programs, human reproduction was taught in segregated health classes more often than in mixed biology classes. Half the schools taught this unit . . . the majority in the 12th grade.

But curiosity among students apparently manifests itself earlier than the 12th grade, because most of the informal programs covered this topic in the 10th grade, a fourth of the schools dividing the material equally between biology and health classes. Among the informal programs in the junior high schools only a few taught this topic.

Menstrual hygiene

This topic was taught almost exclusively to girls, although one out of four schools with planned programs taught it to boys in health classes.

In planned programs discussions of menstrual hygiene appeared most frequently in the 12th grade, while in the informal programs the topic appeared more often in the 9th and 10th grades, with 42% of the junior high schools introducing it in the 7th grade. Three out of four schools taught menstrual hygiene in the health class, and one out of four also taught it in the home economics class.

Seminal emissions

A unit on seminal emissions appeared in half the boys' health courses and in a third of the girls' health classes in the planned programs. Less than 20% of the informal programs included it. Relatively few schools introduced the subject before the 12th grade.

Masturbation

Schools treated the subject of masturbation in almost the same manner as they did seminal emissions. A few schools with incidental sex education programs presented it in the 10th grade.

Heredity and eugenics

About half the schools we studied teach heredity and eugenics. Half those with planned programs covered the subject with boys and girls separately in health classes, the other half with mixed groups in biology classes. Schools with informal programs usually included heredity and eugenics with biology.

There was considerable variation in the grade where the subject was taught . . . about an equal number of schools indicated the 10th, 11th and 12th grades.

Prostitution

Half of the schools with planned programs, but less than 15% of those which taught sex education only incidentally covered the subject of prostitution. Most frequently it was taught in segregated health classes. Only a few schools introduced it before the 12th grade.

More large schools in urban areas covered this topic than did small schools in rural communities, indicating perhaps that the greater accessibility of

Ed.M., Harvard, Dr.P.H., University of Michigan. Fellow, American Public Health Association. Author of Fundamentals in Healthful Living. *Professor of physical education at Pennsylvania State College. Father of three girls.*

Arthur F. Davis

---

prostitution in cities required city schools to make a greater effort to warn students of its dangers.

Venereal disease

More schools taught about VD than about prostitution, most often in 12th grade health classes with boys and girls separated. One school in 10 taught the subject to mixed biology classes in the 10th grade.

The problems of adolescence

Over half the schools with planned programs and a third of the schools which provided sex education only incidentally taught their students about the physical, emotional and social changes of adolescence. Most of them presented the subject in health classes, although many presented it to girls in home economics classes.

Did the schools with planned programs fail to recognize early enough the needs of adolescents to discuss their problems? It would seem so. For the schools with informal sex education programs—those who depended largely on their students' questions to introduce a topic like this—most frequently reported that they discussed the problems of adolescence in the 10th grade . . . the others planned to wait until the 11th and 12th grades to introduce the subject. The lag in the planned programs became even more dramatic when we found that over half the junior high schools taught their 9th-grade students about the problems of adolescence, and another 25% introduced the topic as early as the 7th grade.

Dating, petting and necking

Schools handled these topics about the way they handled the discussions of adolescence. While fewer schools introduced the questions of dating, petting and necking, those with planned programs again showed a lag by delaying them till the 11th and 12th grades.

Students in schools without planned programs most often raised questions about dating, petting and necking in the 10th grade, and 40% of the junior high schools covered these subjects in 9th-grade girls' health classes.

Holds graduate degrees from the University of California at Berkeley and Pennsylvania State College. In charge of physical education for men at Eastern Illinois State College.

John W. Masley

Courtship and engagement behavior

Generally, schools discussed this topic in the 11th and 12th grades. About 40% of those with planned programs taught a unit on courtship and engagement behavior in the health course. Those which provided sex education only informally covered the topic in boys' health classes and girls' home economics classes.

Marriage

The schools handled discussions of mate selection and adjustment in marriage in much the same way as they did those on courtship and engagement behavior. Most of them reported that they covered the subject in the last two years of high school.

One school out of 10—whether it handled sex education methodically or informally—discussed courtship and engagement behavior, mate selection and adjustment in marriage in social studies classes of both boys and girls . . . apparently finding this course a satisfactory avenue of approach to these questions.

Less than 20% of the schools with planned programs discussed planned parenthood (family-spacing). Those which provided sex education only incidentally mentioned planned parenthood very infrequently. Where taught at all, it was taught to boys and girls separately in their 12th-grade health classes and in girls' home economics classes.

Interviews with the principals whose schools did not include this topic revealed that they felt the teaching of planned parenthood was not one of the school's responsibilities.

Pregnancy and infancy

A third of the schools with planned programs of sex education taught the hygiene of pregnancy to their girl students, and a fifth taught it to boys. They covered it in their health classes, most often in the 11th and 12th grades. The schools which provided sex education informally taught the hygiene of pregnancy only to their 10th-, 11th- and 12th-grade girls in health classes.

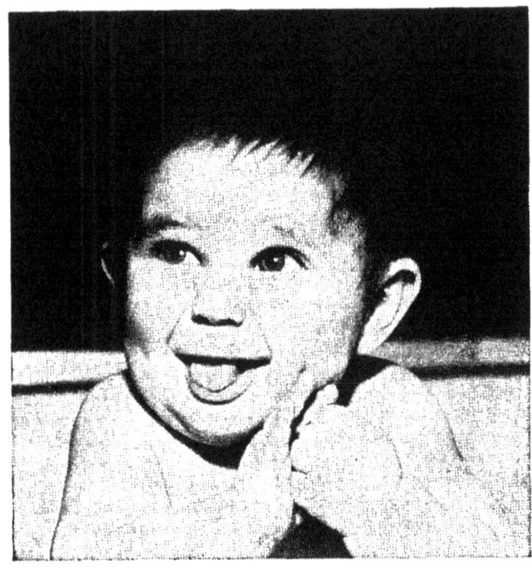

Infant care—almost entirely a girl's subject.

The schools—regardless of whether they planned their sex education programs or not—taught infant care almost exclusively to girls. A little less than half of them covered the subject in home economics classes, fewer in girls' health classes. They divided about equally on the grade—the 9th through the 12th—in which they taught it. A few junior high schools introduced the subject as early as the 7th grade, but the majority of them covered it in the 9th grade.

Sex education—a family responsibility

A third of the schools with planned programs stressed in 11th- and 12th-grade segregated health classes the family's responsibility for the sex education of children. Only a few schools which provided sex education informally discussed this topic, most frequently in the 12th grade.

When a school—whether its program was planned or incidental—taught this subject in a class containing both boys and girls, it used the social studies course as a vehicle.

Most of the sex instruction—planned or informal—in the public secondary schools of Pennsylvania was provided in already established courses. Fewer than 3% of the schools set up special courses either in sex education or family life education. The greatest amount of sex education was provided in health classes . . . but biology, home economics and social studies courses also proved useful channels. Boys and girls shared equally in receiving sex instruction.

Although it seems to us in passing that schools with planned programs cover more material on sex education than do those which provide sex instruction informally, we set out to report present practices rather than to evaluate programs.

What kind of teachers?

Our survey disclosed that about as many women as men provide sex instruction in the Pennsylvania schools. Half the women teachers were married, 90% of the men.

When the survey was made, the women had been teaching more than five years, the men more than nine. Apparently, school principals are assigning the teaching of these subjects to their older and more experienced teachers . . . undoubtedly reflecting the view that those providing sex education should know and understand young people.

The schools with planned sex education programs reported that 56% of the men who taught these subjects and 46% of the women had special training and experience in teaching health education. About half the men had specialized in physical education, biological sciences or general science. A third of the women had specialized in physical education or home economics.

The schools which provided sex education only informally reported that about 45% of the men who handled sex topics had training or experience in biological sciences, and another 45% had specialized in health education, physical education or general science. Women teachers in these schools had about the same qualifications as their counterparts in schools with planned programs.

"How were the teachers in the sex education program in your school chosen for this work?" we asked. More than half the principals replied that their criteria were training and personality. About 40% said they had selected teachers with specialized training. Few said they had selected sex education teachers solely because of personality.

Are their questions answered soon enough?

Summarizing our findings

What did we learn from our study? The evidence seems to warrant eight generalizations about the status of sex education in the public secondary schools of Pennsylvania:

- Students in the larger secondary schools receive a greater amount of planned sex instruction than do those in the smaller schools.
- Lack of qualified teachers hampers the development of a sex education program more than any other factor. Parental and religious objections are less effective obstacles.
- Teachers and school administrators were first to recognize the need for sex education in the schools. They also took the lead in planning how, when and what to teach. In planning their sex education programs, schools have used community resources in a rather limited way, although a few have asked the help of doctors and nurses.
- The schools place the most emphasis on the physiological aspects of sex. If they touch on the psychological and sociological aspects of the subject at all, they do so to only a limited extent.
- The schools provide the preponderance of sex instruction in the 11th and 12th grades. Is this early enough to be of greatest value to the students?
- Schools with planned programs cover sex education more comprehensively than do those which rely on their students to introduce the various topics.
- The schools are giving their more experienced teachers the job of sex education. Those trained and experienced in health education, physical education, biological sciences, general science and home economics provide most of the sex instruction that is given.
- The number of schools with planned programs in sex education is encouraging. We hope it indicates a trend toward the inclusion of sex instruction in the secondary school curriculum.

Questionnaire

I. General information

1. Name of School——————————; County ——————————
2. Principal of School ——————————————————————
3. Person filling out questionnaire————————————; Position——————
4. Type of Secondary School. Indicate by (X).

2-Year High School	——	4-Year Junior High School	——
3-Year High School	——	4-Year Junior-Senior High School	——
4-Year High School	——	5-Year Junior-Senior High School	——
2-Year Junior High School	——	6-Year Junior-Senior High School	——
3-Year Junior High School	——	Vocational High School	——

Others (Please specify) ————————————————————————

II. Development of sex education

1. Do the pupils in your high school receive any planned instruction in sex education? Indicate by (X). Yes ——— No ———
2. If the pupils in your high school do not receive any planned instruction in sex education, are provisions made for any type of informal or incidental instruction in this area? Indicate by (X). Yes ——— No ———
3. If your high school does not have a planned program of sex education, what factors are hindering or preventing the development of such a program? Indicate by (X).

Lack of Qualified Teachers	——	Objection by Religious Groups	——
Curriculum Tradition	——	Objection by School Board	——
Do Not Feel Need for Sex Instruction	——	Objection by Civic Organizations	——
Administrative Policy	——	Others (Please specify)	——————
No Room in Curriculum	——		——————
Objection by Parents	——		——————
			——————

4. If your high school has a planned instruction program in sex education, who were among the first in your community to recognize the need and take positive action in the development of the sex education program in your high school? Indicate by (X).

Students	———	Parent-Teacher Association	———
Parents	———	Civic Organizations	———
Clergy	———	Health Council	———
Faculty	———	Others (Please specify)	——————
School Board	———		——————
Curriculum Committee	———		——————

5. What were the more helpful resources used in the development of the **sex** education program in your high school? Indicate by (X).

Specially Qualified Citizens
such as:
Physician(s) ——
Dentist(s) ——
Public Health Nurse(s) ——
Social Hygiene Lecturer ——
Ministers ——
Parents ——

Local Hospital ——
Community Library ——
Local Board of Health ——
State Board of Health ——
Adult Community Study Groups ——
Voluntary Health Organizations ——
Others (Please specify) ————

Specially Qualified Teachers
such as:
Biology ——
Health Education ——
Physical Education ——
Home Economics ——
Social Sciences ——
Others (Specify) ————

6. In the development of the sex education program in your high school, who of the following were more helpful in planning the program? Indicate by (X).

Physician(s) ——
Dentist(s) ——
Public Health Nurse(s) ——
Clergy ——
School Administrators ——
Teachers ——
Parents ——
Students ——

School Health Council ——
Curriculum Committee ——
School Board ——
Parent-Teacher Association ——
Civic Groups ——
Others (Please specify) ————

III. Instruction program

1. What topics are covered in your high school's sex education program? In the chart on the following page please indicate under section A the code number which describes the extent to which each of the topics listed on the left is discussed in the teaching areas listed across the top of the chart. In each of the appropriate cells under section A, place the code number indicating the extent of coverage. If the topic is covered in a class where there are only boys, indicate your response in the row labeled BOYS; if the topic is covered in a class where there are only girls, indicate your response in the row labeled GIRLS; if the topic is covered in a class where both boys and girls are taught together, indicate your response in the row labeled TOGETHER.

   Under section B, further indicate by (X) the grade or grades in which each topic is covered, either for boys in a separate class, girls in a separate class, or in classes where boys and girls are taught together.

CODE
0—Not at all
1—General
2—Extensively

		A. Teaching Areas									B. Grades					
		Agriculture	Biology	General Science	Health Education	Home Economics	Physical Education	Social Studies	Special Lectures	Others (Specify)	7	8	9	10	11	12
Anatomy of Generative Organs	Boys															
	Girls															
	Together															
Animal Reproduction	Boys															
	Girls															
	Together															
Human Reproduction	Boys															
	Girls															
	Together															
Menstrual Hygiene	Boys															
	Girls															
	Together															
Seminal Emissions	Boys															
	Girls															
	Together															
Masturbation	Boys															
	Girls															
	Together															
Heredity and Eugenics	Boys															
	Girls															
	Together															
Prostitution	Boys															
	Girls															
	Together															
Venereal Diseases	Boys															
	Girls															
	Together															
Physical, Emotional & Social Changes in Adolescence	Boys															
	Girls															
	Together															
Dating, Petting, Necking	Boys															
	Girls															
	Together															
Courtship and Engagement	Boys															
	Girls															
	Together															
Mate Selection	Boys															
	Girls															
	Together															
Adjustment in Marriage	Boys															
	Girls															
	Together															
Planned Parenthood (Family-Spacing)	Boys															
	Girls															
	Together															
Hygiene of Pregnancy	Boys															
	Girls															
	Together															
Infant Care	Boys															
	Girls															
	Together															
Family Responsibilities for Sex Education of Children	Boys															
	Girls															
	Together															

IV. Personnel

1. The chart below is designed to investigate the backgrounds of those persons who contribute to the sex education program in your high school. Space is provided for fourteen individuals and you are requested to submit information for all persons in your school who contribute to the sex education program. For example, if you have three persons who have responsibilities in the sex education program, answer for persons 1, 2, and 3 in the first three columns, *using a separate column for each individual.* Do not identify the persons by name.

	1	2	3	4	5	6	7	8	9	10	11	12	13	14
Male Indicate by (X)														
Female Indicate by (X)														
Married Indicate by (X)														
Single Indicate by (X)														
Teaching Experience (Years)														
Children (Number of Offspring)														

SPECIALIZED TRAINING OR EXPERIENCE IN WHICH OF THE FOLLOWING FIELDS. Indicate by (X).

	1	2	3	4	5	6	7	8	9	10	11	12	13	14
Health Education														
Physical Education														
Recreation														
Medicine (Doctor, Nurse)														
Biological Science														
General Science														
Social Science														
Guidance Work														
Home Economics														
Agriculture														
Others (Specify)														

2. How were the teachers in the sex education program in your school chosen for this work? Indicate by (X). On the basis of special training ——— On the basis of a well-rounded personality ——— On the basis of training and personality ——— Others, specify ———————————————

———————————————————————————————

3. If a workshop course of training in family health and human relations including sex education were offered in colleges of the Commonwealth, do you believe that your community or school would cooperate by encouraging properly qualified persons to attend this course? Indicate by (X). Yes ——— No ——— Undecided ———

M.S. in child development and family relationships, Pennsylvania State College. Director of the Rochester (N. Y.) YW's teen-age program.

Phoebe Eleanor Forrest

Dating and Rating

by Phoebe Eleanor Forrest

Human relationships have been the subject of many books, debates, discussions and experimental studies. These relationships begin within the framework of the family and increase in their scope and complexity as the individual reaches various levels of development. From the fact-finding report of the 1950 White House Conference comes the statement that in each stage of a child's development there is a central problem that has to be solved, temporarily at least, if the child is to proceed with vigor and confidence to the next stage.

Adolescence is one of these stages of development. During this time the young person begins to relate himself to another person . . . and his relationships, especially with members of the opposite sex, assume an increasingly important role. By making a successful adjustment in these relationships he is preparing himself to develop more skills and resources, to enrich his role as a date, as a mate, and finally as a parent.

It is within this period of development that the adolescent can build habits of thought and action which will bring happiness to the future home partnership.

Dating is significant

From the point at which the adolescent views life there are few problems more central than those concerned with "Whom shall I date and how can I rate?" The significance of learning more about the dating behavior of adolescents is established when we recognize that creative marriage and family relationships develop from successful adjustments made by the individual in these earlier years.

One of the most outstanding characteristics of the adolescent is his awareness of and development of heterosexual interests. In our American culture *dating* is the term given to the process by which these interests are developed. The definitions of *a date* are as varied and numerous as are the personalities of the people involved . . . but dating, in general, can be an experience which holds the prospect of satisfying some of the deepest human needs.

If we believe that dating is a process by which the individual learns to adjust not only to the other person but to the social environment around him, then a knowledge of the dating patterns and activities in a specific community will help us to understand some of the forces to which an adolescent must adjust.

High school dating patterns

There were two main reasons for attempting this study of the dating patterns and activities of high school boys and girls.

- First of all, for teachers, group workers, parents and other lay or professional people who are working directly with high school students—whether in planning a family life education course, group discussions, co-ed conferences or canteen activities—it becomes increasingly important to know the problems, concerns and patterns of high school students as they date and try to rate with other students.
- In addition, we are interested in learning more about the role of the parent and the parent-adolescent relationship as it is affected by the dating process.

The dating patterns and activities described here may or may not be similar to dating patterns which exist elsewhere. We hope, however, that these findings can be added to research conducted in other parts of the country . . . and that together the facts will contribute to our understanding and appreciation of the adolescent dating pattern as a part of our culture.

The experimental group

We selected the junior class in a high school in Pennsylvania as the group to study so that teachers in the high school would be able to use our findings in planning courses and activities for the students' senior year. Their anonymous answers to a questionnaire supplied the raw material for our study.

Frequent talks "around the fringes" with teen-agers, conferences with teachers in the high school, discussions with parents, plus my three years' experience as director of a teen-age program provided a background for constructing the first draft of the questionnaire.

A pre-test of this first draft in a high school in a neighboring community showed that certain questions had to be revised, others omitted or added. Later we gave the final questionnaire to the high school students during their home-room activity period at school.

The schools of the borough in the community studied are part of a joint school system which includes five neighboring townships. The children from

Dates today—
a home tomorrow.

the outlying areas come to school in busses which arrive at 8:00 and leave at 3:15. The children from the outlying townships make a 68-mile round trip. The enrollment at the high school in 1951 was 171 10th-graders, 160 11th-graders and 151 twelfth-graders.

Of the 70 boys and 69 girls—from 14 to 18 years old—who answered the questionnaire, about half lived in town, while the rest lived in the surrounding area. Most of their parents had received education beyond grade school and the majority had three or more children. Only 18% of the students came from homes affected by the death, divorce or separation of their parents.

Four of the points we especially wanted to study were:

- The high school students' definition of the term *dating.*
- The reasons given by teen-agers as to why they date.
- Their attitudes toward dating.
- The characteristics they believe help to make a person rate and be popular with his friends in high school.

What is dating?

How do today's teen-agers define dating? As much of the literature points out, it is a phenomenon which has arisen during the 20th century in American

and girl. These three—along with parties and teen-age canteens—were favorites with the group we studied.

Similarity of religious faith does not seem to be an important factor in the dating life of these students. Other research has indicated that common religious beliefs are felt to be more essential and are more desired in marriage than in dating.

Parents and their dating children

In moving from childhood to adulthood, adolescents are trying to adjust themselves to patterns of living that fall within the range approved for them by society. As they are adjusting, they reveal much of all they have learned through experience in the most intimate cultural grouping . . . the family.

Who usually determines the time they come in from dates? The girls indicated that their parents usually set the time, while the boys felt that it was the responsibility of the girls they were dating.

Over half these girls and boys earned their spending money by taking part-time jobs. More girls than boys indicated they received an allowance from their parents or asked their parents for money when they wanted it.

Confiding in parents

In our concern to educate for better family living we recognize the importance of a relationship between *both* parents and their children which permits and encourages youthful confidences. More of these students discussed their dates with their mothers than with their fathers. Studies reported at the White House Conference likewise emphasized that the relationship of both boys and girls was more intimate with their mothers than with their fathers and that girls discussed things more freely with both parents than did boys.

One of the most significant findings in our study is the fact that approximately half the boys and a quarter of the girls did not discuss their dates with either parent. A fifth of the boys discussed their dates with no one.

Family arguments

What did students argue about? They had more disagreements with their mothers than with their fathers, usually about these matters:

- How late to stay out?
- How often to date?
- Who should drive the family car?
- Why not help more around home?

Most of the students felt it was necessary for their parents to approve of the person they were dating and to know where they were going on their dates.

A boy likes single-dates.

A girl likes double-dates.

Two other findings of significance to those interested in family relationships are:

- More than half the group were not encouraged by their parents to entertain their dates at home.
- More than half the boys and 26% of the girls felt that their parents were uninterested in their dating life.

Popularity ingredients

What does a teen-ager think he must do to be popular? What are the characteristics which enable a person to rate?

Boys and girls agreed on the four characteristics they ranked as contributing the most to popularity. They felt it was important for a person . . .

- To be friendly, courteous and respectful.
- To have a sense of humor.
- To be a good conversationalist.
- To be able to be a follower as well as a leader.

Smoking was considered least essential by both boys and girls, as were "enjoying liquor in groups" and "dating popular students only." Few boys indicated that it was necessary for a person to "come from the right family" (8% of the boys, 18% of the girls) and "belong to a clique" (11% of the boys, 20% of the girls).

Many never date at home.

Few girls felt it was necessary to pet (3% of the girls, 11% of the boys) and to neck (11% of the girls, 30% of the boys). Many more boys (31%) than girls (11%) were "not sure" whether or not petting increased a person's popularity.

Did they think good looks or attractiveness an essential "rating trait"? Fifty-four per cent of the boys and 38% of the girls thought so. "Being active in a lot of clubs" was essential to 42% of the girls, to 29% of the boys.

In short, there are patterns of essential and non-essential characteristics which adolescents believe contribute toward popularity in high school.

Implications of our findings

- Homes and schools should provide satisfying heterosexual group activities for youngsters in their early teens.
- In planning youth programs and activities, families, schools and community agencies should not continue to ignore the accepted fact that girls mature socially faster than boys.
- Boys and girls need to talk out their problems with adults who will listen sympathetically.
- It is unfair to try to treat all teen-agers just alike.
- If we would really understand and work with teen-agers, we must continue to study them.

Unfinished business

Our original plan was to study the correlation between a student's participation in extracurricular activities and the frequency of his dates. Since time did not permit this, I recommend that it be the subject of further study. Additional research might cover the correlations between the adolescent's dating pattern and the socio-economic status of his family, his ordinal position in the family, and his residence in a rural or urban community.

Of considerable value would be a study comparing teen-agers who date to those who do not . . . to determine what factors in the adolescent's personality and environment influence his relationship with the opposite sex.

Rating and dating patterns

Do not sign this form. Answer every question.

1. On the average, how often have you dated this school year?
   ——— every night
   ——— more than once a week
   ——— once a week
   ——— twice a month
   ——— once a month
   ——— not at all

2. Do you date mostly someone in the: (check *one*)
   ——— freshman class
   ——— sophomore class
   ——— junior class
   ——— senior class
   ——— high school graduate
   ——— do not date

3. Do you *usually* date someone: (check *one*)
   ——— within your same neighborhood
   ——— another part of town
   ——— from area surrounding town
   ——— do not date

4. Have you ever dated a college student? Yes ——— No ———

5. How did you meet these college dates?
   —— through family
   —— through friends
   —— at work
   —— at church
   —— at dances
   —— haven't dated college students.
   ———————— (list others)

6. If you had your choice, would you rather date a high school student ——— or a college student———?

7. Do you feel shy or ill at ease with the opposite sex?
   ——— usually, if so when?————————————
   ——— sometimes, if so when?————————————
   ——— never

8. Maybe your dates are yet to come. If you don't date, what are your reasons?
   ————————————————————————
   ————————————————————————

9. What *two* nights in the week do you date most frequently? ——— ———

10. In your opinion, what is a good time to end a date on a school night ———, on weekends ———?

11. Who determines the time you must come in from your dates?
    ——— you
    ——— your parents
    ——— your date
    ——— your crowd
    ——— don't date
    ———————— (list others)

12. Are most of your dates?
    ——— single dates
    ——— double dates
    ——— group dates
    ——— don't date

Many never date at home.

Few girls felt it was necessary to pet (3% of the girls, 11% of the boys) and to neck (11% of the girls, 30% of the boys). Many more boys (31%) than girls (11%) were "not sure" whether or not petting increased a person's popularity.

Did they think good looks or attractiveness an essential "rating trait"? Fifty-four per cent of the boys and 38% of the girls thought so. "Being active in a lot of clubs" was essential to 42% of the girls, to 29% of the boys.

In short, there are patterns of essential and non-essential characteristics which adolescents believe contribute toward popularity in high school.

Implications of our findings

- Homes and schools should provide satisfying heterosexual group activities for youngsters in their early teens.
- In planning youth programs and activities, families, schools and community agencies should not continue to ignore the accepted fact that girls mature socially faster than boys.
- Boys and girls need to talk out their problems with adults who will listen sympathetically.
- It is unfair to try to treat all teen-agers just alike.
- If we would really understand and work with teen-agers, we must continue to study them.

Unfinished business

Our original plan was to study the correlation between a student's participation in extracurricular activities and the frequency of his dates. Since time did not permit this, I recommend that it be the subject of further study. Additional research might cover the correlations between the adolescent's dating pattern and the socio-economic status of his family, his ordinal position in the family, and his residence in a rural or urban community.

Of considerable value would be a study comparing teen-agers who date to those who do not . . . to determine what factors in the adolescent's personality and environment influence his relationship with the opposite sex.

Rating and dating patterns

Do not sign this form. Answer every question.

1. On the average, how often have you dated this school year?
   - ——— every night
   - ——— more than once a week
   - ——— once a week
   - ——— twice a month
   - ——— once a month
   - ——— not at all
2. Do you date mostly someone in the: (check *one*)
   - ——— freshman class
   - ——— sophomore class
   - ——— junior class
   - ——— senior class
   - ——— high school graduate
   - ——— do not date
3. Do you *usually* date someone: (check *one*)
   - ——— within your same neighbor-hood
   - ——— another part of town
   - ——— from area surrounding town
   - ——— do not date
4. Have you ever dated a college student? Yes ——— No ———
5. How did you meet these college dates?
   - —— through family
   - —— through friends
   - —— at work
   - —— at church
   - —— at dances
   - —— haven't dated college students.
   - ——————— (list others)
6. If you had your choice, would you rather date a high school student ——— or a college student———?
7. Do you feel shy or ill at ease with the opposite sex?
   - ——— usually, if so when?———————————
   - ——— sometimes, if so when?———————————
   - ——— never
8. Maybe your dates are yet to come. If you don't date, what are your reasons?

   ————————————————————————

   ————————————————————————
9. What *two* nights in the week do you date most frequently? ——— ———
10. In your opinion, what is a good time to end a date on a school night ———, on weekends ———?
11. Who determines the time you must come in from your dates?
    - ——— you
    - ——— your parents
    - ——— your date
    - ——— your crowd
    - ——— don't date
    - ——————— (list others)
12. Are most of your dates?
    - ——— single dates
    - ——— double dates
    - ——— group dates
    - ——— don't date

13. Do you dutch treat? Never ——— sometimes ——— usually ———.

14. Do you enjoy dating people older ——— younger ——— same age ———?

15. At present, are you (check *one*)
——— dating with different persons?
——— going steady with one person? How long? ———.
——— engaged, when do you plan to marry? ———
——— married, how long have you been married? ———
——— do not date.

16. Check ONLY if going steady!
A. Do your parents approve of your going steady? Yes ——— No ——— Aren't concerned ———
B. Do you think you will eventually marry your current steady? Yes ——— No ———

17. Do you think most couples go steady because they like to have continuous dates ———, to rate among students ———, because they think they are in love ———, they like each other more than any one else ———, (list others) ———————————————

18. At what age did you begin dating? ———

19. Do you belong to a clique? (A group that does things and goes places together) Yes ——— No ———

20. Do you usually date within the same group that you pal around with in school? Yes ——— No ——— Do not date ———.

21. Where do you usually get your spending money? (check the *usual* way)
——— regular allowance from parents
——— ask parents when I want it
——— earn it by working at home
——— earn it on a job. What kind of work do you do? ———

22. Do you discuss your dates more with your mother ———, your father ———, both ———, neither ———? It neither, with whom? ———

23. Do you entertain your dates at your home ——— or are you entertained at their home ———?

24. At what age would you like to be married? ———

25. Where do you get your best ideas about how to be popular on dates?
——— from parents
——— from brothers and sisters
——— from classmates
——— from older friends
——— from reading articles in magazines (such as "Seventeen," etc.)

26. Do you smoke? Never ——— Sometimes ——— Usually ———.

27. How do you feel about your date smoking?

——— do not care if my date smokes
——— prefer my date to smoke
——— do not date
——— do not like my date to smoke

28. Do you drink? Never ——— Sometimes ——— Usually ———.

29. How do you feel about your date drinking?

——— do not care if my date drinks
——— prefer my date to drink
——— do not date
——— do not like my date to drink

30. Would you say that most of your dates are:

——— enjoyable
——— boring
——— satisfactory
——— do not date

31. What three things do you do most frequently on dates? Check only *THREE.*

——— go to movies
——— go to parties
——— go riding in car
——— go out to eat
——— make your own fun at home
——— engage in some sport, such as swimming, etc.
——— go dancing
——— go walking
——— do not date
——— do something else, such as ———————————

32. List the places that you go to *most often* on dates:

1.
2.
3.
4.

33. List things that have recently caused disagreements between you and your parents. Do not limit this just to your dating life.

1.
2.
3.
4.

34. Are most of your disagreements: *(check one)*

——— with your father
——— with your mother
——— with both parents

35. Do you feel your parents' marriage has been:

——— very happy
——— as happy as most married couples
——— unhappy

What do you think a person must do to be popular in high school? Be sure to check each item:

	Agree	?	Disagree
36. Be good-looking or attractive			
37. Have a sense of humor			
38. Be smooth in manners and appearance			
39. Belong to a clique			
40. Know how to dance well			
41. Have a good line			
42. Come from the "right" family			
43. Date popular students only			
44. Be active in a lot of clubs			
45. Smoke			
46. Neck			
47. Pet			
48. Have many partners at a dance			
49. Be in demand as a date			
50. Enjoy liquor in groups			
51. Be friendly, courteous, respectful			
52. Be able to be a follower as well as a leader			
53. Be able to entertain the gang at their home			
54. Be a good conversationalist			
55. Be a good dresser			
56. List others			

Check YES or NO to the following questions:

Yes No

—— —— 57. Should a girl ask a boy for a date?

—— —— 58. Should you date a person your parents do not approve?

—— —— 59. Should your parents know where you go on your dates?

—— —— 60. Do you avoid dating a person of a different religion?

—— —— 61. Do you have a "curfew" hour on your dates?

—— —— 62. Do your parents encourage you to entertain your dates at home?

—— —— 63. Have your parents provided space and equipment for such entertaining?

—— —— 64. Do you feel your parents are genuinely interested in your dating life?

—— —— 65. Do you think a mixed party should have a chaperone?

—— —— 66. Do you look upon your high school dating as successful courtship for marriage?

—— —— 67. Does your family own a car?

—— —— 68. Have you and your family worked out an agreement for sharing the family car on date nights?

—— —— 69. Do you think your parents are too strict about your dating habits?

—— —— 70. Do your parents usually know when you return from dates?
—— —— 71. Do you think high school parties tend to imitate college affairs?
—— —— 72. Do you use college facilities for dating or recreational purposes?
—— —— 73. Does your family rent rooms to college students?
—— —— 74. Have such roomers helped you get dates?
—— —— 75. Does the use of the phone cause disagreements in your family?
—— —— 76. Do you enjoy going on "blind" dates?
—— —— 77. Have you ever had a "pick-up" date?
—— —— 78. Do your parents approve of your dating a college student?

Place a check mark in the first space if you participate in the following activities and a check mark in the second space if you hold an office in the group.

Member	Officer		Member	Officer	
———	———	Yearbook staff	———	———	Church groups
———	———	School paper	———	———	Commercial club
———	———	Tri-Hi-Y or Hi-Y Club	———	———	Debating squad
———	———	Cheerleading squad	———	———	Honor society
———	———	Class plays, operettas	———	———	Class officer
———	———	Band, orchestra, glee club	———	———	Athletic Association
			———	———	F. H. A.
———	———	Varsity sports	———	———	F. F. A.
———	———	Student council	———	———	Dramatics
———	———	Church Door Canteen			

Other activities ————————————————————

* * * * * * * * *

Age: ———; Sex: Male ———, Female ———; Grade: ———;
Course: General ———, Business ———, Vocational Ag———.

Do you live in town ——— Outside of town ———
Religious preference: Protestant ———, Catholic ———. Hebrew ———, Other ———, None ———
Occupation of father ——————— Place of occupation ———————
Occupation of mother ——————— Place of occupation ———————
Number of brothers ———, sisters ——— in family
Your position among the children in your family is (encircle) 1 2 3 4 5 6 7
Has either of your parents been divorced ———, separated ———, widowed ———, remarried ———
Is your health excellent ——, good ———, fair ——— or poor ———?
Check the highest year of schooling your parents completed:

Father	Mother
——— grade school	——— grade school
——— high school	——— high school
——— college	——— college
——— graduate study	——— graduate study

VD Movies and Beer

Social hygiene makes the rounds

by Mrs. Uxenia S. Livingston

Will tavern habitués share their alcoholic hours with health education workers? Will owners of night spots offer VD films with their beer?

These are some of the questions that challenged the Missouri Social Hygiene Association in its efforts to reach the vast "unreached" of St. Louis' Beaumont area. We had no doubt that the Beaumont people needed social hygiene information . . . no doubt that only a daring, unconventional approach could do the job. But was bar-hopping the answer?

We decided to take a chance. The Subway Gardens, a midtown tavern in a congested Negro district was to be the "opening night" locale. The owner, a family friend, courageously gave us permission to show "Feeling All Right" and the Jackie Robinson short on VD.

It took weeks of negotiation with neighborhood theaters, the motion picture operators' union, the city health department and night workers at the Subway Gardens before 70 guests there saw the films on September 29, 1951.

An attentive group

In the gloom I could make out attentive faces watching the films. When the showing was over, one neatly dressed woman looked up reflectively from her glass of beer to say with assurance, "You ought to show these films all over the world. Everyone should know these facts. And thank you for the pamphlets." Others joined her in showing their appreciation of the Missouri Social Hygiene Association and the municipal health department. They were proud they could help in making St. Louis free of VD.

And when I mentioned that our main concern is for healthy, happy family life several people asked for publications on family harmony.

With a broad smile the tavern manager, who probably had shared my earlier trembling, came over to me and asked for a return showing. This was the kind of encouragement we needed. Now we could be more venturesome.

Their enthusiasm

Between September 29, 1951, and October 16, 1952, we filled 12 engagements, mostly during the fall months. During this time our stagefright melted before the warmth of our audiences' response. They got over any qualms they may have felt in being brought face to face with a realistic health message during the hours they reserved for escape . . . and were enthusiastically vocal:

"Yes, I'll pass out these handbills."

"We need shows like this. When will you be back?"

"Where can you get these blood tests? How often?"

Most of them are Negroes of the lower income group. On week-ends they crowd into these dirty, dim interiors, sometimes mere basements, where they drink cheap alcohol to the blaring notes of juke-box or combo. The tavern owners, usually white men, are helped by Negro managers.

A lady is present

We have to be ready for the unexpected. In one place the manager asked us to move over. "The police are here to stop a fight. We're sorry this had to happen tonight," he said. In another spot a bibulous admirer shouted down a noisy fellow with the reminder that a lady was present. "This is education. We need it," he said. Then he turned to me, "Say, I like your looks. When'll you be back?"

All types, all personalities. If we estimate correctly, about 822 in all. Some, fashionable, attractive, congregating in three of the better places, were more restrained in their comments. One woman assured me that if we needed a donation for this good work, we could call on her any time.

Kudos to the tavern-owners

This widespread approval of patrons is most gratifying to tavern-owners who put public welfare before business success. Their risk of customer displeasure was a real one, and we shall not forget their cooperativeness . . . tangibly expressed in their distribution of over 4,000 pamphlets.

Without cooperation we could not give one showing. Even one evening's presentation requires several contacts. In one case we arranged for 12 interviews before the stage was set. We still have our sights fixed on a tavern

---

M.A., Eden Seminary. Studied social work at Hull House and the University of Chicago. Health educator, Missouri Social Hygiene Association.

Mrs. Uxenia S. Livingston

which has been so consistently crowded that after three visits, we have not been able to get within speaking distance of the manager.

The St. Louis Health Department has been of inestimable help to us, always willing to cooperate, reflecting the cordial and productive relations that have existed between our agencies through the years.

Not the least of my satisfactions comes when I return to the office to hear Mrs. Josephine Hart Brown, our executive director, say, "Uxenia, you're doing a fine job that takes courage. Be very careful. I'll go with you whenever possible."

Or when I hear Dr. Harriet S. Cory, our beloved pioneer, say, "I'll go with you on some of these dangerous trips."

Though we have no way of checking the final results of these tavern experiments—just one phase of the Missouri Social Hygiene Association's activities—we believe that we've accomplished much in "reaching the unreachables." And they become touchingly proud when I tell them after the showings and discussion that they are all members of an overall committee on "Passing-On-Information."

In one evening's time the attitudes of these tavern habitués toward VD have changed. We've seen them become aware of this health menace . . . of the fact that it can hit them, that it can be easily treated, that it can be controlled.

CREDITS

Photo courtesy Canadian Information Service (Malak), p. 97.

Photo courtesy U. S. Navy, p. 98.

Photo courtesy LOOK Magazine (copyrighted), p. 105.

Photo courtesy British Information Services, p. 109.

Photo courtesy Community Chests and Councils, p. 114.

Photo courtesy Acme, p. 115.

Photo courtesy Bristol-Myers, p. 123.

Photos courtesy Ewing Galloway, p. 127.

San Jose's committee links police and public

by A. P. Hamann, City Manager and Ray Blackmore, Police Chief

The citizens' advisory committee of the San Jose (Calif.) police department has completed its first year of existence as an integral part of our civic life. We are more than satisfied with the accomplishments made possible by this association of citizens and law enforcement officers, for they are doing well what they set out to do . . .

- To foster a closer relationship between the people of San Jose and their police department.
- To stimulate city-wide interest in educational programs designed to help the individual protect his life and property.
- To pool information useful to the police in controlling detrimental influences.
- To tell the public about the steps taken by the police department to control vice and crime.
- To act in a consultative capacity on policies suggested by the city administration and to determine whether they would prove beneficial to the community.

The committee came into being when we called together representatives of the clergy, merchants' association, PTA, the press, radio, labor, veterans' organizations, dads' clubs, and government agencies and explained why we needed them . . . to help us cope with the social aspects of crime aggravated by economic conditions and a vast increase in our population. We emphasized that we wanted them to help us in our job of controlling crime, not to dictate policy nor to interfere with normal police functions.

In this first year, the 29-member committee has helped the police set up such diverse projects as a lecture series designed to help retail clerks prevent shoplifting, a bicycle safety program for juveniles, and for both adults and high school students an educational program to prevent drug addiction.

The committee serves as a kind of clearing-house of information, passing on to the public information about prostitution conditions and relaying to the police what the citizens have to say. This two-way channeling of facts assures the police of public support in their efforts to suppress vice and gives them valid leads on prostitution activity. The information they now get from citizens is authentic, unlike the anonymous tips and leads that used to waste their time.

Success without reservation

In the opinion of all concerned San Jose's citizens' advisory committee has proved an asset to the police department, and no doubt it will become a permanent part of our civic life. The response by public-spirited citizens to our suggestion that they take a permanent part in law enforcement work has been gratifying to those of us who are their municipal servants. This is especially true as they have come to recognize that many of the difficulties faced by the police today have developed into social problems . . . and as such can be successfully combatted only if there is mutual understanding and a desire by citizens and their law enforcement officers to aid one another.

Now the San Jose police department knows it has strong backing . . . knows it won't be smeared with unjust publicity . . . knows it need not fear the machinations of prostitution racketeers and middlemen.

We light the way for others

Other police departments, long tolerant of vice in the mistaken belief that citizens want it, would do well to study San Jose's plan. If their record is clean, they should have no qualms about committee interference. Instead, they will enjoy the confidence and support of a satisfied community free of prostitution and related activities.

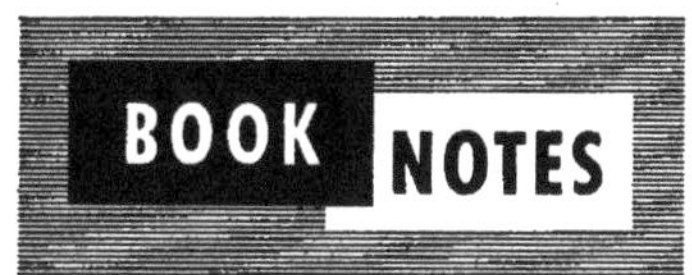

Elizabeth B. McQuaid

Readings in Marriage and the Family, edited by Judson T. and Mary G. Landis. New York, Prentice-Hall, 1952. 460p. $5.65.

Here is a prize package of 75 articles by almost as many authors, each of whom has made a substantial contribution to the study of marriage and the family.

Margaret Mead leads off in part I with a report on the contemporary American family. Emily H. Mudd and Malcolm G. Preston bring the volume to a constructive and hopeful close with articles on education, counseling and research. In between, a star-studded list of contributors presents a variety of points of view backed up by research.

The book's 16 parts include, among others, studies on dating and courtship practices, mate selection, marital adjustments, wife-husband-child interaction, mixed marriage, women's roles and sexual behavior.

Most of the selections are recent and all are readable, although the emphasis on research in marriage and the family limits the usefulness of the volume somewhat.

This volume would be an unusual and valuable text. Students of family life will certainly find it helpful as a reference. It fills in the gaps and unifies the subject since the terms *marriage* and *family* have become loosely applied to a multitude of topics.

Whether the general public will get much out of these readings is a question, for the authors presuppose a reader with considerable background.

The articles are stimulating because of their divergence of viewpoint . . . "you pays your money and you takes your choice." English, Waller, Mead, Bossard, Ogburn, Kingsley, Levy, Kirkendall, Murdock and dozens of others are at their brilliant best.

Section XIV, "Standards of Sexual Behavior," is a hard-hitting, candid, realistic treatment of the sexual mores of our day. In the last section the article, "Penicillin Is Not Enough," is of special interest to social hygiene readers.

This is the kind of publication that looks easy to assemble, but isn't. It is the kind that made the reviewer say, "Now, why didn't *I* think of that?"

Elizabeth S. Force
Toms River (N. J.) High School

Growth and Development of the Preadolescent, by Arthur Witt Blair and William H. Burton. New York, Appleton-Century-Crofts, 1951. 221p. $2.25.

The authors recognize that while the psychology of adolescence has received much emphasis, preadolescence has been largely neglected. Both are experienced and competent educators and administrators, Dr. Blair at North Texas State College, Dr. Burton at Harvard. Their major considerations include:

- The changing social insights of the preadolescent.
- The preadolescent and his subjection to strong cultural impositions.
- Physical growth and its relation to behavior.
- Intellectual development and its relation to behavior.
- General characteristics of preadolescence.

Particularly suggestive is the tentative list of characteristics of the period. The section on guiding the development of the preadolescent includes general principles and corollary practices recommended for dealing with children of this age. Likewise, the suggestions to enable parents and teachers to react constructively to the emotional and social difficulties of preadolescents should be helpful to both groups.

The volume is written simply and should be readily understood by educated parents as well as teachers of various degrees of experience. It should also be helpful to social hygiene workers concerned with parent-children guidance programs and problems.

Jacob A. Goldberg, Director
Social Hygiene-Division
New York TB and Health Association

Family Life Education in School and Community, by Elizabeth McHose. New York, Columbia University (Teachers College), 1952. 182p. $3.50.

Dr. McHose indicates in her introduction that the approaches used in this book to solving problems in family living are not patterns to be followed since each community must work out solutions to meet its needs.

Various plans indicate in conversational style how the efforts of school and community personnel may be combined successfully to meet complex problems in social living. The author gives concrete illustrations of experiences in family life education that have been carried out in communities of various sizes.

She emphasizes the need for mutual understanding by parents, teachers, pupils and community workers of the plans in order to direct the efforts of all cooperatively and constructively toward the attainment of common goals.

The latter part of the book is particularly helpful as it indicates the reefs and buoys in working out a family life education program. The author shows how the community can appraise itself and keep its aims clearly in the foreground so that all concerned may understand the challenges and the progress made. Only by frequent inventories can a community know what efforts have shown results, what problems still must be solved. Then it can make plans to give parents and children the help they need to attain happy and satisfying family relationships . . . to the greater personal and social health of the community.

Mary B. Rappaport
Associate in School Health Education
New York State Department of Education

Women, Society and Sex, edited by Johnson E. Fairchild. New York, Sheridan House, 1952. 255p. $4.00.

The position of women in American society today was the subject of 13 lectures at Cooper Union, here published. They cover social, psychological, political and educational problems, with a final chapter on fashions.

As is usual in such a series, a few of the lectures are perfunctory, and many of them cover familiar ground, the reader knowing what to expect when he sees such names as Margaret Mead, Lena Levine, Marynia Farnham and the like. On the other hand, the book gives a broader view of its subject and a greater variety of interpretation than would be found in the work of any one author.

George Lawton contributes a good discussion of emotional maturity in wives, Ralph J. Wentworth-Rohr makes some telling points in analyzing "Momism," William G. Niederland explains a few of the disastrous results of woman's attempt to repudiate her sex when he talks about psychological disorders of femininity and masculinity, and Gertrude P. Driscoll has words of comfort for women without men.

Harold Taylor argues the need for radical reform in the educational programs now offered for women, but it transpires that he does not want to see them given any substantial preparation to meet the problems they will actually encounter. He merely rings the changes on the old story about "increasing her insight into human affairs," and so on. Training women to be "good wives" would, in his opinion, "be the best way to make them otherwise"—a beautiful paradox indeed!

Failure of the editor to tell something about the 13 contributors is a serious omission. The average reader would like to know the background of those presented to him as authorities.

Paul Popenoe, Secretary
American Institute of Family Relations

Handbook on VD, by Carroll T. Bowen, M.D. Coral Gables, Fla., University of Miami Press, 1952. 66p. $1.25.

In this brief book Dr. Bowen describes the various venereal diseases for the laity. Any such attempt demands experienced judgment in the selection of material to be presented. From his large experience in talking to lay groups, Dr. Bowen provides information that he has found his audiences need.

To this reviewer it seems that more space might have been given to what the author calls "frozen blood tests for syphilis"—persistent positive tests in spite of good treatment. Such seroresistance is a cause of anxiety and trouble to many patients, and it is important that both physicians and the laity recognize that the persistence of positive serologic tests for syphilis does not necessarily mean a persistence of the disease.

Dr. Bowen defines most medical terms, but he makes no effort to do this for antibodies or to explain seroresistance in syphilis by analogy with the persistence of antibodies in other diseases that have been cured or arrested. He is to be congratulated, however, in bringing this subject to the attention of his readers.

To the syphilologist it may seem unfortunate that such incorrect statements as "some organisms (causing syphilis) reproduce themselves as often as every 20 minutes" when it has been fairly well established that the treponema pallidum divides only about once in 30 hours. Such an error, however, is of minor importance in an excellent presentation of material written clearly and forcefully in language that can be understood by anyone with a moderate education.

Evan W. Thomas, M.D., Medical Consultant
New York State Department of Health

The Wonderful Story of How You Were Born, by Sidonie M. Gruenberg. New York, Doubleday, 1952. 39p. $2.00.

Of the many publications on the story of life for little children, I consider this presentation of Mrs. Gruenberg's outstanding.

It is a unique combination of scientific information with attractive appeal. It is geared to the little child's interest and understanding. And best of all, it fairly radiates wonder and joy as it unfolds the "really true story of where babies come from."

In a warm, personal, non-technical manner, the grandmother conveys to the little child the marvel of how he—like all his family, friends and every living person—first began from a tiny little egg, not larger than a tiny dot (well illustrated by a dot visible only under a magnifying glass).

The wonder is continued that this tiny egg, from which the little child began, contained nearly everything that made him himself—his knees, elbows, toes, fingernails, tears, smiles and the ability to grow from a little, helpless infant to a boy or girl and later to a man or woman.

The story of how this tiny egg grew in a special place in his mother's body, which was his first home and where he received food, air, was kept warm and protected; the various stages of his development; how his mother's body adapted to his growth and prepared for his birth; the joy of both father and mother awaiting his arrival; the simple explanation of his birth—all told in a non-sentimental, accurate and delightful way—will captivate a child as much as any fairy tale. He will wish to hear it again and again.

The second part of the story includes the need of a father and a mother to start a baby. The simple explanation of a boy and a girl as male and female, the description of body differences, the maturation of ova and sperms, the role of the tiny sperm "*melting* with the tiny egg," starting the egg to grow into a baby and passing on to the baby hereditary factors from his father and mother and all his ancestors back to the time people began . . . the wonder of it all cannot fail to fascinate a child as well as many adults.

The latter part of the book skillfully describes body growth and changes of the pre-adolescent period, the stages of growth in feelings and interests, and the individual's need to grow out of younger ways of loving into grown-up ways naturally leading to marriage.

The description of married love in the closeness of both heart and body, resulting in the coming of children and the beginning of "another kind of new thing—the *family*—where love surrounds the children just as love surrounds the joining of the sperm and egg" well illustrates the spiritual aspect of parental love and family living which should be the heritage of our children.

This book should be welcomed by all parents who wish to give the story of life to their children in a truthful manner that will fill them with wonder and respect for the universal plan for the continuation of life.

Mabel Grier Lesher, M.D., Educational Consultant
American Social Hygiene Association

Helping Children Understand Sex, by Lester A. Kirkendall. A Better Living Booklet. Chicago, Science Research Associates, 1952. 49p. 40¢.

Parents who are uncertain how to handle the sex interests of their children will find many pointers here to clear up their doubts. Dr. Kirkendall says, "Sex education is unavoidable . . . it's a continuous process . . . it can be easy." Beginning with the problems of the pre-schooler, the booklet progresses to those of the teen-ager and concludes with a discussion of the need for cooperation between community agencies if a proper sex education program is to succeed.

Equipped with bibliography and informally illustrated with clever drawings, this booklet, despite its size, runs a comprehensive gamut.

Personal and Community Health, by C. E. Turner, Dr. P.H. St. Louis, C. V. Mosby, 1952. 9th edition. 659p. $4.25.

One chapter, *Familial Hygiene*, will acquaint college students with such social hygiene concerns as preparation for family living during childhood and adolescence, the reproductive system, the reproductive process and physiological developments at puberty and marriage.

Providing necessary health information for the job, the home and the community, profusely illustrated, with a summary and bibliography at the end of each chapter, the book concludes with a glossary, index and appendix on the control of communicable diseases, including VD.

Into Your Teens, by Helen Shacter, Gladys Gardner Jenkins and W. W. Bauer, M.D. New York, Scott, Foresman, 1952. 352p. $1.53 (for teachers). $2.04.

Designed to help 13- and 14-year-olds solve their problems—whether dating difficulties or otherwise—this eighth-grade textbook is part of a series on health and personal development.

Three units that cover differences in rates of growth, social needs and family conflicts are "Teen Troubles," "Understanding Yourself and Others" and "Living in a Family." Engaging cartoon-type illustrations bring home to teen-agers the right and wrong way of dressing, making friends, going on that first date. There are few who will not recognize themselves in many of the awkward, earnest, puzzled figures. Two pages of dating do's in color differentiating between the boy's role and the girl's ought to bolster the confidence of eighth-graders.

The teachers' edition contains 186 pages of discussion material, including a bibliography.

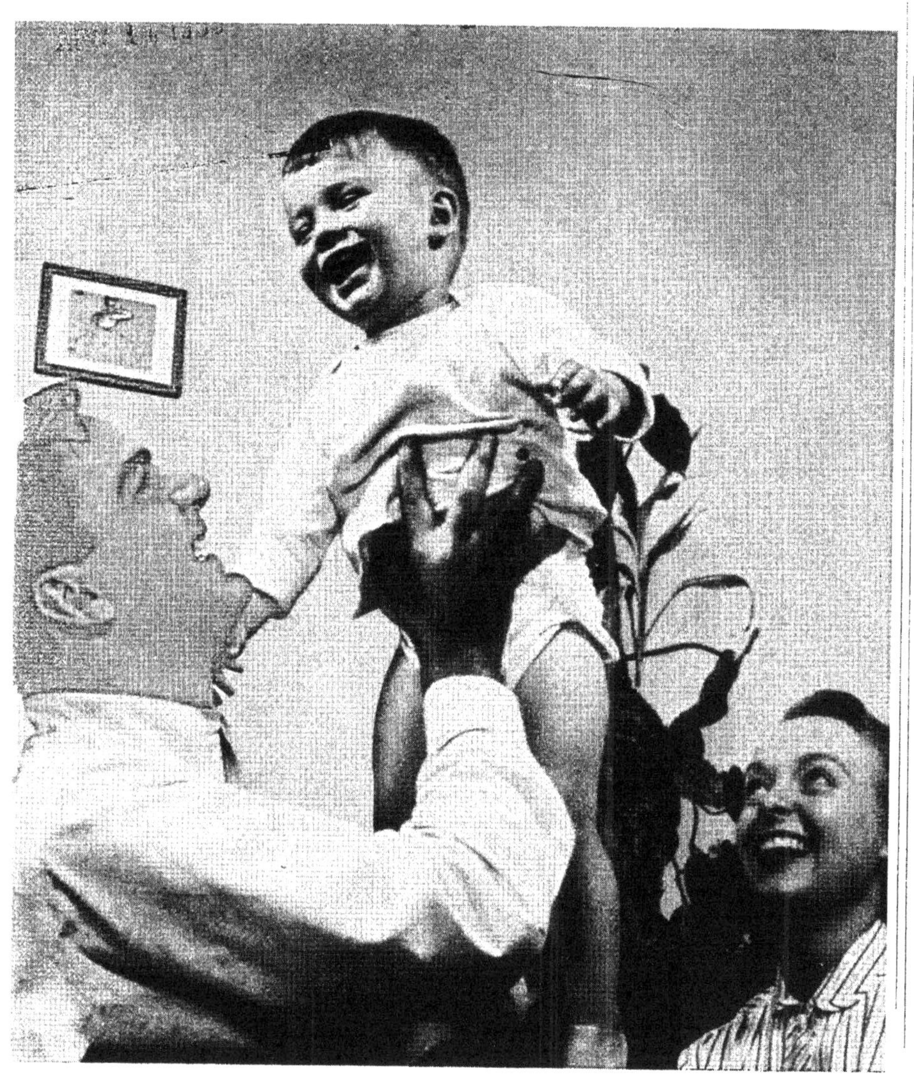

journal of SOCIAL HYGIENE

vol. 39 april 1953 no. 4

IN THIS ISSUE

APRIL 1953

About our cover . . .

Twenty-second of a series of Journal covers on family life . . . photograph courtesy of *Today's Woman.*

THE JOURNAL OF SOCIAL HYGIENE

official periodical of the American Social Hygiene Association, published monthly except July, August and September at the Boyd Printing Company, Inc., 374 Broadway, Albany 7, N. Y. Acceptance for mailing at the special rate of postage provided for in Section 1103, Act of October 3, 1917. Entered as second-class matter at the Post Office at Albany, N. Y., March 23, 1922.

VD in Israel

Immigration and the control problem

by Joseph Hirsh

Israel is part of an historic land mass, the Middle East, which is regarded as the ancient seat of western civilization. From earliest times this land mass has been the crossroads of cultures and the bridge over which the East moved westward and later the West moved eastward. As a consequence, beginning first with the Christian era and then with Mohammedanism and their attendant crusades and hegiras, it has also been the world crossroads of disease and the object of continuous imperialistic wars and internal revolutions.

Physically Israel is a study in contrasts and contradictions. At its widest it is only 50 miles across, at its narrowest only 12. Compared to more familiar geographical and political areas in the United States, Israel is equal in size to New Jersey. It is only one-sixth or one-seventh as large as New York or Florida and one-fortieth the size of Texas.

Like the land itself the people are a contradiction composed of diverse, divergent and often appositive strains. There are the early pioneers and the late refugees. There are the politically informed (of every political conviction) and the ignorant. There are the western-oriented sophisticates and the starkest representatives of backwash, underdeveloped countries. There are the religious traditionalists and the iconoclasts.

There are these and many more strains that co-mingle, clash, threaten one another in many subtle ways, yet strive in their common goal for survival—not only for themselves but for those who have flocked to Israel in recent years.

A safe harbor

With the birth of the new nation began the task of the "ingathering of the exiles." Actually, for hundreds of thousands of victims of Nazi and Communist persecution and for those living in other hostile countries, Israel meant safety and refuge where none existed anywhere else in the world for them. Thus began one of the physically unparalleled programs in the history of mankind.

One of the first laws enacted by the Israeli Parliament was the "Law of Return," giving every Jew the right to immigrate to Israel. Since the establishment of the state in May, 1948, the Jewish population has more than doubled . . . from 650,930 in May, 1948, it jumped to 1,596,000 at the end of last May.

A staggering health problem

During the first four years of its existence Israel admitted without qualification any Jew desiring to come. Along with the healthy came thousands upon thousands of so-called hard core cases—people acutely ill with skin diseases and open tuberculosis, those actively and acutely infected with malaria, intestinal parasites and trachoma, as well as many who were chronically ill or disabled, the lame, the halt, the blind, the mentally ill, the unemployed and unemployable for health reasons.

The relationship of the recent immigration to Israel's major health problems is clearly demonstrated in a random sample of almost 50,000 recent Yemenite emigrés. In this group there were 1,000 active cases of pulmonary tuberculosis, 18,000 cases of syphilis, between 25,000 and 30,000 cases of trachoma, between 10,000 and 14,000 cases of schistosomiasis, between 15,000 and 20,000 cases of acute or recurrent malaria and between 7,000 and 8,000 cases of tropical ulcer.

Their homes are tents but they dwell in the land of their fathers.

VD Control Officer, Mediterranean Theater, World War II. Visited Israel in 1950 and 1952. Executive Secretary, Medical Advisory Board, Hebrew University-Hadassah Medical School, Jerusalem.

Joseph Hirsh

After the ingathering of the rescued survivors of Nazi concentration camps in Europe, a considerable portion of the surviving Jews from the Balkan countries arrived. All the Jews of Yemen and most of the Jews of Iraq were brought in, and immigration from North Africa and Iran has not yet ceased.

New restrictions

This policy of unrestricted immigration, dictated by the urgent need to save Jews from persecution and annihilation in certain countries perforce underwent some changes in 1952. A decrease became necessary for economic reasons. But health also dictated this action. As a consequence, the present policy calls for a prospective immigrant to be medically examined in the country of his origin . . . only a reasonable proportion of old and handicapped persons will be allowed to immigrate to Israel.

Two factors—the improvement of economic conditions in Israel or the worsening of conditions of Jews outside the country—will lead to the lifting of these restrictions. But the newcomers already in Israel pose alarming problems.

Hundreds of thousands have come from countries with a very low cultural standard, where a democratic regime is unknown and where the citizen does not enjoy even the most primitive services in education and health. Even in these countries Jews were considered second-class citizens. As a consequence many of them were illiterate and ill.

The co-mingling in this "tight little island" of Israelis differing so markedly in background, cultures, values, habits, literacy and language is fraught with tension and danger, aggravated by restrictions and shortages of goods, commodities and housing. The settled population feels threatened by the newcomers. The newcomers, on the other hand, many of them in temporary camps and feeling the national austerity in the extreme, are too easily inclined to compare their own low standard of living with the relative comfort of the settled population.

Frustration, a certain degree of bitterness and the suspicion of being discriminated against are results which cannot easily be avoided. They must be

Israeli nurse, immigrant mother, English hospital.

faced in their social, psychological and medical contexts. These factors have a direct bearing, moreover, on venereal disease problems and their control since they relate to the acceptance or rejection by many of the people of the seriousness of these diseases, their willingness to undergo treatment and their intellectual and emotional responses to educational stimuli concerning the cause, nature, spread and prevention of VD.

VD in Palestine

When Palestine was part of the Ottoman empire prior to World War I and in the years following under the British Mandate, the venereal diseases were not subject to compulsory notification. As a consequence there is no accurate way of estimating the extent of the problem. A recent report of the Israeli Ministry of Health states that the "venereal disease problem scarcely existed among the Jews in Palestine" prior to 1948. This view would be seriously contested by American and British venereal disease control officers in the light of the number of contacts reported by Allied troops stationed or on rest or convalescent leave in Palestine during World War II.

Despite this difference of opinion there is no gainsaying the fact reported by the Israeli Ministry of Health that "with the start of mass immigration from Eastern countries where certain treponematoses are even epidemic, the position has changed."

The only statistics available on the subject before 1948 are those furnished by the Workers' Sick Fund of the Histadrut (*Kupat Holim*). This voluntary health insurance fund, which furnishes comprehensive medical care to over 600,000 workers and their families in Israel today, reports that from 1937 to

1945 the venereal disease incidence rate per 100,000 of the insured population varied between 0.12 and 0.33 for syphilis and 0.36 and 0.64 for gonorrhea.

Incidence of venereal disease in Israel

Since the establishment of the new state in 1948, statistics on the current picture are beginning to be available. Beginning in April, 1949, all new immigrants 15 to 50 years old passing through the clearance camp of *Shaar Ha Aliyah* in Haifa, the main port of entry into Israel, have had routine serologic tests for syphilis and clinical examinations by dermatologists of the government health service.

Screening examinations in the Shaar Ha Aliyah Camp

	1949	*1950*
Number of persons tested	68,800	80,000
Percentage of cases of syphilis detected by blood tests and clinically confirmed	0.79	0.68

In December of 1950 the reporting of venereal diseases became compulsory. In view of the mobility of the new immigrants and the fact that both the general population as well as segments of the medical profession had to be educated to the importance of notification, the incidence reports for 1951 and 1952 cannot be regarded as reliable. The Ministry of Health reports that "the total number of cases of syphilis can only be estimated approximately as being about 14,000 in 1952, that is, about one per 1,000 of the population."

Approximate distribution of the different stages of syphilis in 1951

	Percent
Early syphilis (stages 1 and 2)	2.5
Late and latent syphilis	85.0
Congenital syphilis	1.0
Stage not known	11.5

Not indicated in the table is the fact that bejel, a non-venereal type of syphilis, endemic and in fact epidemic throughout the Middle East, is of growing importance in Israel, especially within the last year with the arrival of tens of thousands of new immigrants from Iraq and Iran.

Grateful acknowledgment is made to Dr. Theodore Grushka, Professor of Social Medicine, Hebrew University-Hadassah Medical School, for the statistical and other interpretive data presented here.

In a recent report Dr. Czerniak, VD control chief for the Ministry of Health, summarized incidence data on syphilis and deaths from syphilis for the calendar years 1950 and 1951 and for the first nine months of 1952:

Notified cases of syphilis and deaths from syphilis from 1950 to 1952

Year	*Cases*	*Deaths*
1950 (I-XII)	1,024	12
1951 (I-XII)	1,238	5
1952 (I-IX)	706	11

Stages of notified cases of syphilis from 1949 to 1952

Early syphilis (stages I and II)	150
Latent and late syphilis	2,144
Neurosyphilis	812
Lues congenita	91
Treponematosis endemica (bejel)	25
	3,222

Sources of infection in notified cases of syphilis

Source of infection	*1949* [1]	*1950*	*1951*	*1952* [2]	***Total***
In Israel	—	1	11	28	**40**
Abroad	201	826	1,123	323	**2,473**
Unknown	53	197	104	355	**509**
Total of notified cases	254	1,024	1,238	706	**3,222**

[1] Approximately last quarter only.
[2] First three quarters only.

To cope with this situation a number of programs have been established. Some are new to the country and in their nascency and under the limitations of personnel and funds cannot be adequately judged. Others have a long and effective history.

VD control programs

Shortly after the Ministry of Health was created it set up a venereal disease control section. When compulsory reporting of these diseases was enacted in December of 1950, a confidential central card index system was established in the ministry.

One of the early orders of business of the new Ministry of Health was the consideration of a national Venereal Disease Control Act . . . it has yet to become law.

The government control program is essentially therapeutically oriented and revolves about treatment centers. Treatment is provided free of charge in 19 government municipal and *Kupat Holim* skin clinics and in the skin departments of hospitals. Drugs for the treatment of VD are distributed free of charge to public clinics and private doctors. In addition, procaine penicillin is distributed free to *Kupat Holim* for the treatment of its members.

Prevention

In two areas only is the government's venereal disease program oriented toward prevention. The first of these is an extension of the work carried on for many years by the maternal and child clinics of Hadassah and the *Kupat Holim*. In these clinics, many of them still run by these organizations independent of the Ministry of Health, the antenatal program routinely calls for serologic tests. This program has been continued by the government in those health centers taken over from Hadassah as well as those which it has newly established. The government, moreover, has standardized serological methods in all of the 28 laboratories (5 government, 2 Hadassah, 10 *Kupat Holim* and 11 private) rendering such service.

Quantitatively the effectiveness of the VD control program in the antenatal clinics has been questioned. In 1950, for example, only 16,525 expectant mothers registered with these clinics . . . in that year there were 36,004 live births. While there are no figures concerning expectant mothers who are members of Sick Funds and obtain antenatal care in their outpatient clinics, a real discrepancy and gap exists in the blood-test program.

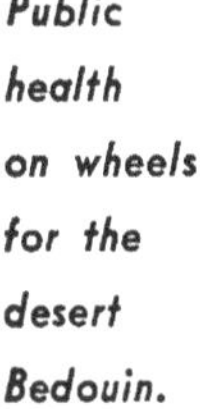

Public health on wheels for the desert Bedouin.

The second preventive aspect of the venereal disease control program involves the new immigrants. A primary concern, to be sure, has been to treat and render noninfectious the new cases of venereal disease. But to do that it has been essential to discover precisely who is infected. Thus, the screening and diagnosis of new immigrants has become a necessary and salutary first step.

The most conspicuous lack in the preventive aspect of the VD control program is health education. As yet only lip service is given to this activity. As a function of general health education or as an integral part of the venereal disease control program it is nonexistent. Although there is pressing need for this service under the unique conditions in Israel today, neither funds nor personnel are available.

Venereal diseases and new immigrants.

In recent years the immigrants have posed a special problem on several scores. In the first place, as a consequence of illiteracy and language difficulties there has been an unwillingness on the part of some to commence treatment. In the second place, among those who have been treated and rendered non-contagious—now the practice for all immigrants coming into clearance camps—and are settled in rural communities in distant corners of the country it is difficult to maintain contact and adequate follow-up. These difficulties could be overcome partly by the use of penicillin aluminum monostearate and newer antibiotics, but in the light of the present austerity in Israel it is not possible to obtain in quantity these relatively expensive agents.

The nurse — she knows what stamina these new immigrants need.

Desert garb and handsome face—the Bedouin.

The present policy of the government, however, is to render non-infectious as many cases as possible and to follow up long-term treatment as best as it can.

Trained social workers trace contacts through the district health offices . . . and the social workers, rather than physicians, follow up. The cases diagnosed at the clearance camp are reported to the health offices of the district in which the immigrant will be settled. Since many of these districts are in remote and little-traveled areas of the country, the difficulties in following up these cases are enormous. Despite the fact that the immigrants may be "settled" they are often extremely mobile within as well as outside the district, so that continuity of treatment is also difficult. With limited government clinics available in some of these remote districts, the Ministry of Health has made an effort to offset this difficulty by arranging with the *Kupat Holim*, which has set up clinics in many of these new settlements, to treat VD even in the non-insured.

The recent revision in the immigration policy has had a salutary effect on the VD problem in that the government renewed an earlier regulation requiring every candidate for immigration from abroad to be medically examined (including examinations for venereal disease) prior to his departure for Israel. Visas are not now being granted to persons actively infected with the venereal diseases.

Although not directly an effect of this revised immigration policy, there has been in recent months a more rigid approach to venereal disease control, particularly in applying screening tests, which are now standardized and regularly made of all immigrants at the reception camps, all army recruits and all admissions to hospitals throughout the country.

Beersheba's Hadassah Hospital . . . a haven for all.

Venereal diseases and the Arab population

There are about 100,000 Arabs in Israel today, most of them Moslem and most of them, despite continuous contact with their Israeli neighbors, leading culturally independent lives. There are few professionally trained Arabs and as a consequence they use the health services made available to all by the government and private organizations. The Ministry of Health reports that "only in places inhabited mainly or exclusively by Arabs have special services been provided. This is done by consideration of their special needs and not as the result of a discriminatory policy." To satisfy their special needs, moreover, the government has arranged for special courses for Arab nurses, teachers and social workers to prepare them to work among their people.

Those Arabs who are members of the General Worker's Union enjoy all of the services of the *Kupat Holim*. In addition, Hadassah hospitals and clinics have traditionally and continuously made their services available to the Arabs.

Within the last few years the Ministry of Health has opened in areas inhabited mainly by Arabs four mobile clinics for the Bedouin tribes in the Negev and for certain villages in western Galilee, and 23 permanent clinics, each staffed by a physician and a nurse who render free medical care and dispense drugs and pharmaceuticals without charge. The government has enunciated a general policy, moreover, imposing no restriction whatsoever on the admission of patients to its hospitals.

Thus Israeli's venereal disease activities, both preventive and therapeutic, are available in equal measure to Arab and Jew alike.

A man and his sons— the new Israel.

Summary

Despite the fact that the venereal diseases are endemic in the Middle East, such statistics as are available for the period before 1948 indicate a relatively low incidence among the Palestinian population. With the creation of the new state in 1948 and the unparalleled immigration into the country there is believed to be a significant increase in these diseases. Epidemiologic data are still inadequate in evaluating the seriousness of these diseases in the whole Israeli public health picture.

The full medical resources of the country have been mobilized to cope with the VD problem:

- By law, the venereal diseases are reportable.
- All immigrants are screened, and case-finding has been highly developed.
- Inadequacies exist in follow-up as well as in public information and education.
- Treatment programs by voluntary agencies supported from abroad are generally of a high order.
- Treatment programs by local agencies indigenously supported are limited in funds and personnel.
- The government program has these same limitations.

Nonetheless, the mobilization of public and private resources and their sound orientation toward both prevention and therapy indicate that the future program will develop along effective lines.

As grandmother and clubwoman she returned to college for an A.B. and M.A. Formerly a kindergarten principal, now dean of girls at Thomas Jefferson High School, San Antonio.

Mrs. Payton Kennedy.

Family life education in San Antonio

by Mrs. Payton Kennedy

"Everything is taught in the San Antonio high schools except the things you have to know."

This rather bitter statement started the whole thing. It was made in a physiology class by a boy in summer school. As a result, the class formed a committee to call upon the superintendent of schools to ask that he add a course in family relations to the curriculum. It was an unorthodox method of getting a course into a school curriculum . . . but it worked!

Of course, the boys didn't know that the groundwork for such a step had been laid by various foresighted people in the community over a period of years . . . that educators all over the country are coming more and more to realize the school's responsibilities in training for better family life. But the boys provided the spark that started the fire. Because of their appeal to their superintendent family life education became a highly successful part of San Antonio's high school curriculum, and for six years it has been growing and developing.

Just what is this program? For one thing, it is probably not like any other one in existence. Why? Because it not only was requested by students, but it was and is planned by students. So often adults sit down and decide just what young people need and give it to them whether or not the young people see any need or use for it. Not this time! And one boy is probably responsible for their having a part in the planning, for when he heard about the new course he yawned, "Aw, it won't be any good. Some ole teacher will decide what to teach."

Something alive

And the "ole teacher" who heard him answered in her own mind, "Not if this ole teacher can help it, the course won't be planned by teachers. This is going to be something alive and real, something that will help boys and girls to think, develop values, build attitudes, throw light on the darknesses of human need. With God's help, maybe this course can draw back a little the curtain that is usually between youth and age so that they can communicate with each other. Maybe it can help young people develop perspective a little earlier, see things as they really are, build the self-confidence they must have to face life's problems and be able to distinguish between the real and the tinsel.

"Of course, age has responsibilities toward young people," the ole teacher thought to herself. "We want to tell them the things learned through the ages. We want to point out to them that civilization has resulted from human restraints. We no longer eat like pigs in a gutter. It is only after religion put restraints upon free physical expression of emotions that man has become capable of unselfish love, that physical expression of love has become wholly satisfying to the basic needs of man . . . for love, security, recognition and change. No one gets any sense of security out of a week-end affair, no sense of belonging, of adequacy, no sense of personal worth and success, no feeling of long-lasting satisfaction. It is only in a happy, permanent marriage that these needs are met in the love relationship.

"In this chaotic world of ours, where everything that is familiar is fading away, we have to face facts. We want to reassure the kids, to help them, to pass on to them the things we know, *but we can't do it unless they want us to.* This course is not going to force it down their throats. We'll find out what *they* want, what they *think* they need. This is going to be dominated by them!"

With this determination in mind, the teacher and a planning committee of school administrators called a series of meetings of students representing each high school in the city. Under the expert leadership of a family life consultant furnished by the state university, these boys and girls thoughtfully and intelligently planned San Antonio's basic course in family life education.

What did they want? What did they plan? They wanted to know how to get along better with their families, how to be good parents, how to have a successful marriage; they wanted to learn everything about dating from

A boy's request sparked the San Antonio program.

We can show them the road.

manners to petting and beyond. What they really wanted is what the whole world wants, a formula for happiness . . . and no one has it. But we do have guideposts, information that will help us along our way. That's what they asked for and that's what the course has tried to provide.

Neither to ignore nor to emphasize

In the last six years, over 7,000 boys and girls of varying backgrounds—economic, cultural, religious and racial—have sat down together and discussed the problems of life and living in a modern world with its pressures and confusions and have tried to sift the chaff from the wheat. It has never been a course in sex education as such, but it has never skipped discussing problems involving sex. As these arise naturally in discussing problems of life, teachers present them in a carefully non-stimulating manner, without emphasis or diminution.

Since young people are so much interested in being good parents, teachers have built on this foundation in handling delicate subjects. Whenever a subject arises of a quite personal nature, the teacher guides the discussion so that the class becomes a class in parent education. "Someday you as a parent will need to understand how your child feels. . . ." And the discussion is impersonal and objective, non-stimulating and unembarrassing.

The teachers do not go more deeply into a topic than the children seek to go, but they never fail to respond frankly and openly to the needs of members of the class. It is true that children bring with them to class as many backgrounds as there are children, that each is at his own level of maturity. But San Antonio's experience indicates that there is a mass of information that can be so imparted that each child assimilates what he is prepared to assimilate . . . when properly done, group guidance covering intimate material has fine results.

To marry tonight?

On the opening day that first year the teacher was outlining the possibilities of the course and mentioned that they would discuss going steady. A little girl interrupted her excitedly. "Oh, do we study that?—When? I'm going steady . . . she's going steady . . . and she's thinking of it and"—the clincher—"*she's* got to decide whether or not to marry her boy friend tonight!" What was the lesson for the day? Going steady, of course. The outcome: a sweet, little, innocent 16-year-old—who had to decide tonight whether to marry a drunken, divorced, 21-year-old she didn't even like when she was away from him and who couldn't think when she was with him—did not marry that night!

Of the many approaches used in these six years, the one which has proved itself is the one that says here are the facts, make your own decisions. One young fellow at the end of the term said this, "I've waited all term for you to tell us what to do, and you never have, but when we get through with a subject, there is no doubt in our minds as to what is right."

They act it out

Role-playing has been very successful. Suppose the lesson is on family relationships. The teacher asks students to volunteer for the parts of mother, father, older brother, sister and little sister. The players receive no instructions, just the outline of a typical situation. With no lines except those they think of as they go along, they act out the situation to some kind of conclusion.

Suppose a teen-age daughter asks to do something that *some* parents would find objectionable. With that, they're off. The "worst" boy, morally, in the class is a good one for "father." (Peculiarly enough, it never fails that the boy the teacher wants to play a certain role will volunteer.)

And the result? No child emerges from an experience like that without understanding his parents' viewpoint better. One time a youngster who was always complaining about his girl's parents' restrictions came out of an experience of role-playing with this comment, "Heck, they aren't careful enough."

Going steady . . . a major question.

Shortly after this type of class experience, the teacher frequently hears parents say that their children are becoming much more cooperative. Then they ask, "Just what are you doing in that class to change my child so remarkably?" Actually the teachers don't prompt the students to apply their new insights at home. Their new behavior is the by-product of thinking.

Life as it is

All through the course, if there is a theme, it is . . . what do you believe, what do you want from life, what is worthwhile, what are your goals, what will help you attain them? All of the 7,000 or more boys and girls have indicated they want to be respected citizens and almost all of them have said they want marriage and children and stable family life in their future. The whole course emphasizes the positive approach to problems . . . acceptance of life as it is.

In a class there are always those who have had experiences that might bring feelings of guilt, so teachers must make a real effort to help them realize that what is past must be accepted, that it is only the present and future over which we have any control, that it is futile to make a whipping-post of ourselves, that for practical purposes it is good mental hygiene to forget mistakes except for the lesson learned from them.

Before the teacher brings up anything of an intimate nature, she makes sure there is real rapport between herself and the group. Even then, when these subjects arise, she makes a conscious effort to get the tone just right for unembarrassing, frank and highly serious discussion. Everything must be right. Otherwise, instead of helping children, the teacher injures them. And in that case the community, the parents, would be justified in killing the program.

When both sides of a question are given free expression, the discussion leader has to be certain that no question is left dangling and that no wrong values will be imparted, only good ones. Six years' experience in doing this has convinced the teachers in San Antonio that there will never be a class when boys and girls will not air to advantage the right attitudes and right values. It has never failed, and the teacher can clinch the convictions of the class by using the non-directive—"So you feel. . . ."

Exploiting others

The responsibility of all boys to girls—all girls, good, bad and indifferent—is always brought out in one way or another. "If boys must have experience, which one of you will wish to have your daughters serve the next generation?" That's a pretty effective question. When they discuss the dumb little sophomore who wants to be popular and will do anything for a date, I ask, "Can you take what she has to offer and not bear any responsibility for your behavior?"

Values and attitudes are what we are trying to build. What kind of values

The 'worst' boy plays father.

and attitudes? The good old-fashioned kind the churches are still teaching, the kind the American Social Hygiene Association is trying to promote, the kind the YMCA and the YWCA believe in, the kind psychologists and psychiatrists like the Sadlers tell us we must have to do a good job of living, the kind called mental hygiene.

But wasn't this supposed to be what the youngsters want, not what adults decide they should have? Yes, that's it. The kids want these things. The teens are idealistic years. Teen-agers want to believe in things, they want reassurance that the teachings of their church and parents are sound. In San Antonio's classroom in family life education they find that their peers, their contemporaries, really approve the teachings of home and church.

Personal integrity

The boys convince the girls they respect only those who keep themselves for marriage, who practice integrity all up and down the line in living. The girls give the boys some insight into feminine psychology . . . their usually hidden but quite serious desire to find a boy who also has kept himself for marriage, who also practices personal integrity in many varied ways. The class makes it possible for boys and girls to develop insight into the feelings of each sex that would be utterly impossible elsewhere.

They leave their class convinced that they will make a better job of marriage than they would have made without the course. Although no organized follow-up study has been made, 'informal questioning of hundreds of former students about the value, in retrospect, of the course indicates that they continue to rate it highly and consider it a good influence upon their lives.

Individual counseling, too

Youngsters who are in the middle of soul-searing problems come to the teacher for personal counseling. The teacher devotes half her time to group work and half to individual counseling. At the students' request, we have abandoned the single-pronged approach—classes only for seniors—for a two-pronged approach including a course for younger students as well as the one for the seniors. The course for the younger group is primarily concerned with family relationships,

Almost all of them looked ahead to marriage.

self-understanding and dating. The course for seniors is devoted more to preparation for marriage, with emphasis upon the problems arising from values, attitudes and emotional maturity rather than physiological facts.

The course for seniors is taught once a week to students who enroll voluntarily. It carries no grade and no credit. The students come from their library period to the class. In the beginning only one teacher taught the course in five high schools, but as the demand grew greater and greater two teachers were assigned to six high schools, each going to three schools.

Three teachers—three backgrounds

What about the teachers? They must be happily married and must be parents. The San Antonio administrators decided on these qualifications immediately. But what about their training? Would they have to be especially trained? When San Antonio embarked upon its pioneering way, none of the colleges offered specific training for prospective teachers of family life education.

To date, there have been three teachers, all equally successful. Each holds a counselor's certificate. One was a high school math teacher, one a junior high teacher, I a social science teacher who had also taught kindergarteners and commerce students.

When the decision to offer the course in family life education was made, my first job as the first teacher was to prepare the teaching material.

What did I do? First I corresponded with 23 school superintendents over the entire country to find out what was being done elsewhere. I read books and more books. I consulted young people themselves, listening, taking notes at a series of meetings with students. Then I went to Stephens College to write the course and develop concrete lessons under the expert supervision of Dr. Henry Bowman, a nationally known leader in family life education.

Dr. Bowman gave unstintingly of his time, knowledge and wisdom, and pointed out possible pitfalls to avoid as well as methods of proved value to use. (My two successors have also gone to Stephens for this short-term training.)

Back in San Antonio

When I returned to San Antonio, I sat down with the presidents of all the Parent-Teacher Associations in the city high schools and went over in detail specific plans for the new course. They gave enthusiastic approval.

All was ready. What would happen? No one really knew, for San Antonio was truly pioneering. San Antonio is a cosmopolitan city with many ethnic groups, a city of many religions. Would such a course be acceptable to the community as a whole? Would it help young people or hurt them?

I took a prayerful attitude into the classroom when I started this trail-blazing undertaking, and my successors have continued that attitude through the years that have passed. Each of us has felt very keenly the tremendous responsibility of this type of teaching.

What was the reaction of the students? They swarmed to enroll, and have continued to vie with each other for the privilege of being in the classes for the six years that the program has been a part of the curriculum. They have made anonymous, careful, written evaluations each term. While not one has failed to endorse the course, it is from their constructive criticisms and suggestions in the classroom and on the evaluation sheets that the course has evolved into its present form.

A revision

During the process of teaching family life for five terms to over 3,000 boys and girls, I have completely rewritten and revised the subject matter—all in the light of the students' suggestions plus what I learned from teaching the course. Schools and colleges over the entire country have requested the course of study. Almost all the colleges now teaching family life education have placed it on their library reference shelves. Many schools have indicated that they intend to use the same material.

Approval from everyone

Not a single parent has made a formal call of protest to the school officials . . . not a single church has protested. On the contrary, there is definite evidence of either enthusiastic or tacit approval by the many varied churches in the city. It is probably accurate to say that San Antonio has accepted family life education as a worthwhile educational contribution to the welfare of the young people of the city. It even seems safe to say that family life education not only is accepted in San Antonio but is capable of further growth and expansion in the future.

In the beginning the course was not identified with any school department, but as time passed it became clearer and clearer that the work was group guidance with implications of group therapy. Family life education is now a bona fide, respected part of San Antonio's guidance program. The teachers are officially called counselors and they work with both individuals and groups.

Thousands of boys and girls say . . .

When thousands of boys and girls write that a course has meant more to them than anything they ever experienced before in their entire lives—those who have been out of school for some time still say the same thing—it seems reasonable to conclude that courses like this, carefully planned and carefully taught, should be available to young people all over the country.

Although it is a discussion course, each lesson progresses from topic to topic, forming a well-rounded whole when complete. Starting with personality, we progress to the problem of maturity, move from there to family relationships, then to dating and its manifold problems, then to standards of morality and the facts of reproduction, and finally to marriage, life philosophy and worthy goals.

If this project has proved anything, it has proved that what needs to be taught can be taught . . . if we make the effort to do it.

San Antonio—a cosmopolitan city of contrast.

Mental Health

Second of a series of chapters from Preinduction Health and Human Relations, new curriculum resource for youth leaders by Roy E. Dickerson and Esther E. Sweeney.

For the Instructor

This section, designed to motivate young people towards achieving maximum mental health, offers some basic concepts about the genesis of behavior and the ability of human beings to change their behavior by using their emotions positively in their unique task of self-development.

One fundamental of good mental health is that the individual must recognize the role of emotion in human life in order to understand, focus and control his emotions and thereby achieve his own and society's goals.

He can develop that recognition in group discussions which emphasize that in the process of growing up one increasingly gains the satisfactions of self-realization, even though one must relinquish some of the attitudes and behavior patterns of immaturity.

It is essential to good mental health that one understand basic human emotional needs and drives and the morally and socially acceptable ways of satisfying them. The instructor or group leader can promote this precept by emphasizing that the process of striving towards mature development gives the individual an opportunity of achieving independence and self-reliance and that working towards these goals need not be carried on in a spirit of revolt against parental or other authority because independence and self-reliance are one's right, duty and privilege.

A primary, guiding principle for all people striving for sound emotional health is that they should gain insight into themselves, their own behavior and its motivations. One of the first things the instructor can do in assisting young people to develop insight is to help them realize that emotional problems are part and parcel of living and not evidence of one's being warped or "different."

Young men and women need to feel confidence and ease in asking for help with their emotional problems. The instructor can help them realize that accepting counseling services when the problems of growing up seem particularly difficult to manage is a normal, sensible procedure, not an admission of defeat, an evidence of abnormality nor a kind of disgrace.

Unless they understand that the achieving of maturity is a gradual and continuing process, they can become easily discouraged. The instructor needs

Military service tests their maturity.

to reassure them and to emphasize the roles played by reason, judgment and choice in the handling of emotional drives and impulses.

A specific goal of preinduction education for mental health is the development of perspective on the present national emergency and on the special demands it may make on mental health resources. With this perspective, young people will view their service in the Armed Forces and their jobs in business or homemaking as a challenge requiring maturity and offering further opportunity for growth.

This section is based on the principle that mental health is a totality, an inseparable relationship of mental, physical, social, intellectual and spiritual health factors. Mental health is not achieved in a vacuum; it relies upon physical health and development, spiritual orientation, the use of intellectual capacities and a complex of social adaptations. It is therefore a challenge to the individual . . . not a grim acceptance of the "burden" of growing up.

Reactions to be Anticipated

As young people begin to see that their feelings towards people and situations are rooted in their childhood experiences, they will need help in resisting the temptation to evade responsibility for their current behavior by rationalizing. The immature person may all too readily conclude that he is a victim of childhood experiences and for that reason neither responsible for nor able to change his present behavior.

The instructor can help young people in realizing that no one has had a perfect childhood and that many of the small child's feelings of rejection and insecurity grow out of his limited understanding of the world around him. Although these feelings often persist, insight into the ways by which the individual gains love, recognition and security today can offset the feelings one has grown up with. Even the young person who actually had little love, security or recognition in childhood can still gain them in the world in which he now lives. But to a large extent he will need help from his teachers and other adults in understanding that they recognize his worth and achievements and feel affection for him.

The instructor needs to be aware of the potential danger of too much self-examination and analysis by students in their discussions of personality, emotions and mental health in general. For the young man or woman who up to this point has had but little concern with the "whys" of his thoughts and feelings, self-focus can lead to an introspective questioning of every motive and feeling and to doubts about what may be perfectly normal and natural.

Keeping in mind the adage, "a little learning is a dangerous thing," the instructor can protect students from the upsetting effects of too much soul-searching.

Mental Health and National Well-Being

It is important that the instructor or group leader realize the crippling effect of poor mental health on the individual and the nation.

Mental hygiene received its first great stimulus in World War I. When increasing numbers of "shell-shocked" men were returned from the front it became apparent that the screening they had received as draftees had been inadequate. The screening, for physical fitness and gross evidence of mental illness or deficiency, had excluded personality factors.

This experience, which showed that personality problems and their genesis needed exploring, gave great impetus to the mental health movement in this country . . . a movement aimed at preventing mental ill-health rather than at mere diagnosis and treatment.

By World War II the Armed Forces realized that personality deficiencies can be more crippling to an individual and to the services than loss of limb. From the outset, each selectee in World War II was carefully screened for

Must he be a victim of his unhappy childhood?

personality factors which under stress or radically changed living conditions might precipitate him into neurosis or psychosis.

It quickly became apparent that the mental hygiene movement, despite every effort to reach into the lives of all our people, had not as yet achieved vital significance in the homes, schools and other institutions that influence the growth and development of young people.

More than 856,000 men (17.7%) between 18 and 37 years of age were rejected for mental disease out of 4,828,000 total rejections from the beginning of Selective Service to August 1, 1945. This figure does not include rejections for neurological conditions nor for mental deficiency. Moreover, the term *mental disease* as applied to those rejected did not in all instances mean acute mental illness; it included those personality disorders that made the individual a poor risk for military service.

Since no screening process is perfect, many service people in World War II were still to be found in military hospitals, in the guardhouse or brig . . . in difficulties because of deep-rooted mental habits and attitudes.

Military training is strenuous. It calls for mature personality and for adaptability and cooperativeness to a degree not usually demanded in civilian life. Furthermore, military manpower needs are such that the individual cannot always be assigned to the duties or places he prefers.

But the Armed Forces are not blindly regimented. Individual classification and assignment in the Armed Forces have been brought to a level far higher than that which prevails in most civilian businesses or industries. Moreover, except in actual combat the Armed Forces provide a rounded program of duty, rest and recreation for service personnel.

But the lack of privacy in the Armed Forces, the pressures of group living and the necessity of living under military regulations may cause unhappy emotional reactions in some young people. Life in the Armed Forces is a radical change and may require time for adjustment. Most young men and women take it in stride; those who continue to feel upset are not necessarily mentally ill. They may, however, need help to deal effectively with their emotional reactions.

Young people need to understand that the job of living is not easy or simple for anyone at all times. They also need to understand that their problems are not unique and do not mean that they are "different" and in a sense disabled because of them.

Emotional reactions such as anger, fear or jealousy are normal. But when they are protracted and overpowering, absorbing the individual and his energies too greatly and creating poorly-defined but deeply-felt anxieties, they become real problems. Young people, whether in civilian or military life, therefore need to be encouraged to seek consultation and guidance services on serious personal problems.

A rounded program of work, rest and recreation.

For Use with Students

The word *personality* has many meanings. One reads that Gloria Glamour is Hollywood's newest "personality." Yet Miss Glamour's true personality is rarely displayed on the screen. She must be Joan of Arc, Clara Barton, Elizabeth Barrett Browning or Queen Guinevere . . . never herself.

Figures in public life are described as "charming personalities" by those who have barely met them. Advertisers promise that a dress (produced in 10,000 lots) will "bring out your personality." These are but superficial aspects of personality.

Personality is the sum of the qualities, attitudes, habits and interests and of the physical, spiritual and intellectual characteristics that make up a particular individual . . . an individual with a separate and distinct identity. Personality must be viewed within the context of an individual's environment, his relationships with people, personal problems, sense of responsibility and ways of expressing his inner drives. His deeds, feelings and reactions combine to make him completely different from every other human being.

Background of Personality

Every child brings into the world a gift from his parents . . . inheritance. Less is known about human inheritance than animal inheritance. While it is possible to study thousands of insect generations in a few years, the observation of human inheritance is usually limited to a couple of generations.

Physically, people inherit a good deal from their parents . . . complexion, color of eyes and hair, skeletal structure, stature tendencies, facial characteristics. Some of one's father and mother, grandparents and great-grandparents—of even more remote ancestors—is in everyone's physical make-up.

But the total personality of a human being also owes a great deal to his environment. From birth, the people around a child; the care, love and protection they give him; his needs and the degree to which they are adequately (or inadequately) met . . . all exert their influence on his personality and his feelings towards the world.

The Physical Element in Personality

Physical factors can affect mental attitudes and, conversely, mental attitudes can affect physical health. A well-rounded personality is easier to achieve when one has excellent health. Headaches, upset stomachs, malnutrition, poor muscle tone and fatigue may have destructive effects on one's ability to get along with people and to function at one's best.

Since physical defects may have a marked effect on personality, they should be corrected if possible. If neglected, crooked teeth, bad posture and other remediable defects may cause the individual to be unduly self-conscious about his appearance and may affect his social ease and poise.

Some physical defects, of course, will yield only slightly to treatment. These too affect personality depending on whether the individual views them as a challenge or as a cause for self-pity, social withdrawal or other unwholesome behavior.

Most people know many individuals who have wholesome personalities and achieve productive and successful lives despite their physical handicaps. Their successes show that by meeting problems and rising above them one can develop fine personality.

The foundations of physical health and fitness are laid in an individual's childhood by the care and nurture he receives; by the exercise he gains in crawling, walking, running and later playing with other children; by the many health and safety measures his parents take. Later it becomes his responsibility to maintain maximum physical health and fitness. The extent to which he accepts this responsibility indicates his emotional maturity.

Class Discussion

- Why does each person on an athletic team need to be in good physical condition?
- How does physical fitness affect one's school work? One's activities in church groups? One's club activities?
- Why is physical health important in marriage and family life?

Good health for good personality.

The Intellectual Element in Personality

Mental or intellectual equipment differs from person to person. Personality reflects the way people regard their intellectual equipment and the use they make of it.

As a factor in personality brilliance of intellect is important only to the extent to which the brilliant person uses his mind constructively and accepts brilliance for what it is . . . a gift he has not earned, a personal responsibility. Normal intellect must be similarly regarded . . . as an endowment that carries personal responsibility.

No one should belittle a person of limited intellect. Everyone knows people whose kindness, consideration and generosity so far outweigh their intellectual limitations that one nevertheless respects, loves and enjoys them. Furthermore, everyone knows people who gain respect and relative success by putting their capacities and talents, however limited, to fullest use.

In contrast is the naturally gifted individual who fritters away talent because he has no worthwhile goals or ambitions. Immature or spoiled, he may believe he is superior to hard work; his philosophy may become "the world owes me a living." His mistaken self-appraisal may lead him to shirk the responsibility of his talents by lazy, wishful thinking.

The human mind, like the rest of the human organism, responds to repeated experience, to habit. The contributions intellect makes to a mature, stable and wholesome personality depend essentially on good habits of study, reflection and thought. The best mind in the world would be like a runaway horse—out of control and even potentially dangerous—unless tempered by good habits and self-discipline.

The field of psychology has made it possible to test individual skills, aptitudes and intellectual capacities with considerable accuracy and success. Where there are large numbers of people about whose capabilities it is necessary to make some initial estimates—as in the Armed Forces or huge defense plants—psychological testing is valuable in making preliminary decisions on job placements and responsibilities. But testing provides only broad-scale measurements, not a complete assessment of a person's capacities and ability to use himself productively.

Class Discussion

- Cite examples of jobs that may not require unusual intelligence but do require conscientiousness, personal interest and application.
- Name some figures of history who despite good intellect and prominence displayed poor personality and character traits.
- Discuss the part intelligence plays in controlling anger and in helping to solve problems.
- What is the role of intelligence in dating, courtship and marriage?

References

- *Learning to Live with Others*, by Alice and Lester D. Crow, pp. 75–91.
- *Personal Problems*, by John B. Geisel, pp. 119–138.
- *Better Ways of Growing Up*, by J. E. Crawford and L. E. Woodward, chaps. 2, 3 and 9. (Questionnaires particularly useful.)

The Social Element in Personality

Family background, customs and traditions; national and community codes; economic, educational, cultural and religious patterns affect the individual as a social being and contribute to his philosophy of life.

The child's social development begins as he first plays with other children and learns to know his relatives and friends. His personality is influenced by these relationships and by the things his playmates—and adults—consider important. Their values cause noticeable group and social consciousness, even in a very young child.

Later, the group becomes increasingly important, fostering one's opinions on movies, recordings and fashion fads, one's feelings about school and one's ideas of what constitutes a good time. The attitudes of the group have cogency for the growing boy or girl and motivate much of his or her behavior.

Generally speaking, young people tend to share their parents' views on moral values. But since their friends may also influence their moral attitudes, young men and women need to realize that they should not buy good standing in the group at the cost of their principles. By following the group to the detriment of one's convictions, one can fail to acquire a fine and mature personality.

Class Discussion

- When should you demonstrate the courage of your convictions, regardless of what others may think?
- Name 10 great national figures who were children of poor families, yet who greatly influenced our society.
- All the boys in John's class plan to send orchids to their partners for the senior prom. John simply cannot afford it. What would be the mature way for him to handle his problem?
- Mary is a "natural-born leader." Generally her ideas are good and are so presented to her classmates that they are perfectly agreeable to going along with them. Once in a while she becomes a trifle bossy. How can her group handle this problem in a mature way and at the same time help Mary to be more mature herself?

References

- *Personal Problems,* by John B. Geisel, pp. 193–203.
- *Better Ways of Growing Up,* by J. E. Crawford and L. E. Woodward. pp. 138–147.

The Emotional Element in Personality

Emotions—feelings—influence people strongly. The emotion of love, for example, influences men and women to make great sacrifices for each other. A child's love for his parents may make him carefully hoard his pennies and nickels (that might otherwise go into bubblegum or new jacks) for their Christmas or birthday presents. Mature love of country and affection for his buddies will make a man willingly risk his life in combat.

Emotions can also influence people in destructive ways. Anger can motivate harsh and cruel words or acts. Fear can create such envy and jealousy of another's success that it embitters the individual and makes him ungenerous and unkind to a competitor.

To develop a mature personality it is necessary to understand emotion and its powerful influence in one's life—an influence that can make one work for fine goals and help one in achieving them.

One often hears the expression, "He's his own worst enemy." Many people are their own worst enemies because they let emotion guide their behavior to the exclusion of reason, judgment and experience.

Fear, for example, is a normal emotion experienced by everyone. Fear can serve human beings; it alerts them to danger. But the man of proved ability who won't take a better job for fear of possible failure is allowing emotion to rule his life to his detriment.

Emotional growth is part of total personality development. It is of such vital significance in both civilian and military life that the Armed Forces consider the individual's emotional tone to be as important as his physical health and fitness. The Armed Forces try to find out the feelings of prospective recruits about people and things, and try to estimate their use of emotion to build or destroy, and their use of reason, judgment and experience in guiding emotions. These factors, brought out in initial interviews, are clues to the likelihood of an individual's successfully adjusting to military life.

In much the same way, increasing numbers of civilian personnel directors are attempting to forecast (through pre-employment interviews by psychologists or psychiatrists) the degree of success they may expect their employees to achieve in meeting day-by-day job responsibilities, in getting along with both colleagues and supervisors, and in handling pressures and emergencies.

Class Discussion

- In a job interview, Sam reveals the following things about his experience: (1) he "never got above PFC in the service because the

Spiritual experiences are part of growth.

What greater love?

top sergeant had no use for men who weren't 'regular army'"; (2) he's changed jobs a good many times because he "had to take the first thing that came along after the war and never could afford to be out of work long enough to pick and choose"; (3) he's leaving his present job because his supervisor is "a nagging, unprogressive type, who gives you no chance to get ahead and show what you can do." How would you rate Sam as a prospective employee?

The Spiritual Element in Personality

The spiritual growth of an individual is inextricably tied in with his emotional growth and social development . . . and with his environment. His aspirations, values, creative abilities and aesthetic appreciation, and his ability to relate himself to his Creator and his fellowmen will be deepened and enhanced by happy emotional growth.

Early in life a child begins to make choices of behavior, exhibiting the root development of conscience. His first choices—whether, for example, to eat a piece of candy now or wait, as his mother has said, till after dinner—are motivated by his desire to hold his parents' love and approval and by his fear that they may withdraw that love and approval.

Later the child adopts his parents' values about right and wrong and begins to use considerably more thought and judgment in making his choices. He is also influenced by the example, aspirations and ideals of his parents and other adults he admires.

As he grows up, his church experiences or his contacts in clubs and young people's groups with spiritually oriented people his own age or older continue to affect his spiritual growth and development.

The Armed Forces' character guidance program is a concrete recognition of the desire of young people to develop their inner lives—the spiritual element in their personalities.

Class Activity

- Student panel to discuss "How a Wholesome Moral and Spiritual Life Affects America's Strength."
- Quiz-the-experts session with community representatives or school instructors to answer students' questions on physical, social, spiritual, intellectual and emotional growth. A psychologist, psychiatrist, physician, psychiatric social worker, health and physical education teacher, social studies teacher and clergyman are suggested for the panel.

References

- *Learning to Live with Others*, by Alice and Lester D. Crow, pp. 65–73.
- *Personal Problems*, by John B. Geisel, pp. 45–50.
- *The Armed Forces Character Guidance Program*, American Social Hygiene Association, 1790 Broadway, New York 19, N. Y.
- *Character Guidance in the Army*, available from the Department of the Army, Pentagon, Washington 25, D.C.
- *Moral and Spiritual Values in the Public Schools*, Educational Policies Commission, National Education Association of the United States and the American Association of School Administrators, 1201 Sixteenth Street, N. W., Washington, D.C., pp. 17–80.
- *Better Ways of Growing Up*, by J. E. Crawford and L. E. Woodward, pp. 182–213.

From Birth to Age Two

From the moment he is born a human being has feelings and desires and reacts to his environment. Before birth the infant in the mother's uterus has nothing to worry about, nothing to strive for. He is supplied with nourishment and oxygen in balanced amounts. He lives in comfortable equilibrium, in perfect safety and physical ease.

But birth upsets this passive, secure and balanced existence . . . upsets it abruptly. For as soon as the child is born, his whole being must adjust immediately to the job of surviving. In his new environment he must depend on others for physical comfort, nourishment and a feeling of safety. Even his supply of oxygen may, at first, be a trifle hard to get.

The little baby is self-centered and spends his early months eating, sleeping, and gradually exploring the world around him. His job is staying alive and growing, and he devotes himself to it fully. If he is hungry and food is not forthcoming, he cries. If he feels frightened—babies are known to be afraid of falling—he also cries.

He is largely aware of his parents simply as kind and loving hands that caress and pet him, feed him, keep him warm and comfortable, and make him feel safe. He comes into the world needing care, love and protection and he comes prepared (so far as his limited physical resources permit) to fight a little for what he must have. Parents (or sometimes substitutes for parents) give him food and physical care, and he commences to feel and accept their love.

The little baby, so helpless at birth and for a time thereafter, soon begins to move about his world, explores it, explores himself—his fingers, toes, ears—and gradually becomes aware of his parents as people. As he crawls and walks, begins to eat in his highchair and talks a little, he continues to get help and support from his parents. He commences to have more outgoing feelings for them, to love and wish to please them, and to be loved by them.

The infant's need for love (and later his need to love) and his limited but gradually more evident fight for what he must have to survive are sometimes called the basic drives. Since it is essential to every human being to protect himself, aggression—the capacity to fight for what one needs and to fend off danger—is manifest as something very fundamental and essential. Some psychiatrists think a child's first sign of readiness to do something in his own behalf—to fight or be aggressive—is sucking the breast or bottle. In any case the continuance of the human race depends upon the basic drives of love and aggression.

Almost concurrent with the child's first displays of his drive for love and his drive to fight is his meeting with frustration. No matter how quickly

Her parents think . . . her playmates say . . . these are all molding her.

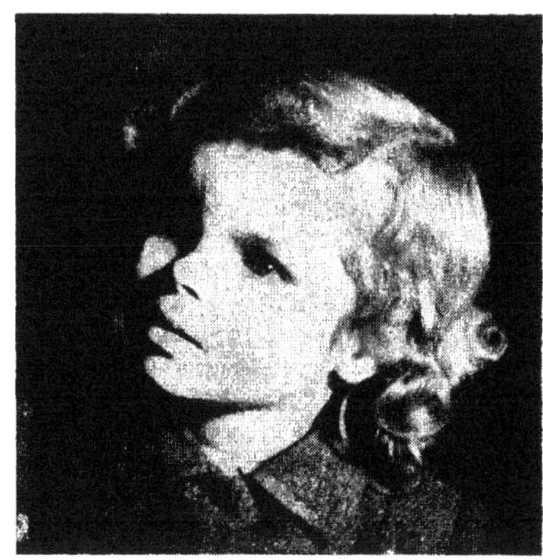

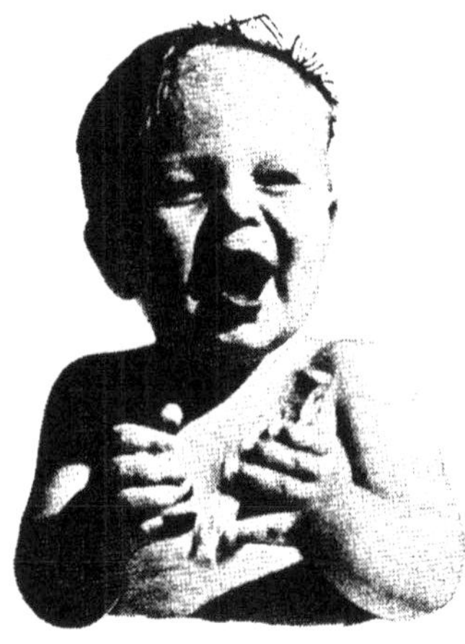

At first the infant loves only himself.

the mother may respond to the baby's need for food or for diaper-changing, the infant (whose sense of time is not yet developed) feels thwarted because her response is not instantaneous. One big job all parents have is to help their children in their early years to realize that everyone experiences frustration in one situation or another.

The mother and father teach the child that he cannot always have the things he wants and may have to accept substitutes. Or that he cannot have what he wants immediately but may be able to have it later. They help the child to handle frustration positively, showing him how he can use a frustrating failure as a stimulus to solving a problem. For example, a collapsed house of blocks is a frustration, but wise parents help the child to try new ways of balancing and supporting the blocks so that he ultimately builds a structure that will stand.

Parents also teach their child that in some situations one can only "grin and bear it." This is part of their job in helping the child to grow up, to use his emotions constructively, to control them and to focus the energies they create on positive goals.

Sometimes the best efforts of parents to demonstrate love to the child, to make him feel secure and to give him recognition fall short of their goal. Unfortunately, the child's limited understanding of his new world may cause him to feel that he is not loved, that he isn't entirely secure or that people do not recognize him.

He may actually be deprived to some degree of the satisfaction of his needs . . . by family problems, for example. A mother's long and serious illness may mean that she cannot be with her child as much as she wants to be. The acute illness of another child in the family may consume practically every waking moment of both parents.

Almost every child feels at one time or another that he is not loved, recognized or entirely secure. This may be for real reasons or because he is unable to understand and rightly interpret every word, action, gesture, tone of voice or other form of parental expression. Most people therefore grow up with some uncertainty about the extent to which they are loved and recognized, and few, if any, have absolute, inner security.

If the child's feelings of rejection, insecurity and lack of recognition are very deep-seated, he may have considerable difficulty in growing up emotionally. As an adolescent or young adult he may need help to recognize his worth and ability to meet life and its problems before some of the feelings he had as a little child can be offset.

What the little child does to cope with feelings of rejection, insecurity and lack of recognition varies and depends on how consistently he feels these things. Sometimes these feelings persist into adulthood in spite of the fact that the adult has many daily proofs that he is actually loved and accepted. Sometimes the methods he used as a child to alleviate his feelings of rejection and insecurity become the behavior patterns of later years. This means that the chronologically mature person may still behave like a child because he is emotionally immature.

For example, the small child just out of babyhood may feel a little unsure about things. He may wish to remain a baby since he still identifies parental care with parental love. Some older people too desire such dependence. They are fairly self-centered and in a sense still want to be babies. Unless one recognizes the significance of wanting to be babied, helpless and waited upon, this immature behavior may continue and interfere seriously with one's career, marriage and family life.

If the little child feels insecure, he may become unduly afraid of new things and new experiences. Conversely, to reassure himself he may try to be daring and brave.

The small child who is unsure of recognition may clamor for it. Older people often do the same thing—demand the limelight, monopolize conversations, boast, etc. Or the little child may try to meet his problem another way. He may commence imagining situations in which he is recognized, powerful and important. Daydreaming in an older person is much the same thing.

Again, the child, feeling unrecognized, may decide that he cannot and should not be recognized—that there may be something wrong with him or that he is just plain bad. He may try to be inconspicuous, withdraw from people and grow less and less self-confident. One carryover of these emotional patterns into later years is acute shyness and aloofness. Another may be a generalized feeling of being in the wrong, of feeling guilty even when one has actually done nothing wrong. Or the adult may doubt his own abilities, even though these may be excellent.

Similarly, a child who doubts that he is loved—even though this feeling may stem from misinterpretation of his relationships with people—may react in a variety of ways. He may try his level best to please everybody so that they will be forced to see what a good child he is and to love him. In older people, one sees the same pattern in the boy or girl who is perfection itself, who tries to appease everybody or possibly even to "buy" affection in one way or another.

Sometimes the feeling of not being loved causes the little child to take an I-don't-care attitude or to feel that if others don't love him he might just as well dislike them. Or he may try to command love by bossing other youngsters.

While it is true that childish feelings and their resultant behavior patterns are often seen in emotionally immature adults, people need not be the victims of their early feelings, nor need they persist in the behavior they adopted as little children. As they recognize they are clinging to childish feelings and behavior, young people can begin to use reason, judgment and their capacity for evaluation in handling their emotions and behavior. Unlike the little child, they have the advantage of considerable experience in living, in knowing people, and in achieving things on their own . . . all this can assist them in attaining a high level of maturity.

Young people can appreciate that the drive for love and the drive to fight are the bases for many of man's highest and most rewarding actions. They can readily recognize that marriage and family life depend upon the drive for love, as do their friendly, affectionate feelings for others, acceptance of social responsibilities, patriotism and brotherhood. But it may be more difficult for them to recognize immediately the rewarding elements in the drive to fight because the word *aggression* is so often associated with war and even with unwarranted attack on the helpless.

Aggression is the force that makes an individual stand up for what he knows is right, resist attack, meet various kinds of danger and when necessary go into combat for his country. But aggression also embodies much more. Properly channeled, it is the self-assertive power behind study and research, art, invention and all those careers and endeavors to which men devote their lives.

Class Discussion

- What constructive ways can people use to win attention and approval, love and affection?
- How do "the life of the party" and "the smart aleck" who knows all the answers defeat their desire for recognition?
- How can a young person get help on his problems of growing up?
- How do envy and jealousy relate to feelings of personal inadequacy?
- What are some constructive ways to overcome shyness?
- Are our emotions harmful, in themselves?

Mixing with the group . . . how easy is it for them to learn?

Age Two to Six

The child between two and six has a host of new experiences.

Increasingly conscious of his parents, he normally forms strong and lasting attachments to them. As he feels loved and happy and secure with both his father and mother, he begins to want to be like them, especially like the parent of his own sex. The small boy finds in his father an ideal of manhood. He imitates his father in play and in his gestures and facial expressions. The little girl sees in her mother an ideal of womanhood. She tries to be like her mother, wants to help with household duties, wants to dress like her, and often plays the role of mother with dolls and with other children.

But there are times when the small child's understanding is too limited to grapple with the seeming contradiction between parental love and parental authority. Since the child is too immature to place sensible and safe restrictions upon himself, his parents must do so. Their authority is usually kind, firm and loving, and the child—even though he regrets the restrictions—accepts his parents' right to exercise control.

Generally the child has little real difficulty in accepting parental authority . . . he even finds it a reassuring support. But there are times when he may interpret it simply as depriving him of something he wants or as a sign that his parents do not love him. At times, his parents may contribute to these feelings, not realizing that their voices may be harsher than necessary and their disciplines too firm.

If the child identifies the exercise of authority with the withdrawal of love, he may respond by revolting, disobeying or acting wilfully. Or he may try to appease, to be a model child. Either course may become a behavior pattern and affect his later attitudes towards discipline and authority. The person in

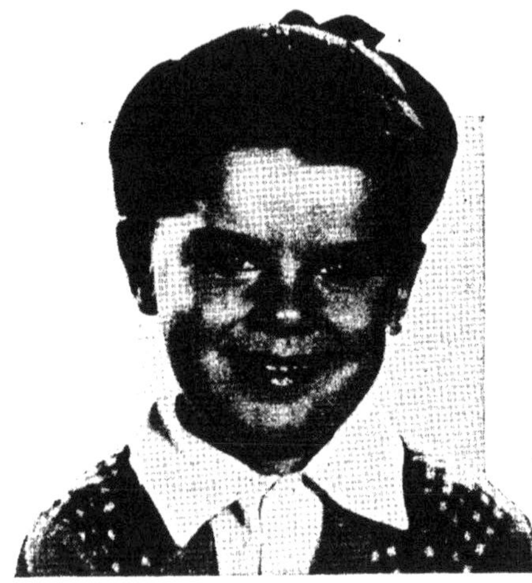

The appeaser—to him authority means the withdrawal of love.

revolt is not happy; nor is the appeaser. Both must gain insight into why they behave as they do and attempt to work out mature ways of living comfortably with authority.

It is during these years from about two to six that many children meet the challenge of new brothers and sisters. Wise parents prepare the little child for the arrival of a new baby, attempt to interest him in the story of how life begins and do their utmost to reassure him about his continuing place in their affections.

Yet it is almost impossible to prevent the small child from having some feelings of worry about his ability to hold his parents' love and recognition. As he observes the care and time the new baby requires, he may feel left out and ignored. Parents who realize that some temporary rivalry is bound to exist between the child and the newcomer do not try to force the 2- or 3-year-old to accept the baby right away; they simply increase their efforts to make the older child feel safe and loved. Gradually the older child does accept the new baby, and his earlier feelings of jealousy are replaced by growing interest in the newcomer.

The child's way of handling the challenge of new brothers and sisters may be repeated later in meeting other people who seem to threaten his security and his place in the affections of people he admires. If he learns that he does not lose status and importance by the arrival of a new baby and if he learns that his parents' affections can include more than just one child, later he will be able to realize that other adults can love and respect him, yet include other people in their regard.

At two or three, a youngster begins to widen his social horizon, to make friends. This is the period of learning to share experiences with brothers, sisters and playmates. Although he now begins to be less self-centered, he is not always ready to share toys and to work and play with his new friends. It is at this stage of learning that the group acts to some extent upon him, for if he won't learn to play according to the rules (and there *are* rules, even though crude and simple) the group may isolate him or punish him in one way or another.

Most children learn fairly quickly to get along with the group. But some react to group pressure by deciding they would rather play alone, others by over-submitting to group rule. The effect of these early reactions is often apparent in later years in the boy or girl who decides he or she is too good for the group or who will do practically anything to gain the group's approval.

The child who fits comfortably into group living—learning first lessons in sharing, unselfishness and generosity, yet acting on personal initiative from time to time—has little difficulty in social adjustments later on. He works happily and productively with three or four schoolmates on a research project, works in his club on producing a play, gets along comfortably in his job, adjusts well to life in the Armed Forces and fits easily and quickly into any new social group.

Class Discussion

- Mrs. Jones frequently says to her boy when he misbehaves, "Wait till I tell your father about this." What effect would this be likely to have on: (a) Mr. Jones; (b) their little son? Discuss.
- When the Smiths' baby was born, Mrs. Smith thought that young Johnny, age 3, would learn to love the new baby more quickly by hearing her say to friends and relatives, "Johnny is crazy about Billy." Discuss.

Age Six to Thirteen

Going to school opens new doors on life for the child. To some extent, his first experiences in playing with other children prepare him for meeting the new group of youngsters he finds at school.

But he may not be quite so ready for a new factor in his life . . . the teacher. The teacher is an unknown quantity and for the first few days he may have some difficulty in understanding her role in his life. Usually he learns fairly soon that she is an adult friend, someone with authority who nonetheless is willing and eager to help him, ready to support and encourage his efforts. A teacher plays an important part in a child's life, and quite often a child who has felt unsure of himself or, for one reason or another, unloved begins to gain confidence and a feeling of acceptance and recognition because of her.

For some children—those who have developed patterns of trying to remain dependent or of occasionally regressing into babyhood because their status with their parents has not been altogether clear to them—school may look like a very big jump into growing up. For a while they may show signs of dependency

Seven-year-olds want friends of their own sex.

either at home or in the school . . . "forget" how to dress themselves and revert to eating and talking like two-year-olds.

The way some children react to early school experiences becomes their later way of reacting to most new situations. Many people find a new experience rather frightening . . . a new class in school, a first dance, a new job, or a first trip away from home. This is not very unusual since most people have some fear of the unknown. But when people try to avoid a new experience, get severely upset about it or become over-dependent on old ways, places and people, they need help in working out a mature and happy approach to new situations.

From about six to thirteen, girls are chiefly interested in relationships with other girls, and boys with boys. This is normal, wholesome emotional growth. During these years, while home and family continue to be important to the child the group takes on increasing importance. Girls enjoy each other's company, like to belong to the same clubs and Scout troops, and want to spend as much time together as possible. Similarly, boys want the same kind of close association with other boys in clubs, teams, camping and other social and athletic activities.

Towards the latter part of this period, boys are likely to be interested in gangs. Gangs are normal, and when their purposes are wholesome they go a long way towards developing group loyalty, cooperation and mutual helpfulness. Some gangs are destructive and encourage antisocial forms of aggression. Some young people who have developed patterns of revolt and hostility towards people and situations use gang life as a way of taking out on society their own fears, uncertainties and doubts.

Many youngsters of 12 and 13 begin getting into serious difficulties that could be prevented if they realized that all around them are wise and helpful people with whom they can talk out some of their feelings of anger, envy and dislike.

These people (leaders of youth groups, teachers, guidance counselors, clergymen and, even better, their own parents and relatives) have been through the job of growing up. They understand many of the problems youngsters face and can aid them in redirecting their emotions into constructive and happy ways of living.

Class Discussion

- Suggest some steps in thinking, reflecting and planning that a person can take if he feels uneasy about these situations: (1) meeting his mother's bridge club when it meets at his home; (2) moving into a new community; (3) taking a first job in an office or industrial plant.
- How can experience in a group increase self-reliance?
- Jack belongs to a gang called the Blockbusters. Recently some of the boys favored an organized fight against the Red Devils, another gang, in order to force a merger. How can Jack show leadership and maturity in bringing about this merger without violence?
- Jim didn't get caught but he was with his gang when they broke street lights on the avenue. He feels his crowd is headed for trouble; he feels he is too. Suggest how he might meet this situation.

Puberty and Adolescence

Home, school, club and community interests are strong in the young adolescent. A new interest, part of normal emotional development, begins to be apparent . . . interest in the opposite sex.

The physical changes of puberty occur at about 12 or 13 in most girls, a little later in most boys. Emotional interest in the opposite sex, however, does not necessarily coincide with physical development. Some boys and girls continue to be chiefly interested in only their own sex for another year or two. For others, interest in each other precedes pubertal changes.

But the years of adolescence are generally characterized by mutual interest between the sexes and consequently these years bring new problems to growing boys and girls. For several years immediately preceding adolescence young people play and associate almost exclusively with members of their own sex; the behavior of boys with boys and girls with girls is informal and casual. By the time they are entering their teens courtesy, dress, etiquette and social behavior present interesting new challenges.

Adolescence also offers opportunities for realizing the satisfactions of growing up. As the adolescent begins to take his place in the adult world, he finds he has a chance to show more self-reliance and self-direction.

But one's eagerness to demonstrate independence and make decisions may sometimes cause hasty and inconsiderate action. The young adult may attempt more than he can yet manage with due regard for his own and society's best interests.

Dating is one aspect of growing up that demands careful thought and planning. Emotion can get out of control more quickly than many young people realize. The drive for love is strong, yet only when it is controlled can it achieve the best personal and social ends. Maturity requires consideration for the other person and realization that it is as dangerous to play at love at 18 as it was to play with matches at eight. Mature use of the sex impulse means deferring the satisfaction of sexual desires to the right time, place and circumstances. It means recognizing moral issues and being guided by moral values in order to fulfill properly the ultimate goals of marriage and family life.

Since maturity is so essential to the job of being an effective citizen, a young person should make every effort to develop insight into his own behavior and motivations, to arrive at an honest evaluation of his development, and thereby to increase his confidence in meeting life, including the demands of the national emergency.

Service to his country requires many changes in a young person's everyday way of living. These changes in turn make demands on his inner resources of strength and stability, and call for self-mobilization attuned to national mobilization.

A century ago men and women the age of today's 12th graders pioneered the Far West, defended covered wagons from attack, built homes and raised families in the wilderness. They met real problems with all the maturity at their command and used each new situation and circumstance to accelerate their development. Today's young people are just as capable of playing their part in the nation's progress and in the defense of its homes and shores.

Just as they are beginning to enjoy the companionship of the opposite sex, young men (and some young women) are being called upon to deal calmly and thoughtfully with the problems that arise when they start military service. Wise use of off-duty time will help them offset the feeling that military life deprives one of normal social life. USO's, churches and hospitable homes offer many opportunities for wholesome relations between the sexes, for good times in good company.

Marriage

Defense mobilization also calls for mature thinking about marriage. A precipitate marriage can hurt both the young man and woman. The post-World War II divorce rate reflected the haste that had marked many wartime marriages. Most of these divorces were painful for the young couples and created serious problems for their children.

Budgets and orange blossoms— she's planned for both.

Although every decision to marry or to defer marriage while the man is in service must be made individually, young couples should reflect on some of the following questions especially when they consider marriage under pressure of the emergency:

- Have they known each other long enough and observed each other in enough different situations to be certain they are ready for lifelong partnership?
- Are both really weaned from dependence on parents?
- Have they realistically planned details of daily living . . . budgets, insurance and possible medical costs?
- Have they had experience in making and abiding by important decisions?
- Has experience proved them capable of facing real hardship?
- Have they decided whether the wife will accompany her husband to military posts or remain at home?
- Are they prepared for the husband's possible overseas duty, which might mean protracted separation?
- Have they faced the possibility, however remote, of his being killed or permanently disabled?

Mature, panic-free analysis of these problems will give young people a sound and confident basis for carrying through their final decision to marry or to wait a while.

Class Discussion

- Discuss the qualities that go into friendship. Are boys and girls as capable of true friendship with each other as they are with members of their own sex?
- What do you think about love at first sight? Discuss blind dates.
- What do you think about going steady at 15, 16 and 17 years of age?
- What are the values of double-dating?

Class Activity

- Distribute cards on which the Crawford and Woodward questions (*Better Ways of Growing Up,* pp. 254–257) have been typed. Have students answer them in two-minute talks.

References

- *Learning to Live with Others,* by Alice and Lester D. Crow, pp. 93–111.
- *People Are Important,* by Floyd L. Ruch, Gordon N. Mackenzie and Margaret McClean, pp. 47–76, 192–237.

CREDITS

Photos courtesy of Hazel Greenwald, Hadassah, pp. 145–155.

Photo by Ewing Galloway, p. 158.

Photos courtesy of USO, pp. 159, 169.

Photo courtesy of the Health Insurance Plan of Greater New York (*New York Times*), p. 162.

Photo courtesy of the San Antonio Chamber of Commerce (Harvey Patteson & Son, San Antonio), p. 164.

Photos courtesy of the Department of Defense, pp. 166, 175.

Photo courtesy of the Pitt Photo Library (Corsini), p. 167.

Photo courtesy of the Canadian Information Service (National Film Board), p. 174.

Photo courtesy of the British Information Services, p. 177.

Photos courtesy of the Community Chests and Councils, pp. 181, 184.

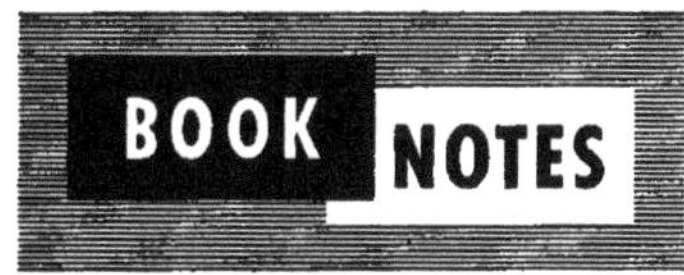

The Habitual Sex Offender; Report and Recommendations, by Paul W. Tappan. Trenton, New Jersey Commission on the Habitual Sex Offender, 1950. 69p.

This compact work is more than a technical report of a governmental committee; it is a solid, documented analysis of the problems, facts and fallacies connected with the social aspects of the sexual deviate. The report presents a program for combatting sex offenses not only by suggesting realistic legislation for dealing with apprehended offenders, but by setting forth a plan for treatment and prevention as well.

The committee very carefully examined the existing legal and psychiatric definitions of *psychopath* and the administrative experiences of the 13 states having sexual psychopath laws. They hoped to arrive at some legal and clinical basis for their recommendations and at the same time avoid any mistakes other states had made in facing the same problem. They concluded that no uniform legal nor clinical definition of *sexual psychopath* existed, and that the majority of the sex offender laws were ineffective or completely inoperative.

The committee then went on to make suggestions based on consultations with Kinsey, Sutherland and Ploscowe and on the results of three studies . . . one in which they questioned psychiatrists, one in which they queried New Jersey high school principals about the extent of abnormal sex practices, and a third in which they polled parent-teacher groups for opinions concerning treatment.

In its most noteworthy section the report destroys some common myths about the sex offender, particularly that there are "thousands of homicidal sex fiends abroad in the land" who are "over-sexed" and who progress to increasingly serious types of offenses. Such fallacies are the major stumbling-block to a sound legislative and preventive program in this field.

Donald J. Newman
University of Wisconsin

American Health Directory, by Henry Hatton. Washington, D.C., Public Affairs Press, 1952. 96p. $2.50.

Listed under subject headings, alphabetically arranged, are the names of pertinent health organizations. Social hygienists will find of interest such headings as sex education, social hygiene, prostitution and venereal diseases.

Phantasy in Childhood, by Audrey Davidson and Judith Fay. New York, Philosophical Library, 1953. 188p. $4.75.

This is a stimulating book to review since it permits a closer look at the approach to childhood which comes from the psychoanalytic school of Melanie Klein. It shows enormous sensitivity to children, their problems and their instinctual demands. It is extremely rich . . . . full of descriptions of situations and quotations of children's remarks, illustrating the concepts behind the understanding of child development.

The titles of the chapters are a good illustration of the major emphasis of this book—The World in Black and White, The Influence of the Real World, The Mouth as a Centre of Feeling, Some Meanings of Excretion, Genital Feelings and Phantasies, Phantasy in Middle Childhood, and The Living-Through of Phantasies.

I was particularly interested in the second chapter, since it was my impression that this book gave insufficient emphasis to the role of the ego in relationship to phantasies . . . the child's capacity to judge, to learn by experience, to understand and to cope with outer reality. Even in this chapter, a good deal of "reality" was related to the emotional relationship between parent and child, and did not take into account the kind of phantasies provoked today by radio, television and books, which influence the child's means of meeting his own needs, in relation to the specific environment to which he has to adjust.

I think this is an excellent book for the experienced child therapist. I do not think that it will serve well the public at large, who will, I think, be unable to follow a discussion of phantasy in childhood condensed to such a degree to the earliest years of life and connected to such an extent with specific problems of child growth.

Peter B. Neubauer, M.D., Director
Council Child Development Center, New York City

The Family in Various Cultures, by Stuart A. Queen and Johns B. Adams. Philadelphia, Lippincott, 1952. 280p. $4.50.

This book provides a wide and interesting variety of facts about the steps leading to marriage and the marriage and family system in various cultures. The range is indicated by some of the chapter headings: The Hopi Family, The Kwoma Family, The Ancient Hebrews, The Early Christians, and The English Colonists in America.

Here we have invaluable teaching material. If we are to educate soundly for marriage and family life, there should be clear-cut concepts of the factors which constitute success in these relationships. One of the best ways to develop these concepts is to study marriage and family life in other cultures for the sake of seeing clearly the advantages and disadvantages. Out of such a study a better conception of values and goals in our own culture should emerge, thus enabling youth to think more clearly about the kind of marriage and family life one should prepare for and strive to achieve.

The book is a must for the teacher or other adult who wishes a better basis for evaluating our own cultural patterns and for teaching youth.

Roy E. Dickerson, Executive Secretary
Cincinnati Social Hygiene Society

Henry VIII—A Difficult Patient, by Sir Arthur S. MacNulty. London, Christopher Johnson, 1952. 202p. 18s.

In presenting interesting aspects of the life and time of the scholar-king, the author gives him credit for great contributions to the advancement of medical science in England.

He believes Henry did not have syphilis and relies on authorities long since dead to support this belief. No modern syphilologist is quoted. More surprising, the author accepts without question the Columbian theory of the introduction of syphilis into Europe and asserts that Francis I of France had syphilis.

Both points are open to doubt. The weight of evidence is against both assumptions.

Charles Walter Clarke, M.D.
ASHA's Executive Director Emeritus

Your Community's Health, by Dean Franklin Smiley, M.D., and Adrian Gordon Gould, M.D. New York, Macmillan, 1952. Rev. 454p. $5.50.

One chapter, Community Problems in Sex Hygiene, gives a brief history of legislative efforts to abolish prostitution, which, the authors claim, has endured because of man's supposed need for intercourse without responsibility. The authors refute the misconception and reprint "The Case against the Red Light" from the *Social Hygiene Legislation Manual,* published by ASHA in 1921.

The modern program to counteract prostitution and its concomitant, VD, includes the treatment and rehabilitation of prostitutes, adequate recreation facilities, effective legislation, proper sex education and economic opportunities for women.

The authors touch upon the recent gains made against VD and devote some space to the need for sex education.

The Modern Family, by Robert F. Winch. New York, Henry Holt, 1952. 522p. $6.00.

Dr. Winch has approached his study of the family as an anthropologist, a sociologist and a psychologist. Psychiatric aspects of family interaction also appear. The author's avoidance of highly technical terminology makes the book useful to the layman, but he is not talked down to.

After picturing family life in other cultures, the author uses flashbacks to compare the modern family with the primitive and to interweave his anthropologic and psychologic analyses. The reader feels he can learn much by studying these so-called uncivilized peoples.

By presenting the family as a cycle and by the frequent flashback to other cultures, the author welds the book together. This readable and comprehensive study, a worth-while contribution to the social hygiene literature, accomplishes very nearly all the author claims for it in the preface.

A. Eleanor Thompson, Librarian
Course in Family Living and Sex Education
University of Pennsylvania

About You, by Marjorie C. Cosgrove and Mary I. Josey. Family Living Series, Volume I. Chicago, Science Research Associates, 1952. 80p. 96¢.

About You is a combination work-book and text-book for junior and senior high schools. The content is organized around various phases of personal and social adjustment, with the major emphasis on mental and social aspects of wholesome living . . . healthy personality, getting along with one's family, friends and the opposite sex, succeeding in school, solving one's problems, and planning for the future.

The authors suggest a variety of approaches for making objective studies of personality development and progress toward emotional maturity.

About You is a refreshing, stimulating and welcome contribution to the material now available for teachers and adolescents on constructive ways to go about meeting the emotional and social challenges of growing up. The one regret is that physical health is not interrelated with mental and social health as a personality asset and a significant factor in securing and holding a job. This omission from the chapter, Planning Your Career (which includes a chart on job-success traits), was disappointing.

Lula P. Dilworth, Assistant in Health Education
New Jersey Department of Education

journal of SOCIAL HYGIENE

vol. 39 may 1953 no. 5

IN THIS ISSUE

MAY 1953

About our cover . . .

President Soekarno of the Republic of Indonesia and Mrs. Soekarno with their two oldest children. Twenty-third of a series of Journal covers on family life . . . photograph courtesy of the Republic of Indonesia.

Harriett Scantland, *Editor*
Elizabeth McQuaid, Assistant Editor

Eleanor Shenehon, Editorial Consultant

THE JOURNAL OF SOCIAL HYGIENE

official periodical of the American Social Hygiene Association, published monthly except July, August and September at the Boyd Printing Company, Inc., 374 Broadway, Albany 7, N. Y. Acceptance for mailing at the special rate of postage provided for in Section 1103, Act of October 3, 1917. Entered as second-class matter at the Post Office at Albany, N. Y., March 23, 1922.

Subscription price: $3.00 per year. Single copy: 35¢.

University of Nebraska and Johns Hopkins alumnus. Formerly medical officer, U. S. Marine Hospital on Ellis Island, and VD control officer for Michigan. Now chief of the VD division, USPHS.

James K. Shafer, M.D.

The Outlook for Venereal Disease Control

by J. K. Shafer, M.D.

I should like to compliment you who attended the recent National Conference on Social Hygiene for once again bringing into sharp focus the countless problems of our environment which so materially affect human behavior. We are completely aware of the impact of these problems on venereal disease control in this country . . . particularly because our personnel and financial resources are so directed that our federal venereal disease division must concentrate largely on the medical, epidemiological and informational aspects of this control problem. We appreciate the work of your groups in education, in the home, in the church and in public health.

With full recognition of the impact of your cooperative efforts, I report with considerable pride the accomplishments of our venereal disease control program.

For the country as a whole I think that syphilis has in the recent past been brought under a considerable measure of control. The reservoir of undiscovered and untreated syphilis in the United States is declining. While we estimate it today to be slightly over two million persons, it is about one-third lower than it was 10 years ago. This is the result primarily of intensive case-finding and educational activities, which dry up the streams of new syphilis that feed the reservoir.

Why a decline?

It is an outstanding accomplishment of recent years that venereal disease rates have declined consistently during a period of mobilization. This is phenomenal in medical history. Nonetheless it develops logically from the simple fact of preparedness. When the present mobilization period began, the armed services, the state and local health departments, the American Social Hygiene Association and the Public Health Service were prepared for it. . .

- We had case-finding and prevention techniques which had proved their effectiveness.
- We had reliable diagnosis and effective treatment.
- We had sound education for the civilian population as well as the military, plus good epidemiologic intelligence.
- Most important, our efforts were united in an efficient, working relationship backed with joint operational experience.

You will be interested to know that at present state health departments have assigned 150 public health workers to military establishments, defense-impacted areas and recreational areas frequented by military personnel and defense workers. These men are especially trained for interviewing and field investigation work, and they are charged with the responsibility of keeping their areas of assignment free from venereal disease.

You will also be interested to know that as a result of the activities of these men and of the parallel activities of the defense establishments and neighboring health departments, VD rates among the military in the continental limits of the United States are lower than ever before.

Since 1940 there has been a steady decrease of over 50% in deaths due to syphilis. Since 1933 infant mortality due to syphilis has been reduced by

During mobilization VD rates have declined.

92%. Even more impressive, the infant mortality rate due to syphilis has been declining much more rapidly than the infant death rate from all causes.

Although we run the calculated risk of being premature in our estimate of the treatment program, we nevertheless take a certain pride in the fact that during the present fiscal year the transition from inpatient to outpatient treatment will have been completed. To provide services comparable to those furnished by the rapid treatment centers, a network of prevention and control centers is being established throughout the country.

Obviously, it would be unsound to return diagnosis, treatment and epidemiology to all of the 3,000 local clinics which once existed throughout the country. However, it is sound to select a few existing clinics for consideration as VD prevention and control centers. Those selected should meet the following requirements:

- Be located in high prevalence areas and in communities which are transportation hubs.
- Provide trained personnel and facilities for successful interviewing.
- Be able to render full-time medical service, with consultative and technical services to private physicians who request them.
- Afford education and training opportunities. The best location for a center would be in or adjacent to a medical school or medical school hospital.

Location of centers

In a low-prevalence area a center may not be necessary. There, the health departments may wish to provide more service to private physicians in order to bring them more completely into the control program.

Utilizing the newer, shortened treatment schedules, these centers will serve areas within and immediately surrounding the larger cities on a regional basis. We estimate that to provide the services required approximately 70 centers will be needed. About 35 now are operating in those areas where the VD problem is most acute. The coming fiscal year should see the prevention and control center program well established and providing satisfactory services.

Gonorrhea is still here

We are pleased to report the preliminary results of an accelerated case-finding approach to gonorrhea. Many of us recall that in 1947 and 1948 the concensus was that gonorrhea was no longer a public health problem. Passage of time and accumulation of experience have dictated the necessity for a new look at this most perplexing problem.

The District of Columbia, New York City, Philadelphia and several other large urban areas are applying a new technique to gonorrhea control—"speed

Ping-pong and revolving-door infections— how can we prevent them?

zone epidemiology." Essentially it is a process of restricting the interview search for female contacts to the period of time (approximately **six** days) when the male patient is assuredly infectious. Only females contacted during that period are sought by the interviewer.

The investigation process begins by telegram or field investigation as soon as the interview is completed. Contacts respond to telegrams within 24 hours or are brought in by field investigation within 72 hours. All contacts are treated on epidemiologic evidence, with the patient and contact both receiving injections of 600,000 units of penicillin in oil with aluminum monostearate. Effective blood levels are established for at least 72 hours and prevent the possibility of ping-pong infection.

Thus far the results of this "transfusion" to gonorrhea control are encouraging. We hope to extend the procedure widely in order to achieve the offensive against this most control-resistant of the venereal diseases.

A new penicillin

Again demonstrating the rapidity with which changes in VD control are introduced, I am happy to be able to report recent studies with a new penicillin, called bicillin, which indicate that single injections of 600,000 units will produce effective blood levels for 10 to 14 days, and 1.2 million units will remain effective for 28 days. Thus even this new gonorrhea control technique may assume a change of pattern.

Injections with the new penicillin will also protect the patient against reinfection over a substantial period of time . . . and now a single injection treatment for syphilis seems completely available, reducing the need for repeated visits to outpatient centers.

The danger of complacency

Inevitably, we must face the fact that we too have problems facing us. Among our major concerns in venereal disease control is the sense of false security which our successful efforts thus far seem to have inspired among both health officials and the public.

Recent events along the northwest coast of Europe remind us that there is a wide difference between restraining a threat to life and controlling it. For hundreds of years the Dutch people have waged continuous war against the North Sea and have had admirable success in restraining it from inundating vast areas of Holland . . . yet unforeseen and unique circumstances of wind and tide destroyed in a matter of hours the work of centuries.

In venereal disease control we have worked hard to erect a workable system of dikes behind which we have been able to restrain and slowly reduce a vast reservoir of infection. But like the deep ocean currents venereal disease in the human body and in society is often hidden and frequently undetected. Our experience with the new controls has been brief. What new pressures may be brought to bear against our present dikes are unknown.

The undiscovered

One thing is certain. We still have an alarming volume of undiscovered syphilis and gonorrhea in the population. Both are diseases which have been

How does the private physician fit in?

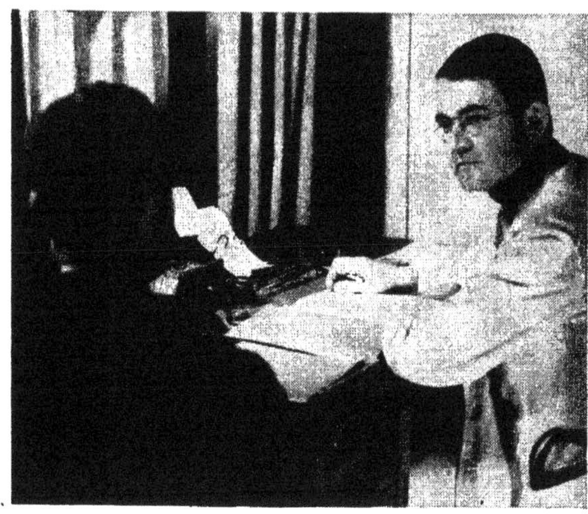

An injection of penicillin, or years of costly care in an institution?

with mankind for thousands of years. At present we have no immunizing agents for syphilis or gonorrhea . . . nor do we see evidences of any new social or moral trends which will eliminate opportunities for spread of these diseases.

In fact, if the rate of illegitimate live births is any indication of sexual promiscuity, there has been a steady and alarming increase of 73% from 1938 to 1947, with unofficial figures for 1948 and 1949 maintaining this trend. Considering the high marriage rates during the war and postwar period—which resulted in decreases in the total unmarried female population—this increase in illegitimate births is all the more cause for concern.

With each new generation

Although bacteriological immunization for venereal disease has not been achieved, we look to you for a social immunization stemming from your splendid activities in public education. One of the frustrations for those of us who are engaged in public information and education is our inability to determine the true results of our work except in the most general of terms. How many people did not become infected with venereal disease in the past year because of public education we shall never know.

We do know, however, that education is an eternal process. A new generation is always pressing forward . . . and for them the old truths must be reiterated with at least the same force and certainly with improved techniques.

From abroad

One must remember too that the increase in international mobilization and the ease of international travel increase the likelihood of importing syphilis from countries where early syphilis is not under control. This importation of syphilis is a distinct threat which, if not carefully watched, could readily undo our control efforts and result in new epidemics across our country. However, VD control activities are now taking on significant shape in other countries, and these parallel efforts will undoubtedly work to our advantage in future years.

A late syphilis decline

A recent review of the costs of late syphilis indicates that our program is extremely profitable in terms of eliminating vast public expenditures for the maintenance and care of those disabled by syphilis.

For example, if the rate of first admissions to mental institutions because of syphilitic psychoses were still at the 1941 rate of 6.6 per 100,000 people, there would have been admitted to state mental hospitals during 1950, 9,914 patients with psychoses due to syphilis instead of only 3,751. We may assume that venereal disease control from 1941 to 1950 prevented 6,163 persons from becoming neurosyphilis casualties in 1950. Since the average patient's stay in a mental institution is about 10 years and the current maintenance cost is $790 per year, these 6,163 persons who were saved would have cost the American public more than $49,000,000 in institutional care.

Dollar savings

Cumulative admissions to mental hospitals for psychoses due to syphilis over the same 10-year period would have been 27,000 persons. Applying a somewhat lower rate to this group—about $761 per person per year—our cumulative savings to the taxpayer for institutional care of the syphilitic insane alone would amount to some $200,000,000.

There are of course other savings—both in dollar and human values—which we are unable to estimate. We are safe, however, in feeling that these savings represent only a fraction of the total dollar benefits of venereal disease control over the last 10 years.

Economy a must

These figures point up another very grave concern regarding our future activities. More than ever before we are confronted with the necessity for rigid economies in government. There will undoubtedly be less money available in fiscal 1954 for grants to states for venereal disease control. At this point we do not know how much less, but we may be sure that the reduction will be substantial. In order that this reduction amount to a true economy and not a radical curtailment of essential activities, it will be necessary for all of us in public health to exercise the utmost care and ingenuity in utilizing our diminishing resources for venereal disease control.

As economy dictates the need for innumerable decisions in the coming months, we will find no formula which will render all decisions right. I would hope, however, that economy considerations would not result in across-the-board reductions in resources. Priorities must and will be given to those most productive control activities which contribute to finding and bringing venereal disease to diagnosis and treatment.

The goal

In the months to come we shall be fortified in our efforts by the accomplishments of the past years and by the assurance that our joint efforts will become continuously more efficient and effective. Our challenge, it seems to me, is to match any decrease in resources with an increase in our determination that this public health battle shall not be abandoned before we have achieved complete control of the venereal diseases.

I Choose to Believe . . .

I choose to believe that the time is coming when every American child will have a real opportunity for a good education, good health and for a promising economic future.

I choose to believe that the time is coming when every American family will have the opportunity for the fuller and richer life that should be the heritage of every American.

I choose to believe that the time is coming when every American will feel that he is a shareholder in our democracy and that he has a real stake, therefore, in developing and preserving it.

I choose to believe that the time is coming when the people of America, by pulling together, will be closer to the brotherhood of man than they have been in their entire history.

We must have a basic faith in the soundness of the judgment of people.

We must have a basic faith not only that our democracy can work but that it is the best system that has been devised by free men for free men.

We must acquire the courage to renew our faith in democracy and to meet our obligation of service to it.

More and more we must translate our democratic faith into democratic action.

It is my deep conviction that the hope of democracy lies in the local community, and that as our local communities are strong, so will our America be strong. It is in the local community that our problems must be attacked and solved rather than at some distant headquarters in the state or in the nation.

It is of the utmost importance that the people of any community understand the total problems and opportunities of their community. If all groups in every community can get together to discuss, work, and plan to solve their local problems our democracy would become so strong that it will not only be able to meet every challenge, but it will actually grow stronger with each challenge.

—R. B. ATWOOD, President
Kentucky State College

Family life education—whose job?

by Laura W. Drummond

For more than a generation family life education has appeared in one way or another in our public schools. With the acceleration of social change, the complexities and dislocations associated with two wars and a major economic depression, many educators and community groups have become concerned with developing a positive program to buttress the family as an institution . . . and to help its members develop healthy personalities, sound values and effective ways of working together.

The family is the most powerful educational agency in developing the attitudes and relationships basic to democratic living. One's mental health and physical vigor are largely dependent on one's early experiences in one's family. The purpose of family life education is to work with families and communities in developing the emotional climate, environment for growth and learning experiences which will strengthen the positive values in family life important in our times.

More than sex

What is family life education? An examination of the literature reveals much confusion of terms.

Some believe that family life education is a new name for sex education and believe therefore that it places major emphasis on physiology, human reproduction and genetics. With this narrow orientation some have considered family life education a touchy subject, emotionally charged and associated with taboos. Certainly an understanding of the facts of life and love, one's sex role and the emotional aspects of sex is an essential part of family life education, but it is not the central emphasis. Family life education is more than a synonym for sex education.

History and culture

Still others see family life education as primarily an historical and comparative cultural study of the family as an institution. This concept emphasizes population trends, folkways in different cultures and subcultures, and the three D's—divorce, desertion and delinquency—rather than the companionship aspects of family living. Surely background facts from anthropology and sociology make important contributions to family life education, but they do not provide the central focus.

Sometimes family life education and home economics seem to be used as interchangeable terms. In fact, the items listed in the *Education Index* for

1929–1932 identify family life education with factual knowledge, skills and abilities associated with homemaking and parenthood. More than 65% of the articles listed in this volume appeared in periodicals sponsored by and for home economists.

Home economics did much of the pioneer work in family life education. Today family living is still the focus of home economics. Home economists play an important role in family life education by providing young people and adults with learning experiences close to the realities of home life and significant in personal daily living: These experiences are designed . . .

- To help boys and girls and men and women to understand themselves.
- To help them develop satisfying relationships with their peers and relatives.
- To help them recognize their personality needs.
- To help them to share in homemaking and child-rearing.
- To help them strengthen family living in their homes and communities.

Home economists see their role as leaders and partners in family life education . . . not as a vested interest claiming the exclusive responsibility for this important aspect of education.

If family life education is broader than sex education, more concerned with companionship than with the institutional aspects of the family, more inclusive than home economics, then how can it be described?

Family life education deals primarily with interpersonal relations and is concerned with emotional maturity as well as physical well-being, with personality development, with the forming and changing of attitudes and with ways of living together within the family and in family-community life.

Much is involuntary

Education for family living is inevitably a part of the whole learning experience of an individual. It begins at birth in relations within the family and continues, without benefit of paid instruction, on the playground, in the school bus, at the juke joint, on the job and in Golden Age Clubs. Many concepts of our role, our values, our ways of feeling about ourselves and others are "caught, not taught." Our response may be positive or negative, in conflict with and even destructive to family life.

Education in interpersonal relations is too important to society to leave to chance. A positive program of family life education is an inescapable obligation of our schools.

Schools and colleges have been slow to assume responsibility for family life education. In 1944 the Metropolitan School Study Council called this a pioneer field in the school program. Five thousand educational workers in

Is sex education the whole story?

60 school districts found fewer examples of good school practices leading to the improvement of family living than in any other of the 12 areas of school learnings.

Nevertheless, in 1940 the United States Office of Education found that 65% of all girls graduating from senior high school had taken some work in homemaking. Although boys too are members of the family and as parents will share the responsibility for homemaking, probably not more than 2% of the boys in secondary schools are enrolled in homemaking education today. Elementary schools tend to have incidental rather than planned programs in this area, and only a few employ consultants to work with teachers, parents and children in improving family living.

What about adults?

It is heartening to know that over half a million adults in 4,000 schools and close to a million adults in groups served by the Cooperative Extension Service are working together on problems of home life . . . but one wonders about millions of other men and women who turn to neighbors, druggists and bartenders for help with baffling problems of family living.

Whose job is family life education? Does it belong in any one department or discipline? Is it appropriate for only one sex? Is family life education important at only one particular period in life? Is it an imperative for only the 60% for whom life adjustment programs are planned? If the response to these questions were a sharp, definitive "yes," the answer to "whose job?" would be easy.

Family life education which releases each individual to grow in self-understanding, to clarify his own values and those of his family, to gain deeper insight into his attitudes, to make decisions and work cooperatively in the

The school bus— it plays its part in education for family life.

family is an important and complex job. It requires the best leadership available in school and community.

Toddlers, too

Teachers in nursery schools and kindergartens have an unusual opportunity to work with children and parents in family life education. This does not mean merely providing a doll corner or playhouse or reading stories about children in Japan. It means helping boys and girls to see how their behavior affects others, to understand and enjoy the coming of the new baby, to accept responsibility for their routine tasks, and to share in homemaking activities according to their interest and ability.

Specifics

In the elementary school the classroom teacher is constantly educating in family life, whether she realizes it or not.

When she listens to what happened at home last night and helps Sally feel accepted and accepting toward her family, family life education is in process. Learning to handle fractions by measuring mother's travel in the kitchen as she prepares dinner after a day at the office is an exercise in understanding mother and fatigue as well as arithmetic. Writing a letter to daddy in Korea may be a way of releasing feelings of resentment at being different from the others who have fathers at home. School projects which encourage learning to help with family marketing, to check the laundry and to get along with brothers and sisters may all be a part of positive family life education.

A number of teacher-education programs now require that all prospective teachers take at least one course in home and family living so that they will feel more adequate and resourceful in helping children to learn from experiences significant in their home living. Some school systems are employing home

Ph.D., Columbia University. Author of Youth and Instruction in Marriage and Family Living. *Former director of home economics at Temple University and Pennsylvania State College. Now professor of home economics, Teachers College, Columbia University.*

Laura W. Drummond

---

economists to help teachers plan with children and parents experiences rich in learning and satisfaction for the whole family.

To help boys and girls deal effectively with their own concerns in home and family living—at the time when they emerge, and in a way meaningful to them—is the function of the classroom teacher, regardless of the child's grade or the teacher's specialization.

Early enough

In many secondary schools family life education is recognized as a vital part of the core program which is scheduled before most students leave school.

Today some boys and girls are dating in their early teens, going steady in high school, marrying and having children before achieving emotional maturity and economic independence. Eleventh and 12th-grade courses in family living may come too late to serve some of the boys and girls who want them most.

Important in general education in both secondary schools and colleges are functional programs of family life education built on the concerns of young people and led by emotionally mature men and women who know the real problems of families today and who understand themselves, their own biases and blind spots well enough to be free to help young people work constructively and creatively on family life problems as they see them.

But the core program does not alone fulfill the needs of young people for family life education. Specialists as well as generalists make unique contributions.

For instance, through the study of communication young people can be helped to see the importance of words and their meanings in strengthening or weakening marriage. They can be helped to understand that expressions of love and hate are a normal part of human relationships in the family.

Eagerly she awaited his coming. Eagerly she cares for him now.

Play-acting may help release tensions and develop insights into why we behave as we do. Contemporary novels and classical literature reveal to children how other families live.

In social studies boys and girls can become aware of the effect of mobility on family life, and the relation of housing to aggression, aesthetic satisfactions and the need for privacy. The study of parent-child relationships in other cultures and our own, dating and rating, and changing mores helps boys and girls gain perspective for their practices and problems.

Of immediate practical value to those ready for wage-earning is the study of social security, taxes, health and life insurance as they affect the individual and the family. The impact of the lengthening life span, living with three generations, planning for aging parents, and considering annuity provisions in different types of jobs are all aspects of social studies which deal directly with interpersonal relations.

Integration

Mathematics classes can help young people understand credit, home loans and installment buying, not merely in terms of interest rates but in terms of mental health and their effect on relationships. Appreciation of art in daily living, developing skills for creative experience in the home, becoming sensitive to the emotional impact of color and design in surroundings, dress and social life are a few of the many contributions of art education to family living.

The relation of effectiveness on the job to one's experiences in the family, anxieties, a good or poor breakfast, and emotional satisfaction or frustration at home are part of learning in business education. Boys and girls need to examine job opportunities in terms of what they mean for the kind and quality of family living they want.

The study of other languages can be a real source of understanding different ways of living, and can contribute to understanding and getting along with neighbors of different ethnic and racial strains. Health education, economics, the sciences, the school cafeteria and guidance service, and all the other aspects of the school program can play a significant part in the school-community program for family living.

Home economics

Of course, home economics as a specialization is closely identified with the school's program of family life education.

Not only do home economists serve as family life consultants in elementary schools and as members of the faculty team in core programs, but also as teachers of homemaking classes for high school boys and girls, out-of-school youth and adults. Their education in psychology, sociology, economics, biological and physical sciences and the humanities, coupled with professional courses in child development, family relations, home management, housing, nutrition, foods, clothing and textiles provides for an unique synthesis of disciplines focused on family living.

Through family-centered teaching, home economists help boys and girls appreciate the complexities of human relationships and operating a home. These young people develop ability to manage resources of time, money, energy and materials in actual life situations and in terms of family values. They

Shall we teach home economics to boys?

Companionship—the warp and woof of family life.

find satisfaction in mastering skills which serve the needs of the family, sustain feelings of personal worth, and lead to new creative experiences at home.

Most important of all, in informal group work in home economics boys and girls learn to work together on problems of home and family living important both to them and society.

Whose job?

Whose job is education for family living? Everybody's . . . school administrators, teachers, pupils, parents, custodians. Each has a place on the team working toward the goal of better family living in our town, in America and in the world.

• • •

CREDITS

Photo courtesy of U. S. Public Health Service (Krutch), p. 197.

Photo courtesy of Cleveland Health Museum, p. 203.

Photos courtesy of Standard Oil Company (New Jersey), pp. 204, 207, 214.

Photo courtesy of the Children's Bureau (Philip Bonn), p. 206.

Photo courtesy of Australian News and Information Bureau, p. 208.

Photo courtesy of Community Chests and Councils, p. 217.

Photo courtesy of United Service Organizations, p. 219.

Photo courtesy of Family Service Association of America, p. 228.

After 10 years

Helping Prostitutes Help Themselves

by Mazie F. Rappaport

In our 10 years of working with promiscuous girls and prostitutes in the protective services division of the Baltimore Department of Public Welfare, we have not been able to find or define "the prostitute personality." · Prostitutes do, however, have a common denominator—their inability to develop with another human being a relationship with meaning and continuity. The promiscuous girl has many men but not one on whom she can really count.

It is not and it cannot be a matter of indifference to an American community that within its boundaries there are widespread promiscuity and, inevitably, venereal disease. Promiscuity is not an acceptable way of life whether the community be a city, state or nation—rural or urban. Attitudes towards sex, marriage, divorce and the role of the family shift, change and grow . . . thoughts and feelings are reorganized and reoriented, fear of change is balaneed by recognition of need for change, laws are amended, social mores modified. What stands sturdily resisting obliteration, however, is the importance of the family, the base on which the community is built and builds its future.

You and I

The relation of people to each other as expressed in the family, then, is the milieu in which we live, in which we express our wants and needs, our hopes, our disappointments and our satisfactions. It is in relation to others that each of us finds his purpose, his definition. It is in our relationships that we create our democratic society—a society which requires not that we be like our fellow man, nor that we agree with him, but rather that we respect him for what *he is* and for his own unique place and role in society.

To carry this role—which we must carry as we give and take—we must have known a relationship which helped us find *our* own worth and dignity, *our* own importance as a human being. Most of us are able to do this because of the care and affection we had very early in our lives. If our parents failed to help us develop the ability to relate to another person, or if some catastrophe warps our ability to relate to other people and for the time being we cannot trust and "be" with other human beings, we are then unable to give and take in home, school or community in a socially useful and satisfying manner.

It is this—just this—which leads a person into anti-social behavior. Sometimes he expresses his frustration in mental or physical illness; more often—because he is unhappy and unable to get along in his family and community—in delinquent or criminal behavior. As he shifts from being responsible for his own conduct to railing against laws and limits, blaming others for his unhappiness, he begins to live *against* rather than *with* his fellowman. He begins to destroy rather than create.

Girls outside the law

When women get into this kind of anti-social activity they almost always become involved in sex delinquency. During periods of stress, particularly during wars, when the promiscuity rate rises and the number of arrests for prostitution increases, a community begins to act.

The Baltimore Venereal Disease Council, a civilian mobilization committee interested in the reduction of venereal disease in this community, was formed late in 1942 to integrate community forces in a comprehensive program of venereal disease control. Aware of the inevitable relation between VD rates and promiscuity and prostitution, this council accepted responsibility for three kinds of activity:

- Vigorous repression of prostitution.
- Improvement in VD case-finding, treatment facilities and methods.
- Development of a case work service for prostitutes and promiscuous girls who wanted help in trying another way of living.

A permanent protective service

In response to the council's recommendation for the establishment of a rehabilitation service, a protective services division was set up in June, 1943, in the Department of Public Welfare.

While World War II gave the impetus for organizing this service for prostitutes and promiscuous girls, it was not a temporary service nor war project. For this reason it was set up in a going public agency. It took its form and location in welfare rather than in health so that applications and referrals would not be limited to the venereally infected or suspected, but would include all who wanted to come whether or not they had syphilis or gonorrhea. Consistently it has always been offered to those who come voluntarily from health, social and law enforcement agencies and to those on probation following trial and sentence.

Since 1943 we have worked with thousands of girls referred from many and all kinds of agencies. We keep in close touch with the Health Department's venereal disease clinics, with the courts, the policewomen, the women's penal institutions . . . and are known as Baltimore's resource for working with promiscuous girls and prostitutes.

Some want a normal, wholesome kind of living . . . others aren't interested.

We interpret "those who might want to come" not as the promiscuous girls who seek us out—because delinquents rarely seek help from a social agency—but rather as those girls who respond ever so slightly to our offer of help. We try to reach them wherever they are, and we tell them how the service works, what it gives, what it will expect and require of them. We say that we know how to help promiscuous girls change their way of living, that we have helped many girls and women.

There have also been many who have not wanted or used our help. Some of them could not, some would not do what we required. To these we had to say that we would not work with them because they were not seriously trying to do anything about their problem.

Prostitution and promiscuity

The terms *promiscuity* and *prostitution* are often used synonomously in speaking of the woman sex delinquent. Actually, *prostitution* is a legal term. In Maryland it is a violation of the law, described as "the giving of the body for hire." Involved in prostitution there is always promiscuity. Whether it be prostitution or promiscuity (with no legal adjudication) the same serious and dangerous self-destruction takes place for the girl.

The girl who is sexually promiscuous does not permit herself to have any meaningful relationships, and finally she cannot have them. Her use of aliases, leaving her clothing hither and yon, frequent moving from one address to another . . . all these may suggest her need to evade police officers and family. But more likely they reflect her lack of self-respect, her inability to put down any roots or even to let her personal possessions have any real meaning. This is what is damaging to the girl and to society . . . for a human being to become so trapped in what she is doing, and so lacking in identity that she cannot or does not care what she is doing.

Beneath the hard shell, the casualness or the sharp and ready humor of the promiscuous girl there is likely to be an unhappy, bitter person no longer in control of her own life. Many of these girls give a history of broken families. They could not bring their troubles into their homes. They could not get from home, school, church and community the resources to help them live creatively and usefully. Their sense of values is warped. They trust no one, not even themselves. They cannot bear themselves as they are. They cannot stop this self-destruction, this psychological suicide, until something or someone on the outside puts a halt to their activities.

Through the years

Through these 10 years the type of girl we see has changed. There are fewer non-residents now, fewer girls who have left small towns to come to a large city to work or to follow servicemen to neighboring camps. Those we see now are more likely to be residents, Baltimore girls. Some have been in state training schools. Some are adolescents defying parental authority, resisting in the usual way for girls . . . in sex delinquency.

Though the type of girl has changed, our way of working has remained substantially the same. Whether she is the out-of-town girl who during the war came in on a truck or the girl who has always lived here, she responds to the same treatment. She wants the "stuff of living":

- An address for which she can have respect;
- A job which uses her capacity and in which there is supervision, regular hours, a known salary and opportunity for advancement;
- A medical examination and, if necessary, treatment in an established clinic, and
- Consistent and dynamic help from a social worker who knows how to hold her firmly.

These are the things that make it possible to help these girls and women get a sense of their own dignity and worth.

Ten years of consistent working with promiscuous girls have given us a substantial experience. We have worked during outright war and through a disturbed peace. We have made several changes in the protective services division during these years to reach promiscuous girls at an early stage in their delinquency . . . to strengthen parent-child relationships . . . and to help adolescents returning to the community from the four state training schools take more responsibility for their behavior.

Getting at the roots

During the war our emphasis had to be on the many girls and women who were getting into trouble in Baltimore, which had a high venereal disease rate and many defense plants and army camps. But even in those days we had set our sights high . . . we knew we had to develop this service on a wide base, emphasizing more and more the preventive aspects.

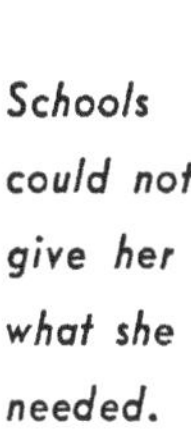

Schools could not give her what she needed.

In 1946, when we lowered the age limit of applicants from 16 to 12, we began to work with *young* sex delinquents, adolescent girls going to the VD clinic for treatment and those brought in as contacts. We made it a matter of policy that we would work with children under 16 only if we could also work with their parents or responsible relatives.

And then in 1948 we merged the Department of Public Welfare's two protective services—that for girls and that for children. This administrative change came out of our conviction that neglect and delinquency are close allies, each feeding on the other. It has been our feeling that if we can work with the parents of young neglected children we may be able to break into this vicious circle. What has come out clearly since the services merged is that most prostitutes and promiscuous girls neglect their children if they have children . . . and more important, girls and women are promiscuous because they themselves were neglected children. When they are sent to us now they are the end result of past neglect and the beginning of another generation's neglect and prostitution.

Training-school children

Early in 1949 we opened our protective services division to boys and girls from the four state training schools who were trying to live once again with their families. While the boys and girls are still in the training schools, we begin to work with their families, who have been informed of the possibility of their return home soon. We know that the returning children will need help and that their families will need it too, if they are to live happily in the community. We see these children not only as adolescents who have been in trouble but as future parents, and we want to help them develop their independent strengths for their approaching responsibilities.

Recently I reread a paper I wrote in 1945, "Towards a New Way of Life," which appeared in the JOURNAL OF SOCIAL HYGIENE in December of 1945.

My conviction now, years after writing it, remains the same as it was then . . . a new way of life *is* possible for many promiscuous girls and prostitutes.

These have been fruitful years, not only for the girls and women who have used our help but also for us who have worked with them. From these girls we have renewed our faith in the resilience of human beings. We have tested many ways of helping them and have learned from experience that what works best is directness, firmness and infinite patience in holding a girl to the choice that is truly hers—to learn to live more usefully and happily by taking responsibility for her behavior, or to risk getting into further trouble.

It's not easy

When Jenny Green rails against moving out of her former apartment or when Betty Jones hates gluing soles on shoes in a factory, when Mitzie Allen finds it impossible to get to a clinic at a specified time or comes in an hour late for her appointment . . . we know that these girls are beginning to sense how really rugged it can be for them to work with us during a year of probation. Whenever we require a girl to move we help her find another place. Whenever we rule out a job as being hazardous for the girl who has been in trouble—the job as waitress, barmaid, night club operator and other jobs with irregular hours, liquor, tips—whenever we say no to such a job, we must help her to find a less hazardous one.

We know that a trip to the clinic can be frightening in that it may confirm the result of behavior she has not allowed herself to face. And breaking her appointment with her worker or keeping this worker waiting for an hour tells us how little such a girl trusts another person to help her and how fearful she is of another's control and authority. Throughout our year with her she needs to ask herself over and over again, "What's in this for me?"

Some jobs are ruled out.

Graduate of the University of Chicago and Pennsylvania School of Social Work. Administrator in medical social work and delinquency. Supervisor of protective services in the Baltimore Department of Public Welfare.

Mazie F. Rappaport

She must also begin to feel and know that our belief in her, our willingness to stick by her through thick and thin, our unwillingness to let her misuse our help . . . all this is geared to helping her make an important and responsible choice for herself.

It's up to her

For these girls and women, so deprived in their relationships, change comes slowly and unevenly. Change towards accepting responsibility for one's own behavior can come about only when one learns to trust another person. When we accept a girl for our service, we have decided that she has the capacity to use this help. We expect a great deal of her. Our expectation of her puts a value on her, a value often unknown to her, as yet unaffirmed by her. In this *she* has everything to gain and *we* can certainly risk this much.

Everything we do in our protective services must help girls develop a capacity for living with other people in an orderly, useful and happy way. To do this, they must be able to live with themselves. The socially maladjusted, unhappy girls and women who come to us saying "Just tell me what to do and I'll do it" have a long hard road ahead. Conforming to a set of rules is simple, but it does not bring about the deep fundamental change in behavior which the girls themselves must produce with our help.

From casting stones

The world has moved faster and further in changing its attitude toward women offenders and children than it has toward other offenders. In shifting from punishing to rehabilitating the prostitute, the community has placed new responsibility and new trust in social case work.

As I think back over our 10 years with prostitutes, I feel certain that many prostitutes and promiscuous girls can change their way of living and that social case work can help these girls to be useful, happy people, able to take their place in family and community as human beings who can live with and in rather than against the social code. This paper is dedicated to the girls and women who have been able to change their way of living. To them we pay awed respect for what they have been able to do. It has not been easy.

Mental Health

(continued from April)

Second of a series of chapters from Preinduction Health and Human Relations, new curriculum resource for youth leaders by Roy E. Dickerson and Esther E. Sweeney.

Emotional Conflicts

Every human being experiences emotional conflicts. When the conditions of living make it impossible for people to satisfy certain of their drives, conflict results.

Implicit in both the drive for love and the drive to fight is the drive to be recognized as a person . . . the so-called ego drive. Impulses, urges and desires grow out of these drives. For example, people want to achieve success, make friends and gain social approval, help others, solve problems, respect themselves, find protection when afraid, rest when tired and so on.

From early childhood everyone encounters conditions that seem to thwart his desires. One soon learns that the more he can socialize his drives, the more comfortably he can live. For example, since hunger and thirst must be satisfied if a person is to survive, his drive to preserve himself makes him seek food and water; but social living prevents him from simply snatching food and wolfing it down. Everybody needs sleep; but only the little baby drops off to sleep just any time.

The fact that drives can be gradually brought into line with social requirements, environmental conditions and the moral code does not mean that they disappear. They are merely sublimated or redirected. Nor could we live without these drives. They are the motive power of human existence. But conflict occurs:

- When any two of an individual's drives or emotions clash.
- When any drive or emotion clashes with morality or the conventions of society.
- When any drive or emotion is opposed by the physical conditions around the individual.

For example, there is illness in a family. Mary's help is needed to free her mother to nurse the sick. Mary wants to help. At the same time, her dramatic club is planning a play and she needs time for rehearsals. Mary's love for her mother and family and her drive towards achievement are in conflict. This is conflict between two drives.

John is ambitious, eager for good grades. But he has been sick for several weeks and missed school. His chances for high marks are poor . . . he may not even be able to pass. Under the school's honor system he could cheat and probably get away with it. John's conflict lies between his drive for success and the demands of the moral code.

On a skiing expedition in the mountains Henry gets separated from his party. He tries to find them or get back on the trail. Still lost at the end of the day, he is spent with fatigue and hunger. He wants desperately to lie down and sleep for a while, though he knows the danger of freezing to death. His conflict lies between his drive to preserve himself, by resting, and the physical conditions around him.

Learning to deal with conflicts is the major task of growing up. Finding solutions satisfying to oneself and society is everyone's lifetime job.

Reflection is vital to the resolution of conflicts and the problems they create. A welter of emotion merely hampers thoughtful problem-solving. As long as one is merely *feeling*, he remains the victim of his emotions. When he begins to reflect and sort things out, starting with an attempt to face and state for himself just what his conflict is, he is nearing resolution.

Mary (above) has to sort out the issues in her problem and her desires about them. She wants to help at home and she wants just as strongly to be in the school play. Before arriving at a decision, she must look at the alternatives and at the possible compromises. Can she appear at fewer rehearsals and still be in the play? Can she get up an hour earlier and by carefully budgeting her time do enough housework to be able to attend rehearsals? She may have to decide to forego the play in order to carry out her responsibilities at home. But it will be *her* plan, arrived at after *her* analysis and evaluation of possible

Big boy or big baby— he can't make up his mind.

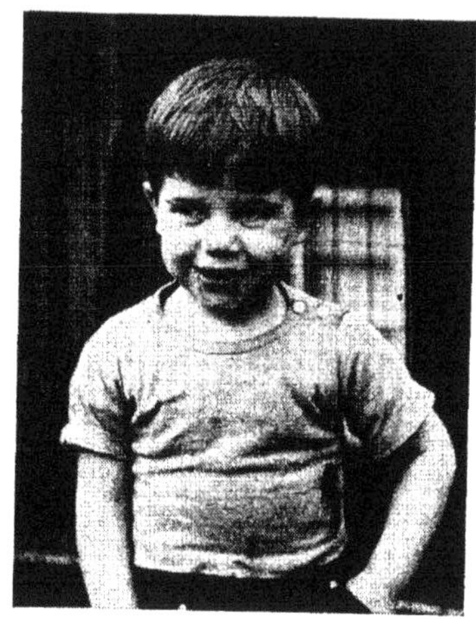

solutions. Then she can move into action, with some disappointment perhaps but without unhappiness or a feeling of conflict.

Class Discussion

- What do people gain from meeting and resolving their conflicts?
- If a person seeks the advice and experience of others in solving problems, does that mean he is weak and unable to handle his own affairs? After one seeks advice, who makes the final decision?

Dependence vs. Independence

The desire to become independent of one's parents opposed by the desire to remain dependent upon them is at the core of the maturing process. One's method of resolving this conflict largely determines what kind of person one becomes.

It is understandable that this conflict should exist. The small child receives everything from his parents . . . food, warmth, protection, love and recognition. As he grows older and can do more things for himself, he still relies heavily on the emotional and physical support of his parents.

Later, as he moves into adolescence and becomes more interested in social contacts and activities outside his home, he naturally wants more independence. Parents seem to hinder him in what he wants. Parental guidance now looks like domination. The young adult loves his parents but resents what he sees as their interference. This is normal. He loses sight of the fact that his parents are responsible for continuing to guide and help him and forgets that even now they are his support in time of worry or trouble.

But if people remained dependent upon their parents, they would be unable to assume the responsibilities of adulthood and the later responsibilities of getting married and becoming parents themselves. The young person's conflict is this: while he consciously or unconsciously wants the care, protection and support of his parents and wants to continue to depend upon them to meet many of his physical and emotional needs, he wants also to stand on his own feet and be independent of his parents.

Parents experience a similar conflict. They want their children to grow up, yet their love and attachment often makes it difficult to watch this growing up and apparent growing away.

Resolving the Conflict

Ordinarily time, experience and understanding resolve these conflicts. Both the parents and the child learn that it is possible to love each other dearly, to respect each other and to recognize each other's worth without the child's having to remain a child.

Does he have to surrender his principles?

When a child has been insecure or has not received enough encouragement to move gradually but consistently towards self-reliance, his wish for dependency may persist into adulthood.

On the other hand, some parents who are fearful that their child will not become self-reliant quickly enough try to push him towards independence when he is far too young. This Spartan approach deprives the child of the pleasure of satisfying his need for dependency in his early years when dependency is normal. His unfulfilled wish for dependency may then also persist into adulthood.

Almost Everyone

The conflict between the desire to be dependent and the desire to be adult and independent exists to some degree in practically everybody. Its resolution is gradual and requires the same approach as any sound resolution of conflict: recognizing and analyzing the problem; weighing possible solutions; evaluating alternatives in order to arrive at the one that will be best for the individual and yet considerate of parents and other people; and moving into action.

No one should assume that a person is helpless or totally unable to deal with problems because he seeks guidance and calls upon the experience of others to help him meet his conflicts. Teachers, guidance counselors, clergymen and sometimes psychologists and psychiatrists are needed to assist with emotional problems just as lawyers, doctors or dentists are needed to help on problems in their special fields. No one feels inadequate when he goes to a dentist with an aching tooth; no one should feel inadequate when he seeks counsel on aching feelings.

Class Discussion

- John, age 20, has never had a date with a girl. He prefers to go out with his parents or stay home with them, reading, listening to the radio or watching TV. Discuss.
- Will is in the Armed Forces. Back home his mother washed and mended his clothes, sent his suits to the cleaner, put his room in order every day. Whenever his homework was difficult she or his father helped him. When Will offered to do any jobs around the house, his mother declined his assistance. Now Will is having a hard time in the service and is frequently gigged for lack of personal order and cleanliness and for poor military housekeeping. Discuss.
- Mary thinks it's grown-up to meet her boy friends away from home, to return late from dates, and tell off her parents when they try to discuss these matters with her. She threatens to leave home whenever she feels her parents are trying to control her. Discuss.
- Henry's troubles in the Armed Forces are all with officers and non-coms; he gets along well with the men in his outfit. The officers, as far as Henry can see, are out to make life hard for him; their orders seem silly and capricious, and he thinks most of them dislike him. What are some of the factors you see in Henry's difficulties?

Meeting Conflicts

Young people need to be aware of some of the unproductive means by which people try to meet emotional conflicts. Most people resort to these means, either as a matter of habit or on occasion. They are "outs" that must be guarded against and discerned when they present themselves as easy and comfortable ways of solving conflicts. Using these outs and failing to recognize that one is doing so may retard one's development into a mature person.

Surrender

John loves Mary and wants to marry her. He's afraid they will have trouble managing on his income. Instead of trying to work out the conflict between his love and his fear, he walks away from the whole thing. He gives up the idea of marriage and breaks off with Mary . . . hc surrenders. His action solves nothing.

But sometimes surrender can be used well, when it is thought about and appears to be the best solution. Jim wants to finish law school. His father is seriously ill. Medical expense is mounting and income diminishing. Jim loves his parents and wants to help; he also wants to finish law school. After thinking out ways of trying to help and yet continue his education, he sees clearly that he cannot do both right now. He surrenders to the stronger of his drives, the drive to help. This is a positive use of surrender.

Surrender can also be used positively when the conflict lies between the individual's desires and the moral code. Henry is in the Armed Forces. He wants the approval of the men in his outfit; he wants to be considered a good sport. A group suggests going to a roadhouse known to be a place of prostitution. His conscience says no. Surrender to the dictates of conscience is not only a sound course here but is a positive way of solving conflict.

Compensation

Compensation is another means of dealing with conflict. Like surrender, it may be a good or a dangerous course.

The athlete stricken with polio who puts all his energies into study and becomes a scholar is compensating well.

The unsure person who tries to assert his importance by bullying and dominating others is overcompensating. Instead of solving his problem of insecurity, he creates new problems for himself by giving others reason to dislike or snub him.

The man who meets the normal, natural fear of combat by bragging that he doesn't know what fear is is overcompensating. The man who is equally afraid but becomes the company's best marksman is using compensation productively.

Class Discussion

- Harry is a veteran of World War II. He lost his vision in combat. He had never tried writing, but now he's working on a novel and he's already sold one short story. Discuss some of the less adequate ways in which he might have dealt with his problem.
- Lucy's parents are having a hard time financially. By various means she gets them to scrimp and do without to buy pretty clothes for her. She is proud of the fact that she is one of the school's best-dressed girls. How could Lucy productively use compensation, rather than overcompensation, to satisfy her desires?

Daydreaming—Escape

Daydreaming is another poor way to handle conflict. Getting away from it all in daydreams—in fantasies where one is the richest boy or girl in the world—only defers the resolution of conflict. Books, movies, TV and radio—all perfectly good forms of entertainment—can be over-indulged in as escapes from problems, as flights from reality.

Unhappy, immature people sometimes turn to harmful physical satisfactions as another out. Excessive drinking, overeating, spending a large amount of time in bed, and misusing the sexual impulse are some examples.

Now and then everyone uses daydreaming or escapes of one kind or another. Imagination and the capacity to identify with other people, real or fictional, can be used constructively . . . in the creative arts, in study and in molding one's ideal of the kind of person one wants to be. But when daydreaming and other escapes become the habitual ways of dealing with conflict, they prevent maturing.

Class Discussion

- How can people use to advantage their interest in books, their dreaming and admiration of great characters?
- Bill wants to study medicine, to become a great doctor of international reputation. In high school he took only the minimum of science courses; he is doing the same in college. He daydreams about himself in a white gown in the operating room of a hospital, teaching eager students or even older physicians. How can Bill unite his dream with reality?

Rationalization

Everyone recognizes the person who could always have done better but for some accident of circumstance. He's the person who could have passed the examination but for the fact that the teacher didn't like him, who could have made the team but for the weather the day the coach tested him.

The young man who wouldn't have a date with Mary "if she begged him" (after Mary had declined his invitation) is also recognizable.

So is the young man in the Armed Forces who "wouldn't be a lieutenant if they hung the bars on me" but who actually failed in his efforts to get to Officer Candidate School.

Through self-deception and self-justification such a person camouflages the truth. Rather than admit failure, he creates a reasonable picture of what he wished had happened and in time comes to believe his creation. As a result, he never sees the true cause for his failures and simply lays himself open to more defeats and the necessity for more "reasonable excuses."

The term for this process is rationalization. It is another child-like way of dealing with conflicts. Most people rationalize every now and then, finding good excuses or high-sounding reasons for their failures or self-indulgences. As a practice it is a deterrent to emotional growth.

Class Discussion

- There's an old saying, "It's a poor workman who complains of his tools." Discuss.
- Among Aesop's fables there's the story of the fox who couldn't reach a bunch of grapes he wanted. Thwarted, he declared they were probably sour grapes anyway. Relate this to the process known as rationalization.

Conversion

Illness can serve as another out or evasion of the job of solving conflict. By an exchange (conversion) of physical illness for emotional pain one unconsciously uses his body to help escape meeting and dealing with conflict. This is called conversion.

The person who invariably has headaches at examination time or the serviceman who goes on sick call whenever a hike or extended maneuvers are scheduled may need to think about illnesses as being rooted, perhaps, in more than just physical causes. If a person is using illness as an out for conflict, he may need professional help to assist him in sorting out physical factors from possible emotional factors and in learning to face his problems.

Class Discussion

- Susan has been a week-end guest at the Smiths' country home. She has not had a very good time; she caught a slight cold because of not having enough blankets and she had a rather poor evening at the country club dance where she didn't know anyone. When she gets home she is "simply too sick" to write a bread-and-butter letter to her hostess. What may Susan be doing? What may be her real problem?

Repression

Sometimes people try to pretend to themselves that their emotions and drives simply do not exist. This process is called repression. Bringing one's emotions under control, a basic human job, does not mean banishing them. It means using one's emotions and the energies associated with them for one's own good and for the good of others.

A person is using repression when he attempts to deal with the pain of conflict by "forgetting" something he finds painful to remember. An unpleasant task that conflicts with more pleasurable activities is easily forgotten. People sometimes forget to write letters to others whom they fear or dislike. Or they may forget an episode that caused them to be afraid of trains or automobiles, yet manage to keep as far away as possible from both.

Rigid repression of the sexual impulse is not the way to control the sexual drive. One has to reckon with its existence and deal with it . . . by substituting satisfactions that are socially and morally acceptable, by deliberately deferring sexual gratification until the right time, place and circumstance, and by sublimating the sex-love impulse in creativity, acts of love and generosity towards others.

Class Discussion

- People who have good cause for anger quite generally control themselves. Is this repression? Is it good or bad? What can one do about angry feelings?
- Is military combat unleashed or controlled aggression? How can one use aggression in solving problems and in learning new things? Give examples from your own experience.

Regression

Regression—the wish "to be a child again, just for a day"—is another immature way of handling conflict.

Unnecessarily prolonged convalescence, childish helplessness and acute homesickness may all indicate regression as a way out of conflict. The person who resorts to crocodile tears or temper tantrums to get what he wants is regressing . . . using the tears and rage that in his childhood used to bring people running to see what was wrong.

Because the small child usually could do little for himself, people responded to his tears and anger and gave him comfort and help. But an adult can do things for himself and can rise above the temptation to regress into childish emotional displays when conflicts or frustrations confront him.

Class Discussion

- How can homesickness affect a serviceman's usefulness? Why should one try to conquer homesickness? Suggest things a serviceman could do to relieve homesickness in a mature way.

Emotional Health

All behavior represents an effort on the part of the individual to satisfy some need. But behavior that is unsocial or that deviates from the normal is an effort to meet a need in an ill-chosen and unconsidered way.

For example, a boy may feel a need to demonstrate his power. Instead of showing constructive leadership—by becoming a class officer or a Scout leader—he may choose to become the head of a gang that steals, destroys public property or behaves generally in a malicious way.

Even though one's emotional needs have not been satisfied to the fullest (and very few human beings do experience complete satisfaction), the person who wants to get the most out of life can use reason, experience, judgment and moral choice towards trying to achieve emotional satisfactions in the best way.

It is important for young people to think about some of the factors that make for good emotional health and indicate emotional growth and maturity.

Emotions and the Nervous System

Human emotions are inseparable from the total human organism. The nervous system plays an important role in feelings and emotions. The development of physical habits and skills involving the brain and nervous system, which enable a person to react quickly and alertly in everyday situations, is essential to good emotional health.

People sometimes get into an emotional panic when they come close to having an accident, for instance. For this very reason schools routinely have fire drills, and communities have air raid drills. Such practices help people to develop automatic responses and calm behavior should disaster occur. More than one burning school has been safely emptied of all children because the children accepted the situation calmly as just another fire drill and followed the established routine as a natural habit.

A healthy nervous system is best maintained by rest, sleep, variety in work and recreation, the treatment of physical defects that may cause nervous irritability, and the development of a habit of concentrating on problems at hand.

The Emotionally Healthy Person

The emotionally healthy person has certain attitudes and characteristics that are discernible in the way he regards himself, other people and day-to-day situations.

He has a good opinion of himself. He neither denies nor overestimates his capacities and character. He sees room for self-improvement. This challenges rather than depresses him. His sense of humor makes him view himself objectively and permits him to be amused at his own foibles when others expose them. He sees the absurdity that often exists in human situations, yet does not despise others for the weakness or foolishness that creates such situations.

While not a Pollyanna, the person of sound emotional health is, generally speaking, cheerful and self-confident. These qualities, of course, largely result from his capacity for meeting emotional problems and for growing through that experience.

Such a person enjoys the company of other people and respects them whether he happens to like them or not. He refuses to permit prejudice to come between him and his fellowmen and refuses to sit in judgment on them. He may, and sometimes must, disapprove of what they do, but he feels no unhealthy compulsion to tell them so unless it is his clear duty to do so. He does not actively dislike people for their faults, knowing that one can "hate the sin and love the sinner."

Although the emotionally healthy person enjoys work, play and cooperative activities with others, he is not lonely when by himself. Because he is self-sufficient, he can use privacy and solitude for his hobbies and for reflection, planning and sorting things out in his own mind.

Others' opinions of him are important to him, but they do not throw him into panic and alarm if they are not uniformly approving. He weighs criticism as objectively as possible, tries to determine its validity and uses it in his efforts to improve himself. He does not dwell on criticisms nor resent the person who made them.

Habitual daydreaming— it solves nothing.

He does not delay facing his problems. After thinking them through, he arrives at his decisions and abides by them. But he is flexible, capable of altering decisions when he has been wrong in the first instance or when situations change.

Although the emotionally healthy person has good habits of work, rest and recreation, he doesn't permit habit to become his master and is adaptable enough to interrupt a routine or change a method when necessary.

A person with good emotional health has a philosophy of life that helps him do his best at all times. Into this philosophy of life—not necessarily fully developed in a young person but nevertheless a guiding factor in his behavior—go his spiritual values and his attitudes towards himself, other people and society generally. His philosophy guides him in viewing the world around him, in evaluating current history, in planning his own future and in making the best possible contribution to his community and country.

The emotionally healthy person is not perfect. He is not free from emotional upsets. He has moments of jealousy, anger and laziness, and he may have occasional outbursts of temper and vindictiveness. He may meet some of his problems quite incompetently. He may occasionally resort to unproductive ways of handling his conflicts.

But he shows his emotional health in the way be generally behaves, generally views things and people, and generally meets problems. The speed with which he picks up and begins all over again after a mistake, the way he learns from a mistake and the effort he makes to understand the reasons for his behavior are evidence of the tone of his emotional health.

Class Discussion

- How are the following related to emotional immaturity: temper tantrums, keeping to oneself, lack of consideration for others, vengefulness, jealousy?
- Why are hobbies important to good emotional health?
- Is the same kind of recreation day after day apt to be as emotionally unhealthy as the same kind of work? Discuss.

Class Activity

- Administer self-quizzes: "How Do I Rate in Mental Health?" and "How Level-Headed Am I?" From *Better Ways of Growing Up*, pp. 131–33.

Reference

- *People Are Important*, by Floyd L. Ruch, Gordon N. Mackenzie and Margaret McClean, pp. 238–78.

Problems Everyone Encounters

All human beings encounter personal and emotional problems. Since people are generally somewhat reserved about them, an individual often fails to realize that others may have concerns like his own. Having problems is a common human experience, normal to living, and capable of contributing to one's growth and development.

Doubts, worries, fears and other problems get out of hand only when they take up too much of the individual's energy, attention and time.

Class Activity

- Have students list anonymously their 10 major problems. Papers should be identified only as male or female. Tabulate problems. A listing of the major categories and types of problems will help students to see: (a) that many people have the same kinds of problems; (b) that problems which boys usually think of as boys' problems and which girls usually think of as girls' problems are in many instances common to both sexes.

Insecurity

No one feels completely secure at all times and under all conditions. Even the person who is self-confident in most situations may experience insecurity and uneasiness under other circumstances. The opera singer, so self-assured in her performance and among other artists, may feel insecure in ordinary social relationships.

Parents neither over-solicitous nor indifferent.

Despite the best possible intentions, parents are sometimes unable to provide children with maximum inner security. It often happens that the child draws erroneous conclusions from occurrences in his childhood and from them derives lasting feelings of insecurity.

By their eagerness for their child's success, parents may unwittingly foster his feelings of insecurity. Often they establish and overemphasize too high standards of scholarship, personal appearance or behavior, then disapprove too strongly when the child fails to measure up. These fairly common parental attributes may lead a child to feel that he can never meet his parents' standards, that he is no good and somehow inferior. Because of these feelings of insecurity and inferiority he may develop a persistent sense of uneasiness with all who, like his parents, symbolize authority. In adulthood, this uneasiness may cause him to identify every employer or military officer as another "parent" who may disapprove.

Interestingly enough, the very opposite of parental disapproval can also cause feelings of insecurity. When parents encourage overdependency, wait on a child constantly and overprotect him from experience with everyday reality, they may cause him to become unsure of his ability to do things for himself and to handle ordinary situations.

Feelings of uncertainty or inferiority and lack of self-confidence are problems that can be met. When such feelings are deep-seated, bother a person much of the time and keep him from working and playing effectively, he may need skilled professional help to deal with them.

But most of the time problems will yield to one's own analysis, thought, planning and action. The boy or girl who dreads addressing the assembly in school may need to recognize that at least part of this uneasiness may come from the unsuccessful experience of trying to speak without careful preparation.

The boy or girl who never knows what to do or say when meeting a person for the first time may have to work up a stock of conversational openings about recent movies, sports events, TV and radio programs and the like. So-called small talk bridges much awkwardness, and each encounter with new people, whatever the degree of success, gives one added confidence and ease.

Class Discussion

- Betty, who has lived with her grandparents for quite some time, is the sort of person adults praise and enjoy. They like her grown-up manner and are happy to include her in their conversations because they find her interesting and intellectually mature for her age. But at high school Betty is rather unhappy and ill at ease. She is aloof from her classmates and they in turn leave her pretty much alone. Her reputation is that of teacher's pet and grind. What can she do to make a secure, comfortable place for herself with her class?

Reference

- *Personal Problems,* by John B. Geisel, pp. 131–51.

Fear

Fear is one of the most common human reactions. Not only is fear normal; inability to feel fear is abnormal. Young people should view fear calmly and objectively and recognize its value in life. They need also to realize that fear—unless faced and dealt with—can drain one's energies and prevent one from living in the most productive way.

Since no one lives in a perfectly safe and protected environment, fear serves the important role of warning a person, alerting him to danger and giving him a chance to prepare himself to meet it. Fear creates physical reactions which protect the individual. It releases various chemical substances in the body which make him more energetic and ready to act on his own behalf . . . to run faster or fight harder.

Some psychiatrists believe that fear is innate and that even the newborn baby is afraid of loud noises or of being insecurely held.[1] Others hold that

[1] *The Psychology of Childhood to Maturity,* by J. G. Williams, New York, Grune and Stratton, 1946.

What fun the new plaything! And what danger, they'll learn.

during very early infancy the child develops fears of being deserted, of not being loved and of being punished or injured.[2]

Since surviving is a baby's big job, it seems logical that even a tiny infant should have some reaction to any possible threat to survival and that that reaction should be fear. Anything or anyone disturbing the baby's limited equilibrium, in a world in which both literally and figuratively his feet are not yet on the ground, threatens him. Threat in turn sets in motion the life-saving reaction of fear.

As the child grows older and learns that some things new to his experience are also dangerous, he develops a healthy fear of fire, of sharp instruments that may injure him and of heights from which he may fall. All this learning of fear is good. It is only when fear gets out of hand that it can cause harm.

As the individual learns through the process of discovering danger in new things, he begins to sense that there may be other dangers not yet encountered. He may now have a new fear . . . a generalized fear of the unknown. What people do not know nor understand may loom as a threat. Such fear, when fraught with nagging uneasiness and disquiet of mind, becomes anxiety.

There is another factor in acquiring fear. As the little child begins to live more and more in the world of other people, he may begin to react to their disapproval by feeling that if they disapprove of him at all, even a little, they will withdraw their love completely. This adds social fears to the child's fear for his survival and his possible fears of the unknown.

The tragedy of fear is not that it exists, for it can be a blessing, a safeguard and a protection. The tragedy lies in the fact that most people are afraid of

---

[2] *Emotional Problems of Living,* by O. Spurgeon English and G. H. Pearson, New York, Norton, 1945.

being afraid . . . they think others will consider them inadequate and cowardly if they admit to fear.

Whenever people are able to realize that their particular problem is one everyone else experiences they can deal better with it and get perspective on it. Knowing that fear is everybody's problem helps to remove the fear of fear.

Because of his feeling of inadequacy or misgivings about the unknown, a young person may become timid and fearful about meeting new people and new situations. His fears can be reduced . . . by obtaining information in advance about the people or situation he is to meet. Before applying for a job, he can find out the requirements and evaluate his qualifications in the light of these requirements. Then, properly informed and properly groomed, he can approach the interview with confidence.

One can use many such practical measures to place new situations in focus and reduce or eradicate fears about them.

Some boys and girls are frightened by pubertal changes. Yet knowledge of the facts and dissipation of any superstitions and mistaken ideas about menstruation, seminal emissions, etc., will usually eliminate fears about these processes.

Trying to repress fear—pretending it doesn't exist—solves nothing. On the contrary, a person may become paralyzed by fears he fails to meet and act upon.

Fear should be the signal for mobilizing one's body and mind for action whether one is afraid of an oncoming train, of playing at a piano recital or of the possible displeasure of one's boss. Action is action whether it takes the form of planning, organizing one's ideas, laying out a whole campaign for better relationships or practicing for a recital. But it is usually not enough merely to think about, plan and organize ways of meeting one's fears; one must act. The best campaign one can map out won't do much good on paper or in one's mind.

Acting on fears, rather than freezing up, is the self-disciplined, self-directed and self-determined way of meeting fear. To save himself, the person in danger of losing his life in a fire must think and must direct and discipline his actions. If he panics, he may die. But if he weighs alternatives for escape, perhaps takes a calculated risk, he is using fear productively, and is thinking and acting in his own behalf.

A positive adjunct of fear is courage. It is quite natural for young people entering the Armed Forces, especially when the country is in danger, to wonder whether they have enough courage to meet what may be required of them. The question of courage is worth thoughtful consideration.

First of all, everything one does now to meet ordinary fears and anxieties is conditioning for the future. Each fear overcome by thinking, planning and action increases one's feelings of self-confidence and courage.

Secondly, a certain amount of fear is normal in combat or any hazardous situation. That is the self-protective mechanism at work. The man on the front lines who takes foolhardy chances which may cost him and others their lives is probably overcompensating for his fears, not meeting them. The man who knowingly and willingly sacrifices himself to save others has converted his fear into action at the highest level of courage.

Thirdly, training in the Armed Forces is designed to protect the individual. A serviceman's job is not just fighting the enemy; it's saving himself, too. Conditioning in the Armed Forces is most carefully worked out to develop alertness, lifesaving reflex actions, a high degree of neuromuscular coordination and those military skills that will protect the serviceman to the greatest possible extent. This conditioning reduces fear by preparing the mind and body to mobilize quickly to meet danger.

Courage is the readiness to fight for what one values. It is the use of aggression to gain the things one wants, needs or considers worthwhile, whether those things are personal achievement, social approval or, in war, the defense of a way of life that one cannot bear to relinquish.

Young people need to be aware of another facet of fear. Sometimes one experiences vague, general feelings of fear, possibly accompanied by some or all of the physical manifestations of severe fright . . . rapid respiration, palpitation of the heart, profuse sweating or upset stomach. Yet the individual does not know precisely what he fears . . . he only knows the feeling of fear. He needs help. If he has been trying to repress his fears, he may experience the symptoms of anxiety and yet be unable to identify his problem. Generalized feelings of anxiety need to be treated by competent professional people.

Class Activities

- Administer self-quizzes, "How Self-Confident Am I?", "How Self-Reliant Am I?", "How Can I Gain More Self-Confidence and Self-Reliance?" from *Better Ways of Growing Up*, pp. 121–25.
- Essay on "Something I Used to Fear but No Longer Fear" or "How I Can Use Intelligence to Fight Fear."

Class Discussion

- How can fear help the individual?
- Why should fear lead to activity? What is likely to happen to the person who simply tries to bear fear without action or who tries to repress it altogether?
- How can people study their fears?

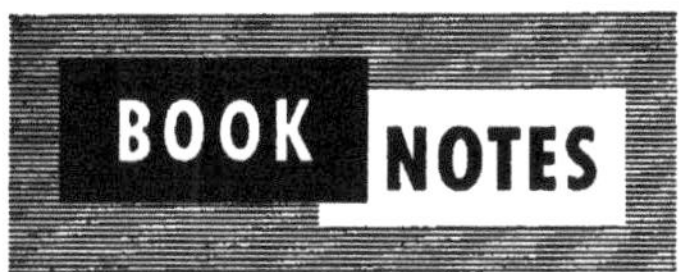

by Elizabeth B. McQuaid

The Cincinnati Report. Cincinnati, Council of Social Agencies, 1952. 276p. $2.00.

This appraisal of the social services of Cincinnati and Hamilton County (Ohio) shows a need for:

- Adequate, coordinated services to the family as a unit.
- A system of coordinated social services for families, children, unmarried mothers.
- Research to determine adequate services for people between 15 and 24.
- Rehabilitative treatment for adults who contribute to the delinquency or neglect of children and sex offenders.

Among the recommendations requiring priority action are these:

- Adequate social planning and coordination of service.
- Aggressive steps to remove hazards contributing to family problems and breakdown.
- A research project to clarify the problems of the so-called "untreatable families."
- A study to determine the feasibility of establishing adequate family counseling services in key tax-supported agencies.

In appraising the county's social services, a committee studied the self-evaluations of 148 public and private agencies and the reports of 22 subcommittees on which over 600 citizens served.

Among the most telling aspects of their report are the comments that follow a description of each agency's services. Prepared by the appraisal committee, they represent a synthesis of agency-citizen thinking all the more valuable for its democratic approach. The Cincinnati Social Hygiene Society is commended for its role as a distinctive department of the Public Health Federation in developing a program which "has long commanded respect here and elsewhere."

Family Life Education Kit. Sharing Sex Education with Children, A Guide for Parents. *Recordings* (two 12-inch vinylite recordings), by Gloyd Gage Wetherill, M.D. San Diego, Calif., Heath Printing Company, 1952.

The Family Life Education Kit includes a manual or guide and two 12-inch recordings, one designated for children 4 to 8 years old and one for children 8 to 12 and older.

The author's purpose and approach are best described in a statement that in the development of the project he has had the cooperation of more than 1,200 parents and teachers interested in meeting "a keenly felt need of helping children understand the sex aspects of wholesome living."

The manual opens with a series of drawings illustrating in simplified form the physiological phases of reproduction. The text consists of 14 chapters on selected subjects which Dr. Wetherill states "originated from a study of the actual interests of children." The titles of the chapters indicate the scope of the book: Growing Up, Menstruation, Emissions, Mating, Pregnancy, Development of a Baby, Birth of a Baby, Feeding of a Baby, Twins and the Dionne Quintuplets, Heredity, Family Living, Friendships, Conduct and Other Interesting Things. Each chapter begins with an overview written in simple narrative form. Then follows a series of pertinent questions and answers. The answers are accurate as to information and, for the most part, clearly stated.

An appendix to the manual contains a vocabulary of 100 selected words and definitions which the author terms "generally advisable for this age group."

The emphasis throughout the manual is mainly upon physiological facts. There is, on the whole, relatively little attempt to integrate the physical with the emotional and spiritual aspects. Most persons will agree that it is highly important for children to receive facts when they are ready for them . . . but aren't we thinking in terms of the whole child? The child's feelings about sex and his interpretation of facts are of paramount importance for they color his attitudes and behavior as they concern sex.

If he is ready for facts, it is essential that his new knowledge should fall into proper perspective in his mind. He is ready also for some understanding and appreciation of the interrelationships of the biological, sociological and psychological aspects of sex and for sound interpretation on his own level.

The foreword suggests that older children may find this manual helpful. Certainly facts are presented in terms readily comprehensible . . . but it is questionable whether the latter chapters offer the most effective psychological approach to the child over 12 or whether he will find the material as presented sufficiently satisfying emotionally.

The recordings are planned to gear in with the manual. In designating Record No. 1 for the child 4 to 8 and No. 2 for the child 8 to 12 and older, the author recognizes the variance in the maturation rate among children. But many persons will differ with him as to the suggested age span. The mode of approach to the usual 4-year-old needs to differ vastly from that to the 8-year-old.

At intervals the listener is invited to turn to specific drawings in the manual. This too raises a question. Will the drawings be appropriate to the comprehension of the child? It would seem that a number of the drawings are far beyond the comprehension of the usual 4-year-old.

Moreover, the recorded situations are not always convincing. The conversation is often stilted because of the too-obvious attempt to bring in situations or concepts which the author evidently felt should be included.

Certainly parents and teachers who are seeking sound factual information for use with children, particularly as it may concern the physiology of reproduction and correct terms, will find this kit helpful. The inexperienced person might well be given words of caution as to its limitations and the possible pitfalls involved in its unwise use.

Elizabeth McHose, Associate Professor
Health and Physical Education, Temple University

Courtship and Marriage, by Francis E. Merrill. New York, William Sloane, 1949. 360p. $2.85.

This study of the social relationships anticipating and characterizing marriage concerns in the main the uniformities of behavior determined by American society.

Written primarily for college students by a Dartmouth professor, the book discusses courtship as a social relationship, romantic love and sex, courtship and marital choice, economic roles, biological roles, parents and children, affectional roles, broken roles (divorce) and strengthened roles (adult and higher education and marriage). There are reading lists and an index.

Teens . . . How to Meet Your Problems, by John and Dorathea Crawford. New York, Woman's Press, 1951. 162p. $3.00.

Here are sympathetic discussions of young people's problems, personal, family, social or school. Out of his experience as educator and counselor Dr. Crawford draws case stories to convince his readers that no problem is unique.

Glands, Sex and Personality, by Herman H. Rubin, M.D. New York, Wilfred Funk, 1952. 205p. $2.95.

Designed to give the average intelligent lay reader some of the important facts about glands, this book avoids technical terms when possible and has an attractive, readable style.

In general, the material is accurate. Examples are often quite extreme, and there is a tendency to overstress the importance of the endocrine glands and the role they play. The discussion, A Man's Change of Life, seems to overemphasize some of the symptoms and indicate that they occur frequently.

Chapter 19, How Hormones Affect Your Behavior, assigns the endocrines an important role in criminality, juvenile delinquency and mental disturbances which is as yet unproved. On page 175 a statement—"It is worthy of note that in many of our mental hospitals a good percentage of patients have shown evidence of endocrine disturbance, and treatment with adequate hormones has enabled them to be discharged or paroled"—is not in accord with the opinion of most psychiatrists. The results of endocrine therapy in mental disease have been, on the whole, disappointing, although there still remains the possibility that endocrines do play an important role in some of the little-understood types of functional mental disorders.

The book as a whole seems overoptimistic as to what can be done by endocrine therapy. The glossary of technical terms is useful. The book can be, in general, recommended for its purpose—to give the public further knowledge of the relationship of the endocrine glands to personality and behavior.

Karl M. Bowman, M.D., Medical Superintendent
Department of Mental Hygiene
The Langley Porter Clinic

Understanding Your Child, by James L. Hymes, Jr. New York, Prentice-Hall, 1952. 188p. $2.95.

This guide to understanding and enjoying youngsters is a real contribution to the growth and happiness of the family—as a unit and as individuals. Parents and teachers will find reassurance in the author's observation that "people are made and remade with every passing day." The light touch of the author, a professor of education and father of three, is ably seconded by the merry sprinkling of drawings by H. W. Doremus.

The Adolescent and His World, by Irene M. Josselyn, M.D. New York, Family Service Association, 1952. 124p. $1.75.

In *The Adolescent and His World* Dr. Josselyn has written a fine, readable and helpful book that should appeal to a large audience. Parents will find it promotes insight into the teen-age world. Teachers and students of human personality will appreciate its worth. And the more intelligent teen-agers will read it profitably.

If it were not for one chapter, *Sex Education and Sexual Behavior,* this could be classified as one of the better books on teen-age personality . . . we could put it in libraries throughout the country, and then sit back and hope it would have a wide circulation.

This chapter has two vital weaknesses that demand challenge. Unless carefully read and analyzed, it could damage the cause of group work, which includes sex information as well as the promotion of sound life values and attitudes. In all fairness, it should be mentioned that Dr. Josselyn probably tried merely to present the material in a thoroughly objective, unbiased, scientific manner, but the result is a confusing and contradictory point of view quite likely to be misunderstood by the average reader.

The chapter on sex education gives the impression that group work imparting sexual information is damaging. Dr. Josselyn actually does not say that . . . she says that a series of lectures on sex as such cannot be given to young people without harmful results.

This is not news. Years ago we learned that purely sex information courses were stimulating and conducive to experimentation . . . but it's a different story when sex information is given as part of material on the psychology of human adjustment. The reader may, however, gain the impression that the author condemns all group work dealing with intimate subject matter. If so, this book would do serious damage to a great cause.

The group approach in schools

In the last few years great strides have been made in family life education in the public high schools through the group approach. The course in marriage at Toms River, N. J., is a notable example of this technique, as is the health education program in Oregon. San Antonio has had an outstandingly successful family life education program which has stood the test of five and one-half years and 7,000 student enrollees.

This has not been done without taking a positive stand against promiscuity—which leads us to the second half of the criticism of Dr. Josselyn's chapter.

She seems to believe that sex mores in the United States have radically, drastically changed as the result of wars and other pressures ... . that complete sexual freedom for both sexes may be around the corner. No one would argue that changes have not occurred. The degree of change is what is challenged.

Parenthetically, if Dr. Josselyn wants any evidence about sex mores in America, let her come into any high school where an unmarried girl's pregnancy has become known to her fellow-students and see what happens to her in the halls at the hands of her so-called free and easy peer group.

We may talk a great deal about—and in small groups accept—sexual freedom, but the great middle class in America still clings to the basic moral teachings of yesteryear. According to the standards of youth, a girl may kiss, may pet a little, but she is expected to retain her virginity. Family life education is helping boys and girls to accept the religious single standard and to reject the outmoded double standard.

Outmoded by what and by whom? By the findings of research studies on successful marriage, by men like Kinsey who have shown the class levels of sexual behavior, by studies like the one made in San Francisco on promiscuity.

Dr. Josselyn states that acceptance of sexual freedom would not necessarily be undesirable. If such is the case, then churches and organizations like the American Social Hygiene Association would do well to fold their tents and quietly fade away. They are passé and have no place in the modern scheme of things.

But she is wrong! Human beings have basic needs for love and security and recognition that can never be met by temporary sexual alliances.

Principles to live by

Certainly, no work can be done to help confused young people either individually or in groups unless there are basic values and attitudes rooted in sound mental hygiene and religious concepts to impart along with specific information, sexual or otherwise. People have to have something to believe in and live by in order to make good, sound life adjustments. This chapter could easily induce a young reader to believe that the author thought moral restraints wholly unnecessary.

Self-restraint, sexually, is not harmful if it is thoughtfully chosen as a way of life before marriage, not from fear but because of the desire for the best. Lack of restraint has yet to prove its harmlessness.

This is a good book to read if it stimulates your thinking. It is bad if you passively accept it *in toto*.

Payton Kennedy, Dean of Girls
Thomas Jefferson High School, San Antonio

Your Marriage and the Law, by Harriet F. Pilpel and Theodora Zavin. New York, Rinehart, 1952. 358p. $3.95.

This is an important book for laymen in an area in which there are too few books even for professionals. It presents the gamut of legal problems that men and women encounter who become engaged, get married, engage in sexual relations, have children, become involved in family disputes, separate and seek divorces.

Part I covers legal problems involved in engagements and breach of promise actions, rules with respect to who may marry, procedures for getting married, interpersonal relationships and property obligations of husbands and wives. Part II presents materials on the obligations and duties of parents and children toward each other, and problems involved in illegitimacy, artificial insemination and adoption as well as a postscript about estates and wills. Part III, The Sex Side, considers problems of birth control, abortion, sterilization and criminal aspects of sexual expression. Part IV contains data on separation agreements, annulments and the manifold problems involved in divorce, homegrown and migratory.

Since the authors have attempted to cover many different areas of pre-family and post-family legal problems, the specialist might find the material on some points a bit thin. However, the book is not intended as a handy guide to the law for laymen. It is not a substitute for legal guidance by trained lawyers. It simply seeks to block out the contours of a vital area of the law affecting men, women and children, and to spot the many booby-traps.

It is to be hoped that the men and women who read this book will lend their voices to the growing demand for a rational revision of the crazy-quilt, illogical patchwork which passes for family law.

Morris Ploscowe
City Magistrate, New York City

Courtship and Love, by William S. Sadler, M.D. New York, Macmillan Company, 1952. 195p. $3.50.

Here is must reading for all teen-agers and their parents. Its simple, easy-to-read style readily appeals to the average high school and young college student. The author does not answer questions about dating, courtship and love, but rather discusses the problems openly and frankly so that the young adult is better able to make a more satisfying decision.

The author, a psychiatrist with 40 years' experience in counseling young people about their premarital love life, gives detailed consideration to dating, mate selection, courtship, engagement and preparation for marriage. In a chapter on Predicting a Successful Marriage Dr. Sadler says, "When we clearly recognize and honestly face our personality difficulties, we can do a whole lot to insure happiness by correcting these shortcomings before the marriage vows are plighted." He is optimistic about the ease with which personality difficulties can be corrected . . . however, facing the facts and accepting each other as real live people with many imperfections are important to the success of a marriage.

Some very sound counsel is given the young couple in the chapter on Starting Married Life. The importance of planning together, learning the business of real cooperative living and avoiding "matrimonial stagnation" are dealt with in an optimistic, realistic way.

The book has a good brief bibliography on preparation for marriage, and it is well indexed.

Marrietta Henderson
Coordinator of Family Life Education
Asheville, N. C.

Parents, Children and the Facts of Life, by Henry V. Sattler. Paterson, N. J., St. Anthony Guild Press, 1952. 270p. $3.00.

The author states that this work was written for and by parents, the latter being responsible for practical hints in the book. Father Sattler approaches sex instruction from the Catholic viewpoint, which considers sex attitudes a complex of religious, moral, emotional, psychological and physiological factors. A discussion of these factors constitutes the heart of the book. Following each chapter are cases for discussion and questions.

The tone of this book is one of simplicity and frankness. The author provides a step-by-step approach for explaining to children the process of conception and childbirth, including the part played by the father and mother. He emphasizes the necessity for associating sex with God and therefore regarding it as good and sacred. A detailed explanation of sexual morality is set forth in two chapters.

Father Sattler's approach should discourage parental puritanism and encourage a broader and more intelligent attitude toward the sex instruction of children. There is a preface by Reverend Francis J. Connell, dean of Catholic University's school of sacred theology, and an index.

John J. Kane, Ph.D.
Assistant Professor of Sociology
University of Notre Dame

journal of SOCIAL HYGIENE

vol. 39 june 1953 no. 6

JUNE 1953

About our cover . . .

June wedding. Twenty-fourth of a series of Journal covers on family life . . . photograph courtesy of the United Defense Fund.

Harriett Scantland, Editor
Elizabeth McQuaid, Assistant Editor

Eleanor Shenehon, Editorial Consultant

THE JOURNAL OF SOCIAL HYGIENE

official periodical of the American Social Hygiene Association, published monthly except July, August and September at the Boyd Printing Company, Inc., 374 Broadway, Albany 7, N. Y. Acceptance for mailing at the special rate of postage provided for in Section 1103, Act of October 3, 1917. Entered as second-class matter at the Post Office at Albany, N. Y., March 23, 1922.

Prostitution—then and now

by Paul M. Kinsie
Director of Legal and Social Protection
American Social Hygiene Association

Every now and then someone asks, "Has any real progress been made in the United States against the prostitution racket?"

And the same person almost invariably adds, "It's always existed . . . always will . . . it can never be eradicated."

Perhaps eradication is outside the realm of possibility. However, many experiences of this atomic age were considered impossible years ago. Assuming that prostitution cannot be completely eliminated, we know it *can* be reduced to a minimum . . . and held to a minimum.

In many cities in the United States today commercialized prostitution has reached that irreducible minimum. To measure the progress that has been made let us compare current conditions to those that existed years ago in practically all communities. A person has only to be old enough to remember his hometown shortly before the first World War, or be willing to accept the opinions of those who were in their late teens or older in those days, to see the contrast.

No need for camouflage

Young people used to be exposed to open and flagrant commercialized prostitution. In most cities—large and small, from Maine to California—red-light districts or comparable conditions thrived. Houses of prostitution were also scattered through business and residential areas, usually within easy distance of the main part of town. Streetwalkers patrolled the principal and secondary streets night in and night out. The back rooms of saloons were hangouts for prostitutes who openly accosted all comers. They took their trade to hotels or rooming houses nearby, whose owners or managers rented rooms exclusively for immoral purposes.

Steerers and ropers circulated about the tenderloins, directed trade to brothels and similar places, and boasted about the new stock that was always available. Very frequently they accosted their customers in full view of police officers on post, because they knew that those for whom they hustled had the green light to carry on their illicit activities.

Their accosting was open and above board, their sales talk similar to that of circus barkers.

Steerers got weekly salaries; other go-betweens got commissions on each customer they provided. Pimps lurked nearby in case a customer became obstreperous . . . and incidently computed the number of customers the girls entertained to be sure that they were not holding out.

From chuck steak to tenderloin

Tolerant municipal administrations permeated with graft and corruption made such conditions possible. Scarcely a person connected with the racket escaped without paying his or her way. The revenue that flowed into the pockets of corrupt politicians and law enforcement officials ran to millions of dollars. Vice districts became known as tenderloins after a police official who was placed in charge of a vice area in a large city, boasted: "I've been eating chuck steak all my life . . . now I can afford tenderloin."

The owners of brothels—as well as procurers, pimps and some policemen—also grew wealthy. The prostitutes themselves, almost always in debt, eked out a mere existence . . . though they accommodated an average of 30 customers a day, and their daily earnings usually amounted to from $20 to $60.

Prostitution underworldlings always had their eyes on new stock and used every means to recruit it. Recruitment was not always easy; frequently they had to use strong-arm methods. Hardened prostitutes helped to induce and coerce green girls into the business . . . and taught them all the tricks of the trade.

Most brothels in the smaller cities harbored at least five inmates. Those in larger cities had as many as 10 or 20, and sometimes 30. Twenty-four hours a day, seven days a week, month after month they were on duty. Those who lived on the premises paid exorbitant rates for room and board and were compelled to buy necessities and knick-knacks from peddlers who split the overcharge with the operators. In addition, the inmates had to divide their earnings 50-50 with the operators of the houses.

In some cities the inmates lived at home and reported for duty in day or night shifts. They usually preferred late hours since they did most of their business after dark.

Frequently their pimps appeared on the scene to collect their earnings and then escorted them to hangouts where they compared notes with others in the racket and discussed their common interests.

A former exploiter—one who used to operate houses of prostitution in various large cities and made a fortune in the racket, and now because of reduced circumstances operates a small hotel legitimately—spoke about the racket in the good old days and compared conditions then with those of today . . .

Decent people want their children to grow up in a wholesome environment.

"Today it's a real scandal to take money from women. Taking it from bookies or other racketeers . . . that's a different deal.

"The difference is like day and night. There ain't one town anywhere in the country today like it was years ago. Don't care which one . . . Chicago, Detroit, New York, Frisco, New Orleans, Portland, Seattle. They're not like they used to be. The racket really is shot . . . people are smarter . . . cops are better educated. The public now won't stand for the racket the way they did 20 or 30 years ago."

In his inimitable way he compared present conditions phase by phase with those of years ago. His was not just one man's opinion. It represented the consensus not only of many big wheels formerly in the racket, but those currently associated with it.

The American Social Hygiene Association's records in the last four decades bear witness to this metamorphosis. During this time ASHA has repeatedly surveyed prostitution and allied conditions in practically every city of any size at all in the United States and its territories and in many foreign countries.

As far back as 1914, members of the prostitution underworld began to see the handwriting on the wall. The published reports of various vice commissions exposed the intolerable conditions that existed. An enlightened public demanded new legislation to curb white slavery. Injunction and abatement laws found their way into the statute books of many states and darkened many red-light districts.

The Draft Act of 1917 prohibiting prostitution near military installations proved to those in the racket that the federal government was interested in suppressing commercialized prostitution. Exploiters and prostitutes also well remember the vice repressive laws that were enacted in 1919, 1920 and 1921 just as the vice interests were striving to stage a comeback and recoup some of the losses they suffered during World War I. Some of the bigshots who realized the public was gradually lowering the boom on their racket, deserted the ranks and sought refuge in the more lucrative operations of the prohibition era.

Although conditions in many cities were still far from satisfactory in the 1920's they were considerably better than they had been a decade before. Fewer brothels were tolerated; most had fewer inmates. Exploiters, pimps and others associated with the business did not flaunt their connections with it and managed to have stand-ins take the rap when spurts of law enforcement took place.

"Never give up" seemed to be their slogan in those years.

When World War II was on the horizon during the national limited emergency, when military establishments were being reactivated and industrial plants were converting to meet defense needs, hope once again ran high in most prostitution circles. They envisioned flourishing trade facilities, and flocked into cities and towns frequented by servicemen or defense workers.

For a while they prospered. Newcomers in the racket apparently did not know about the setback their predecessors received during World War I. Oldtimers either forgot it or believed that if repressive measures menaced them they would be able to weather the storm in one way or another.

Surveys conducted by the American Social Hygiene Association during 1940 disclosed unsatisfactory conditions in 43% of the communities frequented by servicemen and defense workers. Flagrant activities developed. Once again prostitution interests overplayed their hands. When the local authorities began enforcing the law one brothel-keeper in a fairly wide-open community commented . . .

> "Give hustlers an inch and they'll take a yard. They're never satisfied when they're getting a break . . . they'll overdo it. Result? The public starts breathing down the law's neck . . . and down comes the lid."

In city after city the greed of those in the racket started a wave of law enforcement. Prostitutes and those who exploited them were on the move. Mobile or floating brothels developed. Individual women drifted from one town to another. Some were accompanied by their pimps. Others travelled alone. They avoided most of the so-called tight towns and sought haven in out-of-the-way towns with *laissez faire* policies toward prostitution.

Evidence that servicemen were their main targets stimulated public indignation. Again the federal government found it necessary to intercede.

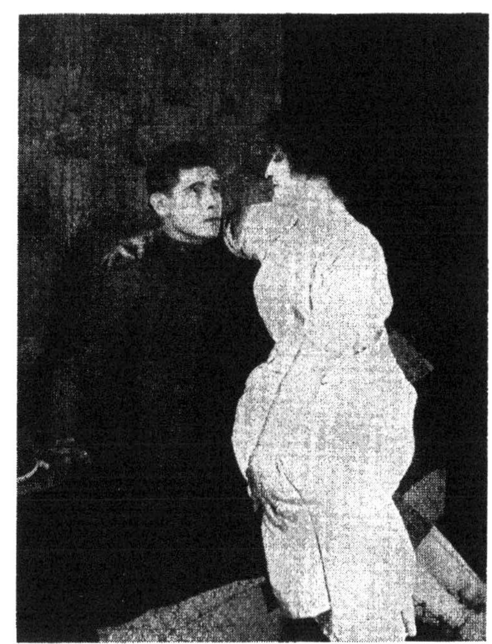

As far back as 1917, prostitution was prohibited near military camps.

The May Act

A division of social protection was created in March, 1941, in the Office of Defense Health and Welfare Services. Shortly thereafter Congress passed the May Act and the President signed it in the interest of "a united effort for total physical and moral fitness." The Secretaries of War and the Navy described in detail to state governors the official stand of the two departments, and the federal government in general, on the repression of prostitution.

Passage of the May Act—which prohibits prostitution within reasonable distances of military installations—caused consternation in underworld circles. The prostitution racket received its real shock in May, 1942, when the War Department invoked this law for the first time in 27 counties near army camps in rural Tennessee . . . because local and state officials either could not or would not effectively repress prostitution. Later 12 counties in North Carolina received the same treatment.

The FBI, which had charge of enforcement, met periodically in many sections of the country with law enforcement officers, military representatives of the government's social protection division, the American Social Hygiene Association and other voluntary agencies, and with key citizens. They discussed prostitution conditions from reports furnished by the American Social Hygiene Association, and stressed the necessity of enforcing laws affecting prostitution near military areas. As a result of the wide publicity given these conferences the prostitution

Acquainting the community leader with prostitution facts . . . this job the federal government asked ASHA to do.

underworld, which did not fully understand the provisions of the May Act, saw FBI agents behind every lamppost.

The 680 surveys of commercialized prostitution conditions made by the American Social Hygiene Association in 526 communities in 1942 revealed that in city after city law enforcement was again taking hold. When the war ended in August, 1945, commercialized prostitution had reached an all-time low. In many places it was almost entirely eliminated, and the Army and Navy reported their lowest VD rates in wartime history.

A new upsurge

The war had scarcely ended when the racket again began to blossom forth. The grapevine spread the word that the battle against commercialized prostitution was over and that the vigorous campaigns against it were wartime measures.

Brothels that had been closed reopened. Bellboys, cabdrivers and others resumed their role as go-betweens. Some did so openly, others cautiously, depending upon how efficiently the laws against prostitution were being enforced.

Prostitutes made their appearance in hotels, subject of course to the calls they received from go-betweens. Certain taverns became hangouts for promiscuous women and girls.

Once again an upward trend in prostitution activity was evident. Once again public opposition waned, and in consequence law enforcement relaxed.

But in 1948 when the United States stepped up its defense program the need to prevent further deterioration in conditions became obvious. The Interdepartmental VD Control Committee appointed by President Roosevelt during the war met again in May, 1948. Representatives of the Army, Navy, Air Force and Public Health Service—with ASHA as an advisory member—carefully weighed the facts regarding conditions inimical to the health and moral welfare of servicemen and civilians.

In a resolution the committee requested the American Social Hygiene Association—as the sole voluntary agency in the field of social hygiene—to do five things:

- "To act as advisor to . . . the National Defense Establishment in matters pertaining to civilian community education and the repression of prostitution.
- "To continue and expand services to supply confidential data regarding prostitution conditions in the environs of military establishments.
- "To give consideration to performing the functions of the Social Protection Division which no longer exists.
- "To make available to the Armed Forces, on request, educational material and advisory services.
- "To bring citizen support to good law enforcement, social treatment and individual health education through the home, the church, and the school."

Although there was a renaissance of commercialized prostitution in many cities during the first three years after the war, prostitution was neither so extensive nor so readily accessible as during the period between the wars. Brothels were far less numerous, go-betweens were less aggressive, and individual prostitutes who solicited in bars, taverns, and grills exercised care in the selection of trade.

Since 1948 conditions have vastly improved. Last year only 86 of the 343 militarily significant communities we surveyed were tolerating unsatisfactory prostitution conditions.

Generally speaking, the larger cities have held the line against the racket. More efficient police departments, better courts and highly organized public opinion are responsible for the satisfactory conditions that prevail in the larger communities. Many small towns and some medium-size cities, and the surrounding areas, are the trouble spots.

In most communities today young people are not exposed to the demoralizing influence of flagrant activities that youngsters encountered years ago. Even in some of the worst cities where law enforcement is lax it takes diligent search to find a prostitute.

Unfinished business

Cleaning up a city to the point where finding a prostitute becomes so difficult that the average seeker must spend considerable effort, time and money to locate one, and risk danger of arrest, is about as much as can be done in law enforcement against prostitution.

•

But the job is far from finished. Constant vigilance is required to keep vice at a minimum. The spadework done in years gone by is paying dividends . . . dividends in health and moral welfare not only for members of the Armed Forces, but for all who want to live in wholesome surroundings.

The job of maintaining a clean environment, which all intelligent people desire, is not only the duty of law enforcement authorities but the responsibility of the citizens of each community. Frequently wheels within wheels, "connections," political tie-ups and other interference with law enforcement against commercialized prostitution are discouraging factors to honest and efficient officers who want to discharge their duties as their conscience dictates. If they don't play ball and become part of the system, they are penalized by being relegated to some unimportant post out of the way of those who work hand-in-glove with the prostitution racketeers.

Wherever and whenever a community tolerates commercialized prostitution, permits it to exert its demoralizing influence and allows it to make its contribution to the spread of venereal diseases, Mr. and Mrs. John Public share the responsibility. If they insisted as forcefully on efficient and vigorous law *enforcement* against commercialized prostitution as they did on getting the laws on the books, they could reduce prostitution to the irreducible minimum . . . and hold it there.

Real law enforcement—it's up to the public.

Education for Marriage within the Anglican Church

by the Rev. Canon Hugh C. Warner

A man once came to me with a story of a marriage that seemed very near the rocks. He was sure his wife had ceased to love him. She was all "shut up" as he put it . . . bitter in her resentment against him, cross and scratchy with their two children, exasperating to herself as much as to those who lived with her.

I was able to have a long talk with her, and she told me much about her childhood. She had lost her father when she was three, and her mother did all she could to protect her from the assaults of the outside world by keeping her close to herself all the time. When nearly five years old, she passed a pram in the street with a tiny baby inside. Her mother stopped to look, and lifted her up to have a peep. She turned to her mother.

"Mummy," she asked, "where did that baby begin before it got into the pram?"

To this day she could remember, she said, the queer way she felt when her mother flushed scarlet and pulled her violently away by the hand.

"That's a question," she said, "nice little girls don't ask. When you get to be a bigger girl, you'll learn all about it."

There were repercussions

She never did "learn all about it." She had done something by asking this question which had, mysteriously enough, made her mother unhappy and cross.

As she grew older she learned odd bits of information about human reproduction from older girls, but always in an atmosphere of secrecy and furtiveness. Was it surprising that in her marriage she failed to accept fully and gladly that expression of married love which unites husband and wife as no other relationship between two people can ever do? There was no happy home because there was no happy marriage.

Since 1944 the Church of England has maintained a Moral Welfare Council, commissioned by the Church Assembly to consider all matters affecting sex, marriage and the family.

With a small central staff dealing with education for sex and marriage, this Council has instituted courses of lectures for men who are later to be ordained in the theological colleges of England and Wales. For clergy who never had such instruction in their younger days there are clergy schools organized on a diocesan basis to help priests take advantage of the openings in parochial life to prepare young people for marriage.

Reproduction . . .

a gift from God.

When one examines cases of marriage breakdown it becomes clear how many of these are due not only to character deficiencies like selfishness, which themselves arise from bad upbringing, but also to a wrong attitude toward sex. This wrong attitude develops so often, as we have suggested, out of early experiences in childhood when questions about reproduction are first asked.

Many cases of frigidity in women and impotence in men are related to an impure attitude toward sex which has come from stories heard from fellow school-children. Neither husband nor wife afterwards is able fully to accept sex as a God-given factor of immense significance and beauty for each in their relations one with the other.

Therefore, the clergy are encouraged to take every opportunity of getting in touch with clinics to which mothers bring their babies for routine examination, with younger members of the Mothers' Union, with young wives' groups, and with parent-teacher associations connected with local schools, offering to these groups courses of lectures on the general subject—how to answer children's questions.

These lectures form a short course . . . questions about God the first week, about prayer the second week, about death the third week, about birth the fourth week. Two further lectures are given developing sex education generally for children of different ages.

This method insures that discussion of sex is not isolated from the wider background of Christian living and theology. Parents are encouraged to answer their children's early questions, bearing in mind the importance of accuracy and of information sufficient to their years, of complete naturalness and of reverence in the whole treatment of the matter.

This latter point is important because every child born is destined to grow, by the grace of God, into fuller development after the death of the body. This link with eternity reflects upon the human reproductive system through which a child is born and demands an element of reverence in the way we deal with it.

A crucial stage

Then we come to that stage in an English child's education when he moves from the primary school into the secondary school (when he is 11 or older). For the first time he comes in touch with children older than himself who have heard a good deal about sex in undesirable ways and very often are only too eager to pass on their information to younger children. There is no need to emphasize the damage that this so often does.

We therefore suggest that every child of 11 have a simple, accurate and reverent knowledge of the father's part as well as the mother's part in human reproduction. If we do not give the information ourselves, other children will . . . and the damage will be done.

Among the reading materials that we use in our work are seven pamphlets written by me and published by the Student Christian Movement Press. They are:

- Puzzled Parents (for parents)
- Where Did I Come From? (for children over 8)
- How a Family Begins (for girls)
- The Start of a Family (for boys)
- Science and You (for young people 16 and over)
- Sorting Things Out (for young people 17 and over)
- The Christian View of Sex (for students)

The later stages of adolescence need a book in themselves. They are associated with behavior problems, with petting and necking, with how far endearments should go, with all the problems connected with courtship and engagement. The important principle we try to guard here is that Christian standards of chastity outside marriage, and fidelity within marriage, are not arbitrary impositions of dusty maxims by a narrow-minded priesthood . . . but that they are the articulations of living experience itself.

Limitless and timeless

We try to show how young people's experience of love witnesses to the inner demand which love makes for exclusiveness in the relationship of one with the other, and to that longing for complete self-giving which in its fullness demands a relationship with each other for life, if it is to be self-giving in the fullest sense.

It is at this stage that we have our great opportunity of explaining the meaning of sex in Biblical terms. We show how the story of the Creation offers us a picture of the man-woman relationship, a joint relational unity from the start, made in the image of God. Because it is made in the image of God—who is a

Born in Southern Rhodesia. Graduate of Oxford and Cambridge. Formerly vicar of Epsom, Surrey, and personal chaplain to the Archbishop of York. Now education secretary of the Church of England's Council for Family Life. Father of six and author.

The Rev. Canon Hugh C. Warner

Triune, a Trinity—we try to help them see that man and woman in association with each other are meant to be like this relational picture we have of the Godhead.

With man and woman in marriage we find a bi-unity (one flesh) where each retains his or her individuality but both are caught up into a relationship that makes them one without losing their identity. It is a relationship which is part of the very stuff of life, and can be broken only by the death of one of them.

In this way our young people are helped to see what lies behind the Christian doctrine of the permanence of the marriage relationship. It is also a time when we can show them the meaning of love as something that consists in a sharing of mutual interests one with the other. There is in it also physical desire, part of God's gifts to men, but that is not *exclusively* what is meant by love . . . whatever Hollywood may say to us on the subject.

Finally, there is that specific element of love which is so distinctively Christian, agape—the love of self-committal, where the relationship one with the other is not conditioned by the fact that one of the partners is getting some advantage from the other. This self-committal of one to the other—a matter of the will—is something that is never influenced finally nor completely by the fact that the partner is disloyal. "While we were yet sinners Christ died for us." And so it is with the highest form of Christian love between man and woman. It is an attitude of mind, and something which, once established, goes on because the grace of God is feeding that love with His own nature.

In this way we try to help young people see the meaning of the Christian gospel . . . of the appeal of Christ's love and the meaning of His death. They come to see it in terms of an experience to which they have already had some kind of introduction in their own experience of love.

For the future

When a couple come to put up their banns and the vicar meets them, he should be prepared. As an ordination candidate he should have received careful instruction on how interviews can be arranged . . . generally three of them, two in the vicar's study, one in the church. The marriage service is taken as a basis of the instruction and the priest draws out the implications—emotional, moral and spiritual—inherent in the Christian doctrine of marriage.

The physical side—that outward expression through which the grace of God comes to a married couple in intercourse—has real importance. This is not normally dealt with in detail by the vicar, but he makes it his business to see that the couple have suitable books to read.

In this way the Church of England is trying to tackle education for marriage among the clergy—with the cooperation of teachers, welfare workers and parents—to the moment when a man and a woman are married and within the framework of a permanent marriage begin to work at that which is to be the crowning beauty and the fullest experience of their united lives.

• •

CREDITS

Photos courtesy of Standard Oil Company (N. J.), pp. 243, 246, 248.

Photo from *Fit to Fight*, first Army VD film, prepared by ASHA during World War I for the War Department, p. 245.

Photo courtesy of Elliott & Fry, Ltd., London, p. 252.

Photo courtesy of U. S. Navy, p. 256.

Photos courtesy of U. S. Department of Defense, pp. 259, 260, 272.

Photo courtesy of Arthur Avedon, p. 265.

Venereal Disease Contact Investigation in the U. S. Navy and Marine Corps

by Captain R. W. Babione (MC) USN
and Lieutenant J. P. Ray (MSC) USN

As the number of infectious cases of venereal disease is progressively reduced, contact interviewing and tracing become more and more the most effective tools for finding and eradicating these diseases.

The modern therapeutic agents with their fast and positive control of infectiousness are of no value as a control measure unless the infected are found and brought to treatment before they have had time and opportunity to spread their infection to others. The remarkable reductions in the incidence of syphilis in the last 10 years in many of the leading cities of the United States are due in large part to assiduous case-finding and treatment . . . and in these the Navy has had no small part.

Until very recently investigators have devoted less effort to tracing gonorrhea contacts, and while the incidence of early syphilis has declined one-third to two-thirds, the reported incidence of gonorrhea has increased up to three times or more what it was 10 years ago. This increase may be partly due to improvement in the statistical reporting of gonorrhea cases.

The Navy has also experienced a marked reduction in new syphilis cases, partly no doubt as a result of improvements in the health of the civilian population. The gonorrhea incidence as compared to that 10 years ago shows no such decrease in over-all incidence.

Since the Korean campaign began

Although the average strength of the Navy was lower during the first year of the Korean campaign than during the first year of World War II, the total number of VD cases was just as high. The venereal disease problem is therefore far from solved . . . in spite of the antibiotic age. This high rate, however, is mainly the result of suddenly placing a large segment of the Navy in the Far East, where the only recreational areas were cities with very poor health facilities and far more opportunity for exposure under different conditions and mores than exist in the United States.

Rates in the continental United States continued at a low level after the Korean campaign began, in good measure because of the active cooperation of the Navy, the U. S. Public Health Service, and various local and state health departments in a broad program of contact interviewing and investigation.

Close cooperation between the Navy and the Japanese health departments has resulted in a much more effective tracing of the contacts of VD cases and better diagnosis and treatment following location of the contacts. Improvements in hygiene and sanitation, and more modern laws for the control of prostitution have also had beneficial results. Consequently, VD rates in the Far East have decreased markedly in the last year. As the situation improves, the relative importance of contact-tracing efforts will certainly increase.

Gonorrhea a problem

Naval experience in the continental United States indicates that gonorrhea is not being so well controlled as syphilis. We believe this failure is due to the fact that some local health departments give this disease less emphasis than syphilis. For some years now federal, state and most local health departments have carried on very effective programs of contact interviewing and investigation against syphilis. Although the United States Navy submits contact reports on all contacts named by gonorrhea cases, until recently a number of city health departments did not trace these contacts . . . the usual reason being lack of funds for investigators.

The situation has been improving since the onset of Korean hostilities, probably because of increased awareness of health in mobilization areas.

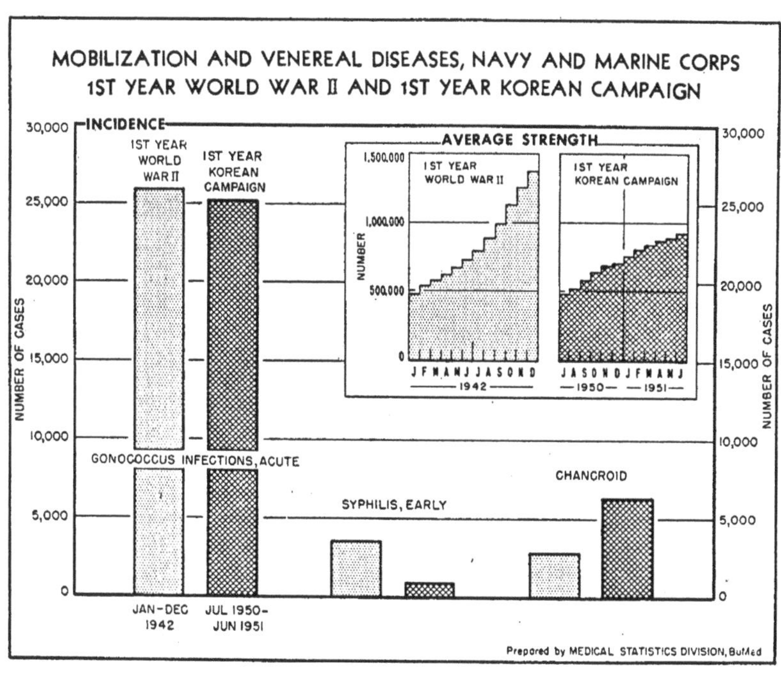

M.D., Western Reserve University. M.P.H., Johns Hopkins. Formerly director of preventive medicine, Bureau of Medicine and Surgery, U.S. Navy. Now in charge of a fleet epidemic disease control unit.

Captain R. W. Babione (MC) USN

Contact disposition is also a civilian operation. It involves medical examination of the contact, establishment of a diagnosis if venereal infection is present, and treatment where necessary. Some health departments treat "on suspicion" on the basis of a contact report from a diagnosed military case. These are the steps that break the chain of further spread. Finally, the results of the investigation are reported to the originating agency.

It is important to have an interested interviewer specifically trained for the job. At times the VD patient may be unable to recall the names of some of his more casual contacts. In such cases the trained interviewer can help the patient recall other things about the contact, the place of encounter and exposure so that the public health department has a few facts that are helpful in tracing the contact.

The U. S. Public Health Service has an excellent school for the training of venereal disease contact interviewers to which the Navy sends hospital corpsmen for a two-week course of instruction. When properly employed as interviewers, these hospital corpsmen are able to obtain the names and addresses of several contacts per case. In fact, one interviewer was able to obtain leads to 24 contacts from one man that enabled health departments in six cities to locate 22 of his contacts. Of the 22, nine were infected with gonorrhea, two had primary syphilis and one had early latent syphilis.

Military-civilian cooperation

All naval units should have at least one corpsman who has received this training. The Public Health Service has recently assigned representatives to certain defense areas to help in coordinating the military-civilian venereal disease control effort. These representatives are to work jointly with the civilian health departments and the military, assisting where possible in venereal disease contact interviewing, training of interviewers and tracing of contacts named by military patients. These workers are assigned through the regional office of the U. S. Public Health Service and the state health departments.

A common mistake is to assume that information obtained by an interviewer is insufficient to warrant the submission of Form PHS-1421 (VD) to a health

Native of Brent, Ala. In the Navy since 1933, an assistant in the Bureau of Medicine and Surgery for five years. Now district preventive medicine officer in the 15th Naval District, Balboa, Canal Zone.

Lieutenant J. P. Ray (MSC) USN

---

department. Most health departments locate at least one-third of the contacts named, even with poor information. The best results are secured when interviewers obtain information on all the patient's sexual contacts during the period in which he could possibly have contracted the disease or passed it on to someone else. Sometimes the incomplete data of several reports add up to a clear lead and to a highly infectious contact.

When a contact investigation is completed or a search abandoned, the local health department reports back on the action taken and the findings if the contact is brought to examination.

It is worthwhile

Trained contact interviewers are able to obtain more contacts and more usable information than untrained interviewers. Health departments report that they are locating a higher percentage of contacts each year, a number of them locating over 50% of the contacts named. Information furnished by the Navy thus helps to eradicate reservoirs of disease which undoubtedly would otherwise continue as a source of infection to civilians and military alike.

We consider the effort to obtain and report information on contacts well repaid. A good interviewer will obtain information on an average of three contacts per case . . . and in such instances an average approaching one new case is often discovered for each known case interviewed. This is believed to be the most promising method of case-finding in most parts of the United States today.

The opinions or assertions contained herein are the private ones of the writers and are not to be construed as official or reflecting the views of the Navy Department or the naval service at large.

Mental Health

(continued from May)

Second of a series of chapters from Preinduction Health and Human Relations, new curriculum resource for youth leaders by Roy E. Dickerson and Esther E. Sweeney.

Problems Rooted in External Causes

Not all human problems emanate from within, although meeting them calls for inner resources. Some problems originate in one's physical or social environment. Some arise when a marked change occurs in one's environment or way of living.

There are other problems—serious illness, grave disappointments, death. Although they arise from circumstances over which the individual has little or no control, he must deal maturely with the emotions these problems bring into play.

The nature of one's ordinary physical environment may often constitute a problem. Owing to housing shortages, many people are compelled to live in crowded conditions. Many others lack the financial resources to live in up-to-date, comfortably arranged homes.

So using one's basic drives as to meet these problems is the healthy course. Love helps one to make the best of things, to be patient and considerate in crowded and awkward living situations. Properly focused assertiveness can be used in planning and carrying out practical and ingenious ideas that make the home more attractive and livable. Further, one can use his drives, ambitions, desires for achievement and earning ability to change the situation . . . if not today, then in due course.

Association with other people may and often does involve problems. The emotionally healthy person enjoys social relationships and tries both to contribute to and profit from them. But the people with whom one lives, works and plays may not be uniformly mature, stable and emotionally healthy.

Everyone has to deal with the problems created by selfish, inconsiderate, demanding or stubborn people. Everyone knows someone who won't play unless he can dominate the situation, who takes to temper tantrums and tears if he feels thwarted in even minor matters or who causes embarrassment by attention-getting behavior at social events. One must often deal with the individual whose ambition, for example, causes him to treat colleagues unfairly and to try to achieve his success on their—not his—efforts, or with the person who thinks humiliation and scoldings will improve the performance of subordinates.

Countless other problems may be created by the people in one's environment and must be met with all one's inner resources. Understanding is one of these. The individual who understands his own problems, drives and emotions can use understanding in dealing with other people. Understanding why people behave the way they do and what their problems and unmet needs may be can help one immeasurably in keeping humor, balance and perspective in human relations.

Furthermore, self-understanding and self-analysis can help the individual to examine his own behavior honestly in order to determine whether the people in his environment are creating the problem or whether he is creating difficulties for himself and blaming others.

Here, as in all human problems, thinking and planning are necessary. The emotionally healthy individual plots a course for himself in difficult personal relationships. Sometimes it may be wisest to remove oneself from the relationship. Sometimes one must yield to another if the issues are minor. Humor and perspective may help one decide that taking things lightly is the best solution. Analysis may also indicate that a wise course is a calm, frank discussion of the problems in the relationship with the other person.

There are perhaps some problems that can neither be walked away from nor talked out with the person who creates them. The majority of officers and non-coms in the Armed Forces, for example, are men with fine leadership qualities, men of established emotional health whom their subordinates char-

The officer must be emotionally healthy.

Give them a reason and they'll adjust to radical change.

acterize as good guys. But in such large organizations as the services it is possible that a few may misuse authority and deal with recruits in a harsh or domineering way. The serviceman must be careful in deciding whether this is actual harshness or a decent, genuine effort to condition and toughen him for the jobs ahead. The raw recruit may fail to see that being able to take it on the chin in a variety of situations is part of military life and that his superiors may view as necessary hardening what he views as domination.

In rare instances where there is apparent justification for feeling that an officer is harsh, the emotionally healthy person will probably decide to grin and bear it and do his level best to avert trouble by top-grade performance. If the situation gets beyond his ability to handle it, the mature thing for him to do is to report it through proper channels.

Disappointment, Illness and Sorrow

Sooner or later all people face grave disappointment, serious illness in their families and the death of relatives or friends. These problems cannot be permitted to overwhelm nor immobilize one. Difficult as they are, they are part of living. The way one meets them is related to growing and maturing.

The fact that an individual may be unable to alter the course of events does not mean that he is unable to meet and deal with their emotional impact. Grief is a normal human reaction of which no one should feel ashamed. It is normal too to feel disappointment, especially when one has put much of himself into striving for something he fails to get. It is normal to worry about sick relatives and the progress of their illness. But indulging in prolonged grief and helpless worry, or responding to disappointment by refusing to make further efforts retards one's emotional growth.

The emotionally healthy person meets sorrow with as much thought for the future as possible, substitutes action for immobility, and so far as he is able substitutes one emotion for another. Interest in and care for the welfare of other members of the family who are equally bereaved is one way of getting into action and substituting one emotion for another at a time of death. Grief, sorrow and bereavement maturely coped with can add depth and understanding to one's whole personality.

Action can alleviate disappointment. If, for example, one is disappointed because of his failure to win the prize for the class essay, he can analyze as objectively as possible the faults of his essay and enter a new competition or start a new piece of writing. The emotional pain of disappointment will not disappear overnight, but it will be reduced by activity and new interests and by the emotions that energize and support those interests.

Response to Change

Marked change in one's environment or pattern of living—new people, new situations and new ways of doing things—may challenge good mental health and require frequent, rapid adjustments. The emotionally healthy person can rely on certain habits of thought, analysis and planning, and on certain attitudes he has already developed. He simply looks upon the whole question of change as a new problem to be met and solved in the best possible way. His flexibility will go a long way towards helping him, as will his sense of humor and generally cheerful outlook.

Life in the Armed Forces, in particular, creates a very radical change in one's living conditions, working conditions and social contacts. Military discipline may present a problem at first, but it can be recognized as essentially no different from the discipline of home, school or business. Moreover, self-discipline is a characteristic of good emotional health, and the boy or girl who enters the Armed Forces realizing that self-discipline is intrinsic to the best military discipline will live comfortably in his new environment.

Young people can view life in the service with better perspective when they reflect that millions of men and thousands of women entered military life during World War II, met such problems as loneliness, homesickness, boredom and lack of privacy and went through the hardships that are essential conditioning and preparation for combat. Yet the overwhelming majority adjusted well and served their country to their utmost.

Human beings are capable of fighting for their beliefs and ideals. They are also capable of adjusting to radical changes in their lives for the sake of their beliefs . . . and of doing so cheerfully.

When viewed as part of the learning process, a change or a new situation assumes its proper proportion in life as a challenge to full use of one's inner resources, as a means of achieving further maturity, and as a potentially rich and rewarding experience.

Conclusion

During the last years in high school one obviously cannot do all the things that will produce a mature personality. But use of insights newly gained, recourse to counseling services if necessary, and conscious effort to continue on the road to adulthood may produce better and more satisfying results than one can immediately foresee.

Young people can be encouraged by the fact that today the emotional health of the nation is recognized as being every bit as important as its physical health. Consequently, the training of teachers, clergymen and leaders of young people's organizations emphasizes mental hygiene and in many instances includes specific techniques of counseling.

Guidance counselors, case workers, psychologists, psychiatrists and many clergymen are specialists in counseling. Young men and women in school, business or the Armed Forces can freely, simply and without self-consciousness bring their problems of growing up to counselors who are prepared to help them to help themselves on the road to maturity.

Reference

- *Personal Problems,* by John B. Geisel, pp. 53–69.

Class Discussion

- Henry has worked earnestly and consistently on his job. His employers say it is necessary to reduce staff and plan to do it by dismissing those most recently employed. Henry must go, although he knows his work has been excellent. Discuss how Henry can handle this disappointing experience in a mature way.

- Margaret's mother is seriously ill and it is doubtful she will recover. There are four younger sisters and brothers in the home. Margaret is deeply grieved over her mother's illness and fears she may die. How can Margaret meet her problem in the best way?

- John had an automobile accident and lost one of his legs. Complications have arisen and it now appears he may never have the use of his other leg. This is a tragic situation for him and naturally he is facing a real and difficult problem. Discuss how he can take steps to meet it.

Class Activities

- Panel of two or three servicemen and women to discuss "Problems I Faced and Met on Entering the Armed Forces."
- Panel of several of last year's graduates to discuss "Some Problems Encountered in Business and How to Meet Them."

Jacob A. Goldberg

Life Memberships Awarded

An honorary life membership in the American Social Hygiene Association was presented at a Social Hygiene Day luncheon in New York City to Dr. Jacob A. Goldberg, director of the New York Tuberculosis and Health Association's social hygiene division.

Similar awards will be made in other cities to:

Major General Edwin P. Parker, Jr., USA (ret.)
Former provost marshal general

Charles D. Bowdoin, M.D.
Venereal disease control officer
Georgia Department of Public Health

G. G. Wetherill, M. D.
Director of health education
San Diego city schools

Mrs. Florence Sands, executive director
Social Hygiene Association of Dayton and
Montgomery County

TO BAILEY BARTON BURRITT . . .

Who has devoted his life to the cause of family health and welfare . . . in his home city of New York . . . in the larger community of the nation . . . and most recently in the international community . . .

Who from the very beginning had the insight to look upon the problems of family health in fundamental terms of the prevention of sickness and the maintenance of positive well-being . . . and who for his achievements in this field is known as a pioneering parent of the family health movement . . .

Who, having originally planned to devote himself to a career in education and having instead been called to service in social welfare, has been teaching the rest of us all of his life . . . by precept, by demonstration, by example . . .

Whose keen mind, great administrative ability, sympathetic understanding of human nature and mature wisdom have always been generously placed at the service of his fellow-citizens, thus putting Americans permanently in his debt . . .

The American Social Hygiene Association, whose policies and program he has long helped to guide, is proud to award this medal for Distinguished Service to Humanity, with the admiration and affection of its officers, its directors and all its members everywhere.

WILLIAM FREEMAN SNOW AWARD

FOR DISTINGUISHED SERVICE TO HUMANITY

Presented to

BAILEY BARTON BURRITT

1953

A Builder of Modern America

by Frank George Boudreau, M.D.

Tribute to Bailey B. Burritt on National Social Hygiene Day

I speak of the institution first, and of the man second. For by his works we know the man. In the old days the institution was said to be but the lengthened shadow of a man. Nowadays every institution owes its existence to several leaders . . . it is the lengthened, intertwined shadows of a number of men. Institutions multiply and flourish when men are free to think, speak and initiate. One man may thus create parts of many institutions, impressing his personality and his character on one or more of their components. So as we pass them by, we recognize that one aspect is the work of William Freeman Snow, another the fruit of Edward L. Keyes, still another the architecture of Thomas Parran.

The friends we meet and work with every day seem like ordinary mortals, commonplace individuals bearing few signs of greatness. But there will be found in some of them such solidity of character, such perception of truth, such ability to influence others that they will in future years have cast large shadows on the wall of history. This, I forecast, will be the fate of Bailey Barton Burritt.

I hope that those of you who come from Boston will forgive my temerity in trying to bring Ralph Waldo Emerson up to date. He lived in a relatively simple society, which science had not blessed with the telephone, the radio, the automobile and television. It is no wonder that his philosophy was somewhat simpler than our own.

What I have been trying to say—and doing it very badly because of interruptions from telephone, radio and television, which permit the intellectual slums to penetrate into our very homes—is that Bailey Burritt has impressed his character and personality on the work of many institutions. As we read their reports or otherwise acquaint ourselves with their work, we recognize here and there the marks of his excellent workmanship.

Trail-blazers

These are all notable institutions, designed to promote human welfare, to relieve misery, to make mankind or a part of mankind whole. Most of them have set their mark on our society by courageous pioneering and painstaking demonstration, so that in addition to promoting the welfare of their immediate clients, they have set a high example for others to follow. Funds invested in them have fertilized the social soil of places far distant from this city. In distant market places they are of good repute.

William Freeman Snow, M.D., a far-sighted pioneer and practical idealist.

Let me begin with the American Social Hygiene Association, since I am its guest today. It was not created at a very favorable period of medical history.

Let me quote two comments on the medical scene which were made just a few years before the turn of the century. Oliver Wendell Holmes, the elder, was accustomed to say in his lectures at Harvard:

> "I firmly believe that if the whole *materia medica* could be sunk to the bottom of the sea, it would be all the better for mankind and all the worse for the fishes."

And Bishop William Croswell Doane, who died in 1913, made it into a rhyme

"Stir the mixture well
Lest it prove inferior
Then put half a drop
Into Lake Superior.

"Every other day
Take a drop of water
You'll be better soon
Or at least you oughter!"

In the period of the first World War none of us could have imagined that far greater advances in the treatment of the venereal diseases than had ever been known would in the near future give us the potent chemotherapeutic and antibiotic agents now in effective use.

William Freeman Snow

The new American Social Hygiene Association grew strong and vigorous. William Freeman Snow achieved what seemed at the beginning to be impossible . . . cooperation of the army, federal authorities, state departments of health, local health agencies, and the people. His view encompassed the whole problem from its origins to its baleful results. Education was his principal weapon, but any tool easily fitted his hand. Our contingents went abroad and with them William Freeman Snow, who never thought a frontier of any kind—local, state, national or international—was an obstacle to progress.

Edward L. Keyes, M.D.
left his impress
on social hygiene.

So with gentle persistence and unshakable determination he shaped one by one the foundations of the great institution the American Social Hygiene Association has become. Courageous and sagacious pioneering, painstaking demonstration, pilot-plants which withstand the most rigorous tests . . . these I believe are still the characteristics and the assets of the association.

I knew of William Freeman Snow before my League of Nations days, but I became well acquainted with him when he began to work actively with the League's social and health sections. It was an experience which enriched me. Today I think of him and of his work and personality with pleasure and gratitude. He lives still in the thoughts and minds of thousands of his friends and acquaintances.

Let me now pass on to another institution, the Milbank Memorial Fund. I am sure Bailey Burritt had been in touch with the founder of the Fund long before he joined the Fund's technical board in 1922, for I find a letter written in 1913 by the founder, to his institution, the Association for Improving the Condition of the Poor. This letter proposed the creation of a department of social welfare, of which Bailey Burritt later took charge.

This was pioneering at its best, for the department undertook a complete program of public health which was so far ahead of its time that it would not seem outdated today. Later he became director of the Association for Improving the Condition of the Poor and on the merger of this society with the Charity Organization Society, the senior executive of the Community Service Society.

Health demonstrations

Between 1922 and 1946 his connection with the Milbank Memorial Fund was very close, for in 1922 he was appointed to the Fund's technical board, and there he helped to plan and supervise the health demonstrations in Cattaraugus County (N. Y.), Syracuse and New York City. The story of these demonstrations is so well-known that I need not repeat it here. It belongs, I think, to the heroic period of public health work when problems were vast and the means of solving them relatively weak, a more equal contest than today.

A characteristic of Bailey Burritt's work is the family health maintenance plan of the Community Service Society. Requested by the health committee of the Community Service Society to review its health program, Bailey reported that certain activities were outmoded. He went on to propose in their place a study or demonstration based in part on the Peckham Health Center. This has become the family health maintenance plan, which is sponsored by the Community Service Society, Montefiore Hospital and the Presbyterian Hospital.

You will be hearing a great deal about this work in the future for it is on the growing edge of public health. It is characteristic of Bailey Burritt to march on a little faster than time marches on and to bring his associates along with him.

These are but examples of Bailey Burritt's fruitful association with forward-looking social agencies. I know of many others, but I am sure that I do not know of them all. Of one thing I am certain: Bailey Burritt's influences on these and other agencies has been for moving forward, for progress, never for standing still or retreating.

What can I say about the man? Many of you know him better than I do and you would be indignant if I did him less than justice. Moreover, it is difficult to describe a building still under construction or an unfinished painting or an organism that is still growing. This is the state of our friend Bailey Burritt . . . he is still growing, still widening his horizon, and he will not hold still long enough for me to get a good picture of him.

Best British Briar

When I first began to smoke a pipe, I tried to find one with the letters BBB branded on the stem. These letters stand for Best British Briar as well as Bailey Barton Burritt. And these two institutions resemble each other in many particulars. For a good briar pipe is a solid piece of work. It has the character which protects it from damage by fire or fall; it withstands with ease all the ordinary vicissitudes of life and it remains sweet despite neglect or abuse. It takes on readily a smooth and lively polish, which fits it for the best society, while it is perfectly at home in less fortunate circles. It brings comfort and satisfaction to its owner and his friends, but it is sometimes disliked by

Long-time social hygiene leader. Former Surgeon General of the U. S. Public Health Service. Now dean of the University of Pittsburgh's school of public health.

Thomas Parran

the pipe owner's wife who is naturally jealous of the high position it occupies in her husband's affections. I don't really know whether the other B. B. B. has suffered in this respect.

The finger of suspicion is often pointed at those from whose lower lip dangles the dissolute cigarette, and a cigar too often stamps its bearer as a wily politician or an uncharitable plutocrat. A wholesome atmosphere of honesty surrounds the man who smokes a BBB. I wonder that more rascals do not assume this disguise.

There is a general belief that a pipe smoker is a friendly, thoughtful individual, whose long pauses between slow puffs indicate that he is cerebrating, that he reflects before he speaks.

I need not carry the comparison any further. You will all have grasped my meaning, which is in essence that Bailey Burritt is a comfortable, friendly, useful person to have around . . . and we hope he will continue to stay around and continue to be as comfortable, friendly and useful as he has always been in the past.

I think that at some time in the future as we look back on this occasion we may all come to the conclusion that Bailey Burritt has been and still is one of the builders of modern America. I wish there were more builders like Bailey, for you may be sure the part of the building he is responsible for will be solid and functional. For he has always believed that institutions exist for the benefit and use of people. Francis Bacon expressed that belief in these words:

> "Lastly, I would address one general admonition to all: that they consider what are the true ends of knowledge, and that they seek it not either for pleasure of the mind, or for contention, or for superiority to others, or for profit or fame, or power or any of these inferior things; but for the benefit and use of life; and that they perfect it and govern it in charity."

The Family . . . Cornerstone of the Future

by Bailey B. Burritt

On accepting the Snow Medal for Distinguished Service to Humanity

I am not at all unmindful of the significance of the honor you have conferred upon me. I am appreciative of this medal because its significance comes in large measure from the fact that it reflects symbolically the great contribution to the wholesomeness of individual and family life made during the long and fruitful career of Dr. William Freeman Snow, the leading participant in the founding and successful operation of the American Social Hygiene Association.

Dr. Snow laid out a very broad program of activity. Personally he enjoyed a very simple and devoted family life. His whole career was dominated by his devotion to the sanctity, purity and stability of family life. He devoted himself to securing those positive factors of wholesome social environment which favor the development of the best in individual and family life.

In his thinking, this involved the guidance of youth in the significance of family life and preparation for establishing happy and meaningful relationships between parents and between them and their children. He was fully aware of the importance of this not only for the future of the family itself but for the future of society as a whole. Because of this, he advocated throwing an educational arm around youth and prospective and actual parents to protect them from the harmful influence of the misuse of one of God's greatest gifts to man . . . the urge to procreate.

Implications of the award

But without further eulogizing the scientific and social heritage which Dr. Snow left us, I should like to mention another reason which makes me cherish this award. In conferring it, you are honoring me. In reality, however, you are doing more than that on this Social Hygiene Day. You are honoring a cause. That cause is the strengthening and protecting of family life by developing the practice of social hygiene. You are emphasizing the fact that the American Social Hygiene Association has a record of accomplishment in this field. You are, I believe, at the same time expressing the anticipation of still greater achievement because of your awareness of the unrealized potentialities of the social hygiene movement in family life.

Much of the work in the past has of necessity been directed to cleaning up, as it were, the backyards of the communities of our country. I mean, by that, of course, the creation of citizen knowledge and understanding of the harm that comes to the individual family and to society from the persistent commercial exploitation and perversion of man's procreative instinct.

Without the customary restraints of their home and community they need social hygiene's protecting arm.

It has not been an easy task. The backyard was full of weeds and rubbish and the commercial exploiters were determined to keep it so. But the wide-open red-light district of my university city of Rochester, N. Y. —'the butt of many uncouth stories and a temptation to many youths of Rochester while I attended the university — is no more.

Licensed or tolerated districts were well-nigh universal in our large cities between 1898 and 1902. They have been outlawed. Various phases of commercialized prostitution as well as brothels and taverns lending themselves to promiscuity are by no means completely extinct. In some places, indeed, they are intolerably bad still, but in the great majority of our cities they are no longer publicly accepted. With some exceptions and occasional lapses, citizens and laymen insist on their suppression.

You are all familiar with the unique services of the undercover studies, which the American Social Hygiene Association makes upon request. These have had a large share in improving the environment of our cities and towns throughout the country. So persistent, however, are the anti-social forces that this important function still requires a substantial portion of the association's too-limited budget and must be continued.

It is all the more important at this time because of the great need of proteeting millions of our young people who are concentrated in military encampments and emergency industrial areas. Here the ordinary environmental restraints of home, school, church and social and civic groups are more or less removed. At the same time, these environments are precisely the places that attract the commercial exploiters of vice with their attendant prostitutes, brothels and other temptations to youth.

The American Social Hygiene Association's studies of prostitution conditions are made only upon the request of the military, the U. S. Public Health Service, municipal officials and responsible civic organizations. The detailed findings—always confidential—enable the requesting groups, with the cooperation of the association, to clean up unsatisfactory conditions.

The importance and volume of this work is illustrated by the fact that although the association made 389 surveys in 342 communities last year, at the end of the year there were still 183 requests from the military services and 41 from the U. S. Public Health Service that we had not been able to fill.

In providing this protective service, we have succeeded only because we have had the continuous and active support of all the military services during two wars, during the intervening periods and in the present defense activities. Similarly, we have had the unqualified support and help of the USPHS and the cooperation of state and local officials . . . including governors, mayors, health officers, police and other officials. Without this backing and without the support of national, state and local health and civic organizations and individual citizens, success would have been meager.

Venereal disease prevention

I have already pointed out that the American Social Hygiene Association's original program was much broader than the suppression of commercialized prostitution. It included the prevention, so far as possible, of venereal disease . . . an evidence in itself of the failure to suppress prostitution and promiscuity. Insofar as this preventive effort failed, syphilis and gonorrhea have not been controlled. Not content with preventive efforts alone, the association has devoted much effort to cooperating with citizen groups and to obtaining their support for public health authorities in providing clinics and treatment facilities to aid in the cure and alleviation of cases which have not been prevented.

Health authorities—national, state and local—have recognized the importance of these health measures and have succeeded in providing adequate treatment facilities in most communities and are constantly improving the use of people trained to discover, discreetly and effectively, exposed cases and bring them unobtrusively under treatment.

The advance of medical science and the use of penicillin in the treatment of syphilis and gonorrhea—in which Dr. John F. Mahoney, health commissioner of New York City, has such a distinguished part—has accomplished marvels in the rapid and much simplified treatment of these diseases. So effectively has this been done that a tendency has appeared among some health officers and other persons to think these diseases are no longer a serious public health problem.

In 1952, however, there were 25,078 new reported cases of syphilis in New York City. This number has increased steadily from 20,489 in 1949.

The reporting of gonorrhea by private physicians is so notoriously neglected that we have no very accurate knowledge of the number of new cases. However that may be, syphilis alone in New York City shows a far greater incidence than tuberculosis. In 1952, for example, the number of new cases of tuberculosis was 7,178, less than one-third the number of new cases of syphilis alone.

Early case-finding

Although much progress has been made in case-finding, still more intensive efforts are now needed to discover early cases of primary and secondary syphilis. Many cases are not now discovered in time to prevent late syphilis and its complications. The public health problem here is wider than the individuals concerned, because if those infected are not discovered while in the primary and secondary stages of the disease, they are in many instances exposing other persons to infection . . . thus adding to the stream of cases that need to be discovered and treated. In short, in spite of the fact that penicillin is so effective in rendering cases of venereal diseases non-infectious, the public health problem of these diseases is far from solved.

The objectives of official and voluntary health services are primarily and fundamentally *the prevention of disease.* The public health aim, for example, in the control of tuberculosis is to prevent it. Can the public health aim of the control of venereal diseases be less? If not, the solution involves increased attention to the educational, social and environmental factors affecting the incidence of VD. The path to prevention lies along the road of a well-informed public.

Education

This leads me to the third historic and present objective of the American Social Hygiene Association . . . education.

The strength of our civilization and the firm stability of society rest fundamentally upon the strength and stability of its biological and social unit, the family. This strength rests in no small measure on the wholesomeness of the relationship between the sexes, both before and after marriage. *This* is the broad objective of social hygiene. Its success depends upon the active and thoughtful pursuit of this objective by parents, the school, the church, the public health agency, and civic and social groups.

*John F. Mahoney, M.D.—
his persevering efforts
revealed the effect
of penicillin on syphilis.*

The association's educational aim is to serve as a stimulating center of educational information. It attempts to gather from far and near the best of experience and make it available to appropriate organizations and individuals. Within the limits of its budget, it necessarily confines its efforts to supplying information and guidance to trained leaders . . . to school and college instructors, public health educators, clergymen, parent-teacher associations, health associations, and other civic and social groups.

This is at once the most fundamental and at the same time the most complex, difficult and delicate function of the association. It has to be pursued energetically but wisely. It requires maximum consultation with experienced leaders of our educational system, public health agencies, and social, religious and civic organizations. At the moment we are searching for an educational leader to direct this important service.

Preinduction health and human relations

The American Social Hygiene Association has recently assembled a manual of suggestions for educational and other leaders called "Preinduction Health and Human Relations." It has grown out of several years' experimentation by the association and the Cincinnati public schools and was edited by Mrs. Esther Emerson Sweeney, ASHA's director of community service, and Roy E. Dickerson, executive secretary of the Cincinnati Social Hygiene Society. It is now being tried out more fully in several places and will be revised from time to time as new experience may suggest and warrant.

Education . . .
most complex and
fundamental part
of social hygiene.

While adapted primarily for use in school systems, the book contains much that is useful for discussion leaders in religious, health and civic agencies. It is a very useful addition to the technical publications made available by the American Social Hygiene Association's education division, whose aim is to help in developing better understanding of the fundamental importance of stable, contented and healthy family life, freed from the handicaps that come with unwholesome, careless, unrestrained relationships between men and women. Upon these relationships rests the difference between healthy and unhealthy families; between happy and unhappy childhood; between a troubled, weak, uncertain society and a sane, stable and healthy society capable of withstanding the inevitable stresses of life and of developing those positive qualities of character which make for a good life in a wholesome environment.

Legislation

Much federal and state legislation and many local police and health regulations have been due to the initiative of the American Social Hygiene Association's legislative committees. For example, the legislation providing for prenatal blood tests as a preventive measure was drafted by the association and passed in many states. Prenatal blood tests are now required by law in 42 states.

The association has also taken an active part in promoting premarital blood tests. Legislation providing for these now exists in 40 states. Many laws for the repression of prostitution, which now exist in every state and territory of the Union, have been enacted with ASHA's enthusiastic encouragement. The association has assembled and made available complete digests of laws relating to the repression of prostitution and to the control of venereal disease. These are periodically revised and afford useful guides to those interested in further progress in these areas.

Syphilis respects no boundaries

The spirochete knows no political boundaries. He travels far and near without cost and without passports by sea, land and air. He joins armies, frolics with tourists and finds his way about with sailors. In these days of rapid transportation of large numbers of people from all parts of the globe, he finds himself at home today in the Far East and tomorrow in the Far West. In spite of protective efforts, he breaks through all barriers.

From a self-interested as well as a humanitarian point of view, the people of America are obliged to take steps to repress him. This is all the more

Symbols of service . . .
national and international.

necessary and all the more difficult because venereal disease is so prevalent in those countries that have inadequate health services. The World Health Organization has accordingly given the control of venereal diseases high priority. The U. S. Public Health Service vigorously assists, and the federal government appropriates modest sums of money for this purpose.

The American Social Hygiene Association, through its international committee, was one of the founders of the International Union Against the Venereal Diseases and has helped support it over the years. At present, a delegation from ASHA is attending a meeting of the Union at Rotterdam.

The association is endeavoring to strengthen public support of WHO's venereal diseases section by raising one-third of the budget for a full-time liaison office for the Union at Geneva, provided other countries raise the other two-thirds. In this way the International Union can bring more substantial citizen support of all countries to WHO's difficult but effective work.

Because of the importance of all these services—and the official and unofficial recognition of the American Social Hygiene Association's contribution to the control of venereal disease and to the fostering of wholesome relationships between the sexes—the United Defense Fund is now providing the bulk of the budget which enables the association to carry on its work. If this summary does no more than stimulate your desire to assist the association's board and staff to realize more fully social hygiene's major purpose of strengthening and protecting family life as a cornerstone of the future, it will accomplish its aim.

May I reiterate my unbounded appreciation of the generous award you have conferred upon me? And may I recognize with you that in reality it is an award to Dr. William Freeman Snow, to Dr. Charles Walter Clarke and to all those who have made possible the accomplishments of the American Social Hygiene Association . . . and carries with it the expression of the great hopes of all of us for the family of tomorrow?

Another point of view

Sex education for adolescents

by Irene M. Josselyn, M.D.

Dean Kennedy presented a thoughtful, thought-provoking review of my book, *The Adolescent and His World,* in the May, 1953, issue of the JOURNAL OF SOCIAL HYGIENE. Her challenge in regard to the chapter on sexual behavior of the adolescent is valid in view of her earlier statement that "the more intelligent teen-agers will read (the book) profitably."

It would seem, however, that her statement should be considered very carefully. I personally would be extremely hesitant to encourage anyone to read the book unless the individual had had considerable orientation to general psychological concepts and unless he or she were able to read it from the point of view of general psychological problems rather than from any personal urge for self-understanding.

For professionals

As indicated in the foreword, the book is "designed primarily for social workers and other professional people—the technical focus of the material presupposes that the reader has considerable knowledge of dynamic psychology." Without either theoretical background or practical experience plus real maturity a person might present the material so that it could create a great deal of anxiety. While the concepts outlined in the book could, I believe, be given to parents and adolescents productively if presented from the point of view of helping the adolescent and the parent, I do not believe that this is the book to accomplish that end.

On the other hand, in view of Dean Kennedy's suggestion that the book be made available to adolescents, one can scarcely disagree with her feeling that the chapter on sexual behavior would be very confusing to a young person. I am not sure that the young person would read into it a permission for promiscuity unless he were trying to find a rationalization for such behavior. Rather than sanctioning promiscuity, the definition of sexual maturity actually rules it out.

From the viewpoint of those of us working with adolescents, however, it would seem important that we try to understand what is happening to them in our culture to help them bridge the gap that occurs between the philosophy of the older generation and the younger . . . whether this is in regard to sexual behavior, social attitudes, political concepts or daily experiences.

It is not a matter of saying that the older generation is wrong and the younger generation right. It is equally, however, unsafe to assume that the older generation has an attitude that in its crystallized form should be permanently maintained through subsequent generations. The adult should not be eager to abandon his own philosophy but he should be willing to expose it to honest questioning by himself as well as others. The adult will be most helpful to the younger person if his own philosophy has the strength of flexibility rather than the weakness of brittle rigidity.

Reactions to a pregnant peer

Dean Kennedy suggests that one consider the reaction of high school people when they discover that one of their peers is pregnant. In my experience the reaction is extremely challenging. I have known some—girls particularly—who get a great deal of vicarious gratification out of the knowledge. Confused in their own thinking, unable to resolve the conflict between their impulse to defy society and to conform to society, they see the unfortunate girl as an expression of their own defiance. As a result, they can enjoy defiance without suffering the consequences.

On the other hand, I have seen many girls react to this situation by becoming frightened and solving the anxiety in a contrasting way. Seeing the tragedy and the punishment inflicted upon the pregnant girl—not only in terms of society's disapproval but more importantly because of the violation of the more basic goal of the young girl—they react with a rigid defense against their own sexual feelings. They reject the girl, cruelly attacking her at a time when she is so in need of help in facing her own situation. By rejecting her they reinforce their taboo against sexual expression. The taboo may then gain a strength that will prevent even a socially and psychologically healthy expression of sex drives. While superficially this reaction is reassuring to adults, it may in the long run be almost as unfortunate as the reaction of the other group who flaunt their acceptance of the pregnant girl.

Were the adolescent mature enough to be objective about the problem, one would see, in my opinion, a quite different reaction in our high school group. The group could deal with it more objectively, recognizing that in our society behavior resulting in pregnancy before marriage creates unanswerable problems. They would then recognize that the girl's behavior expresses some difficulty of hers which they can avoid by a careful evaluation of their own attitude toward sexual behavior. Her experience would not then be a threat to their own patterns. They could see her in terms of her needs with no fear of nor wish for contamination of their own behavior.

That such maturity is more theoretical than actual is of course obvious. Most adults have not reached enough peace within themselves to handle objectively the problem of the unmarried mother.

Let's face reality

Each of us individually would like to have the world a certain way. We all repeatedly have to face the fact that it is not often patterned according to our wishes. The Kinsey report surprised many people who were not aware of the frequency with which the standards of others contrasted with their own. I would suspect that when the long-heralded book comes out disclosing the sexual pattern of women in our culture, many people will be even more surprised. It is important that those of us working with young people face first of all, realistically, the actual facts, try then to understand them and finally deal constructively with our understanding.

Dr. Kennedy suggests in her review also that if the attitude expressed in the book were accepted, the role of those interested in the field of social hygiene would be a futile one. I would feel quite differently.

As indicated in the book, I have many questions about the value or the wisdom of group discussions for the purpose of giving sexual orientation to high school students. There, in my experience, it is more important and safer to handle the problems with the individual. It would seem that one function of the social hygiene group is the continual evaluation of the techniques used in helping high school students finally formulate their own sexual philosophy. Certainly an equally important task is to help parents and other adults dealing with the high school group to understand the problems behind the externally manifested confusion of the young person.

Sexual information given within the framework of a broader course in psychology, physiology or biology undoubtedly has some validity, particularly if it is given before the onset of adolescent confusion. Again, however, how this is done should be constantly re-evaluated.

Why segregation?

One of the questions that is very tantalizing is why—if we are so convinced of the value of such discussions and try to reassure ourselves that they do not have ramifications beyond the point of focus we have established—do we tend to separate boys and girls for such discussions when they reach the high school level? The answer often given is that boys and girls are more comfortable and feel freer to talk under those circumstances. Does that not have some deeper implications than we superficially recognize?

After all, the common goal of all people working with teen-agers is to help them mature into healthy adulthood. We must guard ourselves against being over-confident and being too certain that we have in our generation found the answer to attain this goal. In spite of our best intentions we still see neuroses develop under our eyes. Until that is no longer true we must accept the tentativeness in any approach we recommend.

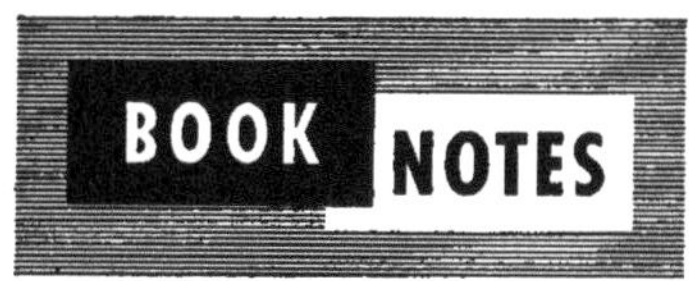

by Elizabeth B. McQuaid

Adolescence, by Marguerite Malm and Olis G. Jamison. New York, McGraw-Hill, 1952. 501p. $5.00.

Teen-agers can't help acting like adolescents—they *are* adolescents! This book is for adults "to help them understand what the adolescent needs to live wholesomely and happily, and to show them how these needs may be met."

The authors give us a picture of the adolescent as he is today—his reactions to the tensions and strains produced by the demands and patterns of his peers, which are often in conflict with the demands and patterns of the adults who influence him. Definite and workable suggestions show adults how to help the adolescent by understanding when to help him, when to leave him alone. The reader is urged to remember how he felt and how he reacted in similar situations when he was an adolescent.

Social and emotional, personal and vocational adjustments of the adolescent are discussed. Boys and girls in this period of physical, mental, emotional and social growth must meet the problems involved in adjusting to life values.

Parents, teachers and others who are living with and seeking to help adolescents will be more aware of their responsibilities as they read this book.

Mrs. Corinne J. Grimsley
Extension Specialist in Family Relations
N. C. State College of Agriculture and Engineering

Health Instruction Yearbook, edited by Oliver E. Byrd, M.D. California, Stanford University Press, 1952. 232p. $3.50.

The contents—273 condensations selected from about 1,500 health articles—include Col. Forrest Braden's article, Steady Pressure on the Prostitution Racket, from the May, 1952, issue of the *Journal of Social Hygiene;* venereal disease figures for fiscal 1951 as reported to the U.S. Public Health Service; and an abstract on the FPM test for syphilis which points out that the test, in giving a negative report, may foster a false sense of security.

The Single Woman, by John Laurence. New York, Duell, Sloan and Pearce, 1952. 267p. $3.50.

Explaining his services as confidante of "more women than the average man meets, even casually, in a lifetime," the author of this pertinent and useful opus says, "I am neither a gigolo nor a psychiatrist." His occupation is listed simply as Catholic priest.

Probably the closest approach to what might be called the "text" of this volume appears on page 266, "There are mysteries of physical pain and moral evil in this world that only unquestioning faith in the wisdom and goodness of an inscrutable God can make bearable." As for an epitomization of the author's more mundane thesis (while admitting that "as a priest" he has "certain very definite views"), two sentences from his preface seem most apt: ". . . I feel very strongly that unless a woman has honest motives for not marrying she should marry if she can. If she cannot, I am certain that she will find complete virginity a far less frustrating solution of her problem than any of the other alternatives which will inevitably be suggested."

In examining the attitudes of those single women who feel that lovers should be taken if husbands are unavailable, Father Laurence claims to think and judge as "a philosopher rather than as a priest." It may be possible for him to effectuate this definite dissociation but such intra-personality changes are as difficult to make as they are rare. Nevertheless, we find his book decidedly readable and plan to use it whenever indicated.

In 1942 Dr. Ruth Reed of Catholic University authored, and Macmillan published, a volume with this same title, *The Single Woman*. Though her style was not as smooth as Father Laurence's, her advice and suggestions ran along similar lines. Both authors write from celibate backgrounds. This may or may not lend authority to their admonitions, depending on the training, experience and belief of each reader. Hence, some case work conferring might well precede reading recommendations.

Ray H. Everett, Executive Secretary
Social Hygiene Society of the District of Columbia

Getting Along with Parents, by Katherine Whiteside-Taylor. A Junior Life Adjustment Booklet. Chicago, Science Research Associates, 1952. 40p. 40¢.

This booklet assures teen-agers that everyone has problems with parents.

When boys and girls try to see themselves as their parents see them, they find their problems become less difficult. The booklet recommends the family council, which gives each member of the family a chance to present his case and to talk over democratically the problems that each sees from a different point of view.

The American Family, by Ruth Shonle Cavan. New York, Crowell, 1953. 658p. $5.00.

Readers who want a survey of the contemporary American family as a base for their social hygiene interests can probably find no better current source than Dr. Cavan's book. Statistics and interpretative data are well blended, the profuse family literature culled and integrated, and the totality presented in succinct and readable fashion.

The American Family is, however, a textbook, as the author's many tables, graphs, footnotes and multisyllabic vocabulary won't let us forget. Perhaps the blame for the academic tone of the book should be placed on the market, dictated by the pedantic needs of text-adopting instructors, not on Dr. Cavan.

The author is particularly skillful in presenting pertinent facts and relatively unbiased descriptions regarding controversial issues. The currently confused family values of the middle class, which some other authors see fit to glorify, get little support from Dr. Cavan. On page 497, for example, she points out the "need to redefine divorce as a valid method of ending an unsatisfactory marriage rather than as a catastrophe because of personal failure and broken vows."

On the premarital sexual question, the author partially bows to Calvinistic mores, but is courageous enough to state that "no widespread social disaster results from premarital sex relations" and that the undesirable effects that may take place are only "*possible* results of premarital sex behavior for *individuals in whose social world it is disapproved*" (page 390; italics ours).

It may be true at times that Dr. Cavan too readily swallows the glib maxims of parent-child "experts." The realistically struggling parent probably won't find much practical help from reading that "the adequate parent is personally mature and well adjusted" and that his relationship to the child should be both "warm and responsible" (page 529). The question is "how?". The author merely reflects, however, the current vague state of our knowledge in such family areas and should be held no more to account than the rest of us for the inadequacy of contemporary family research findings.

Robert A. Harper, Ph.D.
Washington, D.C.

A Marriage Manual, by Hannah Stone, M.D., and Abraham Stone, M.D. New York, Simon and Schuster, 1935, 1937, 1952. 301p. $3.50.

This third edition and thirtieth printing is a revision and amplification of previous issues. A new chapter, Happiness in Marriage, has been added, and the original form—hypothetical consultation in dialogue style—has been retained.

Living in Balance, by Frank S. Caprio, M.D. Washington, Arundel, 1951. 246p. $3.75.

The main purpose of this book is to show how nervous breakdown can be prevented. The author indicates that there are not enough psychiatrists to treat all those who need this help and that many of the ten million neurotics are capable of helping themselves. The root-causes of many of our emotional conflicts are explained in non-technical language.

Problems related to sex, among others, are given careful consideration in many of the 31 chapters, specifically in the following: Avoiding an Unhappy Marriage, Nerves Strain Marriage Ties, Jealousy, Four Types of Neurotic Wives, Four Types of Neurotic Husbands, The Right Attitude Toward Sex, A Bad Marriage Can Become a Good Marriage, and Love Must Be Earned.

This book is well-written, interesting and easy to understand. By applying many of the principles of mental hygiene contained in this book, the reader will better understand himself and other people, and if his complexes are too deep-seated, he may better comprehend the need for seeking the competent help of a trained specialist. It should be a helpful aid to the general reader as well as to the educator, social worker, youth leader and church worker.

H. F. Kilander
Specialist for Health Education
U. S. Office of Education

Making and Keeping Friends, by William C. Menninger, M.D. A Life Adjustment Booklet. Chicago, Science Research Associates, 1952. 48p. 40¢.

From this concise and bright booklet teen-agers will gain insight into some of the positive and negative aspects of making friends. It points out that we have to learn to give love to receive it, and that we learn first from our parents, then from our playmates and later from our friends of both sexes. Unresponsive parents can build a wall within their children that makes them afraid of being hurt, and that insulates them from the give-and-take of later relationships.

Marriage itself is the closest kind of friendship, requiring more discrimination than previous choices of friends, and growing out of mutual interests and attraction.

There are a few warning notes at the end. The phase of emotional "arrested development" that some teen-agers go through is dangerous if they become too attracted to one person of their own sex. New attachments or the help of a counselor may be the answer. Another danger spot lies in the normal desire of young people to follow the crowd. This is fine if the crowd's standards are all right.

The Natural Superiority of Women, by Ashley Montagu. New York, Macmillan, 1953. 205p. $3.50.

The author, a professor of anthropology at Rutgers, marshals a host of facts to prove woman's natural superiority over man and breaks down many myths of male superiority . . . to foster more cooperation and appreciation between the sexes and less competition.

He says that, as child-bearer and child-rearer, woman has the most significant job in the world, a fact that it would be well for man to appreciate. He says that the false standards man sets for woman result in marital breakdown. He believes man would profit exceedingly if he accepted his responsibilities as husband and father more conscientiously.

His iconoclastic chapters on myths of superiority are, on the whole, convincing, but his recommendation that married people enjoy a four-hour working day (both men and women) to cement their personal relationships is, as he recognizes, too futuristic for popular acceptance. With less repetition the book could still make its point that man should not accept complacently the present position of the sexes, that good relations between the sexes are basic to good human relations in all societies.

Exploring Your Personality, by William E. Henry. A Better Living Booklet. Chicago, Science Research Associates, 1952. 48p. 40¢. Special quantity rates.

Teen-agers want to have dates and to get along with their friends, their parents and other adults. But they can't improve their relationships until they find out what they themselves are really like, explains the author, an associate professor at the University of Chicago.

"Your personality is the sum total of you," he says. And it's personality rather than looks that counts in our relations with the opposite sex.

Although parental love and discipline—and parental mistakes—all help to shape young personalities, nothing is irrevocable. The smart teen-ager, once he understands why he acts as he does, can go about changing himself . . . the teen years are good personality stock-taking years, flexible, eager, experimental.

How to Make a Success of Your Marriage, by Eustace Chesser. New York, Roy, 1953. 103p. $2.00.

Doctor Chesser says that "to a great extent you have to learn marriage as you go along," for it has a changing, day-to-day pattern. Some chapters are The Meaning of Marriage, Planning in Advance, Difficulties in the Way, The Middle Years, all of which are practical in their approach.

Lives in Progress, by Robert W. White. New York, Dryden, 1952. 376p. $3.00.

This study of the natural growth of the personalities of three relatively normal people at two different stages in their lives incorporates the biological, psychodynamic and the social and cultural points of view. These investigations are not clinical case histories, but were initiated by the author while teaching at Harvard.

The role of sex in the development of these three people is considered as part of the whole picture. One of the subjects recognized his sexual promiscuity for what it was—a means of escaping from his anxieties, a shoring up of his battered ego. The marriages of the others are discussed.

The author is insistent that man is not only shaped by forces; he is a shaping force, too.

Your Children's Manners, by Rhoda W. Bacmeister. A Better Living Booklet. Chicago, Science Research Associates, 1952. 49p. 40¢.

For parents and teachers, this booklet points out that long-term association with good manners will smooth out much of the adolescent's confusion about dating and general social relationships. The stresses and strains of adolescence are reflected in emotional outbursts that should not be met with answering outbursts, but with reason and understanding born of a realization that the adolescent is reaching toward independence and adulthood. A serene, confidence-building atmosphere in the home is basic.

Some chapter heads are *Friendliness comes first, Sincerity and manners, Etiquette in the nursery* and *Adolescence and manners.*

Preventive Medicine and Public Health, by Wilson G. Smillie. New York, Macmillan, 1946, 1952. Rev. 603p. $7.50.

A revision of an earlier edition, this book contains a chapter on the venereal diseases, specifically syphilis, gonorrhea, lymphogranuloma venereum and chancroid. Syphilis is covered briefly as to epidemiology, prevalence, diagnosis, control, prevention, premarital safeguards, prenatal safeguards and modification of control methods.

The chapter reports a sharp decline in late latent syphilis, a constant level for early latent syphilis and a rapidly falling rate for primary and secondary syphilis—which, the book cautions, may be attributable to treatment by private physicians and lack of reporting. The author concludes that "the most effective preventive measure in syphilis is earliest possible recognition of the disease followed by immediate, adequate treatment."

Your Child and His Problems: A Basic Guide for Parents, by Joseph D. Teicher, M.D. Boston, Little, Brown, 1953. 302p. $3.75.

The author, director of the Child Guidance Clinic of Los Angeles, writes this book for parents, doctors, psychologists and all who deal with children, to point out to them the psychological problems of children and parents. Among the chapters are The Painful Path to Adulthood, Sex and the Child, and Family Stresses and Strains.

Like many before him, Dr. Teicher recognizes that sex education begins with parents' attitudes, and emphasizes that "one must consider not only the child's readiness for information, but the relevance of that information to his thoughts and interests."

There are an annotated table of contents and index.

A Sex Guide to Happy Marriage, by Edward F. Griffith, M.R.C.S. New York, Emerson, 1952. 352p. $3.00.

This guide to the sexual side of married life is written for those about to be married as well as those already married, for however long a time. Robert Latou Dickinson, M.D., introduces the book, and Robert W. Laidlaw, M.D., and Frances W. Dow conclude it with a chapter on marriage counseling in the United States. An appendix on pertinent services and an index complete the volume.

Some chapter headings . . . anatomy and physiology, problems of the engaged couple, control of conception, abortion, some male problems (including a discussion of venereal disease) and sex education.

Our Children Today, edited by Sidonie M. Gruenberg and the staff of the Child Study Association of America. New York, Viking Press, 1952. 366p. $3.95.

One article by the staff of the Child Study Association, prepared by Katherine E. Hyam, traces a child's emotional growth from infancy and stresses that a parent's feelings about sex are exceedingly apparent to the child. Sex education should begin whenever a child asks a pertinent question—which he shall probably ask over and over again. Parental guidance, rivalry, group identification and the need for independence are treated in that order.

Healthy sexuality, the positive goal of today's sex education, involves a gradual process of integrated growth.

This symposium, a successor to *Our Children—A Handbook for Parents,* includes among its participants such names as Gruenberg, Baumgartner, Gesell, Langmuir, Auerbach and Frank.

GRIN AND BEAR IT by George Lichty

Courtesy of the Chicago Sun-Times Syndicate

"You sure the 'bees and flowers' story isn't obsolete, dear? . . . must have been some advancement along that line since we were young."

journal of SOCIAL HYGIENE

vol. 39 october 1953 no. 7

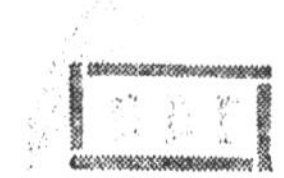

IN THIS ISSUE

OCTOBER 1953

About our cover . . .

Norman Rockwell's Red Feather Family. Twenty-fifth of a series of Journal covers on family life . . . photograph courtesy of Community Chests and Councils of America and the United Defense Fund.

Harriett Scantland, ***Editor***

Elizabeth McQuaid, Assistant Editor

Eleanor Shenehon, Editorial Consultant

THE JOURNAL OF SOCIAL HYGIENE

official periodical of the American Social Hygiene Association, published monthly except July, August and September at the Boyd Printing Company, Inc., 374 Broadway, Albany 7, N. Y. Acceptance for mailing at the special rate of postage provided for in Section 1103, Act of October 3, 1917. Entered as second-class matter at the Post Office at Albany, N. Y., March 23, 1922.

The JOURNAL does not necessarily endorse or assume responsibility for opinions expressed in articles, nor does the reviewing of a book imply its recommendation by the American Social Hygiene Association. Subscription price: $3.00 per year. Single copy: 35¢.

Red Feather Nickels

Consider the lowly nickel—hardy and practical as the alloy it comes from, stamped with the noblest symbols of democracy. Multiply this nickel by over 5 billion—the goal of the Red Feather campaign this year, the means of serving 1,700 communities next year. And the Red Feather campaign, like the nickel, bears the impression of enduring idealism . . .

E Pluribus Unum—One united appeal for 18,500 services . . . no waste, fair distribution.

Jefferson—The Red Feather, too, symbolizes the democratic way.

Liberty—The Red Feather's staunch respect for the individual leaves each community free to choose what services it will support.

In God We Trust—With the Red Feather, the American Social Hygiene Association helps to build America's spiritual resources . . . through strong, stable family life and a wholesome environment for soldier, defense worker, you, your children, your neighbor.

United States of America—Resounding words, they are no more than America's people, 160,000,000 men, women and children aided through one United Defense Fund.

Your nickels can be Red Feather nickels. Save them, watch them grow, send them as dollars to join others in a crescendo of service for all. E Pluribus Unum!

E. A. Roberts

Former president of Community Chests and Councils and of the United Defense Fund. Lawyer, insurance company president, inspiring volunteer.

All together for defense

For peace and freedom: faith and united action

by E. A. Roberts

The last time I opened my mouth in Washington I was standing up in this hotel, speaking to several hundred Washingtonians gathered for the kick-off dinner of the Community Chest campaign. The subject assigned me bore the modest title, "To the Nation and the World."

Since that time, I'm glad to say, I've heard a good many better speeches coming out of Washington on this subject. And I hope to hear many more. That is, if it is true, as some say, that the new administration is just learning the ropes in Washington, and they fondly hope and expect that it will take them at least 20 years to do so.

I didn't feel at that dinner that I was talking to the nation and the world, and as far as I know the Voice of America didn't put me on. I figured that I was talking to a bunch of veteran volunteers, like myself, and I was glad to give them what comfort and cheer I could. But perhaps in a sense I *was* talking to the nation, because there before me was a group of men and women who were demonstrating one of the oldest and finest of our national characteristics . . . and that was a bit of selfless volunteer service to their community through the Chest campaign.

And not only service to their community, but to the nation and the world. For among those dollars they were setting out to raise for the local day nurseries and clinics and Scouts and Y's and services to the old and the sick and the handicapped — among those dollars some were ticketed for the United Defense Fund. They went far beyond the city limits, along with other dollars — from Cleveland and Seattle and Akron and hundreds of other home towns.

They were busy dollars and they did many things. Maybe they helped turn on a light in the window of a USO club in Alaska or in some spot in the Caribbean. Maybe they helped put *out* a light in the window of a brothel off Black Alley, USA. Or buttoned up a warm wooly coat on a shivering Korean kid. Of course they were deflated dollars — worth about 53¢, I'm told, compared to the old-fashioned 100¢-dollar. But I think every UDF dollar was up to par in that very old-fashioned currency, human kindness.

I'm glad to be back in Washington again. As I look at you I see some familiar faces from St. Paul and Chicago and San Francisco, and a lot of other cities I know and like. I wouldn't be surprised if once again, I'm talking to the nation. If the Voice of America is listening, it can safely tell the world. The ears of the world, friendly ears and hostile ears, are bent in the direction of the United States these days . . . and it would do both kinds good to tune in on a meeting like this.

Pilgrims all

Let me say again that it's good for all of us to be in Washington. There's still a bit of the pilgrim in most Americans, and Washington is a national magnet for our pilgrimages. We flock here for all sorts of reasons . . . to trudge the historic corridors; to gaze respectfully at the hallowed documents; to peer up at the needle point of the Washington monument; to stand in a kind of awe at the feet of French's colossal Lincoln. Or maybe we come just to see the cherry trees in blossom.

But no matter what our mission, or whether we're young and idealistic, or a little old and cynical and world-weary, few of us pilgrims can escape feeling a little stir of the blood, a glow in the heart, a refreshing lift of the spirit. This is our town, too.

Of course, some pilgrims are too busy to feel any of this. They're the ones who bear in their pockets letters to Congressmen. They warm chairs in the waiting rooms at the Pentagon. They buttonhole senators. They *want* something. Sometimes they're known as the "special interest" groups — the pressure boys.

Well, we needn't look down our noses at them. We too represent a special interest — the health and welfare of our communities back home. And we're a "pressure group" too. Except that we're not putting our pressure on the Pentagon or Capitol Hill. Our business here does not call for legislation, or appropriation, or even senatorial investigation. The only pressure we'll feel in this gathering is the pressure in ourselves, as responsible leaders in our own communities.

Now I admit that a great deal of drivel is uttered about lay leadership, particularly in this Chest-Council movement. You might think we had been divinely appointed. But the truth is that without quite knowing why, we found ourselves one day sitting in a meeting. There was a silence, and to fill the void we say something. Before we know it, we are chairman of the next campaign.

Lights for USO clubs.

I used to think this was an isolated phenomenon that happened only to me. But as the harness has bitten more deeply into my shoulder blades, and I have attended more and more national gatherings, I see my opposite number all over the map. And I conclude that it just can't be fortuitous. There must be something behind it — some design, some plan, by an all-wise Providence to catch, time and put to good sound use what could otherwise be a bunch of free enterprising, free wheeling vice-presidents and insurance hucksters.

So I am not discouraged when I look about me, not to see any Knights in Shining Armor. I know you for what you are — ordinary fellows like me. And yet you bear, and rightly, the stamp of leadership. And it serves you right. For years you've been yelling for more topflight business leadership in Washington. And here you are!

The torch of leadership

This is all to the good. I do not know what qualities of organizational genius, executive and administrative skill you may possess, but I am quite sure that you have one essential quality — the respect of your fellow citizens, and the power, in your own sphere, of influencing people by your words, your personality, your attitude and your example.

Your country urgently needs these qualities today, and I ask you to use them with all the powers in you, in support of our national defense effort.

Now most of us realize that national defense is not to be achieved by the aggressive might of armed forces. Nor is it the modern equivalent of a fort behind which we can hide, snugly girdled by a network of radar burglar alarms. The goal of American foreign and military policy is a positive and purposeful one — to build a just and lasting peace, and to help create the world political and economic order on which such a peace depends. It is a task of unparalleled difficulty and complexity. And with all the admiration in the world for President Eisenhower, Mr. Dulles and General Mark Clark, they can't pull it off — without us, the people. The Defense Department, the State Department, NATO, Point IV, the International Bank are all part of it, but they're just so much dead machinery unless they have the faith, understanding and the active support of all the American people.

And they're not getting it in full measure. And I'll tell you how I know. Because for three years now, I've been privileged to push and pull, sweat and bleed in the company of some wonderful people, including many of you here today, for the United Defense Fund. It's been a desperate, uphill fight every step of the way, and it wouldn't have been if the American people really knew the score of the national defense effort.

I mention the UDF because, in a small way, I believe the public attitude toward it reflects accurately the public attitude toward the total national effort. The UDF is, in effect, off the same piece of goods and the threads are the same — services to the Armed Forces, to defense communities, and to our allies overseas.

We hear quite a bit of talk about "the hard shell of apathy" that seems to encase the American people in their attitude toward national defense. Well, what can *we* do about it?

Seems to me we have two choices . . . we can either crack the shell or crawl in under it. Personally, I look better cracking than crawling. You do too.

For if there ever were experts at the crack-the-shell game, we're in this room. We are experts in overcoming apathy. There never was a time when the American people — or any people — weren't apathetic about reaching into their pockets and drawing out money to give away. And yet last year these same apathetic givers reached down and dug up $260,000,000 for Community Chests and United Funds. *It can be done, and you know how.*

Hand in hand with apathy, a sort of jittery pessimism creeps through our fine land. We are living in a day when the world seems to be teetering somewhere between heaven and hell, and for some peculiar reason a great many people seem to be leaning toward hell. Any time the USSR really wants to step up its propaganda to convince hesitating nations of the imminent decay and dissolution of the corrupt capitalist system, it has only to take the words out of our own mouths. We seem to be so busy condemning, exposing and lacerating each other with charges, countercharges and smears that any harsh remarks from Vishinsky tend to sound like "God bless you." Having discovered a few termites nibbling at the pillars of democracy, some people seem determined to hack down the pillars to examine, the termites scientifically. I sense a jittery, nervous, edgy mood in the land that is infectious, and I don't think I caught it by just working for the United Defense Fund.

From faith

The best antidote that I know for hell is heaven. The best cure for doubt is faith. And the mental health people tell us that the best way to resolve negative doubt and fear is to take positive action.

I'd like to say something about faith. Of all the people in the world, we ought to have the most of it.

- *We can have faith in our national goal.* Because that goal is to establish a just and stable peace for all people. Around our council tables there is no Caesar, no Alexander, no Hitler, scheming to grab territory, enslave people and bring home the loot.
- *We can have faith in our spiritual inheritance.* And by that I mean the central religious concepts that human life has value, with dignity, and that men are brothers and that God is their father. That concept was not imposed on us by a Central Committee . . . it has come down through the ages, from the sages and prophets of Judaism, and to some of us it was most perfectly taught and lived by Jesus Christ. It is embodied in every ethical concept that distinguishes man from animal, and civilization from the jungle. Abuse it, deny it, crucify it, that spiritual inheritance is alive in you. Perhaps it will surprise you to know that it was what brought you here today.
- *We can have faith in our institutions.* The spiritual concept is written into the Declaration of Independence and the Constitution of the United States. It finds expression in the law of the land, in our schools, churches, hospitals, scientific laboratories, and all the good and helpful services that men and women of understanding and insight have created.
- *We can have faith in the search* for a method of achieving peace by something other than war. And let me tell you this is something new. And I suggest it for the quiet contemplation of those who think we've explored everything, discovered everything, invented everything and tamed everything, and that there are no challenges left for the adventurous spirit of man.

The United Nations is a bit of exploration that may well out-Columbus Christopher Columbus. He believed the world was round, and proved it against a good deal of evidence to the contrary. Through storm and stress and doubt and apathy, Columbus lived to see a new coastline emerge out of the mist. We too dimly see a new continent ahead — the vague outline of a world at peace with itself. The only question is . . . are we smart enough navigators?

Universal as the brotherhood of man is a father's love for his child.

I think we are . . . if we pull for the shore together. And here again I must refer to the United Defense Fund because it represents in its small way the kind of unity that our national defense effort so desperately needs. If the United States is to be worthy of the frightful responsibility of world leadership, the gears of the nation simply have to mesh. The statesmen, the generals, the economists, the scientists, the industrialists and the farmers have to be in on the act. This is the first order of the nation's business.

And the nation's business is UDF business. The United Defense Fund was created because responsible leaders in human welfare, to their everlasting credit, saw what that small cloud over Korea might mean, and looked to their umbrellas. They had reason to know that national defense is more than marching men and more than planes and guns, that it is also the mobilization of the courage and spirit of people, and that it calls for united action by all community forces to strengthen and sustain the health, welfare and morale of the men in uniform, the defense worker and the home front.

We can be proud that the founders of the United Defense Fund didn't rush out and start a new agency. They had the sense to make use of a tested instrument of unity which was the Chest plan and structure. The UDF was a true child of federation, and I'd like to remind you that it looks very much like its dad. It takes the same principles — planning, budgeting and financing — that have worked well for more than 30 years locally, and applies them to the national community.

And I can tell you that since working for the United Defense Fund, I have had a good deal more appreciation for the headaches of United Nations. For in the UDF we have the same problems . . . strong national agencies, with their full share of pride, jealousy and individual drive, and always lurking in the background the itch to go it alone. That they haven't gone it alone — but have voluntarily sacrificed something of the individual freedom of action, and are pulling together in federation's harness — is something of an accomplishment.

But the going has been tough, and still is. The point is, will UDF make the grade? If we can't demonstrate the strength of unity in the relatively small field of health and welfare, where we are the so-called experts, we can't very gracefully gripe about the lack of unity in the Army, Navy and Air Force, or in the North Atlantic Treaty Organization, or in the United Nations.

Faith and unity — short words, but loaded, I've tossed out at you. Here comes a phrase — *Positive action for peace and freedom.* Not just talking, but doing.

Quiz programs are the vogue right now. What would we say if a quizmaster shot this question at us?

What have you done this day for peace and freedom? Not what have you read, mind you, what news analyst have you listened to, but what have you *done?*

I can imagine some of the answers:

- I bought a defense bond.
- I signed up as a civil defense worker.
- I sealed a government contract.
- I gave a pint of blood to the Red Cross blood bank.
- I'm paying a whale of an income tax.
- I'm running an essential business, paying high wages, helping maintain a high standard of living.

'd say that all these belong honestly on the list, and I'd add another:

- I'm an active volunteer in my hometown Chest. I came to Washington at considerable effort to see what I could do along with other volunteers to extend the feeling we have for our home communities to that bigger community, our nation.

Pride in the home town— can it stretch to cover the nation?

Our national community

It's a big idea to grasp, this concept of a national community, hard to feel . . . except, that is, in time of war. Must we really wait for the rockets' red glare, the bombs bursting in air until we feel it? It's so easy to be conscious of the glorious fact that you're from Texas, by God, and proud of it; or from Chicago, or from Virginia, suh. So hard, when things are running along normally, to stretch that pride to cover the nation. In the USO, particularly, we have to wrestle with that problem constructively. There are still a few Chest budget committees, for example, who say, "Yes, sure the USO is a good thing, but we don't have one in our town. Our givers want to see where their money goes."

Do we always have to see things with our physical eyes? Isn't that a part of leadership, to help people see with the inward eyes of imagination and understanding? Faith is the substance of things hoped for, the evidence of things not seen. Haven't we a responsibility to help Americans see the invisible?

The hordes of invisible men

There are a lot of invisible men walking the pavements of cities coast to coast these days. Literally invisible, sometimes, since they're permitted to swap their uniforms for civilian clothes the minute they're off duty.

It was different in my warrior days. We loved to get into those khaki outfits, wind up our puttees and strut our stuff. But nowadays some young fellows feel that the uniform is not a badge of pride so much as a badge of second-class citizenship. Is this true? It sounds pretty bad to me, if it is. Because these fellows are first-class citizens diverted for the moment to an emergency job, but with every hope and expectation of returning to civilian life.

Invisible men or first-class citizens? The clear-eyed see their worth.

We are proud of the fact that we're not a militaristic nation; we have no large, permanent force of professional fighting men, no military caste system. But the surest way to get one is to cut off servicemen from their civilian ties and throw them into a separate herd . . . to throw them together on their own resources, a group apart from the normal life of the community.

Defense is indivisible. The man in uniform may hail from Brooklyn or Dubuque or Seattle. But he didn't sign up to defend Brooklyn or Dubuque or Seattle. He signed up for America. And until every one of our communities realizes that simple fact we're a long way from feeling the sense of national community that we've got to feel if this national defense effort is either national, *or* defense *or* an effort. The USO speaks for the invisible man, invisible only to those suffering from cataracts on the eyes of imagination.

There's quite a vogue these days to put one's personal faith into statements headed "I Believe." Maybe it's because we so often are confused and befuddled that it makes us feel better to get something down on paper. That great newscaster, Ed Murrow, started the vogue, I think, with his broadcasts. And now he has collected and edited a book called "This I

Believe." In it are the personal confessions of faith from men and women of all walks of life — writers, teachers, preachers, businessmen, scientists, generals, actors, musicians and baseball players.

For some reason I was not invited to contribute to this volume, although I note with pride that a fellow-Philadelphian ~~and a~~ Community Chest crony of mine, Albert Nesbitt, was. I am a forgiving fellow, so I have decided to contribute a chapter anyhow. It is an honest statement of a community volunteer, rather well worn but still trudging along. I'd feel better about my essay if you'd all sign it too. Here it is — It's a good deal shorter and simpler than the one Jackie Robinson wrote:

I believe that national defense is the first order of business for every citizen.

I believe in health and welfare services to the home front, and to those who defend the home front far from home.

I believe in the volunteer spirit, as the spark which lighted the torch for the Goddess of Liberty, and can keep it lighted.

I believe in the power of personal leadership, and will put whatever I have at the disposal of my country.

I believe in my country, its fundamental concepts, its institutions, and its people, including myself.

I believe that national defense is not just an escape from war, but includes also a positive search for a fair and just peace for all the world.

I believe in the united way of doing things, whether it's raising money for health and welfare, or raising hell with communism. And finally,

I believe in the last verse of the *Star Spangled Banner* as well as the first. I know the first verse by heart but I tend to mumble the last. And yet it's worth knowing by heart especially in days of national defense:

And thus be it ever, when free men shall stand
Between their loved homes and the war's desolation
Crowned with victory and peace, may the heav'n rescued
land
Bless the power that has made and *preserved us a nation.*

Preserved us a nation. That interests me especially, because I'm from Philadelphia. Philadelphia is a pilgrimage town, too. We have a good many points of interest to show pilgrims. I could lead you, for instance, into a smallish, severely plain little room where a group of men met and created a nation. I'm sure they would resent the idea we hear uttered so often nowadays to the effect that "these are the most critical days ever to face our nation."

You see, the Philadelphia fellows thought *they* were living in the most critical days. They had practically nothing to go on, no "vast national resources," no industrial empire, no allies, no money to speak of . . . and a price on their heads besides. But they created the nation. And they've left it to us to preserve.

The Star Spangled Banner is right. "May the heav'n rescued land bless the power that has made and preserved us a nation."

Some of that power will certainly have to be generated in just plain citizens like us. Bless us, too, and more power to us!

CREDITS

Photo by Fabian Bachrach, p. 290.

Photos courtesy of the United Service Organizations, p. 292, 329.

Photos courtesy of Standard Oil Co. (New Jersey), p. 295, 297.

Drawing courtesy of Infantry Journal (Stephen S. Story, Jr., artist), p. 298.

Photo courtesy of Pitt Photo Library (Libsohn), p. 305.

Photo courtesy of Hawaii Visitors Bureau, p. 312.

HAVE YOU . . .

Renewed your ASHA membership?

Renewed your subscription to the JOURNAL OF SOCIAL HYGIENE?

A. Frank Brewer, M.D.

Chief of the California state health department's bureau of venereal diseases; special consultant to the U. S. Indian Service; visiting lecturer at the University of California.

Dangers of the Antibiotic Cocktail in VD Control

by A. Frank Brewer, M.D.

What are some of the factors influencing favorably the long-term trend in the decline of syphilis?

Antibiotic therapy has made a contribution, but not dramatically nor alone, as pointed out by Dr. Joseph E. Moore in his article entitled "An Evaluation of Public Health Measures for the Control of Syphilis," which appeared in the March, 1951, issue of the *American Journal of Syphilis, Gonorrhea and Venereal Diseases.* The decrease in syphilis incidence in Europe and the United States began almost a century ago and has continued downward since then except during periods of war and civil unrest. Factors other than effective therapy have been responsible for this progress. The fact that the character of syphilis has changed from a virulent acute type of infection to one of great chronicity suggests that by a process of gradual adaptation the virulence of the syphilis organism has decreased, while individual resistance to the disease has increased. Other important factors in the decreasing incidence of syphilis are attributed to the progressive improvement in socio-economic conditions and the application of modern public health control measures.

The modern public health program in venereal disease control includes the finding and treating of infected people, as well as making available to the public information regarding the venereal diseases. These measures have been effective in reducing infant and adult morbidity, mortality and admissions to mental hospitals. These reductions were apparent long before antibiotic therapy and actually began in this country with the arsenical era. Is it wise, now, to curtail these efforts?

California's control efforts

Public health efforts in California are reflected in epidemiologic reports which show that an average of 60,000 reports of contacts and suspects of venereal disease have been processed through the State Department of Public Health each year for the last five years . . . 300,000 individuals in need of medical examination because of exposure to infected individuals or because of a positive routine laboratory test. In addition, approximately 1,500,000 individuals in California are screened annually for syphilis by means of routine laboratory tests, and in each of the last five years the state has distributed enough penicillin to treat an average of 40,000 cases of syphilis and gonorrhea annually. Certainly these are facts that cannot be ignored and show that the public health program has been effective.

California's local health departments have curtailed their venereal disease control programs in varying degrees. Clinic hours, medical and nursing staffs, and even epidemiological activities have been reduced . . . not because the number of patients appearing at clinics has decreased materially, but because of the decrease in the number of patient-visits required to complete treatment.

Patients can now be treated in a period ranging from one to 15 days, with 95% completing treatment in the required time. Before the advent of penicillin, treatment of syphilis ranged from one and one-half to three years, with only 25% completing treatment.

Case-holding under the long-term treatment routine was a major problem, whereas today it is a minor one. Under the long-term treatment, patient-visits were cumulative; therefore, it was necessary to continuously increase the staff. Today this is not true and adjustments have logically been made.

In numbers of patients the fires still burn almost as brightly as ever, and the staff cannot be reduced beyond a reasonable point if we are to continue an adequate control program. The accelerated decline in postwar venereal disease incidence stopped in 1950, when the rate of decrease slowed markedly to the present incidence, approximating that of the prewar days. Therefore, too much optimism is not yet justified.

Trend same for 50 years in America

The unprecedented decline in reported cases of syphilis and gonorrhea during the last seven years has created undue optimism for control in most quarters, with the antibiotics being given great credit in this situation. Are we ready to accept the statement that syphilis is a vanishing disease and that gonorrhea and the other venereal diseases are no longer of public health significance? Undue optimism is, I believe, unwarranted and unrealistic. Neither should we be overly pessimistic. The truth probably lies somewhere between the two extremes.

To predict the speedy eradication of diseases as complex in their clinical and epidemiological aspects as the venereal diseases is indeed unrealistic, while to deny the widespread use of the antibiotic cocktail's influence in the control program is like hiding one's head in the sand. However, proof of this influence is as yet wholly lacking, except by certain inferences.

GRAPH I

VENEREAL DISEASE INCIDENCE RATES
NAVY AND MARINE CORPS, 1900-1949

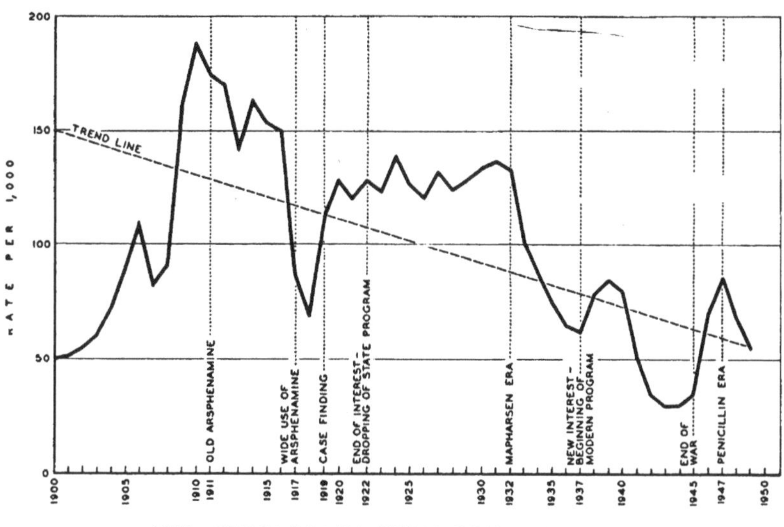

SOURCE DEPARTMENT OF THE NAVY, BUREAU OF MEDICINE AND SURGERY, MEDICAL STATISTICS DIVISION

Graph I shows that the same sort of phenomena has occurred each time a new drug and new interest has been generated in the control of the venereal diseases. (This graph is based on Navy morbidity, probably the best statistics we have in America.) Note that reported cases of venereal disease steadily increased from 1900 to 1910 — when use of old arsphenamine started — and lasted until 1916, the first deadline in our 50-year period. World-wide publicity was given Ehrlich's discovery and thousands of people sought therapy. Interest waned because of cost, toxicity and a relatively high mortality. With the discovery of neo-arsphenamine, again widespread interest was aroused because of lessened toxicity and greater ease of therapy; it lasted until 1922, the end of World War I and the beginning of the first venereal disease control program in this country.

Ten years then intervened with little interest, and sporadic work was done. Treatment was given when requested but with little case-finding either by the profession or by demand of the public or health officials.

History repeats itself with the advent of mapharsen, still less toxic and more easily administered. In 1932 mapharsen was developed, and the Navy and civilians immediately started its experimental use. Again great interest was aroused in the venereal disease program.

In 1935 with Social Security grants we developed the modern venereal disease programs with active case-finding. This period lasted through the war to 1945.

Postwar dislocation occurred, with an increase of the venereal disease rates.

Then in 1947 began the penicillin era. The same general trend can be observed over a 50-year period. The trend line shown here was fitted to triangulated points and smoothed, and you note that little or no change has taken place in the trend since 1910. I want to emphasize again, it isn't the drug alone; it is mainly the interest and public health activities and other factors not easily evaluated that have given us these results. With this as a background for thought let us examine the dangers of the antibiotic cocktail.

Premises—true and false

My first premise is that the real danger inherent in the acceptance of the antibiotics as a cure-all for the venereal diseases lies in the consequent development of the attitude that the problem is solved and no longer of public health significance. Is this a justifiable attitude? Let's examine it.

- Assumption 1. Venereal disease rates are lower in America than at any previous time in history. Conclusion: *Antibiotics are the answer.* Facts: The rate of decline as shown by the trend line is the same now as in the past, and the precipitate drops now are no different than in the eras of other new drugs and activity.

- Assumption 2. Venereal diseases cannot long stand up under the onslaught of such specific drugs as the antibiotics.
  Facts: No disease has ever been treated out of existence. Antibiotics are no more specific than the heavy metals; they are more easily and quickly given and should still further reduce mortality and admissions to mental institutions.

- Assumption 3. Use of antibiotics is so general that we unknowingly cut chains of infection.
  Facts: *Actually unknown,* but some sampling has shown that the average individual does not get an antibiotic oftener than two times yearly and only a few infected individuals would be under therapy at one time.

  The lower socio-economic groups where venereal disease is endemic get most of their antibiotics through venereal disease clinics for specific infections, or in charitable hospitals for other infections. In other words, the middle-income and upper-income groups can afford and use most of the antibiotics. The influence of these drugs in income groups where most of the venereal diseases are found is probably negligible.

  Actually, antibiotics used by groups in which most venereal disease exists, except as used for these specific diseases, could have little or no effect on the spread of the diseases. Exposure rates and sex practices are such that antibiotics, even if used two or three times annually, would at no time by chance alone cut enough chains to materially hinder the spread of the diseases.

I repeat, the trend has not materially changed in 50 years. It has accelerated or slowed according to the interest and effect of those interested in control.

The greatest change that has taken place is our ability to get 95% of cases adequately treated now as compared to 25% formerly. This fact does not alter incidence or prevalence rates, as reinfections can now take place much faster than formerly. Even though we failed to hold 75% of syphilis cases formerly, we did get enough sporadic treatment for them to render most of them noninfectious for long periods of time.

The one great advantage of modern therapy is the cutting down of mortality and complications of the diseases and in preventing prenatal syphilis.

Real danger in abolishing proved procedures

Should we now abolish the practice of taking premarital and prenatal serologies and routine inpatient serologies at our charity hospitals — which has been proposed — all our gains can well be lost. It will take continual case-finding and vigilance to hold our gains. While in the past our interest has fluctuated, never before has it been said these diseases were not a *public health problem*, and herein lies the great danger of the attitudes now developing even among our leaders in public health, education and science. I believe that teachers and scientists can make their

Babies are healthier . . . thanks to modern treatment for prenatal syphilis.

GRAPH II

CIVILIAN CASES OF SYPHILIS AND GONORRHEA
CALIFORNIA, 1940-1952

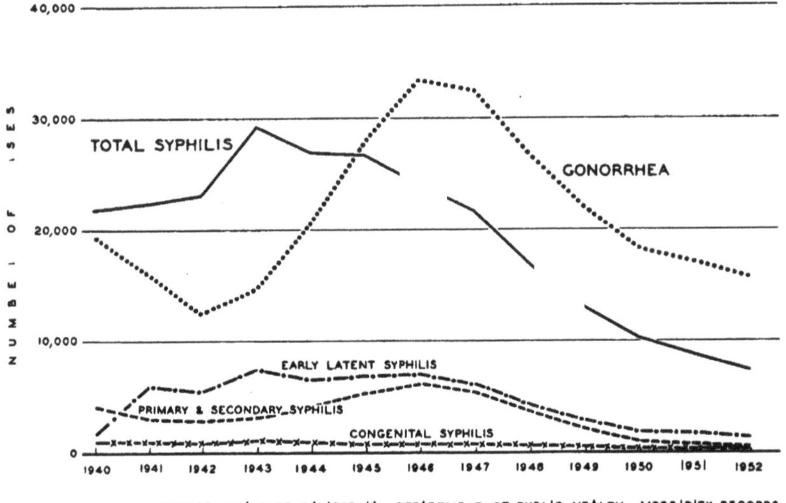

greatest contributions by continuing educational programs at a high level, by being vociferous and persistent in their assertions that a problem still exists, by pointing to the facts, and by continuing their long-range objectives of strong family life units.

Already state and local health departments have lost interest; slowly and surely programs are deteriorating.

Graph II shows the decrease in rates of primary and secondary, early latent and late syphilis and gonorrhea during the last 10 years. You will note the rate of decrease in primary and secondary syphilis is greater than the others. Might it not be lack of reporting or failure to diagnose because of ease of treatment that accounts for our low ratio in infectious syphilis? We certainly are missing most of the new cases or we would not continue to find latent and late syphilis by serology to the extent we do . . . or else the antibiotics in subcurative doses are giving rise to asymptomatic cases of venereal disease.

We have made great gains in the reduction of mortality, admissions to mental hospitals, prevention of prenatal syphilis, and prevention of blindness. Are we now to lose these gains because of our reliance on the antibiotic cocktail to do all our work for us? *It won't, I assure you.*

A social hygiene service . . . personal and marriage counseling

by Mrs. Dorothy W. Miller, Executive Secretary
Massachusetts Society for Social Hygiene

- Is the counseling of individuals who are troubled over the part sex plays in their lives logically a job for a social hygiene society?

That question, often put to the Massachusetts Society for Social Hygiene, calls for an answer based on facts, not on opinion nor precedent nor tradition.

Since 1934, when we instituted personal counseling as a part of our social hygiene services to Massachusetts, it had been our opinion that . . .

- Group and mass health education of the type carried on by a social hygiene society needs to be supplemented by individual guidance.
- Our counseling service is different from and complementary to the services offered by other agencies.
- The people who use our counseling service recognize it as a source of help to them in handling problems involving sex.

Back in 1934 we were pioneers. Before that, a person troubled over the part sex played in his life had usually turned to his clergyman, or doctor, or lawyer . . . when he summoned up enough courage to go to anyone. And it was the exceptional clergyman, doctor or lawyer who was professionally equipped to provide good counsel on sex problems.

We had proceeded with professional caution in setting up the service . . .

- Had backed it with a governing board of distinguished physicians, psychiatrists, educators, clergymen and social workers.
- Had employed a counselor * with the experience, knowledge and aptitude that are singularly effective in helping people solve problems involving sex.
- Had set up sound procedures for keeping records, maintaining the confidences of our clients, referring them to other agencies, consulting, reporting, and in all ways keeping to the high professional standards that are imperative in practicing the art and science of helping people out of trouble.

But by 1950 our pioneering represented only precedent . . . and in days of rapid change precedent carried little authority in itself.

* Lester W. Dearborn.

We had opinions and a precedent. But to answer the question scientifically we needed facts.

So we looked at the record . . . the 347 men and women who came to the Social Hygiene Society for help between January 1, 1950, and December 31, 1951. In two years, 215 women who needed help, 132 men.

Two out of five were between 26 and 35 years old. One in four was between 18 and 25, and one in five between 36 and 45. Only 3% were under 18, only 10% over 45.

Half of them had gone to college or professional school, another 40% had at least a high school education. Only 5% had not gone to high school.

Referrals

Who sent them to the Social Hygiene Society? Two out of five of them had heard of our counseling from relatives or friends who had used our service. In 29% of the cases they were referred to us either by clergymen (5%), by schools (1%), by physicians and psychiatrists (7%) or by lawyers, other counselors and social agencies (16%). Another 26% came to us for individual help after hearing a lecture course given by our counselor. About 6% had learned about our service from our publications or some other source.

What were their problems? This was the crucial question since its answer focuses on the specialized, rather than general, counsel we provide. We found that our 347 clients presented four general categories of problems:

- Those which focused on a situation or need predominantly in the area of sex . . . clients who needed specific information about sex, or guidance in handling sex inadequacy or maladjustment in marriage or a problem of sex not necessarily connected with the marriage relationship.

- Those reflecting the client's need for premarital education and guidance.

- Those which focused on a situation, problem or need not predominantly in the area of sex . . . clients who needed help on some phase of mental or physical health, vocational or social inadequacy, interpersonal conflicts (some marriage-centered, some not).

- Unclassified . . . four clients who were unable for some reason to verbalize their need at the first interview and did not return for further help.

TABLE I

Category	No. of Cases	% of Cases	No. of Conferences	% of Conferences
Focus predominantly in the area of sex	191	55	~~740~~	74
Premature education and guidance	53	15	128	12.8
Focus not predominantly in the area of sex	99	29	127	12.7
Unclassified	4	1	4	.5
Totals	347	100	999	100

Here is a fact that is important . . . 70% of our clients (those in the first two groups) came to us because they wanted help in meeting some situation arising specifically from the role of sex in their lives. Is it logical to assume that people see in the Massachusetts Society for Social Hygiene — which exists to reduce misunderstanding and misuse of sex — an organization uniquely qualified to help them with their sex problems?

Another fact is important . . . during the counseling process one-third of the 99 clients whose main problem was not primarily focused on sex revealed misunderstanding or lack of knowledge of the role of sex in their lives. Is it logical to assume that the reputation of the Masssachusetts Society for Social Hygiene as a specialist on problems involving sex brings to us clients who want help in understanding their sexuality even though they prefer to present another type of problem?

TABLE II

Category	No. of Clients	% of Clients	No. of Conferences	% of Conferences
Marriage-centered situations	173	50	572	57
Premarital education and guidance	53	15	128	13
Situations not marriage-centered	117	34	295	29.5
Unclassified	4	1	4	.5
Totals	347	100	999	100

Nearly two-thirds of our clients (those in the first two groups) came to us for help in making their marriage succeed. Of the 173 whose problems were marriage-centered, 47 came to us with problems not primarily focused on sex. (Twenty-one of these 47 had incidental sex difficulties.)

The remaining 126 clients whose problems were centered in their marriage asked for our help in resolving their sexual inadequacy or sexual maladjustment . . .

- Lack of orgasm (32 clients).
- Lack of interest in sex, sexual ineptitude, etc. (41 clients).
- Maladjustments and conflicts arising from the sex relationship in their marriage (53 clients).

Of the 117 men and women who asked our help on matters not centered on marriage, 52 wanted help in solving some problem of sex . . . homosexuality, masturbation or the sex behavior of some relative or friend. Thirteen wanted information about sex. The others wanted our counsel on improving their physical or mental health, vocational or social adequacy, or relationships with people.

These, then, were the people who had come to us for help, and why they had come . . . 215 women, 132 men. How did we go about helping them?

What kind of help?

For some, who asked only for information, we prepared special reading-lists directing them to the most helpful and authoritative books and pamphlets in the field.

With others, who asked our help in preparing for marriage, we spent many hours in consultation, seeing couples together and separately in successive interviews. During their talks together client and counselor explored the client's family background, his conflicts with his parents or brothers and sisters, his reactions to his upbringing and discipline, his early sex education, his reactions to school, and his associations with his teachers and playmates.

In a kind of sex inventory they review his or her sex experiences in childhood and adolescence, including homosexuality or masturbation, and the present status of the couple's sexual relationships. The counselor describes what may be expected in a good adjustment in marriage, stressing the importance of right attitudes, of understanding the differing psychology of the sexes, of the couple's relationships with other people.

He suggests that they read together selected books and pamphlets, and urges them to have premarital physical examinations more complete than those required by law.

To help clients asking for guidance in making a good adjustment to their sexuality, the counselor works with them through a four-step process of exploration, catharsis, reassurance and re-education.

The first step encourages the client to tell his story, to define his main purpose in asking counsel and to explain what he hopes to gain from it. In listing the client's sex experiences, the counselor pays careful attention to his client's general attitude toward those experiences and to any fears or worries he reveals. In trying to help the client understand himself and why he behaves as he does, counselor and client discuss and evaluate the client's answers to various personality tests . . . crystalizing in the client's mind some of the factors he could not discuss earlier.

If the client's problem is impotence or lack of orgasm, or if there is indication of physiological difficulty, the counselor recommends a thorough medical examination before proceeding on the theory that the cause is entirely psychological or attitudinal. The counselor emphasizes that health problems have an indirect if not a direct bearing on any emotional difficulty, and recommends regular eye examinations, dental care or other medical treatment if the client has had no recent help of this kind.

Almost 20 years

For consultations on selected cases, the counselor turns to a panel of advisers . . . medical, psychiatric, educational, legal. As individual experts and as a panel, they help the counselor with professional opinion and advice.

Since they began our service back in 1934 they have watched schools and colleges begin to offer courses on marriage and family life. They have watched the average American's growing acceptance of sex as a fundamental component of his human nature. They have watched the growing awareness of the value of personal counseling in sex guidance, marriage and family adjustments. Now we must go further and apply scientific research methods to evaluate the reliability of counseling procedures and the effectiveness of this service. That is the next step.

This is the heart of social hygiene . . . the role of sex in life. To teach people to use their sexuality in ways that bring them physical, emotional and social satisfaction . . . that is social hygiene's aim. Up to a point, mass and group teaching work well. Beyond that point, there is need for an individualized approach. It is social hygiene's pride — as well as social hygiene's responsibility — to be able to focus on one individual's particular problem of sex the specialized competence developed over many years.

Eight years after the houses closed

Was "controlled" prostitution good for Hawaii?

by Walter B. Quisenberry, M.D.

Is it good public health practice to tolerate so-called "controlled" houses of prostitution in a community? Does it increase or decrease the venereal disease problem if the houses are closed? Does it protect local girls from sex offenses and rape to have a red-light district? Is there any connection between juvenile delinquency and tolerated prostitution?

These and many similar questions faced the citizens of Hawaii for many years. In this report I will attempt to answer these questions from Hawaii's experience.

The history of prostitution in Hawaii goes back to about 1778 with the discovery of the islands by Captain Cook ("The Honolulu Myth," by Samuel D. Allison, M.D. Journal of Social Hygiene, February, 1946). As western civilization spread to Hawaii, prostitution developed out of what was thought to be a need. The situation had become so bad by 1860 that the legislature enacted a system of regulated prostitution to mitigate the evils and diseases arising from prostitution. The act was not popular, and by 1868 it was permitted to lapse. But when venereal disease became more widespread, the act was revived. Finally in 1905 the legislature withdrew the act.

In 1914 a committee met to study a number of social conditions . . . one of them prostitution. This committee was effective in closing the red-light district in Honolulu in November, 1916.

As a consequence there was a significant reduction in the Army's VD rates in the Hawaiian Department. The average rate from 1913 to 1916 was 81; the average rate from 1917 to 1920 was 51 . . . a 38% reduction in the Army's venereal disease rates after the houses of prostitution were closed.

Within a few years, the houses of prostitution reopened. In the summer of 1930, the military police took charge of a system of regulated prostitution, and in 1932 the Honolulu Police Department took over. The plan, calling for regular medical inspection of prostitutes and police supervision of the houses, continued until the beginning of World War II.

During the first year of World War II, Hawaii was under military rule. Prostitution continued, and efforts toward repression, rather than so-called "control," were unsuccessful.

Social protection

The Council of Social Agencies of Honolulu appointed a social protection committee in 1943 ("Fighting Sin in Paradise," by Ferris F. Laune. Journal of Social Hygiene, February, 1946). This committee studied the problem of prostitution carefully and made recommendations. Finally on September 21, 1944, Governor Ingram M. Stainback ordered the so-called "controlled" houses of prostitution closed.

Many citizens of Honolulu were disturbed over this action. They thought the venereal disease rate would skyrocket. Prominent lay citizens as well as members of the medical profession believed this fallacy too . . . in spite of the fact that the Territorial Health Department had pointed out that professional prostitutes had been the source of approximately 75% of all new venereal disease infections acquired in Hawaii. Many citizens also feared that rape would become rampant and that the streets would no longer be safe for women.

What happened to the VD rate?

The venereal disease rate in Hawaii has always been low for a seaport area. It has been reported that the venereal disease rate for the Army's Hawaiian Department in 1941 was 15 per 1,000. ("Venereal Diseases in War-Time Hawaii," by Samuel D. Allison, M.D. American Journal of Syphilis, Gonorrhea and Venereal Diseases, September, 1947). At the end of that year World War II began. At the close of the first year of the war, the rate dropped to about 5.

In 1943 it declined to 3, and for the years 1944 and 1945, the locally acquired part of the rate was down to 1.5.

In 1942 most infections were acquired in the Hawaiian area. It is estimated that at the onset of the war, at least three-fourths of the 15 cases per 1,000 servicemen in Hawaii were acquired locally. Beginning with 1944, there was a sharp change in this picture, with the great majority of venereal disease cases diagnosed in Hawaii being acquired outside the Hawaiian Islands. In 1944, the total venereal disease rate for the Armed Forces in Hawaii was 4.4, with the locally acquired fraction being 1.5. This was the year during which the houses of prostitution were actually closed. During 1945 the locally acquired case rate remained about 1.5, while the total rate for the Hawaiian area increased to 7.5.

A prompt reduction in the number of venereal disease cases reported to the Health Department was noted following the closing of the houses of prostitution.

TABLE I

Summary of VD Cases Eleven Months Before and Eleven Months After Closing Houses of Prostitution in Honolulu, T.H., September 21, 1944

	Number 11 Months Before	Number 11 Months After
Gonorrhea	1,072	671
Syphilis (primary and secondary)	57	32
Total	1,129	703

For a comprehensive picture of the venereal disease cases reported to the Health Department from 1941 through 1952, see graphs I and II. Graph I shows the actual total venereal disease cases, civilian and military, reported to the Territorial Health Department for the 12 years. Graph II shows the civilian venereal rates per 100,000 population for the 10 years from 1943 to 1952.

Reporting of civilian cases of gonorrhea may be considered somewhat unreliable. The size of the military population in Hawaii during this period was not made known to the Health Department (military rates as stated above were released at intervals) so rates could not be computed for the total combined civilian-military group.

These graphs show reductions in venereal disease cases and rates following the closing of the houses of prostitution in 1944. It will be noted that there was a temporary increase in both cases and rates following the end of the war . . . no doubt because of a letup in military venereal disease control measures. This same situation, which prevailed in many other parts of the world, reached its peak in 1946 and then began to go down again.

There have been steady decreases in both cases and rates since that time, with two exceptions:

- The number of reported gonorrhea cases rose in 1948 but promptly declined again the next year. The cause of this brief upswing is not known.
- During 1952 gonorrhea cases and rates increased, while the syphilis cases and rates continued to decrease. This increase in gonorrhea was due principally to an outbreak on the island of Kauai. Along with this, military establishments in Hawaii reported a slight increase in gonorrhea cases . . . probably because more military personnel were stationed here last year than in the preceding years.

Many factors in VD reduction

Undoubtedly many factors were responsible for the decrease in the amount of venereal disease during and since the war. The closing of the houses of prostitution was probably the most important of these.

During the first half of 1942 the following important steps were taken in developing a coordinated venereal disease control program for Hawaii.

- In February a division of venereal disease control was established in the Territorial Health Department.
- In March a Navy captain was assigned to venereal disease control.
- In May the military governor issued an order relating to the control of communicable diseases, especially venereal diseases, supplementing existing Board of Health regulations. This order called for a coordinated venereal disease control program by the Territorial Health Department, the Army and the Navy.

Allison has reported that the following points were outlined as measures to which particular attention should be paid:

- Immediate reporting of all cases of venereal disease to the Health Department along with the names of suspected sources of infection.
- Examination of all individuals suspected of having such disease.
- Effective quarantine of contagious cases with hospitalization when necessary.

Of course the establishment of the division of venereal disease control in the Territorial Health Department was the first step in coordinating community efforts to control venereal disease. Many other community agencies—including the Council of Social Agencies, the Honolulu Police Department and the military forces—took part. This cooperation brought about the strengthening of treatment facilities and prophylaxis, as well as improved investigation of

GRAPH 1

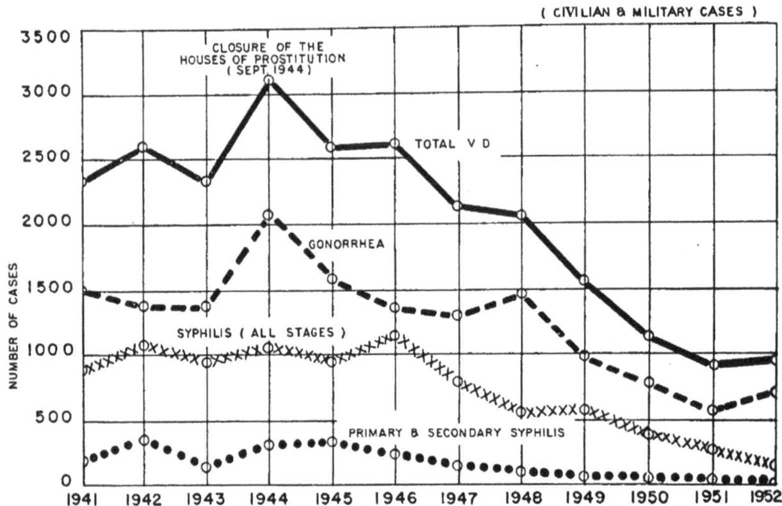

contacts. It initiated a fine educational program designed to reduce the incidence of venereal diseases.

How about sex crimes?

Well-meaning citizens have thought that regulated prostitution is necessary for the protection of decent women and young girls in the community. This has proved not to be true. The repression of prostitution does *not* lead to increases in sex crimes and rape, as statistical analyses of sex crime carried on up to the present time show. Records in other cities as well as in Honolulu verify this fact.

Studies were made in Honolulu of the sex crimes and rape cases in the 11-month period immediately following the closing of the houses of prostitution compared with the 11-month period immediately preceding the closing of the houses.

During this period there was a 24% decrease in rape cases and a 28% decrease in all sex crimes. Allison shows in table II the actual numbers of cases which demonstrate this prompt reduction.

TABLE II

Analysis of Sex Crime Figures 11 Months Before and 11 Months After Closing Houses of Prostitution in Honolulu, T.H., September 21, 1944

	Number 11 Months Before	Number 11 Months After
Rape	29	22
Other sex crimes (exclusive of prostitution)	559	404
Total	588	426

The Honolulu Police Department has continued to study the number of sex crimes and rape cases coming to its attention, and has concluded that there has not been an increase of sex crimes or rape cases since the closing of the houses of prostitution. In table III, Dan Liu, Chief of Police of Honolulu, compares the period beginning three years before the closing of the houses of prostitution to the period following the closing of the houses to the present time. The number of sex crimes and rape cases reached a peak the year the houses of prostitution were closed (September 21, 1944). There was a rapid decline at first, and then in general the decline was maintained with increases and decreases in individual years.

TABLE III

11-Year Study in the City and County of Honolulu

	Rape	Other Sex Crimes Excluding Prostitution
1941–42 (October–September)	10	348
1942–43 "	19	623
1943–44 "	30	617
1944–45	29	452
1945–46	16	433
1946–47 "	17	368
1947 (Calendar year)	17	358
1948 "	13	416
1949 "	14	392
1950	27	377
1951	22	410
Total	214	4,794

GRAPH II

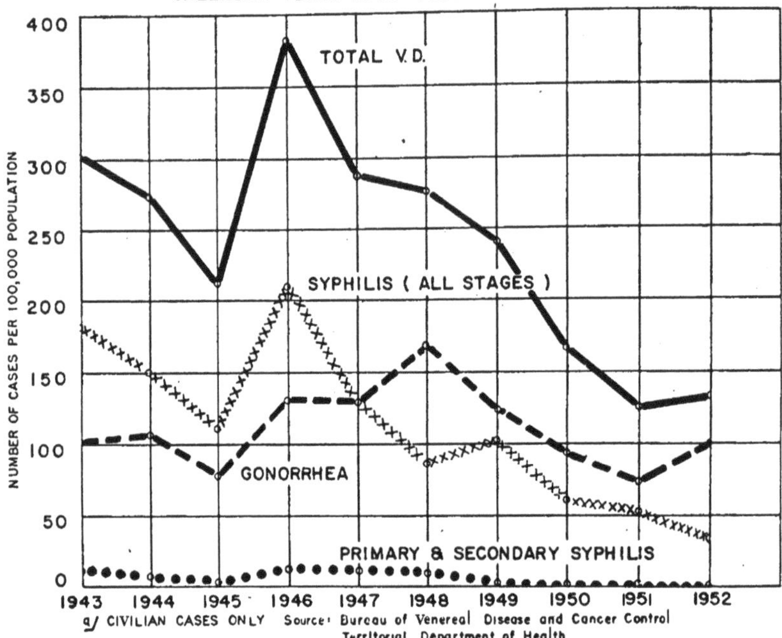

We have shown in Honolulu that the repression of prostitution does not lead to an increase in sex offenses and rape cases in a community. In fact, we had 27% fewer rape cases and 32% fewer sex crimes eight years after the closing of the houses than before.

What about juvenile delinquency?

Certainly the fact that there were houses of prostitution in Honolulu was not a secret to anyone who stayed a while in the city. It was considered somewhat of a tourist excursion to go to one of the parks in town and watch the lines of men waiting to enter and the men leaving the houses of prostitution.

Children could also see what was going on. This must have had a traumatic effect on the minds of those children. Workers in juvenile delinquency have pointed out other ways in which prostitution affects children. Many times when youngsters are in trouble, they will not reveal the working places of their mothers when the mothers are employed in houses of prostitution.

There has been a gradual decrease in the number of juveniles admitted to the territorial training (reform) schools since the closing of the houses of prostitution, according to Mabelle J. Puth, chief parole officer of the Department of Institutions.

Authorities in this field, however, feel that there must have been several factors involved in this decrease. One is the attitude of the judges who commit the juveniles to the territorial institutions: If the judges are concerned about the problems of juvenile delinquency, there will be a decrease in the admissions to the territorial training schools and an increase in the number of cases put on probation. Tables IV and V, from reports of the Department of Institutions, show the admissions to the training (reform) schools of Hawaii for the 11 years from 1941 to 1952. These show the highest number of admissions to the girls' home occurred the year the houses of prostitution were closed, with a gradual decline since that time. The highest number of admissions to the boys' home came the year after the houses closed, with a gradual decline since.

Decrease in admissions

It is clear that there has been a reduction in admissions to the territorial training schools during the last eight years. (Admissions from the island of Oahu only, the island on which Honolulu is located, follow in general the trend for the Territory.) The closing of the houses of prostitution may be one of the many factors responsible for this reduction.

It was proved that certain members of the Honolulu Police Department accepted considerable sums in graft money during the period when the houses of

TABLE IV

Admissions to Girls' Home 1941–1952
Territory of Hawaii

1941–42	67
1942–43	79
1943–44	80
1944–45	88
1945–46	52
1946–47	69
1947–48	50
1948–49	34
1949–50	34
1950–51	27
1951–52	27
Total	607

TABLE V

Admissions to Boys' Home 1941–1952
Territory of Hawaii

1941–42	82
1942–43	96
1943–44	67
1944–45	64
1945–46	116
1946–47	100
1947–48	71
1948–49	40
1949–50	35
1950–51	46
1951–52	43
Total	760

prostitution were tolerated . . . a social evil in itself. At present there is very little evidence of graft connected with the prostitution which is now going on in a limited, clandestine way in Honolulu.

Another prominent evil which goes along with prostitution is narcotics addiction and sales . . . a natural accompaniment to houses of prostitution. The madam in charge of the house may give the girls narcotics when they become tired so they will work longer and make more money for her. After a short period, they become so completely addicted to the narcotics that they will work for nothing, if necessary, only to get their narcotics. The sale of narcotics through the houses is facilitated by the atmosphere which prevails.

Other social ills with prostitution

Prostitution, sex crimes, juvenile delinquency, narcotics problems, and graft are symptoms of social illness. Because the venereal diseases are frequently acquired through prostitution, the health department enters the picture. The alert health department is interested in preventing the basic social illness which breeds these conditions.

Because of the large amount of money that can be made from the perpetuation of these social ills, it is often very difficult to eliminate them from a community. A concerted effort by all community agencies is necessary—with the health department, police and social agencies playing the most prominent parts.

On the basis of Hawaii's experience it can be stated definitely that it is not good public health nor good social hygiene practice to tolerate houses of prostitution in a community, even if they are "controlled." A red-light district does not protect local girls from sex offenses. From a purely public health standpoint, it can be said with assurance that the closing of the houses of prostitution in Hawaii immediately reduced the incidence of early syphilis and gonorrhea cases. From the long-term standpoint, it can also be shown that the number of venereal disease cases reported to the Territorial Health Department—including congenital syphilis cases—has also been reduced. My report, "Potentialities in Congenital Syphilis with Case Presentations," from the Hawaii Medical Journal, November-December, 1949, includes information on the reduction in congenital syphilis cases.

Director of preventive medicine, formerly chief of venereal disease and cancer control for Hawaii's Department of Health

Walter B. Quisenberry, M.D.

Conclusions

Closing of the houses of prostitution was instrumental in bringing about the following improvements in Hawaii:

- A reduction in venereal disease cases and rates.
- An immediate reduction in sex crimes and rape cases, with no increase noted after eight years of repressing prostitution.
- A reduction in juvenile delinquency cases during the last eight years. It is difficult to point out the concrete part played by the closing of the houses of prostitution. Rationally it can be said that there should be a reduction in juvenile delinquency because of improvement in the overall social health of the community.
- A general overall improvement in social hygiene in the community to be realized over many years to come . . . stronger homes and fewer crimes in general. There should also be a reduction in the narcotics problem.
- A reduction in graft in the Police Department.

It can be said with certainty that so-called "controlled" prostitution was not good for Hawaii.

Acknowledgments

The author wishes to give special acknowledgement to the following individuals and groups for their very valuable contributions to the work presented in this report:

- Samuel D. Allison, M.D., dermatologist, Honolulu, formerly director of the Division of Venereal Diseases and later director of the Division of Preventive Medicine in the Territorial Department of Health, Honolulu.
- Dorian Paskowitz, M.D., formerly assistant chief of the Bureau of Venereal Diseases and Cancer Control and until recently acting chief of the Bureau of Venereal Diseases and Cancer Control in Hawaii's Department of Health.
- Daniel S. C. Liu, chief of the Honolulu Police Department, and his force, especially the Morals Squad.
- Ferris F. Laune, Ph.D., secretary of the Honolulu Council of Social Agencies.

- Edward J. Burns, formerly chairman of the Social Protection Committee of the Honolulu Council of Social Agencies.
- Miss Mabelle J. Puth, chief parole officer for Hawaii's Department of Institutions.
- Hubert E. Brown, Ph.D., chairman of the Health and Physical Education Department of the University of Hawaii.
- The present and former staff members of the Bureau of Venereal Diseases and Cancer Control, Territorial Department of Health.
- A host of other faithful community-minded workers in Hawaii who have contributed immeasurably to the progress indicated in this report.

"I'll be glad when my first date is over. Mother says a girl shouldn't ever kiss a fellow on the first date"

Spiritual Health and Development

Third of a series of chapters from Preinduction Health and Human Relations, new curriculum resource for youth leaders by Roy E. Dickerson and Esther E. Sweeney.

For the Instructor

Moral and spiritual health are intrinsic to any view of health that regards man as a totality. The instructor using this material has a three-fold opportunity . . .

- To make a major contribution to the lives of young people by helping them to synthesize the moral and spiritual concepts that have been, both formally and incidentally, part of their previous education and experience.
- To contribute directly to the spiritual growth of youth in the very process of discussing this material, since reflection upon moral meanings is basic to character development.[1]
- To encourage youth to move positively in the direction of those relationships, experiences and opportunities that further and deepen moral and spiritual health, whether they remain in civilian life or enter the Armed Forces.

Young people today face a long period of wars or the threat of wars. They see their government and indeed the whole world grappling with tremendous moral problems that sometimes appear to be merely political, social or economic. They must shortly take their part as citizens in meeting domestic and global crises and will need the strongest moral and spiritual equipment with which to fight for right and decency.

Some will find this equipment in religious, some in philosophical conviction, some in a sound combination of both. But schools and community agencies—as well as homes and churches—have a role to play in guiding youth towards the development of moral and spiritual health. Without health which is morally and spiritually sound it is doubtful if youth will be able to win the battles ahead, to carry on the great traditions of their country or even to live peacefully and comfortably with themselves.

---

[1] *Adolescent Character and Personality*, Robert J. Havighurst and Hilda Taba, New York, Wiley, 1949, pp. 6 and 7.

Reference

- *Moral and Spiritual Values in the Public Schools*, Educational Policies Commission, National Education Association of the United States and the American Association of School Administrators, 1201 Sixteenth Street, N.W., Washington, D.C.

For Use with Students

Every young person wants to get the most out of life and to get on with the job of living in the most confident and successful way. To get the most out of life, human beings must *bring* something to living.

A person who is easily worried, fearful and unsure of himself is a person of poor emotional makeup. So also is one who feels that people are against him or jealous of him or competing with him unfairly, who wears a chip on his shoulder or who, on the other hand, is uneasy about standing up for the simplest of his rights. In short, such an individual is unlikely to bring the best mental health to living.

Similarly, a person whose physical health is poor, who frequently breaks dates because of illness, who loses his chance to compete in school athletics because of inadequate physical fitness, also fails to bring the best possible equipment to the job of living.

But good intellectual equipment, fine physical health, a wholesome mental outlook are still not enough for living. Human beings need spiritual and moral development to round out their total readiness to give to and get the most from life.

What Is Spiritual Health?

Moral and spiritual health has to do with the way people regard their fellowmen; with their individual decisions on what is right and what is wrong; with the development of such positive virtues as truth, kindness, reverence and brotherhood. It calls for their assuming moral responsibility and using their own understanding of the relationship between man and God in the daily fulfillment of their responsibilities toward themselves and other people.

Mahatma Gandhi's words—written and spoken—may be lost to men in a relatively short time . . . his spiritual stature and moral force will last. In England's most perilous hour Winston Churchill held the British people firm in their resolution "to fight on the beaches, to fight in the streets. . . ." His convincing strength arose from his own moral vitality. George Washington, Thomas Jefferson, Abraham Lincoln, Woodrow Wilson—all live forever in American history and tradition as symbols of greatness because of the moral and spiritual values that motivated them.

General Lawton J. Collins, Chief of Staff of the United States Army, said: "The true strength of any army lies in the moral character and spirit of its

Patriotism is more than knowledge.
It is belief and the desire to protect.

soldiers. A man needs a sense of dignity and responsibility. He must know and believe in the ideals of his country, and he must be willing to protect and perpetuate them."

What is true of the strength of an army is true of the strength of a nation. And a nation is no stronger than every man and woman within its boundaries.

Today's Challenge to Spiritual Health

Patterns of American life are undergoing great change. Even before the present national emergency many young people were moving about the country in search of the kind of jobs they wanted, under the most favorable climatic or other living conditions. This movement away from the communities where they had grown up—a movement increasingly accelerated by the national emergency—has usually meant some loss of the personal support normally derived from family relationships and home life and from hometown friendships, churches, clubs and other community associations.

Now still greater numbers of young men and women are entering the Armed Forces or are continuing the movement towards other communities as defense workers. Today it is more important than ever for young people to think about their own inner resources for meeting new and very different people, situations and living conditions. In their new situations it is vital that they think about and discover ways of finding those aids and supports to moral and spiritual development that were hitherto taken more or less for granted.

Those going into the Armed Forces find that their great tradition of emphasis on moral and spiritual health first inaugurated by George Washington is being carried on and implemented. The character guidance programs in the Armed Forces have as their primary objective "the development within each individual soldier (sailor, airman, marine) of a sense of responsibility. This is accomplished first by helping the soldier (sailor, airman, marine) to understand certain basic life principles, and second, by encouraging the discipline involved in applying these principles to life situations." [2]

Young men and women will find that the Armed Forces encourage them to

---

[2] *Character Guidance in the Army*, U. S. Army brochure.

continue their usual patterns of church attendance. Chaplains in all branches are men trained not only in theology but also in interviewing and counseling.

In those military installations where it has not been possible to assign chaplains of all faiths, service personnel find that the chaplain—whatever his faith—is charged with responsibility for group discussions, on a non-denominational basis, of moral and spiritual values.

Young people in the Armed Forces will need to take stock of themselves, however, and to determine whether they are taking fullest advantage of the opportunities for spiritual development offered in military installations and civilian communities.

Young people who have been affiliated with churches at home will want to continue their religious practices, whether in the Armed Forces or in civilian careers. They will find that churches also offer many possibilities for recreation, friendship and, when necessary, guidance on particular problems.

For young people who have never had formal church affiliations there is opportunity to explore the meaning and value of religious experience. No matter where they may be, they will find that their efforts to use community resources in developing the richest spiritual and moral health will be rewarding and will add immeasurably to their total development as well-rounded human beings. Those resources are in churches, in groups such as the YMCA, YWCA and USO, and often in the homes of new friends they make in the course of work or recreation.

Spiritual Foundations of the American Way of Life

The phrase *the American way of life* is so variously used today that the thoughtful student can afford to reflect on the foundations, principles and values underlying that way of life.

Every young person should seek the answers to certain questions: Is the American way of life merely a system of broad, general guides for governing bodies? Is it something that can exist independently—just as an idea—or must it be reflected in the life and philosophy of each individual? Is the American way of life founded on values that are essentially spiritual and moral? If so, does its perpetuation demand acceptance of those spiritual and moral values by each individual?

Every boy and girl in this country is being called upon today to play a serious and important role in the preservation of the American way of life. Many will enter the Armed Forces for its defense. Many will work in industries building armaments to safeguard it. Many will uphold the American way of life in their homes and offices and in their volunteer health and welfare activities.

Thoughtful examination of spiritual foundations of the American way of life and of their meaning in one's own life will make its defense more worthwhile and more assured of success.

Human Personality

The concept of the inherent worth of every human being is basic to great religions the world over. It is also one of the first of the spiritual values in which Americans believe and for which they have fought and died . . . and will again whenever and wherever necessary.

In the American way of life, every individual—rich or poor, learned or ignorant, different from others in his beliefs, politics, way of living and working, racial or national origin—is recognized as a distinct, human personality with certain inherent, inalienable rights.

Recognition of the value of every human being is found in:

- Our Constitution and Bill of Rights.
- Our American aversion to every form of oppression.
- Our common agreement that every individual should have every opportunity of achieving, by his own efforts, a feeling of security and competence in dealing with the problems of daily life.
- Our ever-growing realization that we are one people living in one world.
- Our acceptance of responsibility to provide every child in this country with educational opportunities that meet his varying needs and aspirations and encourage in him respect for himself and others.

Day in and day out everyone can show that he appreciates and accepts the idea of the inherent worth of every human being. In countless ways one can affirm spiritual awareness of this fundamental value.

All people come into frequent contact with others who do not think as they do. Yet differences of religious, political, economic and social beliefs and the expression of them are possible in a free democracy. One does not hate nor oppress nor strive to injure someone because he is or is not a Democrat, a Republican or an independent voter. One may even disapprove of another's point of view, yet not deny him the right of expression nor consider him less of a person because he may be in error.

A student in any class of 40 or 50 boys and girls has daily associations with many who go to different churches, whose families have more or less money than his, whose national or racial origins are different from his. Regardless of differences and despite occasional failures to remember the respect owed each of his classmates, he finds himself well-disposed, on the whole, towards the group and finds them well-disposed towards him.

This may seem commonplace to most young people, yet there are countries in the world where caste systems still thrive, where social distinctions enter into how open and friendly people can be with one another, where children from homes of various economic levels do not attend the same school.

Complete acceptance of the inherent worth of every human being is not always easy to acquire nor maintain. Some young people have to work hard for consistent ability to recognize the worth of people of different color or of people who, for one reason or another, are lacking in personal attractiveness or whose cultural backgrounds and interests are different from their own.

Yet only by incorporating this concept of individual human worth into one's working philosophy can a person insure that he will always be just and fair in his relationships with others, and will sedulously avoid discrimination or even action that might seem to approve another's discriminatory conduct.

Class Discussion

- How do our courts recognize the worth of human beings even when they have violated the law by theft, murder, treason, etc.?
- How is recognition of the value and worth of human beings shown in the maintenance of systems of free public education in this country? In wage and hour laws?
- Name some of the ways in which totalitarian governments have shown their fundamental disregard of the inherent worth of human beings.

Moral Responsibility

Another of the great spiritual and moral concepts Americans accept and upon which the American way of life is predicated is moral responsibility.

While human beings do not always act in accordance with their understanding of right and wrong, approval generally goes to those who follow the dictates of conscience and disapproval to those who do not.

It is considered evidence of independence and maturity when a young man refuses to race a "hot rod" or when a girl refuses to be drawn into casual petting . . . when conscience says "no."

The people of this country are profoundly shocked by the lack of moral responsibility displayed in sports scandals and in unethical practices of some public officials.

A good mind,
a strong body,
a cheerful outlook—
are they enough?

Our entire judicial system is predicated on man's moral responsibility for his acts. Our courts, however—recognizing that human beings are at some times less morally responsible than at others—acknowledge and consider questions of sanity and other special factors in judging criminals.

Moral responsibility does not just grow in the individual without any effort on his part. From early childhood, people begin forming the habit of making decisions and taking the consequences, even when unpleasant. Making firmly-based moral decisions may never become easy and sometimes, in serious matters, may not be accomplished without help and advice.

But the child who learns early that punishment is easier to bear than an uncomfortable conscience develops habits of self-reliance, decisiveness and moral responsibility that later make him a mature, stable, valuable citizen.

One factor in human experience that often causes the individual to make unwise and even immoral choices in conduct is poor perspective. It is right and proper to want to give presents to those one loves. It is appropriate to provide one's family with luxuries as well as necessities when this can be done. But one must put first values first, for to steal or embezzle in order to do these things is obviously wrong and indicates poor perspective. There are men in prisons today who are basically decent human beings, yet who are paying a debt to society because they failed—through immaturity or emotional rather than rational action—to handle moral decisions in accordance with their own consciences.

All people are faced, practically every day of their lives, with numberless decisions calling for the exercise of moral responsibility. The temptation to murder or steal is relatively rare for most people. But there are always the commonplace temptations . . . to lie to save one's face or to keep from being censured for failure or error; to pet on a date "because it's expected"; to engage in illicit sexual relations because someone says, "Why not? Everybody does";

to destroy another's reputation in the course of an afternoon's idle gossip. These temptations require decision-making . . . choice between right and wrong.

Moral responsibility, however, involves more than just decisions between right and wrong. At times it involves assumption of responsibility for other people and their problems. In groups of people one sometimes sees the less mature acting in a cruel and thoughtless way towards one individual . . . making him the butt of their jokes, belittling him, perhaps bullying him. The mature, strong person has a responsibility to put a quick end to such practices against a more defenseless person.

Again, a girl on a date may have to take responsibility for helping her escort to keep from drinking too much or from driving after drinking or from other weaknesses or faults. A boy in the Armed Forces may need to take responsibility for helping an immature young serviceman resist the ridicule of other men when he refuses to go to a house of prostitution with them.

In a broader sense, moral responsibility for others is further demonstrated in individual and public support of Community Chests and special funds for helping people in trouble of one kind or another.

A further aspect of moral responsibility about which young people need to be aware is their obligation to know the issues of the day, to weigh and evaluate them and ultimately to bring their voting power to bear on those issues or to make their voices heard, in other appropriate ways, as citizens.

Class Discussion

- Why does cheating on an examination indicate a lack of social as well as personal moral responsibility?

- How is moral responsibility demonstrated in the U. S. Point Four Program?

- A man is certain that he can get a particular job if he lies about part of his employment experience. What moral principle is involved in his responsibility in this situation? (The end does not justify the means.)

- What questions of moral responsibility are involved in the following: Punctuality on a job? Obedience to orders in the Armed Forces, even if the individual doesn't agree with them? Driving a car? Crossing a street? Game-hunting?

- How does the government assume moral responsibility for those who are unable to take care of their own needs?

by Elizabeth B. McQuaid

Setting Things Straight

In reviewing the summer's crop of new books we noted with great concern a misstatement in *Individual and Community Health,* by William W. Stiles, M.D., M.P.H. (New York, Blakiston, 1953), about the American Social Hygiene Association. To set the record straight we immediately dispatched to Dr. Stiles the letter shown below. A copy went also to his publisher with the comment that we should be happy to hear about their plans for correcting the error.

June 15, 1953

Doctor William W. Stiles
Associate Professor of Public Health
University of California
Berkeley, California

Dear Doctor Stiles:

We have read with considerable dismay the statement on page 358 of your new book that birth control "has been fostered by voluntary health agencies, particularly by . . . the American Social Hygiene Association, inspired by Margaret Sanger."

Nothing in our constitution and by-laws, in our tradition, nor in our publications warrants such a statement. Since its founding in 1914 the American Social Hygiene Association has taken no position on birth control; it intends to take none.

The American Social Hygiene Association derives its inspiration from such founders and early leaders as Doctor Charles W. Eliot, Doctor David Starr Jordan, James Cardinal Gibbons, Jane Addams, Felix M. Warburg, Doctor Edward L. Keyes, Jr., and Doctor William F. Snow; at no time has this organization derived its inspiration from Margaret Sanger.

The statement contained in your book which may be widely read can do serious damage to our program in family life education. We would therefore appreciate hearing from you and your publisher as to what steps you expect to take to rectify the error.

Very truly yours,

Philip R. Mather
President

Making Good as Young Couples, by T. Otto Nall and Bert H. Davis. New York, Association Press, 1953. 110p. $2.00.

This little volume is made up of brief descriptions of 17 marriages that might have failed—and didn't. They are given as real-life stories about such problems as interfaith marriages, in-laws, and "the other couple." It is not clear whether either of the authors interviewed the young couples himself nor what role the counselor played in any of the cases presented.

Dr. Otto Nall is editor of *The Christian Advocate*. Mr. Davis, a businessman, has been associated with the *Christian Endeavor World* since 1931. With this common background, the collaborators agree that the church may exert a positive influence in the lives of young couples.

Discussion questions for each case may make the book useful in groups. The paucity of penetrating insights limits the usefulness of the book as a case volume.

Evelyn Millis Duvall, Ph.D.
Consultant

Physical and Emotional Aspects of Marriage, by C. L. Anderson. St. Louis, Mosby. 1953. 234p. $4.00.

Says Dr. Anderson in his preface, "This book is the outgrowth of repeated requests from college students for information in a compact, readable, semi-technical form on the highly important subject of sex and reproduction as it relates to these young people as normal everyday Americans."

And that is just the information this book gives. It is concise and well arranged. Seldom has an author been able to put so much reliable and readable material in 234 pages. While a little too technical for the popular reader, the book is ideally adapted to college students, who would profit by its perusal.

The author accepts facts and faces reality, but he also dares to uphold ideals. His little book is up-to-date in its biology, sound in its psychology, broad and practical in its psychiatric implications. It deserves to enjoy a wide distribution among present-day college students.

William S. Sadler, M.D.

When You Marry, by Evelyn M. Duvall and Reuben Hill. New York, Association Press, 1953 (rev.). 466p. $3.75.

The increased understanding of marriage and family living as developed during the last seven years is ably reflected in this revised edition. The authors' rich familiarity with their material has enabled them to integrate studies and facts into a book both lay and professional readers will enjoy.

The many readers who found the earlier edition helpful will be interested in the new material—a consideration of the male's importance in the dynamics of family life, a detailed chapter on wedding plans, a brief discussion of adoption, and an expanded treatment of family life education. Format and organization have been revised for easier use, and new technical references at the end of each chapter will be of invaluable help to professional readers in many fields.

Mayo K. Newhouse
Family and Children's Service
Minneapolis, Minn.

Criminology, by Clyde B. Vedder, Samuel Koenig and Robert E. Clark. New York, Dryden, 1953. 714p. $4.50.

The authors have brought together a symposium of the writings of eminent criminologists, from the past down to the present. They begin with Lombroso and Ferri, who laid the foundations for modern criminology by first suggesting that crime has its roots in man's biological makeup and his relation to environment rather than in original sin, moral defects or natural perversity.

The field is comprehensively covered: The phenomenon of crime itself; the criminal, his personality and characteristics, patterns of conduct and possibility of adjustment; probation, parole and others are treated in original and authoritative research contributions. Separate sections of the book consider various phases of crime in the general social structure—including gambling, prostitution and syndicated crime—not only by case histories of individuals but by analyses of particular cities and crime organizations. Here are names, places and events with which the public generally is acquainted only superficially.

Although the primary purpose of the book is to provide students of criminology and those professionally engaged in such work with an authoritative volume containing the best available writings on the subject—it is so designed that it can be used as a textbook—anyone having normal curiosity about this field will find much interesting reading therein.

J. Allan Crockett, Justice
Utah Supreme Court

When Children Face Crises, by George J. Mohr, M.D. A Better Living Booklet. Chicago, Science Research Associates, 1952. 48p. 40¢.

If parents show their children how to meet everyday situations with confidence and courage, crises like divorce won't shatter a child's sense of security. Even minor quarrels between parents can upset and perplex a small child who does not understand that people can love one another and at the same time show hostility to one another. It is necessary for parents to explain to a child that they can get mad but that it is only temporary.

Bitter, recurrent quarrels can seriously affect a child's emotional growth —quarrels that erupt in divorce. The unhappy child is torn between the "good" parent and the "bad," weighed down with guilt, insecure about relationships . . . liable to carry over resentments against one sex or the other into adult life.

Parents should be careful to determine whether divorce is the best step, spare the child painful aspects, foster in him a healthy attitude toward people, try to give him normal family life, and in remarriage, respect the role of step-parents.

The Well-Adjusted Personality, by Phillip Polatin, M.D., and Ellen C. Philtine. Philadelphia, Lippincott, 1952. 266p. $3.95.

This book on preventive psychiatry by a husband and wife team is their second in the field of mental health. Dr. Polatin, a practicing psychiatrist, and his wife, a professional writer, have combined their skills to prepare a useful guide to emotional self-help.

Written for adults only, the book deals with the development of the individual during his student period, and his adjustment to work and to independence. The core of the work examines marriage and plainly indicates the authors' conviction that not all individuals should marry. The authors discuss the rights of parents, opportunities for full psychological maturation in parenthood, and emotional problems characteristic of the declining years.

While directed at preventive psychiatry, the book demonstrates once more the impossibility of discussing healthful living without resorting to the use of sick people as examples of the problems of human emotional adjustment. The authors use a profusion of brief case histories as illustrative material, a technique which, however useful in emphasizing a point, tends to leave the layman with the impression that lasting alterations in human behavior patterns are easily achieved. The difficulty of treatment is indicated in some instances, and in others treatment fails or the goals achieved are only partial. But the physician may feel the attitude of the authors tends to be somewhat optimistic as to the efficacy of brief psychotherapy in solving the problems of the more seriously neurotic.

The thinking expressed in the book represents current concepts of a dynamic theory of interpersonal relationships uncluttered by reliance on references to professional authorities and detailed psychoanalytic theory. The layman interested in mental health and preventive psychiatry will find in this book a reliable interpretation of the professional viewpoint regarding successful living, especially with regard to marriage, children and the home.

Unfortunately we do not as yet have adequate scientific tools with which to evaluate the prophylactic impact of such reading, but most psychiatrists are agreed that intellectual awareness of what influences our emotional life is a definite help in making us healthy citizens.

Robert T. Morse, M.D.

Why Some Women Stay Single, by Elizabeth Ogg. Public Affairs Pamphlet No. 177. New York, Public Affairs Committee, 1951. 31p. 25¢.

Marriage is not a goal but, like singleness, is a way of life. By facing up to her situation, by meeting it through creative and productive activities and by developing her capacity to love, the single woman can become an adjusted, integrated person.

First of all she should understand the reason why she is single, whether it be an extrinsic one or a pathological one due to a dominating, a puritanical or a possessive parent. She may, in her twenties, meet such problems as parental control, financial insecurity or loneliness. As she grows older, she must face realistically the fact that she will probably not marry and that she must make the best of it through job success—work with children, homemaking, social work—friends, hobbies.

No one, married or single, gets everything she wants, and the single woman "has more time and a greater incentive to express her creative effort in wider fields."

The Power of Sex, by Frank S. Caprio, M.D. New York, Citadel, 1952. 229p. $3.00.

Doctor Caprio, who has had clinical experience in psychiatry as a staff physician at Walter Reed Hospital, stresses the relationship of sex to health and shows how sex influences personality from childhood through maturity to old age.

Mrs. Charles H. Babcock **1909–1953**

With sorrow we write of the death of Mary Reynolds Babcock, friend of the American Social Hygiene Association and generous contributor to the social hygiene movement. Wife of a former ASHA board member, mother of four, good citizen, she always gave generously of herself and her resources for the well-being of her fellow Americans.

Mary Babcock was fundamentally a creative person. This creative ability was evident in her strong family devotion, her love for and proficiency in the arts, and her determination that her countless benefactions contribute constructively to the health and welfare of others. Her gifts to hospitals and schools are among her memorials.

Throughout her life she remained a quiet, purposeful person, whose self-effacement and desire for anonymity kept unknown to the public many generous gifts, including those to social hygiene. The American Social Hygiene Association in these words honors the memory of a friend whose fruitful life was ended far too soon.

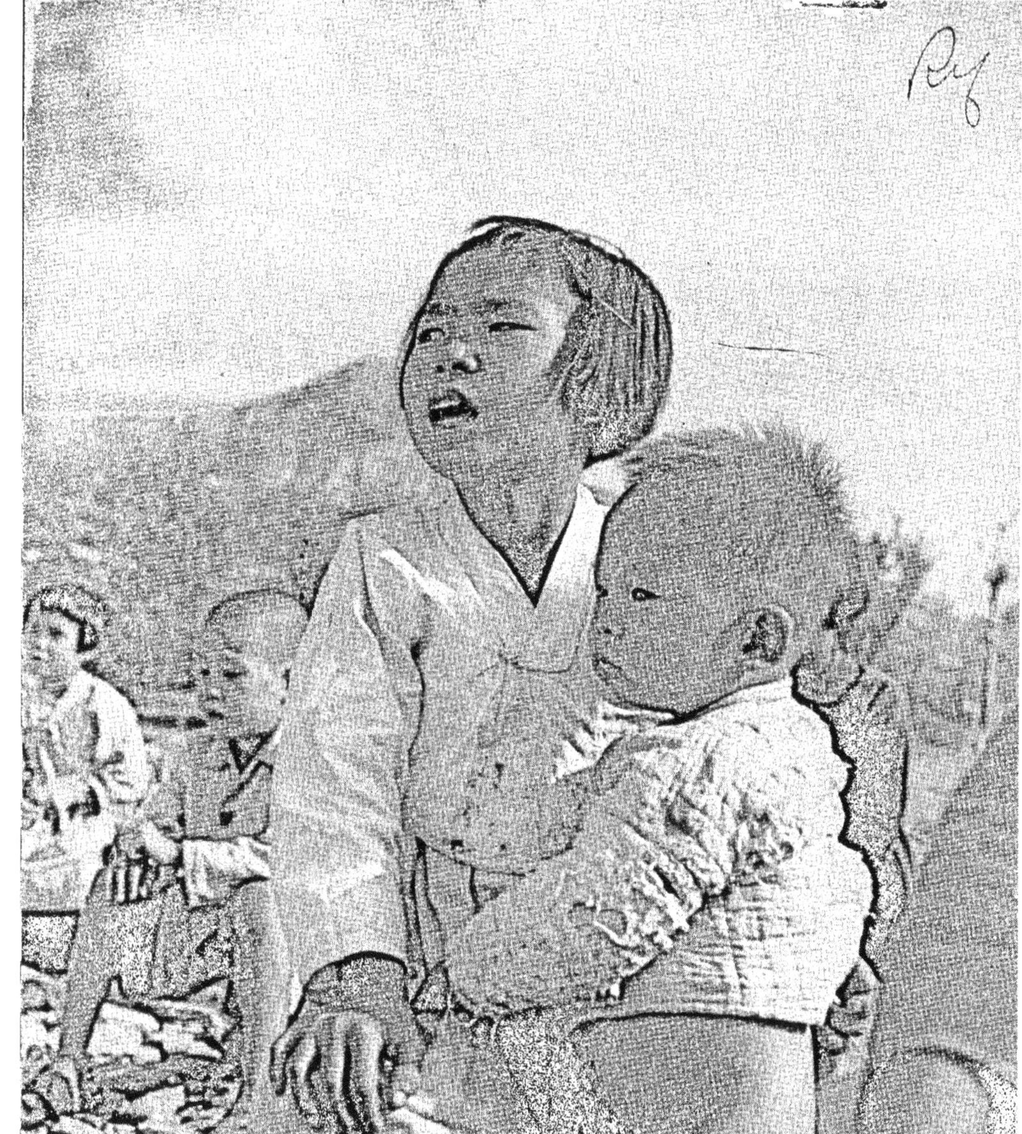

IN THIS ISSUE

NOVEMBER 1953

About our cover . . .

Family life in Korea. Twenty-sixth in a series of Journal covers on family life . . . United Nations photograph courtesy of American Relief for Korea

Harriett Scantland, Editor
Elizabeth McQuaid, Assistant Editor

Eleanor Shenehon, Editorial Consultant

THE JOURNAL OF SOCIAL HYGIENE

official periodical of the American Social Hygiene Association, published monthly except July, August and September at the Boyd Printing Company, Inc., 374 Broadway, Albany 7, N. Y. Acceptance for mailing at the special rate of postage provided for in Section 1103, Act of October 3, 1917. Entered as second-class matter at the Post Office at Albany, N. Y., March 23, 1922.

The JOURNAL does not necessarily endorse or assume responsibility for opinions expressed in articles, nor does the reviewing of a book imply its recommendation by the American Social Hygiene Association. Subscription price: $3.00 per year. Single copy: 35¢.

Ellis F. White, Ed.D.
Director of Education
American Social Hygiene Association

Three cheers for those who try!

What do parents hope for and teachers aim toward at the beginning of every school year? Probably all agree that by next summer boys and girls should be able to read more easily and more widely . . . know more about mathematics . . . write more lucidly and more legibly. They hope their children will know more about the glorious history of our country, about democracy and the meaning of freedom.

Certainly they hope somewhat vaguely, but sincerely, that during this process of learning facts and skills children will become stronger morally and spiritually and better able to adjust to today's complex civilization.

All parents and teachers do not agree about how to help a child develop these intangible qualities. But so long as a parent hands over to a teacher these more personal aspects of his child's life and education, and the teacher in turn declares such matters to be the responsibility of the parent . . . the child will be learning subject matter in a vacuum. Knowledge and skills are important . . . but they're not enough for a good life. The boy or girl whose parents and teachers work together in creating opportunities, at home and at school, that help him understand himself and his function in his family and in the world is going to be happier, healthier and better adjusted.

Yes, it takes work . . . it takes much careful planning to integrate successfully the important aspects of education for personal and family living into the school's curriculum and the home's activities. Good materials are available to the parents and teachers who want to use them. Three cheers for those who take the time to try!

Books and pamphlets in family life education

Dr. Milton Levine finds adolescents naturally resistant to parents, prone to misinterpret simple discussion as criticism. Let them get their books from an outside source, says he, and why not use a super novel as a medium?

The sex education of children is always a difficult problem for parents. In discussing this subject with their children most parents are not only inhibited by their own upbringing, but they face further complicating circumstances. The needs and interests of the children vary as they grow older and the child-parent relationships also change.

The pre-school child brings questions freely to his father or mother and expects a prompt and accurate answer. The school-age child usually asks fewer questions, but will still come to his parents unless he has learned that they resist such questions or give inadequate or incorrect answers.

The adolescent presents a much more difficult problem in sex education. He is at a stage of development when normally he is secretive and resistant to his parents. Simple discussions by his father or mother are taken as lectures and criticisms, and are resented forcefully. And in his desire to appear grown-up and feel grown-up, he hides his concern and lack of knowledge under the cover of "You don't have to tell me. I know all that already."

But unfortunately adolescents *don't* know "all that already," in spite of numerous discussions with their friends and acquaintances.

A little knowledge

It is true that most adolescents know that a baby develops within its mother's body, and they probably know how a baby is born. Comparatively few of them know the father's part in procreation, and none of them, as they enter their teens, can possibly know, much less understand, the sex urges, sex desires and sex passions which they are to experience.

Almost every parent wants his child to know that these sex impulses are normal. But we also want our children to know when and how they can control these impulses and why they must control them.

continued on p. 340

Carol Levine knocks the props from under "helpful" books for teen-agers with their "Sam and Sally" dialogues, likes relaxed parents who can answer a question without reaching for a book, thinks lulls in conversation are comfortable things.

Father and daughter write independently and agree—almost

Books play an important role in the life of every person in our modern civilization. Their subjects extend from trips to Arabia, to the phases of the moon, to adolescents and sex.

Many books are being published today on sex and sex relationships. Those I have read on the "facts of life" from a biological point of view are basically good, but those which try to give hints to "teen-agers" are detestable . . . at least all those I've come in contact with.

To me, the word teen-ager carries with it a lot of unpleasant and often untrue connotations, such as clumsy, spiteful, gawky. I don't think there is a really good word to express this in-between period from childhood to adulthood. Adolescent is better than teen-ager, at any rate.

These so-called "helpful" books seem very ironical to me. Some of the advice, which could be good, is written in dialogue form, implying memorization before the reader goes out on a date. For instance, they give advice on how to act on a date. Do they say, "Act informal, be yourself, make conversation naturally"—or something like this? No. They say, "Sam: 'Isn't it nice out here?' Sally: 'Yes, the air is cool. Do you like baseball?' "

They tell you to bat the conversation around so that it centers mainly on your date, and that every answer should hold a question with it so there shouldn't be a lull in conversation. I think a lull in conversation can say a lot more than meaningless chatter . . . after all, a lull isn't always uncomfortable.

Those books that do give good advice often overstep themselves and finish up in what I think is a very corny "Sam and Sally" method.

Pamphlets are more compact and generally stick more to facts, omitting the "hearts and flowers" many books have.

Books and pamphlets should be used to get facts from, rather than to

continued on p. 341

The toddler looks first to his parents for the answer to his questions.

Very few parents are able to discuss these problems with their teen-age sons and daughters . . . and still fewer adolescent children are willing to discuss these subjects with their parents.

It is obvious then that if we wish to give our children this important information in the right way it must in most instances come from pamphlets and books on the subject or from some outside source the children respect . . . such as a teacher, physician or minister.

Let's read

There are a number of excellent books and pamphlets approaching the subjcet from various angles. As an example one might note the following titles of pamphlets for the adolescent: *Understanding Sex, So You Think It's Love, Dating Days, Dating "Do's and Don'ts" for Girls, Growing Up Socially, Looking Ahead to Marriage, How to Live with Parents, Petting Wise or Otherwise?* and *Dates and Dating.*

These are titles which should be of great interest to all teen-agers and should be available to them. Parents might give them to adolescent children—but parents should not be too surprised nor upset if their youngsters put the books or pamphlets aside unused. This is to be expected in a great many homes, where adolescents are expressing their usual resistance to parental direction and interference.

It follows that these books and pamphlets should be placed in reading-rooms and libraries where teen-agers can read them as they desire without the knowledge of the parents. Teachers, Scout leaders, club directors or others outside the home—whom the children have confidence in and whose judgment they respect—could also give boys and girls these materials.

continued on p. 342

prove facts with. At home an argument comes up, and Mamma says to Papa that adolescents always argue, and then goes to the bookshelf and gets a book to prove what she says is true. Does this book do the proving? Certainly not in the midst of a heated argument.

When the criticism isn't personal

But if a pamphlet is handed out in school, or in a recreation center, the whole situation changes. A lot of pamphlets have a note of criticism in their titles, such as *Learning How to Improve Your Personality.* Maybe it's that at home the title pertains only to you, and suddenly becomes very personal . . . or maybe it's just that it's a lot easier to accept criticism in a group than singly at home.

I think biology and human relations courses in school are very important. These should start at about the age of 11, when there should be a biological course that has just the necessary preparatory facts that will help these pre-adolescent children understand "growing up."

Of course sex should also be brought up in the home, but many parents seem to think the word is taboo. Parents don't seem to realize that at times it's almost as hard for the child to ask a question as it is for them to answer it.

It would be nice to think that every home had informal, relaxed parents in it, ones who could talk about everything and anything with their children. If one of the offspring wants to read the facts in a book—fine. But if he asks a direct question, he will appreciate the information much more if it is answered directly and without the use of an "answer book."

A word about courses

School courses are important mainly to tell those children whose parents haven't yet told them about life. It's better to hear it in school than in a

Books that give "hints to teen-agers" are detestable!

continued on p. 343

Parents should not feel that the adolescent doesn't want this information nor that it is being forced on him against his wishes . . . for all boys and girls of this age level have numerous questions and look for aid in their solution. Children often consider these questions too personal to mention directly to parents or others. They may associate them with a certain amount of guilt, which may be readily relieved by proper information.

The novel as a medium

In a recent discussion with a group of adolescents on their attitudes they suggested that much more might be gained if novels and stories for teen-agers contained the information they need. They thought most books and pamphlets were too much like lectures on do's and don'ts for teen-agers. In their opinion if this same information were presented in the course of a story it would be more acceptable, for they would not only find interest in the story but would identify with the fictitious adolescent who meets the various problems.

If such a book were to be written it would have to be of high quality to merit a large audience and to be included in a list of school reading.

This would be one further approach to the personal education of the teen-ager. It would not take the place of nor supersede books and pamphlets, for these deal more specifically with situations encountered by adolescents. They should still be available for easy reference whenever needed.

A place for books

To expect the adolescent to bring his problems to his parents is generally not realistic . . . to expect him to be completely satisfied after a discussion with a physician, Scout leader, minister or teacher is to expect the impossible. Books and pamphlets attractively presented in a style neither condescending nor preachy—and placed where they may be privately and easily accessible—are among the most important agents in the education and adjustment of the adolescent child.

A native of Spokane, he received his M.D. from Cornell University Medical College, where he is assistant professor of pediatrics. Author of A Baby Is Born, sculptor, musician, father of two girls.

Milton I. Levine, M.D.

A 15-year-old high school junior, she has lived in New York City all her life. Likes children, square dancing, camping, ceramics and the viola.

Carol Levine

---

distorted fashion from friends who aren't even sure what they're talking about themselves.

In high school, it is necessary to go into the subject more thoroughly. The courses should be fairly informal, and each topic in which there is any discrepancy should be thoroughly discussed.

Films often provide clear definitions of things. Most of those I have seen are good, but a few have strayed from biology in trying to make the presentation appear "cute."

A teacher who gives his point of view and thinks that only it can be right, is often disliked by his class. Of course, there are some things that aren't debatable, such as how babies are born, or how many chromosomes there are to a human gene. But other topics—such as adolescent behavior—in one way or another hold more than one point of view and are worth discussing. Often personal problems are interesting topics for discussion, especially those which are of mutual interest to both sexes. And I think both sexes should discuss these subjects in mixed groups.

These courses are stimulating and worthwhile, and if they don't do anything else they answer the direct questions that pamphlets and books can't answer.

Another point that I think has to be brought in here is the companionship

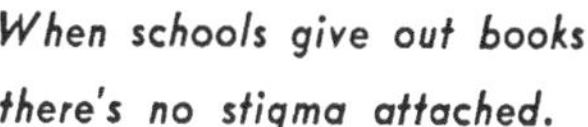

When schools give out books there's no stigma attached.

But it's the human element that counts.

of a counselor, teacher or just an older person, a person who is capable of giving advice, and with whom one has a close enough relationship so that he can talk about almost anything. Some of the things discussed might be much harder to accept from parents, especially if the discussion takes place in front of a brother or sister who is younger and just at the age when teasing is the best weapon in an argument. I feel that it's just so important to have a companion of some sort, who isn't a member of the immediate family and who can act as mediator, critic, complimenter and adviser on those things that are just impossible to discuss with or accept from parents.

Each to his taste

How much more there is to say on this all-over subject, I can't say. Each individual meets different people, and different circumstances. From these varied surroundings he can pick the various outlets that his personality needs. Many other people—a club leader, a clergyman, or maybe an uncle who's young enough to be modern in his approach to life—can and do help guide adolescents.

I think for most people the human element of guiding is much more important than the use of books and pamphlets, but in a lot of cases the latter are also important.

Whoever, wherever or whatever it is, there should be in the life of every growing person something or someone who answers the questions that bother maturing minds.

Catholic marriage forums in New York City

where religion, experience and medicine join hands

by Francis P. Mestice, M.D.

"Please keep up these marriage forums. I can't say enough in praise of them."

"The forum was terrific."

"The forum was helpful and I was able to learn many things."

"If it wasn't for the forum I don't know what I would have done."

These are a few typical reactions from the 26,240 young men and women who have attended marriage forums conducted throughout the Archdiocese of New York during the last five years.

The purpose of the marriage forum is to present in a positive, reasonable, practical manner the Catholic Church's teaching on sex, love, courtship and marriage. The thousands of young people who have participated in the forums came with a genuine desire to learn. Although they acquire new information and straighten out garbled impressions the ultimate objective is the formation of a positive attitude toward marriage.

Who attend?

The primary purpose of the forums is the remote preparation of young people 18 and over to assume the responsibility of marriage. Those already engaged come too, however, and the married take in the forums as well. either as a refresher course or as a source of reliable answers to current problems in their marriage. Non-Catholics, who are cordially invited, eagerly come and are favorably impressed.

Three youth-serving agencies in the Archdiocese of New York, the Confraternity of Christian Doctrine, the Catholic Youth Organization and the Catholic Charities Guidance Institute have joined forces in this venture. The alliance of these three organizations, significant in itself, arose from a solid conviction that the separate efforts of each were severely conditioned by the stability of family life within the Archdiocese of New York.

The forums are held in various areas, and thus far 25 areas—both rural and urban—have been covered, with an average attendance of from 200 to 800 young people.

The forum consists of three sessions on three successive weeks. Sessions for men and women are held simultaneously but separately, primarily because of the difference in attitude of the young women as compared to that of the young men, which is demonstrated particularly by their questions. (The men are inclined to be matter-of-fact, almost calculating in their approach. The young women, on the other hand, are more idealistic.) Forum speakers have agreed that it would be practically impossible to reach and benefit a mixed audience as well as a segregated.

Priest, laymen and doctor

The opening talk—by a priest—considers sex, love, courtship and marriage from a positive point of view and includes an exposition of what is meant by the vocation of marriage, the nature, purposes, qualities of the marriage contract, and the obligations of the married state. The "talking down to," "take it or leave it" approach is studiously avoided and a reasonable, logical "here's why" method of presentation is employed. The speaker gives some practical considerations in preparation for marriage and concludes with a consideration of marriage as a vocation.

The second session is called "The Voice of Experience." Two married people present Christian principles in action in their own marriages. Quite literally they share their lives and hearts with their young audience. They discuss finding and choosing a life partner, courtship, preparation for marriage as a career, necessary adjustments in the first year of marriage, and such down-to-earth questions as getting along with in-laws and shopping to get the most for each inflated dollar. They cover the adjustments that are necessary with the arrival of the first child and their responsibilities as parents . . . and give practical hints for getting the most out of the job of being a parent. Within the broad framework of these topics each lay speaker develops the subject in his own way, drawing heavily from his own experience.

In the third and final session a doctor discusses marriage from a physical and psychological point of view . . .

- Choice of partner.
- Optimum age for marriage.
- Psychological differences between the sexes.
- Emotional content of everyday married life.

With dignity and prudence he points out frankly and scientifically the physical and psychic positives of moral sex life. He stresses the importance of proper and competent premarital medical advice. He gives some attention to pregnancy and to abortion and contraception from the medical point of view.

His talk is not sex instruction in the usual sense, since this subject is considered to be reserved for the privacy of the doctor's office. He does, however, emphasize strongly the sublime place of sex in marriage and the

fulfillment of womanhood which is motherhood. Finally he demonstrates that there is no real quarrel between medical science and religious principles in regard to marriage.

Who are the speakers? The priests are most frequently moral theologians from seminary faculties and the ecclesiastical marriage tribunal.

The selection of the lay speakers is more difficult. "Mr. and Mrs. Big" are definitely excluded because their prominence or wealth could give the impression at least that they are not typical and could occasion the reaction—"It's easy enough for the likes of them." People of moderate means and no prominence save that of successful, happy marriage are selected. Among them are a policeman, a school administrator, an insurance salesman and a lawyer, to mention a few.

The women are generally college graduates and all are homemakers. Their appearance is proof positive that motherhood and attractiveness are not mutually exclusive. One of them is the proud mother of eight redheads; another had four children of her own and then adopted four others. These women particularly can answer with honest authority any question about limiting the size of a family.

The doctors, carefully selected, include obstetricians, gynecologists and psychiatrists.

A question period

At each session the formal talk is followed by a brief intermission during which the young people submit their questions in writing. And question they do! Written questions provide anonymity, do away with embarrassment, and save time, since experience proves that the young people's questions fall into much the same categories at each forum.

The question period is, as would be expected, the liveliest part of the evening. Speaker and audience alike welcome the humorous twist or the

Marriage—a sacrament, a vocation, a contract.

reaffirmation of previously discussed subjects. No matter what type of neighborhoods is represented the questions run much the same.

The priest is naturally asked many moral questions. The questions asked of the lay people vary considerably but always include several about limiting the size of a family because of economic conditions, nights off, working wives . .. . and most of all from the girls—"How do you know when you're in love?" The position of husband and wife in regard to finances and managing the home is a popular issue, too.

The lay speakers give their personal opinion on the practicability of the many and varied theories of child-rearing. Military service as a concern of both the young men and women often governs the kind of questions they ask.

The doctor is always asked about the legend that Catholic doctors are bound to save the life of the child in preference to the life of the mother, particularly in Catholic hospitals. This and other old wives' tales are properly exploded by the doctor during the question period. Frequent questions arise about so-called dangerous pregnancies as well as the practicability of the rhythm method. These and other medical questions are answered by the doctor in a thoroughly scientific and straightforward manner. Time and time again the conclusion that the Catholic Church and sound medical science are in complete agreement is the result of the questions most frequently asked.

Appropriate books and pamphlets are on sale during the forums, and the participants are encouraged to buy at least one publication as a resource to refer to in the future. Again the response has been more than satisfactory.

At the conclusion of each forum a questionnaire sounds out the reaction of the young people. Some of the responses are—

- "Subjects not covered satisfactorily."
- "Did not understand the medical terms."
- "You ducked working after marriage."
- "How do you stop your five-year-old from cussing?"
- "How can I get a man?"

On the other hand, there are responses such as—

- "Grateful for the chance to attend."
- "Everything satisfactory and straight to the point."
- "You don't evade the issue of marriage but hit directly on the subject, keeping me interested every minute."

A link in the chain

Marriage forums are not a cure-all nor the final solution to all the ills that beset our social institutions, particularly the family. However, they have been at least one small step in the direction recommended by the Catholic bishops of the United States in their 1949 statement that "study groups concerned with the preparation for family life should be widely encouraged and zealously promoted throughout our country." An attempt has been made to fulfill the desire expressed by Pope Pius XI in his encyclical on Christian marriage "that all may be thoroughly acquainted with sound teaching concerning marriage."

Ever mindful that preparation for married life is a process that begins in childhood and continues into young adulthood, these forums are presented as an additional help and bulwark to the young men and women of New York who fundamentally want to do a good job as marriage partners and parents.

Yonkers (N. Y.) obstetrician on military leave. Pioneered in marriage forums and participated in college courses on preparation for marriage.

Francis P. Mestice, M.D.

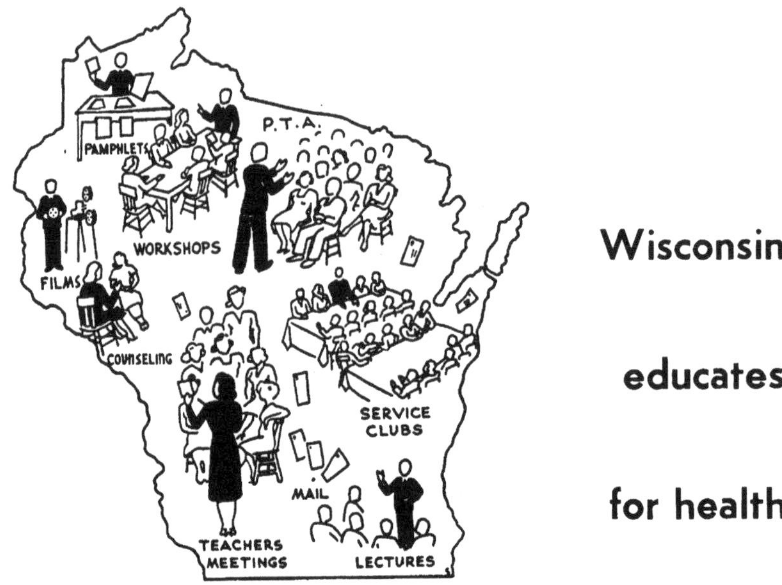

Wisconsin educates for health

by Philip Dykstra

Why has illegitimacy in Wisconsin decreased over 18% during the last 15 years while our neighboring states averaged a 2% increase?

Why does Wisconsin have one of the lowest venereal disease rates in the United States?

Why has Wisconsin had one of the lowest records on divorce rates during the last 15 years?

These were questions that deserved answering early in 1953 when we made a study of illegitimacy, divorce and venereal disease rates in Wisconsin. In each case the answer, it seems to us, is the same . . . a long-range, planned program of sex education, begun 30 years ago and carried on successfully right through years of depression and war up to the present time. The program has changed through the years, of course, as we have increasingly concentrated on encouraging local programs in schools, parent groups and civic organizations, and decreased emphasis on state services.

Since early in the 1920's Wisconsin has had two, three and sometimes four public health educators working full-time on social hygiene. They have traveled thousands of miles each month, met with scores of parent, school and community groups, and discussed sex education and family living with hundreds of thousands of pre-adolescents and adolescents. Their efforts, we feel, have paid off in the wholesome sex attitudes and habits of many residents of our state. These improved attitudes and habits form an important part of health . . . that state of "complete physical, mental and social well-being—not merely the absence of disease or infirmity."

Even if our goals were limited merely to the eradication of the physical ravages of the venereal diseases, we would still be justified in carrying on our education program. But today, with the growing concern for the mental, social and emotional welfare of society, our activities in sex education become even more important. The objective has become three-fold—social, mental and physical.

I base my observations about the health educator's role in sex education on my experiences with the Wisconsin State Board of Health. What we have achieved may not be achieved in other states . . . what techniques we have used may fail for others . . . and what problems we have faced may not trouble others in the least. But they may point up our pitfalls and obstacles to others.

Basic concepts

Let's look first at some general health education concepts. We believe that sex education stands in the same relation to health today as did sanitation and isolation to the control of yesterday's major health problems. Health education is a matter of using modern philosophy and teaching techniques to attack problems which cannot be stopped by building a plant, giving a "shot" or passing an ordinance. We can solve our social hygiene problems only by widespread understanding and individual action.

In dealing with any health problem, social hygiene included, the health educator must remember he is part of a team. Public health physicians, nurses, engineers and sanitarians all join the fight and contribute immeasurably to the success of any public health program. The contributions of a person with formal training in education also are readily apparent.

Educators are not needed to distribute pamphlets, articles or films. They should use these no more than any other member of the public health team. But educators, as consultants, can help make any sex education program effective by systematically using sound educational methods and procedures.

Health education is effective only to the extent that it motivates people to *act.* Knowledge itself is not enough . . . if it were, no doctor nor nurse would die of any disease that could be prevented or cured. When we know what to do, *and do it,* we enjoy the greatest possible security of continued good health.

Keeping these basic principles in mind, health educators in Wisconsin have developed a social hygiene program on two premises. . . .

- That sex education is a small but important part of education for family living and parent training.
- That sex education is best done by the home first, with the help of the church, the school and the rest of the community.

This has always been our belief, practically our creed: Parents are the child's first and best sex educators.

But parents need help in this important phase of their child's guidance—more so today perhaps than ever before. Now the child leaves the home when he is five or six and spends most of his waking hours outside the home. Other community agencies must continually supplement home training.

Thus, the role of the health educator is to serve in an advisory capacity and to encourage community agencies to develop local programs. Quite naturally, his services take different forms in various communities.

In the schools

There is still a need, we find, for outside lectures in sex education. Since the early 1920's, boys and girls in junior and senior high schools throughout our state have heard lectures on sex education. While we now feel that a year-round program in each school is more effective, we cannot break 30 years' tradition overnight, and so we still offer our lecture service to the schools.

In a school that has a program of social hygiene education, we try to encourage a fresh approach and a different interpretation of the subject. In a school where the nature of the subject, a rapid turnover of teachers, or some other factor has resulted in little or no concerted effort in sex education, we offer a wholesome approach to a subject previously considered taboo. Often this is the only wholesome discussion of sex these young people have ever received. In our discussions we do not attempt to overwhelm them with information. Instead we try to develop wholesome attitudes towards sex.

Work with administrators and teachers also receives a high priority in a health educator's social hygiene work. In Wisconsin we constantly meet with individual teachers or groups of teachers to encourage them to include more sex education within their particular curriculum field—not treat it as a separate subject. They are urged to discuss problems realistically with their pupils . . . and whenever the opportunity arises.

In the overall school program we suggest incidental education on the elementary level and integrated information in the junior and senior high years, followed by a regular semester course on family life education in the 12th grade. This course should include some discussion on the important role sex plays in family living. We also urge a realistic personal guidance program for every school as a most important part of social hygiene education.

Native of North Dakota, Hope College alumnus, former teacher and social hygiene worker. Now health education director of Wisconsin's State Board of Health. Father of three, vigorous PTA officer.

Philip Dykstra

Meetings with adult groups are another important part of any state-wide sex education program. Study clubs, discussion groups and other organizations often stimulate community-wide efforts for more wholesome and adequate sex education. Here too health educators properly serve as resources, not as leaders of community action; to be effective the stimulus and desire must come from the community.

Continuous review and survey of current social hygiene pamphlets, books and visual aids is another service we on the state level perform for interested individuals and groups. In Wisconsin we make samples of the better materials available to residents of the state on request. Our health materials library contains over 30 social hygiene pamphlet titles, including many published by the American Social Hygiene Association. Our visual aids library has 41 sex education films, filmstrips and recordings. Several prints of many titles are available. Almost 1,500 groups in Wisconsin viewed at least one of these visual aids last year.

The health educator's activities in sex education should *not* include case work. Most of us are not trained for it. We should make appropriate local referrals to the school principal or superintendent if a pupil is involved, or to a case work agency or child guidance center.

To be effective, the health educator must also coordinate his efforts by cooperating with related state agencies. We in Wisconsin have worked closely with the State Committee on Family Life Education, the State Department of Public Instruction, the State Department of Public Welfare, the University of Wisconsin's extension division, and the Wisconsin Congress of Parents and Teachers, to name but a few. Each has contributed immeasurably to the success of our state's social hygiene program.

We still have problems to solve. Chief among them is the need for encouraging school administrators and teachers to integrate sex instruction into their curricula where it most naturally and logically should be. Reactions to these suggestions are varied. Some say, "Our teachers are unprepared to handle the subject, and even if they were prepared, they don't have the personality to put it across." Others protest, "That's dynamite. This town would never stand for our teachers discussing that subject."

Our position is this: Granted that few teachers are adequately prepared to handle the subject; granted that our teacher-training institutions are perhaps not adequately preparing them; and granted that many teachers could use materials and aids to assist them, still . . . any person mature enough to discuss the subject in a normal and natural manner, without choking up and sputtering, as sex comes up bit by bit in routine classroom situations, is a far better source of information than the street-corner, alley or gutter.

And the opposition

What about the supposed objections from the church and home? These have been vastly over-emphasized, we find. When church leaders understand the modern theories of sex education—that we are not advocating a separate course *per se* but rather integration within the established curriculum; that we are including sex as a small but important part of family life education; and that we advocate taking no stand on the problems of birth control or divorce—then they are usually most cooperative. As for the parents, they are usually the first to admit they want help in handling this phase of their child's guidance and they welcome the aid of community agencies.

This then is Wisconsin's program. Has all this activity produced results? Has sex education been generally accepted in Wisconsin's schools and communities? Can any tangible evidences of its success be produced?

So far as the acceptance of sex education in our schools is concerned, we find an answer in the results of a survey conducted by Dr. Warren H. Southworth of the University of Wisconsin's School of Education in 1950. We quote from his *A Study in the Area of Family Life Education—The Nature of Sex Education in Wisconsin Secondary Schools* (to be published).

"In the spring of the academic year 1949–1950 a questionnaire (concerning the status of sex education in Wisconsin high schools) . . . was sent to all of the 498 public high schools (in Wisconsin). . . . A total of 404 principals (81% of the 498) responded with information from their respective schools. Only 14 of the returned questionnaires had to be discarded for incompleteness or failure to follow directions, which left a total of 390 questionnaires for analysis in this study.

". . . A careful study (of the returns) reveals that a great majority of Wisconsin high schools are offering some instruction in sex education. In fact, only one questionnaire was returned with the notation, 'We provide no sex education in our high school curriculum.' Only eight high schools (about 2.5%) indicated that sex education is presented through a special course. All the rest of the 390 high schools from which questionnaires were received included this subject as incidental or integrated units in such curriculum areas as science, social studies, home economics and physical education.

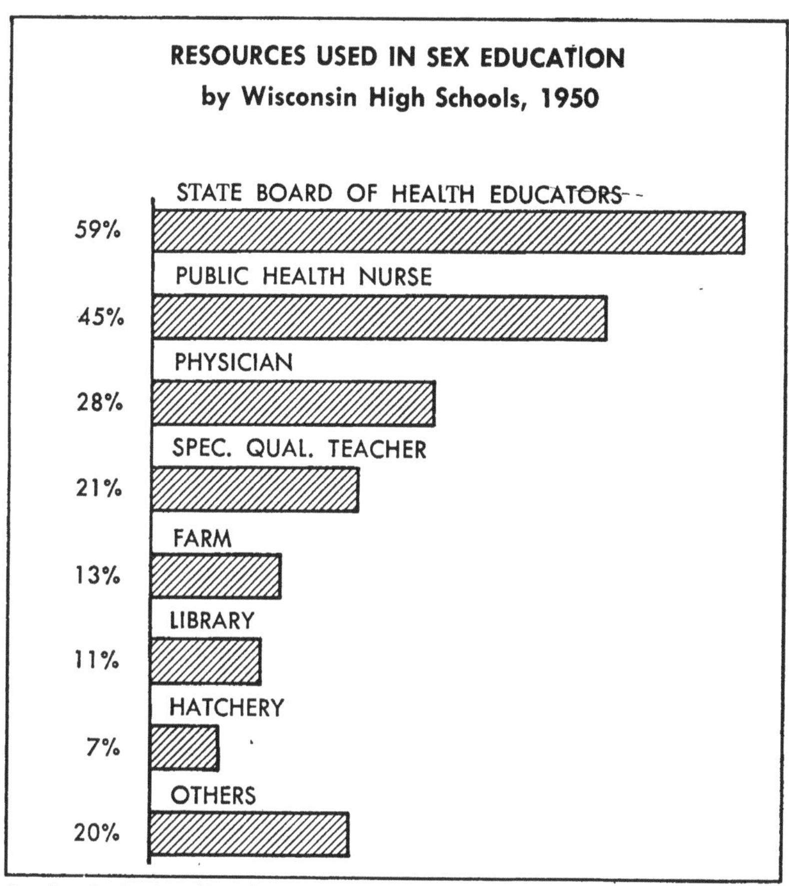

Data from Dr. Southworth's study

". . . The resources used in the sex education program (in Wisconsin) are many and varied."

Note that over half the schools listed health educators as their most helpful resource. Add to this the fact that health educators work closely with a number of the other people and agencies listed as resources by the schools— public health nurses, physicians, health and guidance teachers and libraries. Thus it becomes apparent that health educators are among the most helpful resources in social hygiene efforts in Wisconsin.

Another survey, conducted in 1951 by Ralph Kuhli, former state social hygiene chairman for the Wisconsin Congress of Parents and Teachers, gives us some indication of the social hygiene activities taking place in the communities of our state. One hundred sixty local PTA groups replied to questions about their social hygiene activities during the year.

- 42% of the PTA's reported that they devoted at least one of their regular monthly meetings to a discussion of local social hygiene problems.
- 52% previewed and discussed at least one sex education film.
- 8% conducted a series of community-wide study conferences on sex education.
- 6% reported buying and donating books on sex to local libraries.

Considering all the other community-wide problems in which the PTA has an interest, we think this survey indicated the important place social hygiene programs have in Wisconsin's local communities.

There is other tangible evidence of the success of our state's social hygiene program in Wisconsin's low illegitimacy, divorce and venereal disease rates.

To minimize geographic and economic factors, we compared our rates with those of other states in our section of the country (Michigan, Illinois, Indiana, Minnesota, Iowa and Ohio). The comparison seems valid as Wisconsin is the only state of those listed which has had personnel devoting their entire time and efforts to state social hygiene activities.

During the last 15 years, while surrounding states were reporting an average increase of 2% in illegitimacy, and the nation a 7% decrease, *Wisconsin can point to an 18% decrease.*

During this same period, only South Dakota reported a decrease in its divorce rate. No state, however, in our area has a lower divorce rate than Wisconsin. While the midwest increased 26% in its divorce rate, and the nation reported an increase of 37%, *Wisconsin recorded only a 16% increase.*

Probably the most reliable figures concerning the venereal disease rates are those based on the first million selectees and volunteers for World War II. These figures show that while the midwest states listed above averaged 20.8 cases of syphilis per 1,000 inductees, Wisconsin averaged only 6.3 cases per 1,000. Only one state in the country, New Hampshire, reported a syphilis rate lower than Wisconsin's. Figures based on approximately the same number of inductees during the present mobilization surprisingly show a rate of only 1.1 cases of syphilis per 1,000 Wisconsin inductees.

Yes, we feel that Wisconsin's sex education program has brought results. We realize our efforts cannot take all the credit for these most encouraging results, but we do believe our activities have given impetus to much of the fine work individuals, schools and organizations are now doing throughout the state.

Does sex education really pay? In Wisconsin we think the record proves it does.

American Venereal Disease Control Problems

With emphasis on their epidemiology

by J. K. Shafer, M.D.

The value to the public of preventing sexual contact between a person infected with venereal disease and one not infected has long been recognized. Many people may be familiar with quarantine-like measures which try to control the infected person, or punitive measures like the Danish law of 1866 which provided that those who "practice sexual intercourse, knowing or supposing themselves to be infected, may be punished. . . ." In 1876, the president of the American Medical Association, taking cognizance of European measures against venereal disease, proposed a system of control in all the states, based upon the following points:

- Preventing the spread of disease by using measures that protect the well against the sick.
- Using legal methods of control in addition to treatment by empowering Boards of Health to place persons diagnosed as having venereal disease in hospitals for treatment . . . just as they are empowered to deal with cholera, yellow fever and similar infections.

Although the medical and public health professions slowly began to appreciate the need for a frontal attack on venereal disease, the next 40 years saw little accomplished in the United States toward a national anti-venereal disease program. A few of the more progressive states began to require the reporting of venereal disease during the first two decades of this century, but beyond these beginnings no advances were made toward an effective program until the first World War. By that time experience in controlling other epidemic diseases and in trying to establish active local health units increased to some extent our knowledge about the control of venereal disease.

By 1917

That venereal disease was a significant cause of rejection for military service brought home forcefully the need for steps toward the control of this group of infections. The United States Public Health Service drew up plans for making a start toward a national control program and urged state health officers to begin adopting the necessary measures. What is important to us is that in 1917, before any kind of national program existed, it was clearly recognized that in addition to diagnosing, reporting, quarantining and treating venereal infections it was necessary "to investigate the physical condition of people who have contact with known cases of syphilis."

Speed—a byword in case-finding

Thus by 1918, when a national venereal disease control program had its beginning in federal legislation, we acknowledged the need for breaking epidemiologic chains of venereal infection. It was well accepted that the patient who appeared in the physician's office or the public clinic was but one link in a chain whose length was unknown.

Yet for many reasons we were not ready to exploit our recognition that the patient at hand was our only connection with our total problem . . . the world of infected persons. For one thing, during the postwar years of the 1920's and into the next decade financial support for a national venereal disease control program was non-existent. For another, serious problems of diagnosis and treatment overshadowed our concern with epidemiology. There was also the vexing question of holding patients to the then unknown duration of arsenical therapy. With limited financial and personnel resources, we were necessarily restricted to dealing with problems of diagnosis, adequate treatment and case-holding.

There were other reasons besides those that were technical and administrative. First and most obvious was the natural unwillingness of patients to name their sexual contacts. And beyond that barrier lay the viewpoints and limitations of health workers. Then, as now, it was no great problem to investigate the sexual partner of the individual with syphilis if the partner happened to be a spouse. But we had a very profound reluctance to probe into the sexual life of the person with syphilis much beyond the marital tie, perhaps because further delving seemed an unwarranted invasion of personal rights.

The ostrich attitude

This reluctance was only one aspect of the national traditions and social attitudes which barred successful search for contacts. Unaware of the real character of the sexual behavior of most venereal disease patients, health workers ascribed the reticence of patients in naming contacts to a feeling of shame or to a *bona fide* inability to remember casual sex partners. These rationalizations, which impeded a realistic approach to VD epidemiology, protected the prejudice deep in most of us against the informer . . . the busybody who reveals damaging information about his associates, the man who boasts of his conquests.

Perhaps of more importance, they expressed a profound distaste for the idea that many persons among us had a large number of casual or promiscuous sexual contacts within a short period of time.

Meanwhile, psychiatry, psychology and sociology as well as medicine and public health were showing interest in the venereal disease patient. They began to ask questions:

- What type of person contracts venereal disease?
- What environment does he come from?
- Who are his companions?
- What is his educational background?
- How stable is his sexual pattern?
- What *is* his sexual pattern?

One fact which evolved from both experience and scientific study was that the person with venereal disease usually has a wide circle of sexual partners, some casual, some more or less permanent. Thus, it began to become quite clear that if the health worker asking for contacts does not know this pattern and is content with the naming of one or two contacts, he may miss the source of the infection as well as other contacts to whom the patient may have transmitted his disease. The importance of the patient as a lead into this wide circle of infections was unmistakable.

Our public health program of treatment would be, at best, a holding operation until we bolstered it with sound and vigorous epidemiologic practice and made it a true program of preventive medicine.

A nicely shaded vocabulary

Acceptance of this reality, however, was not the end of our difficulties. We had to develop a language which venereal disease control personnel could use with the sexually unrestricted. The terms used by venereal disease patients were local and idiomatic, sometimes coarse, often virtually unintelligible to outsiders. We had to find words that would not offend decency too greatly, yet would be understandable to the majority of the infected.

Moreover, delineation of the epidemiology of venereal disease is a complicated process. It deals with a complex chain of actions involving many different workers. An error at one point may negate the value of all previous effort. The difficulties become more and more intricate as exchange of epidemiologic information takes place between distant health jurisdictions. This exchange requires a high level of cooperation between our states, thousands of local health departments, health authorities of the Armed Services, Veterans Administration, hospitals and private physicians.

So it was that during its early years our program was relatively ineffective in finding the early case or in uncovering an individual's infected contacts. The bulk of our admissions to clinics, as cases of latent syphilis, had passed the point where treatment could prevent further transmission of infection. For the most part, our program was not reducing the number of new cases which would occur in the future but was merely treating individuals to prevent late disabling complications. In 1941 only 14.2% of the syphilis cases coming to treatment were in the lesion stage.

It was, therefore, painful experience—and not our natural inclinations—which led us to adopt our present epidemiologic practices. When we realized the need for preventing the transmission of infection we assigned top priority to the interviewing of all lesion cases of syphilis for their contacts, to finding these contacts, and to bringing them in for diagnosis and treatment before the disease was spread still farther.

The interview

How did we conduct our work in VD epidemiology? The first step is to interview the patient. It is difficult to describe in detail an interview because the technique varies with each patient. Then too our procedures, developed almost entirely from trial and error, may be partially or entirely inapplicable to the social attitudes in other countries.

I shall restrict myself, therefore, to some of the concepts underlying our activities in venereal disease epidemiology. One of the basic concepts is that any theoretical or *a priori* approach to contact-interviewing or tracing is actually injurious to the success of the program. Because venereal disease is so closely bound up with sexual behavior, theories and practices of interviewing developed for other communicable diseases would not, we believe, be entirely suitable for this program.

Furthermore, we realize that the variations in personality among venereal disease patients demand great flexibility and resourcefulness from the interviewer. We have to rely upon his perception of the kind of patient before him and the kind of approach to which that patient would respond. Consequently, rigid rules for interviewing are kept to a minimum.

Did the patient travel?

An address prepared for the General Assembly of the International Union against the Venereal Diseases, April 21–26 in Rotterdam.

Another principle is that the interview is directed primarily toward obtaining the names and addresses of contacts. Education of the patient about the nature of his disease, alleviation of his personal or social problems, moral instruction and medical guidance . . . all these the interviewer weaves into the pattern of the interview as necessary to motivate the patient to name additional contacts or to increase the amount of identifying information. The interview. is only one part of the service that a venereal disease control center provides, and the educational process, to be successful, must extend beyond the contact interview into other aspects of that service.

A third principle of our interviewing policy relates to the amount of suasion permitted. Naturally, the interviewer makes every effort to obtain the patient's voluntary cooperation, and devises every item of the interview pattern to make that voluntary cooperation inevitable. He never extends himself beyond the point of voluntary cooperation. He never employs intimidation nor threats of legal action, nor conceivably practicable tools like narco-hypnosis. Even use of the quarantine power is rare.

Futility of punishment

Over a period of time these compulsive methods are not effective. To a large extent venereal disease patients belong to a group whose members pass on to one another their experience in the control center. If they speak well of their experience, we may expect future cooperation. If they speak badly, we shall find ourselves confronting patients whose attitudes are completely uncooperative.

For the same reason, the interviewer assures the patient that his information is completely confidential under all circumstances. The interview itself takes place in complete privacy without interruptions.

Two other lessons learned from experience serve to guide the interview. One is that no matter how many contacts the patient names, the interviewer always assumes there are still others yet unnamed. The second is that he seeks homosexual contacts from male patients with the same energy as heterosexual. I might add parenthetically that we have yet to establish a valid instance where syphilis has been transmitted between females in a Lesbian relationship. Here again the experience of other countries may differ.

The interviewer's first step—and this is basic to a successful interview—is to establish a friendly but professional relationship with the patient, reflecting clear acceptance by the interviewer of the patient's sexual behavior. The second step reveals the patient's ability to remember the details of his recent and remote past. The interviewer may praise the patient's memory in preparation for the point in the interview when he will use the patient's ability to recollect to establish the identity of his sex partners. Items of the patient's history not necessarily related to his sexual conduct are also useful in determining the extent of his mobility, particularly during the period when he might have acquired or transmitted his infection.

The interviewer learns about the patient's sexual habits, including frequency of exposure and number of partners, and the terms in which he describes his sexual activity—all indicative of what he may expect when he reaches the critical period of the patient's sexual life.

At this point the stage is set for the fruitful portion of the interview. Using inducements appropriate to the individual patient, the interviewer tries to obtain the names of all contacts in the critical period, beginning with the most recent and working back through the entire period when the patient and his sexual partners might have exchanged infections.

The form seems complex

Once the interviewer gets the maximum contact information it is recorded on a form for use by investigators in finding contacts and for the exchange of information between health departments. These forms have been continually revised as experience has indicated better ways and means of getting and transmitting more complete information.

The 5-part form (figure 1) presently furnished by the Public Health Service to its own hospitals, to the branches of the Armed Forces, and to the United

Figure 1. Venereal Disease Epidemiology Report Form

CONTACT'S LAST NAME | GIVEN NAMES *(And Nicknames)* | CONTACT'S ADDRESS *(Include State)* | No.B-126607

DATE REPORTED | AGE | RACE | SEX M ☐ F ☐ | MARITAL STATUS S ☐ M ☐ W ☐ D ☐ Sep. ☐ Unknown ☐

OTHER IDENTIFYING AND LOCATING INFORMATION *(As Speech, Teeth, Physical defects, Place and hours of employment, Hang-outs, Friends, Relatives, etc., be Specific)*

HEIGHT | SIZE | HAIR *(Color, Style)* | COMPLEXION *(Skin Color)*

DATE OF LAST EXPOSURE | PLACE OF EXPOSURE *(Establishment Name If Applicable)*

PLACE *(And Hour)* OF ENCOUNTER

CONTACT REPORTED BY PATIENT WITH: Gonorrhea ☐ Syphilis ☐ Stage ______ Other VD ☐ Specify ______ | PTNO

CONTACT'S RELATION TO PATIENT: Wife or Husband ☐ Friend ☐ Pick-up no Fee ☐ Other ☐ Specify ______ | INTERVIEWER'S NAME

USE REVERSE SIDE OF FIRST COPY FOR MAP IF HELPFUL

REPORTING AGENCY *(COMPLETE NAME)* | *(MAILING ADDRESS TO WHICH COMPLETED DISPOSITION IS TO BE SENT)*

INVESTIGATING AGENCY ______ **DISPOSITION** DATE OF DISPOSITION ______ WORKER NO. ______

IF INFECTED ENTER DISEASE AND STAGE IN APPROPRIATE BOXES BELOW

CLINIC AND PATIENT NUMBER OR PRIVATE PHYSICIAN:			DISEASE	STAGE
Brought To Treatment	(Previously Untreated This Infection)	X 3		
Returned To Treatment	(Previously Treated This Infection)	3		
Under Treatment At The Time Of Investigation		4		
Previous Treatment Adequate		5		
Refused Treatment		X 5		
OTHER- *Specify*		X 5		

IF NOT INFECTED OR DIAGNOSIS NOT ESTABLISHED, CHECK BELOW

	1	LOCATED - UNCOOPERATIVE (NOT EXAMINED)
	2	NOT INFECTED
	6	CANNOT LOCATE - REASON:
	7	MOVED OUT OF JURISDICTION (Enter New Address On Reverse Side)
	8	INSUFFICIENT INFORMATION TO BEGIN INVESTIGATION
	R 9	EPIDEMIOLOGIC TREATMENT - SYPHILIS
	X 9	EPIDEMIOLOGIC TREATMENT - GONORRHEA
	9	OTHER - Specify

PHS-1421 REV. 3-53 VENEREAL DISEASE EPIDEMIOLOGIC REPORT Form Approved Budget Bureau No. 68-R427.1

States Veterans Administration is fairly complex. The items of the form have emerged from consultation with our field investigators. We sent them a tentative draft of the form and requested criticisms and suggestions. On the basis of their replies, we included all items needed to enable investigators to find various kinds of sex contacts.

If the patient names a sex contact who lives within the jurisdiction of the health department which obtained the contact information, the routing of this form is quite simple and direct—into the hands of the local investigator. Often the interviewer himself may search out the contacts whose names he has elicited.

If the contact lives in an adjacent local health jurisdiction the telephone is usually the quickest and most efficient way to initiate case-finding action. If the contact lives in a different state, telegrams are permissible. By telephone or telegraph the interviewer passes along the information to the unit that will carry out the investigation. In such a case, the form follows through the mail, both to amplify the information forwarded by telephone or telegram and to serve as a control record. Return of the form not only assures the originating health department that the case has been adequately handled but also advises the state health department concerned that its program is functioning efficiently.

The investigator who goes out to find the contact must know his community and the groups of which the contacts are a part. He must know their hours of work and play, their haunts as well as their addresses, the focal points at which they congregate, and the persons who know them and whose leadership they respect. He must be discreet to aviod violations of confidentiality, tactful to

The VD patient . . .
who is he?
where does he
come from?

University of Nebraska and Johns Hopkins alumnus. Formerly medical officer of the U. S. Marine Hospital on Ellis Island, and VD control officer for Michigan. Now chief of the VD division, USPHS.

James K. Shafer, M.D.

prevent embarrassment of contacts by family or friends, and alert to circumvent the reluctance of some contacts to come to the health department.

A procedure recently evolved permits much-needed international cooperation in venereal disease epidemiology. Where venereal disease patients diagnosed in the United States name contacts residing abroad, multiple epidemiologic forms are forwarded to consular offices of the United States, which in turn transmit the necessary copies to the appropriate health authority. These forms originate in military stations of the United States located here and abroad, in medical facilities of the United States Public Health Service, the Veterans Administration, and the United States Coast Guard, and in state and local health departments. The action taken rests, of course, with the health authority where the alleged contact is reported to reside.

Sufficient copies of the forms are available to inform the consular office concerned and the originating station of the disposition of the case and to provide the investigating health authority with a file copy. Incidentally, the United States Public Health Service is eager to cooperate in investigating persons residing in the United States who have been reported as contacts of venereal disease patients in other countries.

(to be continued)

CREDITS

Photo courtesy of St. Brendan's forum, p. 347.

Photo by Edmund Duchene, Brooklyn, p. 348.

Photo courtesy of the Catholic News, p. 349.

Drawing courtesy of Wisconsin State Board of Health, p. 350.

Drawing by Harvey S. Weiss, courtesy of the Infantry Journal (Bernard Liebman), p. 363.

Photo courtesy of Standard Oil Company (N. J.), p. 367.

Photo courtesy of the National Recreation Association (Paul Parker), p. 370.

Spiritual Health and Development

Third of a series of chapters from Preinduction Health and Human Relations, new curriculum resource for youth leaders by Roy E. Dickerson and Esther E. Sweeney.

(continued from October issue)

Human Institutions and Human Beings

If every human being is recognized as being profoundly, individually and separately important, it follows that human institutions are the servants, not the lords, of men. This fundamental of the American way of life is closely related to the moral and spiritual heritage of all Americans. Recognition of this concept in concrete situations affects the moral and spiritual development of each individual.

In totalitarian states, the state itself is supreme, the individual completely subordinate to its needs and demands. The people may be arbitrarily deprived of rights that Americans take for granted . . . the rights to travel freely, to choose one's occupation and place of residence, to gain a fair hearing in the courts, etc.

The fundamental value that holds supreme the inherent worth of every human being has meant recognition of the rights of the individual in this country, sometimes to the disadvantage of the social institution . . . the state.

For example, in time of war the right of the individual conscience is clearly recognized, even though the country needs all possible manpower. Conscientious objectors are given fair opportunities to place their reasons for their position before an appropriate body and to serve the country in ways that conform to the requirements of their consciences.

The Constitution of the United States, the very foundation-stone of the state, was designed to be subject to amendment so that the state might never supersede the rights of the individual. Constant review of the constitutionality of our laws by the Supreme Court is a further protection of the rights of the individual and a further guarantee that our social institutions shall not become the masters of men but shall continue to be subject to them.

All of America's great social institutions—its court systems, state constitutions, school systems, penal systems, publicly supported hospitals—are the responsibility of good citizenship because they have been created to serve men and not the state. It is characteristic of the American way of life that when the people of New Jersey found judicial machinery and other matters of government antiquated and cumbersome, they commissioned citizens to recommend revision of the state constitution.

The majority of members of most school boards, prison boards, hospital boards, etc., in this country are private citizens, not government officials. While most of the great prison reforms and hospital improvements have been strongly urged by the officials of those institutions, vigorous public support of such changes has come about because the American citizen—as part of his tradition—is aware of his responsibility for evaluating and where necessary changing social institutions.

Class Discussion

- How does the citizen's responsibility for voting relate to the concept that institutions are the servants of men?
- Why is it a duty of responsible citizenship to become acquainted with proposed new legislation?
- How could domination of the individual by institutions lead to oppression and tyranny?
- Discuss the following quotation in the light of the concept that institutions are the servants of men: "Democracy is talking itself to death. The people do not know what they want; they do not know what is best for them. There is too much foolishness, too much lost motion. I have stopped the talk and the nonsense. I am a man of action. Democracy is beautiful in theory; in practice it is a fallacy. You in America will see that some day." (Benito Mussolini to the late Edwin L. James of the *New York Times*, 1928.)

Common Consent

Man is unique. He is capable of social relations involving cooperation, planning and, frequently, personal sacrifice for the good of the group. Because man can exercise moral responsibility in matters affecting himself and other persons and because he is capable of putting personal interests aside for the good of others, common consent has become one of the cornerstones and guarantees of the American way of life.

One sees the principle of cooperation—of common consent—at work almost every hour of the day. Three men decide to go on a fishing trip. Each has a special place in mind. They might all go separately or might even all stay home if they were unable to arrive at an agreement. Some give-and-take is necessary in order to carry out the original plan . . . that all three should go together to fish in an agreed-upon place.

In family life, cooperation is essential to comfortable, harmonious and constructive living. Whether the question is which style of architecture for a new house, what period for the new living-room furniture or which park for the family's Sunday picnic, mutual consent is necessary.

This does not mean that everyone is necessarily completely satisfied with the outcome of the decision. It means that some members of the group have agreed to what the others want and are mature enough to abide by the results.

In a country of almost 160,000,000 people the principle of majority decision through representative action has been agreed upon. This does not mean that every majority decision is perfect. Nor does it mean that the decision is everlastingly binding on 160,000,000 people.

The 18th amendment to the Constitution was the law of the land. It resulted from majority action. Subsequently the law was repealed . . . by majority action.

A law that is unjust or unsound can be passed by the majority. That law can also be repealed or amended. Both processes—enactment and amendment—and the orderly working out of them involve recognition of the unique nature of man . . . his ability to cooperate and to accept majority action or, when the issues are grave, to work for the change of majority opinion.

The American system of spiritual and moral values, which places major emphasis on the uniqueness of man and on his inherent worth and dignity, resists the idea that violence is necessary to achieve worthwhile ends and stresses the wisdom and *humanness* of common consent.

This does not mean that force may never justifiably be used. When arbitration, negotiation and every reasonable means of obtaining cooperation and maintaining peace fail, force may have to be used. But it must be force tempered by humanity, regulated by law and safeguarded by justice. Thus, in foreign

We, not the state, are the masters of our schools, law courts, hospitals.

relations, when aggression cannot be controlled by mutual agreement and common consent, it may be necessary for the United States to wage war.

But when war becomes the last resort, recognition of the fundamental dignity of every human being must still actuate the American soldier . . . as it should actuate all human beings.

In reviewing a case presented during the Japanese war crimes trials, General MacArthur said: "The soldier, be he friend or foe, is charged with the protection of the weak and unarmed. It is the very reason and essence of his being. When he violates this sacred trust, he not only profanes his entire cult but threatens the very fabric of international society. The traditions of fighting men are long and honorable. They are based on the noblest of human traits . . . sacrifice."

Class Discussion

- Here is a statement by the late Supreme Court Justice Brandeis: "Democracy substitutes self-restraint for external restraint. It is more difficult to maintain than to achieve. It demands continuous sacrifice by the individual and more exigent obedience to the moral law than any other form of government." How would you apply this to the following situation: The desire of a mob to kill, without trial, a man caught in the act of a vicious and cruel murder and the responsibilities of law enforcement officers under such circumstances?
- How does Justice Brandeis' statement relate to responsible use of voting power? What should every voter think about and try to learn before casting his ballot for candidates for office, before voting on matters submitted to referendum?
- Suppose a boy is overwhelmingly voted into a class presidency. Several students know of strong reasons why he is not worthy of the honor. Majority opinion has already prevailed. How can the students referred to handle the problem with due regard to morality and to the principle of common consent?
- In the Armed Forces, within the discretion of the officer in charge, some matters may be handled on the basis of common consent. Does this mean that all matters should be decided by poll? How are the Armed Forces themselves an outgrowth of the principle of common consent in this country?
- Why can't the President of the United States declare war on his own initiative?

Devotion to Truth

From the concept of man as a unique, inherently worthy individual capable of exercising moral judgment and of accepting moral responsibility for his acts arises the spiritual value of devotion to truth. To blind oneself to truth or to evade the moral responsibility of seeking truth and of using judgment and intellect in that search is to fail to realize the maximum integrity of which each individual is capable.

The American way of life encourages the search for truth and knowledge through its traditions of public education, free press and free assembly. Devotion to the highest truths is guaranteed through freedom of worship.

It is for the preservation of these values—so natural to man, so much part and parcel of his makeup as a human being—that this country is in the forefront of efforts to make the UN's Declaration of Human Rights a reality for all peoples everywhere.

To preserve these values from destruction by totalitarian powers this country has instituted its entire program of national preparedness against attack. Essentially, it is for the continued guarantee of the fundamental rights of man—in a world where many of those rights have been abrogated by force and violence—that young men and women are asked to devote a period of their lives to service in the Armed Forces of the United States.

But devotion to truth does not exist in a vacuum. Everyone has a moral obligation to seek truth, to speak truth and to bring together as much fact and opinion as possible in trying to arrive at truth.

A free press

Channels of communication carry a heavy responsibility in informing and influencing people. Simply because it is free, a free press (including radio and TV) can slant news. But the American press, on the whole, adheres to the highest standards of reportorial integrity, recognizing its obligation of being accurate and truthful in news reporting while reserving the editorial and by-lined column as channels of free opinion. In a national political campaign, for example, a newspaper such as the *New York Times* gives equal coverage to both major parties. In so doing, it maintains truly fair standards of journalism. For ignoring one side of a major issue is just as much a case of news-slanting as publishing a biased, inaccurate story.

The intelligent newspaper reader, on his part, has his own criteria of honesty and fairness. Recognizing that he himself may have certain prejudices which color his interpretation, he reads several newspapers and a variety of editorial opinions in his devotion to truth and search for it. And when discussing with others what he has read, he is careful to make clear where he is citing facts and where he is citing opinions and estimates.

Academic freedoms likewise carry responsibilities. The search for information and enlightenment requires discipline of mind and emotion. It also requires some guidance from mature minds. A young person is not forfeiting freedom in his search for truth because he relies to some extent on the wisdom and experience of others.

The young man or woman who seeks historical truth must search for it in the writings of others . . . he can rarely consult source documents themselves.

When seeking ideas on the nature and responsibilities of man, one must depend heavily upon past and present philosophical scholarship. A young person who seeks religious, scientific or economic truth must be guided, even to some extent directed, by the findings of others.

This does not mean that young people should fail to use intellect, judgment and reason in exercising their basic right to seek knowledge with freedom and honesty. The search, however, may be lonely and possibly less fruitful if not accompanied by some reliance on the honesty and wisdom of other people equally devoted to truth.

Probably no other Armed Forces in the world are so deeply interested in the young person's search for truth as our own. The educational emphasis in our Armed Forces is not the result of a desire merely to polish up American youth's intellect. The Armed Forces are committed to the ideal of a thinking, convinced fighting force equipped through both formal and informal education to know the truth and fight for it.

There's democracy in the majority decisions of free people.

In fair play and good sportsmanship we recognize the equality of all.

Devotion to truth makes other demands on people. What one says, writes or conveys by facial expression or gesture may tell the truth or falsehood. Communication between human beings, in small things or grave, should be honest. Men are not like lower animals, which are unable to live lives of deception because their behavior is so greatly determined by instinct. We can be dishonest . . . but only at the risk of destroying the very meaning of communication.

Both historic accounts of court hearings in totalitarian countries and novels by men such as Arthur Koestler who have lived in those countries demonstrate what can happen between human beings once devotion to truth ceases to be a spiritual value to a government. The big lie is not just a single untruth. It is a systematic sell-out of truth to gain certain ends.

In so-called white lies—the headache used to break an appointment, the other engagement by which a dull invitation is refused, the lack-of-time story to cover a neglected duty—may lie the seeds of greater untruths on other occasions.

Many people are untruthful because they are afraid of consequences of telling the truth. Many tell untruths to ingratiate themselves with people. Other untruths arise from a desire to impress people, to injure people one doesn't like, to cover ignorance and appear to be "in the know." Clearly these reasons stem from immaturity.

In their search for personal growth and development, young people must learn to face the consequences of truth—consequences sometimes painful or uncomfortable—if they are to function in an adult way.

Class Discussion

- What moral responsibilities do editors have in a country where the free press is a basic institution?
- What moral responsibilities do writers have towards a free press?
- Why is public opinion likely to be a stronger controlling factor on such things as salacious or inflammatory literature, motion pictures, etc., than censorship?
- Cite instances of how public opinion created self-censorship in communications. (The motion picture industry's codes; editor's reactions to letters from readers about certain features—columns, comic strips, etc.)
- How do freedoms carry concomitant responsibilities?
- Why are moral and spiritual values important in such studies as contemporary history? Sociology? Homemaking?
- Sometimes people tell untruths "to keep from hurting others." How can one be truthful and yet not hurt others? Discuss in relation to two situations: Jim invites Sally to the junior prom. She has no other invitation but hopes Joe will ask her. In any case, she wouldn't want to go with Jim . . . she doesn't particularly like him. In the second situation, a businessman and his wife have promised to visit friends for the evening. The friends have gone to a lot of trouble preparing for the visit. The husband is tired, worried about business matters, just wants to stay home. He agrees that his wife should go and explain things to their friends.

Respect for Excellence

Since the American way of life is predicated on great spiritual ideals—the essential worth of each individual, his moral responsibility and his consequent obligations to himself and others—it follows that in the American social and educational scheme of things each individual should be assisted towards the maximum development of his mind, character and creativity.

Although human beings, in the words of the Declaration of Independence, are created equal, all are not alike in all things. But this does not mean that anyone in our society is free to classify the people who should or should not receive encouragement and assistance to develop to their utmost. Class distinctions—whether economic, social, religious, racial or ethnic—are inimical to America's spiritual values.

The only distinctions consonant with a democratic society are individual distinctions based on individual behavior, performance and integrity. Even there, it is the moral responsibility of each person and of our whole society to resist discrimination against any individual and to insure that each receives maximum opportunity to develop his potentials.

Under one set of circumstances, a boy or girl may do poor work in school, misbehave in one way or another or appear indifferent to efforts to reach and assist him. Yet under other conditions the same boy or girl may respond well to educational opportunity, work towards the development of his own character, and work with others for his own and the community's goals.

The classroom cut-up may be using diversionary tactics to draw attention away from his inability to keep up with his work. Without understanding and help from his teachers, parents and perhaps his fellow students, he may resort to even more serious behavior in his efforts to keep his actual difficulties from being recognized. With understanding and help, he could deal more maturely with his real problem . . . by tutoring, by more intensive and better-planned study.

No one who believes in the inherent worth of every human being has the right to regard another as "hopeless" or unreachable.

While protection of the individual and the community requires separating from society people who violate the law, our entire judicial and penal system is predicated on the fact that human beings can and do change and that they can realize themselves productively and be valuable to the world even in prisons or other penal institutions. From prisons have come such contributions to society as prisoners' offering themselves as human guinea pigs for medical research programs; creative gifts such as the stories of O. Henry; inventions such as those of David Marshall Williams, who gave the U. S. Army the "short stroke" and movable-chamber principles for its carbine.

Only a penal system recognizing the inherent worth of every individual (even an errant one) could have nurtured such contributions to society.

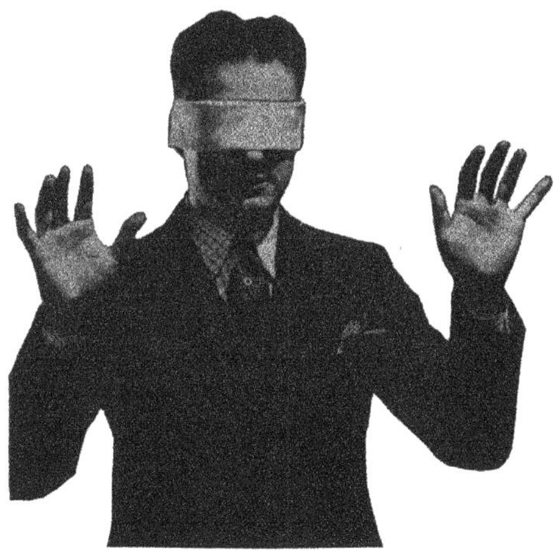

Without discrimination as to race, creed or sex.

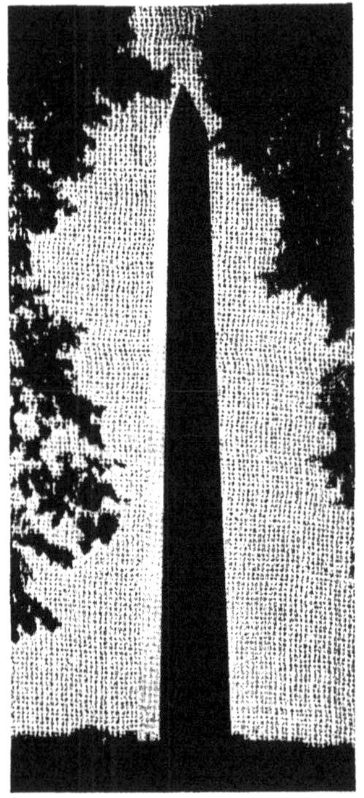

American traditions . . .
public education,
free press, freedom
of worship . . .
in these we reveal
our devotion to truth.

The ideals of individual worth and respect for individual excellence mean that neither money, ancestry, positions of authority and power nor other accidental circumstances create excellence. Youth's effort to achieve excellence of mind, character and creativity is therefore worthwhile, for it is through such efforts that man is most distinctly human and most completely living in terms of his own human nature.

Whether all such efforts receive recognition and praise or whether excellence itself will always be known to other people and encouraged by them will depend on a variety of circumstances. No one can predict.

But the difference between functioning to one's utmost and functioning merely for recognition and prestige is the difference between living in spiritual and moral terms and living for selfish ambition alone. The long nights Abraham Lincoln spent in a draughty, ill-lit cabin seeking knowledge and truth were not aimed at the presidency. They were aimed at self-realization . . . at excellence. What followed was the result of both his preparation and the circumstances of his times.

Today's young people will make tomorrow's decisions. They will vote for men and measures that will either provide or withhold opportunities for people to develop their maximum excellence in mind, character and creative ability.

The United States is still a growing, developing country. All the opportunities for self-realization have not yet been provided for every individual in this nation at the level of each person's capacities. But the spiritual concepts on which the nation was founded are real. They can be made to work more and more consistently for our national goals if our citizens are equal to the effort to reach those goals.

The student of today knows that for himself and for many of his classmates the road to higher learning is not altogether wide-open and easy. He also knows, though, that there is more educational opportunity available to him than there was to his grandfather. Best of all, the student of today knows that in a free democracy initiative and persistence will open doors in business, industry, the professions and trades . . . doors that might be forever closed to him in many other countries.

Because notions of a caste system are inimical to democracy, youth can readily realize that intellectual attainment is not the only kind of attainment worthy of honor in our society. An intellectual aristocracy—or any other kind—is a danger to our very moral and spiritual heritage itself. Worth, dignity, honor, idealism and achievement of the best of which one is capable are still and always will be more highly regarded in the American way of life than mere wealth, intellectual attainment, ancestry or political importance.

Class Discussion

- Why are motion pictures about pioneer life in America, exploration and invention so popular in this country?
- Is a college education essential to a full and successful life?
- Name some of the influences in the lives of young people that tend to develop character. Name some of the experiences that develop character, if used with maturity.
- Theophrastus, a Greek philosopher, said, "Why is it that while all Greece lies under the same sky and all Greeks are educated alike, it has befallen us to have characters so variously constituted?" How would you answer that question?
- Name some great men and women in this or any other country who achieved self-realization and contributed to the welfare of others despite poverty, limited education, personal illness or other difficulties.

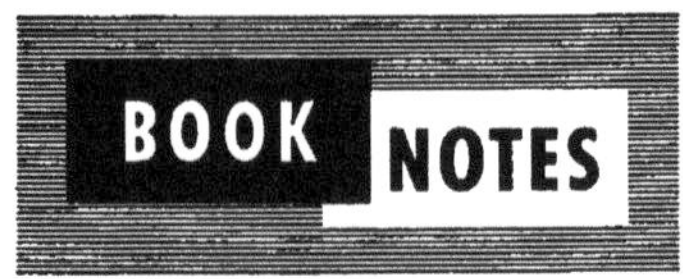

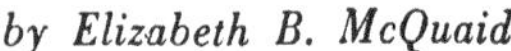
by Elizabeth B. McQuaid

Marriage, Morals and Sex in America, by Sidney Ditzion. New York, Bookman, 1953. 440p. $4.50.

An historical review of ideas—sweeping from the pen battles of the 18th century to the findings of Kinsey and the production of the films "Human Growth" and "Human Beginnings" within the last half-decade—this is an effort to document the proposition that sexual-social problems are indivisible and that social reform movements are always interrelated with sex reform.

Some historians may question the selection of materials used to document these theses and may question the distortion given various reform movements and religious sects by examining them from the sexual facet.

However, in addition to a very detailed presentation of the role of letters, press, pulpit and public lectures in the feminist movement of the 18th and 19th centuries, the book also gives a much-needed historical and social context for the family life education of the 20th century.

For the family life educator whose history goes back only as far as the initiation of the Groves' course in 1926 and Popenoe's American Institute of Family Relations in 1930, or Judge Lindsey and Philosopher Russell's writings in 1925 and 1929, Ditzion's work provides a framework for many of the trends and statistics of contemporary family life education and makes many of the problems appear not so contemporary nor new.

Clark E. Vincent, Ph.D.
University of California

Illustrated Guide to Sex Happiness in Marriage, by Lucia Radl, M.D. New York, Greenberg, 1952. 112p. $1.75.

This little book, well written and most completely illustrated, is a lucid presentation of much-needed factual information for exactly the purpose the author claims. It will be of value to the young married couple and to those approaching marriage because of its realistic, non-emotional presentation of dependable facts and situations they will meet. It should prove a very great help to marriage counselors with its direct, sensible and reassuring approach to their problems.

G. G. Wetherill, M.D.
San Diego City Schools

The Control of Communicable Diseases, by Hugh Paul, M.D., D.P.H. London, Harvey and Blythe, and New York, deGraff, 1952. 526p. $9.50.

The chapter on venereal disease control is the only portion of this book which might be of interest to the student of social hygiene, but we find in it little of practical value. In the limited section on the control of venereal diseases one misses a forthright, organized discussion of the activities necessary to carry out an effective program. One sentence is devoted to contact investigation. The material presented may give the inexperienced some misleading impressions and even contains outright inaccuracies. For example, Dr. Paul states that in syphilis "spontaneous cure does not occur" and that treatment is compulsory in the United States.

There are also important omissions. The author makes no mention whatever of darkfield and cerebrospinal fluid examinations in the diagnosis of syphilis, nor does his comment on the treponemal immobilization test contain reference to the potential significance of this test in specifically detecting latent syphilis and false positive reagin tests. The devastation of late cardiovascular complications of syphilis is nowhere included.

The reader benefits little from the author's inept statements and ends the chapter without positive attitudes on methodology in venereal disease control.

Adele C. Shepard, M.D., M.P.H.
New Jersey State Department of Health

Sex and Marriage, by Havelock Ellis. New York, Random House, 1952. 219p. $3.00.

The name of Havelock Ellis is a landmark in the history of social hygiene, but much of his important work was done more than a half century ago. Inevitably, his significance is now largely historical. This book is made up of essays and to a large extent book reviews published during the later years of his life or written prior to his death in 1939. It is hardly necessary to say that they are dated.

It is not very high commendation of a book to say that it leaves in the reader's mind a vivid impression of the great advances made in the subject since the book was written! But students of social hygiene cannot avoid getting such an impression, while at the same time they renew their admiration for the author's graceful literary style and the humanism which inspired him.

Paul Popenoe
American Institute of Family Relations

Modern Concepts of Communicable Disease, by Morris Greenberg, M.D., and Anna V. Matz. New York, Putnam, 1953. 553p. $6.20.

The chapter on venereal diseases is succinct in its presentation and broad in its scope. Readers should realize, however, that the therapeutic effectiveness of the most recently manufactured penicillin preparations, plus accumulated current knowledge of their effectiveness, have altered treatment schedules considerably since the publication of this book.

However, the material on the fundamental relationship between the nursing management and the medical aspects of the control of venereal disease is especially valuable to nurses, students and general practitioners. The result is a clear-cut, panoramic view of our present-day concept of venereal disease control.

John William Lentz, M.D.
Philadelphia Department of Public Health

The Mystery of Love and Marriage, by Derrick Sherwin Bailey. New York, Harper, 1953. 136p. $2.00.

This scholarly, theological review of biblical and church history concerns getting married, being married, or getting separated and getting married again. The thesis is "one flesh" *henosis*, the harmonious union of a man and a woman.

The biblical *eros*, *philia* and *agape* loves as they become complementary in the marriage relationship provide the setting for a discussion of the significance of sexual intercourse. The combination of the three kinds of love reaches the superlative in this union in "one flesh."

Although the author is an Anglican, his theological and scriptural considerations include varieties of interpretation made throughout the history of the Christian church. It is only in appendix II that the Anglican position regarding divorce rather colors the interpretation of some biblical passages.

This is a compact volume that is much needed by theologians, physicians and social workers, but anyone can read it and forever be freed from any hesitancy or feeling of shame in dealing with this subject, as the author's view of the God-intended pattern of human unity expressed in sex relations becomes clear.

Rev. Fred G. Scherer
Salem, Ore.

Babies Need Fathers Too, by Rhoda Kellogg. New York, Comet Press, 1953. 256p. $3.50.

This book attempts to fill a very large void in the literature on child-rearing. It discusses the place and function of the father in the family, in contrast to the usual emphasis on the mother-child relationship that has failed too often to heighten our awareness of the father's importance.

Of the 19 chapters, four chapters discuss the father or the family, while the rest discuss the child's stages of development and his needs in relation to important experiences. The book therefore is again mostly related to child development—no doubt an important focus—even though the title seems to emphasize the role of the father.

It is written with a good deal of common sense, and is no doubt based on vast experience. It avoids professional jargon, tries to define very simple concepts, and in my opinion does this too much; e.g., in defining a nursery school.

I miss in the book an understanding of the role of the father in our culture—what we expect from the man as the head of the family group—and the cultural values he represents, often outside his own free decision. I also miss a discussion of the marital relationship, and I hope in the future it won't be necessary to write books which speak about "mother" or "father," but which speak rather about the "parents." The role of the father is not understood, unless one knows his role as a husband, because his love for his wife or his discontent will reflect itself in his relationship to his children. When we speak about the family, we cannot discuss one single member without discussing the whole family group.

I am sure this is a book many mothers will want to give their husbands, and so it will fulfill its intentions.

Peter B. Neubauer, M.D.
Council Child Development Center

Management of Chancroid, Granuloma Inguinale, Lymphogranuloma Venereum in General Practice, by Robert B. Greenblatt, M.D., and others. Washington, D. C., Division of Venereal Disease, U. S. Public Health Service, 1953. 2nd ed. 66p. 30¢.

This booklet, of special interest to venereologists, covers each of the diseases of its title in turn, with particular reference to their etiology, incubation period, epidemiology, clinical signs and symptoms, clinical course, diagnosis and treatment. A final chapter on differential diagnosis and a bibliography complete the treatise, available from the U. S. Government Printing Office.

Problems of the Family, by Fowler V. Harper. Indianapolis, Bobbs-Merrill, 1952. 806p. $9.00.

The author, a professor of law who teaches the course in domestic relations at Yale University Law School, uses court decisions, social case work reports, text notes and readings from the literature of anthropology, sociology and psychiatry to show the legal, social and psychological aspects of family problems. His purpose is to give information about the causes of family breakdown, preventive measures available, and agencies and specialists that treat family problems.

An excellent reference book, it is encyclopedic in scope and equipped with glossary, workable index and extensive bibliography, especially suitable for clergymen, doctors, lawyers, teachers, family life counselors, social workers.

Beginning with a history of family organizations from primitive society to the present, the book covers premarital problems and relationships, creation of the marriage relationship, problems of marital adjustment, and family disorganization . . . the last including direct treatment techniques, the socio-psychological treatment of domestic discord and a study of 250 successful families, followed by proposals for full-fledged reform in our divorce laws.

William J. Petrus
American Social Hygiene Association

Whom God Hath Joined, by David R. Mace. Philadelphia, Westminster, 1953. 93p. $1.50.

Dr. David Mace, known widely for his distinguished leadership of the National Marriage Guidance Council of England, is now professor of human relations at Drew University. In *Whom God Hath Joined* he suggests four weeks of daily meditations on the Christian meaning of marriage.

While written principally for couples recently married to be used by them in deepening their love and understanding of each other and of their marriage, the book contains many profound insights which are certain to prove inspiring to all married Christians.

Ministers, leaders of youth groups, and parents will find careful reading of the book well worth while.

Richard E. Lentz
National Council of the Churches of Christ

Marriage, by Earl Lomon Koos. New York, Henry Holt, 1953. 441p. $5.50.

It is to be expected that a book representing a complete rewriting of Professor Ernest R. Groves' first text in marriage education and an attempt to perpetuate Groves' point of view supplemented with newer insights provided by the experience of many instructors and the research findings of the past two decades would be an improvement over the original. Koos' book is that.

It is addressed to the student who expects some day to marry. It contains much to provoke thought and does not pretend to give all the answers. Koos' long experience in teaching and counseling serves as an effective screen for the inclusion of material that students consider pertinent and the exclusion of that which is remote from their needs and interests.

Throughout the book it is apparent that the author realizes that students must make value judgments relative to marriage and marriage preparation and that therefore they need more than an objective and statistical analysis of what is happening to marriage today. Topics such as premarital and marital sexual adjustment, abortion, contraception, mate selection are discussed with balance and perspective.

The style of the book is interesting and simple but not elementary. It is enlivened with quotations from case studies and numerous illustrations. It contains an up-to-date bibliography, a list of audio-visual materials, and many suggestions for student investigation and social drama.

Henry Bowman
Stephens College

Sexual Harmony in Marriage, by Oliver M. Butterfield. New York, Emerson, 1953. 96p. $1.50.

To the degree that there is a genuine need for a clear, frank presentation of the nature and significance of sex in marriage Dr. Butterfield's book, much of which appeared in his *Marriage and Sexual Harmony,* remains a valuable contribution. Of special import is the introduction by Dr. Nadina Kavinoky in which the patterning of sex behavior is stressed as a means of strengthening affectional bonds.

The discussion of sex techniques is factual and remarkably complete in view of the brevity of the text. However, in these post-Kinsey days an increased desire to evaluate sex as a form of emotional communication in marriage seems to have superseded the former curiosity concerning the mechanics of sex.

Bertha G. Gold
Hunter College

Syphilitic Optic Atrophy, by Walter L. Bruetsch, M.D. Springfield, Ill., Thomas, 1953. 138p. $5.50.

The author, clinical professor of neurology and psychiatry at Indiana University School of Medicine, director of research at the Central State Hospital in Indianapolis and a leading authority on the pathology of neurosyphilis, describes the changes in the ocular mechanism which cause syphilitic optic atrophy and shows how this condition (which accounts for 30,000 cases of blindness in the United States) can be prevented in the vast number of persons who now have syphilis.

His monograph, beautifully printed and illustrated, lucid, concise and practical, is an important contribution to modern knowledge of the pathology, diagnosis and treatment of syphilis. His research was aided by grants from the American Social Hygiene Association and the National Society for the Prevention of Blindness.

Charles Walter Clarke, M.D.
Executive Director Emeritus
American Social Hygiene Association

Building a Successful Marriage, by Judson T. and Mary G. Landis. New York, Prentice-Hall, 1948, 1953. Rev. 564p. $5.25.

In the second edition of this well-known college text the authors have succeeded admirably in presenting "in readable form the scientific knowledge that exists about mate selection, courtship and the adjustment problems of marriage."

This edition follows the general plan and scope of the first one. Certain chapters, however, dealing with the special problems of young people have been revised to comply with recent research and current social trends on mixed marriages, premarital sex relations, in-laws and marriage adjustment, and sex education of children. Two new chapters shed further light on the changing sex role and marriage under special circumstances.

With statistics and facts carefully documented, the text is simply written, direct and objective, to be recommended to all young people approaching marriage. Teachers of marriage courses will find most helpful the review questions and selected readings, suggested problems and activities, film lists, socio-dramas and good index.

Elizabeth McHose
Temple University

Personality in the Making, edited by Helen Leland Witmer and Ruth Kotinsky. New York, Harper, 1952. 454p. $4.50.

This book, the official fact-finding report of the Midcentury White House Conference on Children and Youth, summarizes findings of interest to all who work with children—parents, community leaders and social workers.

Its two parts, The Development of the Healthy Personality and The Implications for the Conduct of Social Institutions, contain chapters on the making of a healthy personality, the importance of parent-child relations, and the family. The book asserts that parents' attitudes toward their children determine children's health and personality more than do techniques of child-rearing.

The discussion of education for family life in the schools emphasizes that adequate programs are cross-sections of many subject-matter fields related to the real-life experiences of real people. The report urges that curricula be developed by parents, pupils and teachers; points to the need for deciding who teaches what, for curriculum building and integration, and for adequate family living programs for boys; and reports a slow but definite trend toward homemaking instruction for boys.

When Children Start Dating, by Edith G. Neisser. A Better Living Booklet. Chicago, Science Research Associates, 1951. 49p. 40¢.

If adults are to understand the difficulties of youthful dating, minimize heart-break potentialities and further youthful adjustment, they must realize the significance of boy-girl friendships to teen-age social and emotional growth.

The various steps forward in learning to love—from infancy to adolescence—are traced, and they will be steps *forward* if they are handled wisely. Parents must try to build up a child's self-confidence, for before he can like someone else he must like himself, before he can appreciate a person of the opposite sex he must enjoy being a member of his own sex. Dating popularity is evidence to the teen-ager that he is succeeding in a competitive world, proof that he is liked.

In helping boys and girls to meet each other, the family, school and community groups should invite teen-age leaders to assist in planning activities. Such disadvantages to youthful dating as going steady and petting can be overcome to some extent by positive emphasis on group activities, and much more can be accomplished through discussion than through edict.

THE LAST WORD

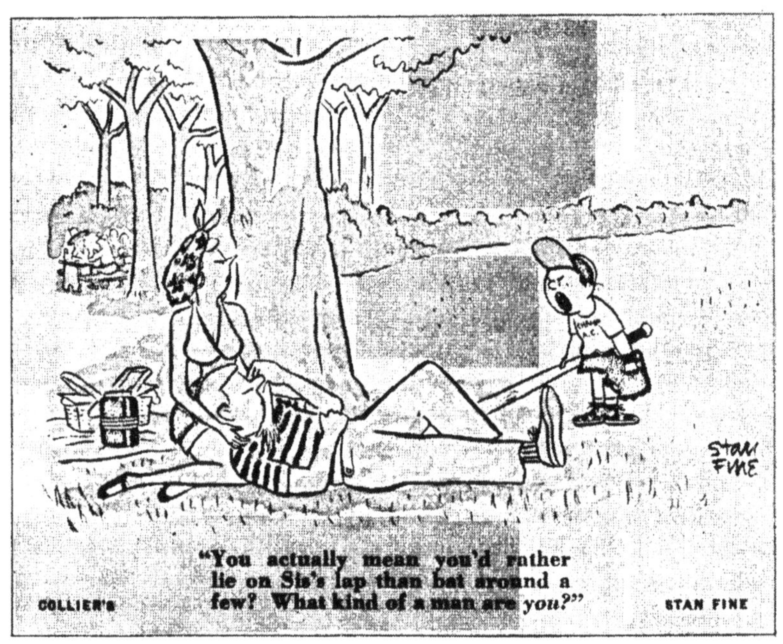

"You actually mean you'd rather lie on Sis's lap than bat around a few? What kind of a man are *you?*"

COLLIER'S STAN FINE

IN THIS ISSUE

DECEMBER 1953

About our cover . . .

The Holy Family, by Jacob Jordaens. Twenty-seventh in a series of Journal covers on family life . . . reproduced by courtesy of the Trustees of the National Gallery, London.

Harriett Scantland, Editor
Elizabeth McQuaid, Assistant Editor

Eleanor Shenehon, Editorial Consultant

THE JOURNAL OF SOCIAL HYGIENE

official periodical of the American Social Hygiene Association, published monthly except July, August and September at the Boyd Printing Company, Inc, 374 Broadway, Albany 7, N. Y. Acceptance for mailing at the special rate of postage provided for in Section 1103, Act of October 3, 1917. Entered as second-class matter at the Post Office at Albany, N. Y., March 23, 1922.

The JOURNAL does not necessarily endorse or assume responsibility for opinions expressed in articles, nor does the reviewing of a book imply its recommendation by the American Social Hygiene Association. Subscription price: $3.00 per year. Single copy: 35¢.

Proceed with Caution

Americans cannot fail to be proud of the brilliant achievements of our official health agencies in carrying forward the nationwide venereal disease control program of recent years. VD rates are down and the appropriations which made the decrease possible have shown a corresponding gradual decrease. This is as it should be.

Historically, control measures have been carried forward by joint action of federal and state health authorities, with funds contributed by both federal and state legislatures. The argument for federal participation is strong: the importance of protecting service personnel and industrial workers in a time of national emergency; the fact that communicable disease in a very mobile population cannot be held within state boundaries; and the need to equalize the cost of control measures between the richer states which can carry the load without undue hardship and those poorer states which cannot possibly do so. This partnership has worked well and has paid dividends in better health for all our people.

In recent months the belief has grown that the time is fast approaching when the states can carry the greater part of the control load alone. The effectiveness of antibiotic therapy, the real reduction in rates, and perhaps also a certain amount of wishful thinking tended to support this belief. It took shape in mid-1953 when Congress cut the appropriation for VD control in the current fiscal year by nearly 50%.

The American Social Hygiene Association is convinced that this way lies tragedy: we still have in this country an estimated 2,100,00 people with syphilis, 110,000 new cases each year. Gonorrhea is probably still the most prevalent of our communicable diseases with the exception of the common cold. If we are to continue to deal successfully with this situation we must seek and find and treat these people.

What the country needs now and should be able to expect from its Congress is a carefully considered plan for the control program over perhaps the next 10 years, with federal contributions determined by foreseeable need. There is no reasonable doubt that—unless the organisms of syphilis and gonorrhea develop strains resistant to penicillin—appropriations can be and will be progressively reduced. Let us temper wisely our efforts to economize on appropriations for VD control.

A parent protests against the experts

by Mrs. Fred McKinney

Present-day parents have an advantage over those of previous generations. We receive from many directions the benefits of an age comparatively enlightened about physical, social and personality development. Most daily newspapers carry at least one syndicated column of advice to parents; radio programs are regularly scheduled; women's magazines feature special articles besides a routine department concerning family problems; parent-teacher and similar groups present a year-round program of speakers in related fields.

We can be, if we listen to all these sources, widely informed . . . and completely overwhelmed.

I believe a large number of parents are compelled, simply by the weight of this quantity of information aimed at them, to take their functions as parents too heavily. We should be aware that we are the direct heirs of a culture which regarded worry as a virtue. In our parents' generation, the person who was free of worry, who dealt with questions as they arose and then forgot them, was charged with taking life too lightly . . . a serious accusation.

In our generation, we consider this cheerful attitude good mental hygiene . . . yet we retain a guilty feeling of evading our responsibilities if we do not worry. So we read the columnists and magazines, listen to the radio experts and our club speakers, and decide we have Problems with our children . . . since everyone else, obviously, is struggling with Problems.

I am not challenging the merits of expert advice, nor the value of making it widely available to the public. I do believe, however, that along with advice we parents should receive some reassurance concerning our effectiveness in our children's lives and some release from the anxieties we feel toward our role as parents.

This is especially true for the parents of adolescents. The experts place much stress on this period . . . its importance in the individual's life and the problems that are peculiar to years of adolescence. This period receives so much emphasis indeed that we hear parents of young children say, "I am enjoying them thoroughly while they're little. But I'm just *dreading* adolescence!"

Anxious children too

Such a situation is unfair to both the parent and the youngster. Granted that at adolescence many characteristics that have gone unnoticed during childhood suddenly come into undeniable and undesirable prominence . . . granted that at this time changes may occur which if not modified or checked will make for maladjustment in adulthood. Nevertheless, it is mutually unfair that parents approach this period in their child's life with apprehension and tension.

Moreover, our children, whom we are after all encouraging to be literate, have access to the same sources of information as we and, according to their personalities, either fancy their role as the center of anxiety for their elders or are burdened by it.

I should like to suggest at this point that the typical parent of adolescents is also, during this period, meeting a personal, physical crisis of greater or less severity. In the average family, one or both of the parents of children this age are approaching or in middle age, a time of life that is crucial for most individuals.

How many so-called adolescent "problems" are real, how many the reaction of a tense, middle-aged person to a quite normal situation? And how many reflect the inadequacies we adults feel about ourselves at this time of life? Just as most of us have lost the physical resilience and energy required to follow an energetic two-year-old all day, so we must admit have we lost some of the mental resilience and energy required to follow that same individual at 16 in his quick shifts between child and adult behavior.

Wife of a psychology professor, mother of Megan, Kent, Molly and Doyne, she's now a freshman at the University of Missouri.

Mrs. Fred McKinney

Most of us find Ogden Nash's "Tarkington, Thou Should'st Be Living In This Hour" a perfect expression of our feelings. The lines . . .

"O Adolescence, O Adolescence,
I wince before thine incandescence.
Thy constitution young and hearty
Is too much for this aged party . . ."

are exactly the words most of us would use at 4:30 in the afternoon when every-one comes in from school.

They can be fun

Perhaps the best solution is to assess ourselves as we are and then sit back and enjoy these teeners . . . because they *are* enjoyable. At no other age does the individual show that wonderful mixture of adult wit and child gaiety that is peculiar to this age. There is an off-beat quality to their actions and sayings that is most entertaining to adults . . . *if* the adults are relaxed enough to be appreciative. They are lively, interesting, stimulating, unpredictable.

(So that no one will think this wafts from an ivory tower, I'll mention here that under our roof there are four children—three in the 14–18 bracket—six radios, three record-players, and a full, professional set of dance-band drums. I know what I'm talking about.)

This enjoyment of our teeners can be genuine if we take the view that we are just one part of a large group working for their well-being . . . teachers, group leaders, physicians, ministers and more remotely related professional workers. We are not alone in our concern for these young people.

Not only is our influence partial, but it must be indirect. I used to think of myself as the foreman of a railroad roundhouse, charged with the duty of clean-

ing and fueling the engines as they come in from their runs and then getting them off on schedule. Like most metaphors, this had its breaking-point: I'm sure no roundhouse foreman needs to cope with young engines panting in an hour late for supper, trailed by two or three hungry engines from other railroads.

So now, with the idea before me that I as a parent am only one of many influences in my children's lives and that my influence must be subtle and indirect, I think of myself as the manager of a high school football team. (I have learned the correct behavior of a team manager from my son, who serves in this capacity.) You see that the field is in good playing condition, all the uniforms back from the cleaners' and mended, and the equipment complete before the game. Then you sit on the sidelines, water-bottles and bandages ready, and watch the game, totally committed to its fortunes.

The rules of the game forbid you to interfere, to coach, to take any part in the action . . . yet you are alert to rush in and apply towels, bandages and deliberately offhand encouragement in emergencies. This is your only opportunity, under the rules, to assist your team.

A little confidence

All parents will recognize how closely this role of team manager approximates their own role, particularly the "anxious seat" part of it. But I believe firmly that it is a privileged seat, with a fine view of the game, and that some of the anxiety can be removed from it if we remember that our players are well versed in the rules of the game and have had all the preparation we can provide. We'll experience pleasure in the game if we remind ourselves that the players are the beneficiaries of the greatest skills in developmental processes yet achieved by the race.

And we should realize that much of our anxiety is engendered by the unintended pressures of our assistants, the specialists, by our heritage of the "virtue" of worry, by the strains of our time of life, and by our too idealistic resolve to eliminate in this one generation the errors of all previous generations.

Police and health cooperation in VD control

The Vancouver story

by A. John Nelson, M.D.

An address before the Pacific Coast International Association of Law Enforcement Officials.

When asked to give an address before a meeting of the Pacific Coast International Association of Law Enforcement Officers, I accepted the invitation with some trepidation. Not having the qualifications to belong to that distinguished organization but having a medical background, I find my views colored by the tremendous advances that have been made in recent years in the diagnosis and treatment of the venereal diseases. On this account, therefore, and if this material should appear to have a professional bias, I would beg your indulgence and plead only my greater familiarity with the medical aspects of these diseases.

Again, there is the added difficulty of attempting to evaluate the part played by the police and health departments respectively in a cooperative control program that from its very nature demands some overlapping of the functions of each. It is, however, a pleasure to make public acknowledgment of the help the Division of Venereal Disease Control has received from law enforcement agencies throughout this province, and particularly from Vancouver's police department.

In evaluating the trend of venereal disease in recent years I used figures summarized in the table on page 391.

These figures indicate considerable achievement in the last five years. British Columbia entered the postwar era with the highest venereal disease rates in Canada. By the end of 1951, however, the rate for all syphilis had dropped 76%, the rate for infectious syphilis 95% and the rate for gonorrhea 26%. It is apparent, therefore, that within five years we have made a particularly successful focal attack upon infectious syphilis, and with some pride we can say that British Columbia has now attained virtually the lowest rate for infectious syphilis among the Canadian provinces.

Effective enforcement

While part of this successful achievement is due to advances in medical science —particularly the advent of penicillin—much credit is also due to the tireless and persistent efforts of British Columbia's law enforcement officers. Thus, while it is true that penicillin will rapidly end the infectious stage of these diseases once the cases have been found, only effective police enforcement can minimize

Cases of venereal disease reported, British Columbia, 1947–1951

	All syphilis		Early syphilis		Gonorrhea	
Year	*No.*	*Rate*	*No.*	*Rate*	*No.*	*Rate*
1947	1,775	170.0	578	55.4	4,039	386.9
1948	984	90.9	252	23.3	3,617	334.3
1949	807	72.4	157	14.1	3,833	344.1
1950	572	50.3	59	5.2	3,653	321.0
1951	467	40.1	34	2.9	3,301	283.3

per 100,000 population

opportunities for transmitting infectious venereal disease ... by suppressing third-party facilitation and prostitution.

Let us study the evolution of the joint VD control program of the police and health department in the city of Vancouver—a large seaport, a great recreational center, with a sizable transient and seasonal population—a focal point for those casual relationships which so frequently result in the acquisition of venereal disease.

To appreciate what has been achieved it is necessary to begin the story some 10 to 12 years back. At that time, conditions in Vancouver were, to say the least, unsavory. Venereal disease was on the increase, and bawdy-houses were flagrantly violating the law and daily spreading fresh infections. Indeed, statistical studies showed that the prostitute was the source of infection in some 25% of all new male gonorrhea admissions to the main Vancouver clinic. The Board of Health, in a limited survey of a group of prostitutes from these houses, found 72% of them infected with venereal disease, while each had in her possession a certificate to the effect that she had been examined by a medical practitioner and was free of infection!

The situation then was sufficiently serious to arouse the Provincial Board of Health to further action. They were indeed fortunate at that time in having as the provincial director of venereal disease control Dr. Donald H. Williams, a man outstanding in venereal disease control. By an intensive program of law enforcement aimed at bawdy-houses, and at certain beer parlors and rooming-houses known to be facilitating the spread of venereal disease, Dr. Williams rapidly reduced the number of venereal infections reported.

Indeed it is not too much to say that Dr. Williams' studies into the influence of prostitution on venereal disease prevalence in Vancouver and the success of abatement proceedings represent an outstanding contribution to venereal disease control and sociology. In showing that the closing of bawdy-houses, and the control of other facilitating premises, brought about a rapid reduction in venereal

Rising postwar VD rates—
then a renewed attack on VD.

disease, he both emphasized the need for law enforcement and demonstrated the excellent results which could be obtained.

A natural division

A question naturally arises . . . what are the respective roles of the police department and public health department in the over-all strategy of attack against the venereal diseases and the various community conditions facilitating their spread? It is at once apparent that the acquisition of venereal disease by any individual comprises two separate entities—first the source or infected individual, and second the situation whereby the source is made accessible to the healthy person.

In the cooperative control program, the source or infected individual is essentially a medical problem, whereas the circumstances contributing to the spread of venereal disease are mostly problems for police action . . . since procuring, living on the avails of prostitution, and operating a common bawdy-house are criminal offenses under federal law. From this it follows that the attack on the facilitation process and the facilitator is primarily a function of the law enforcement agencies.

It is clear, therefore, that in the broad field of police and health department cooperation in venereal disease control, certain functions are assigned to each. The health department has the specific responsibility to control these diseases through the examination and treatment of cases and their contacts. The criminal nature of the facilitation process and the criminal activities of the facilitators come within the jurisdiction of the police department.

That each department may carry out its responsibilities individually, and at the same time play its part in the combined strategy of attack, the highest degree of cooperation is not only desirable but essential. The health department's staff, through their questioning of cases and contacts, will have information about conditions and persons facilitating the spread of venereal disease, which they should relay to the police for corrective action. Conversely, the police in the performance of their duties will come in contact with delinquents and sex offenders who should properly be referred to the health department for an examination for venereal disease.

This kind of cooperation between the two departments on a day-to-day basis should insure the exchange of all available information, to the advantage of both. But this degree of cooperation between two departments can obtain only where each really understands the problems of the other and sincerely desires to make cooperative activities work.

I have referred to Dr. Williams' success in the use of law enforcement agencies to control prostitution and other facilitating activities in the city of Vancouver. Unfortunately, with the war's disruption of social conditions, it was found impossible to consolidate these advances, far less to extend them. In time of war, both departments had other emergency duties and responsibilities and could devote less time to this complex problem. With the relaxation of cooperative activity by health department and police department, the inevitable result was some recrudescence of previous unsatisfactory conditions.

Legislative support

In 1947, however, an even closer cooperation and understanding between the Division of Venereal Disease Control and the members of the Vancouver City Police Department, effected a concerted program of attack on venereal disease which now closely approximates the ideal.

1947 also saw other advances of great assistance to both departments in their joint activity:

- Passage of the revised Venereal Diseases Suppression Act by the Provincial Legislature
- Passage of the Criminal Code Amendment Act, which made possible the imposition of heavier penalties than hitherto for the keeping of bawdy-houses.

The infected person . . .
a medical problem.

These advances in legislation, together with greater cooperation between the two departments, are in no small measure responsible for the success of the venereal disease control program in this province.

Details of joint activity

Skilled investigators interview all patients passing through the health department's venereal disease clinics regarding the identity of contacts, place of meeting, place of exposure and other information about the facilitation process. By referring to large-scale maps showing beer parlors, hotels and cafes, they encourage patients to identify specific premises.

The health department's staff uses all this information in their routine follow-up of contacts. This is primarily a health department responsibility since the police in their attempt to control other law violations cannot be expected to devote a great deal of time to it. Quarterly facilitation reports tabulate and summarize pertinent information obtained from patients about specific premises. These provide the information necessary to enforce action against offending premises.

In many cases the attempt to remedy the unsatisfactory situation is made through professional organizations such as the British Columbia Hotels Association, which disciplines its member hotels. Where beer parlors are involved the Provincial Liquor Control Board usually acts. If these channels cannot take remedial action the police department's morality detail receives the assignment. In this fashion both the source of venereal disease, and the conditions facilitating its spread, are controlled.

Bawdy-houses

Here is an example of how these measures work in practice. At the end of the war the number of venereal infections had increased to an alarming extent. and bawdy-houses had again resumed their nefarious and disease-dispensing activities in Vancouver. Police attention was again directed to these unsavory premises. Early in 1947 after repeated raids by morality officers (who had the support of a subsection of the Criminal Code of Canada relating to the liability of landlords, lessors or agents of premises against which a conviction has been registered for being a common bawdy-house), the several well-known houses repeatedly reported to the Division of Venereal Disease Control were finally closed and have remained closed ever since.

Alumnus of the University of Glasgow and of London's Royal Institute of Public Health and Hygiene. Teaches public health at the University of British Columbia. Directs the VD control division of British Columbia's Department of Health and Welfare.

A. John Nelson, M.D.

Vancouver

The immediate effect was a marked reduction in the number of times bawdy-houses were named as places of exposure. Thus, in 1946, bawdy-houses were named 50 times as a source of venereal disease . . . in 1947, 12 times . . . in the last three years, on the average once a year. The police department has carefully investigated the three and has ruled out in each instance bawdy-house activity. It would appear, therefore, that organized bawdy-house activity is no longer a problem in Vancouver. The results of an independent and objective survey of commercialized prostitution activity in the city made by the American Social Hygiene Association substantiates this belief.

Prisoners are examined

One further joint activity of police and health departments in this city deserves mention. Since September, 1938, the Division of Venereal Disease Control has operated regular clinics for both male and female prisoners at the provincial jail, Oakalla Prison Farm, in the adjoining municipality of Burnaby. All new prisoners received there are routinely examined for venereal disease. This arrangement takes care of prisoners admitted to the provincial institution, but in Vancouver, as in other cities, many persons apprehended by the police are never sent to the provincial jail. Many of these individuals temporarily in police custody are known to be venereal disease contacts whom the VD Division is anxious to examine and treat if infected. It was apparent, therefore, that this constituted a serious gap in our control program.

Fortunately the Venereal Diseases Suppression Act of 1947, which I have referred to, provides for the compulsory examination and treatment of persons

As a global problem venereal disease affects North America

in custody or awaiting trial. Armed with this authority and with the cooperation of the city police department, the VD Division in May, 1947, was able to establish a medical examination center at the city jail, where all women in custody are routinely examined for venereal disease. A public health nurse from the Division makes these examinations each morning before court convenes. At first the examination center restricted its activities to female prisoners, but its unqualified success in uncovering new cases of venereal disease (in the first year of operation 106 (23%) out of 471 women examined showed evidence of venereal disease) led in the following year to a similar examination center for men.

A review of the work done by these jail examination centers reveals their value in case-finding. Between May, 1947, and the end of 1951 a total of 4,329 women were examined in the female center, and 1,930 (or 45%) were found to have evidence of venereal disease. Between September, 1948, and the end of 1951, 6,945 male prisoners were examined, and 560 (8%) found infected when examined only for syphilis.

It is felt that these examination centers are of the greatest value in VD case-finding, and in providing information about contributory social conditions among a certain segment of the population. The degree of cooperation between our departments, in both the setting up and continued operation of these jail examination centers is a model for other communities to emulate.

Unlimited cooperation

I feel that I have demonstrated what can be achieved in venereal disease control by joint activity of the police department and health department . . . and I feel too that there is no limit to this cooperative achievement.

I had occasion to visit a smaller interior city in British Columbia where two bawdy-houses were known to be operating and where, in spite of enforcement action, the local police could not completely close the premises. Investigation revealed that the totally inadequate penalties imposed upon conviction by the court nullified enforcement activities. One bawdy-house keeper with five successful convictions recorded against her had received minimal penalties, mainly fines.

This unusual situation existed in spite of the fact that a section of the criminal code dealing with prostitution provides that a person with three or more convictions for bawdy-house activity becomes subject to a mandatory jail sentence of up to two years. Obviously joint activity by the police and health departments in venereal disease control requires the cooperation of other agencies and individuals, particularly judicial officials.

In this particular instance the health department backed up the police by taking the matter to the attorney-general's department. There it was decided that if another minimal penalty were imposed for bawdy-house activity, the sentence would be appealed in an endeavor to remedy the unsatisfactory situation. This example shows the extent of police and health department cooperation.

Let there be no let-up

In conclusion, may I at this time sound a warning? Venereal disease is still with us in our respective communities, and it would indeed be a tragedy if after having come this far we were to relax our joint efforts at control. Venereal disease still presents a problem, both from within and without. Within, the proprietors of commercialized vice stand ready to profit from any relaxation on our part. Without, venereal disease is still widely prevalent in many parts of the world where control programs have barely begun to grapple with the problem. So long as these diseases remain global in their distribution they constitute a potential danger to the communities of North America, particularly if there is a further social upheaval brought about by war.

The price of success in the war against venereal disease is constant vigilance against its incursions, but it is my fervent hope that whatever may lie in the future, police department and health department, shoulder to shoulder as joint guardians of the public safety, will stand ready to meet the challenge of these diseases.

American venereal disease control problems

with emphasis on their epidemiology

by J. K. Shafer, M.D.

(continued from the November issue)

It is our experience that the application of interviewing techniques can be sharpened through careful training of interviewing personnel. To meet our need for trained men and women, schools of interviewing are operating where clinic populations are adequate for teaching purposes. Students attend from civilian health departments and the Armed Services . . . forming an additional tie between our civilian and military venereal disease programs.

Prerequisites for a successful interviewer are, as we see it, a good educational background, intelligence and an honest desire to do the work. The training schedule in the schools is crowded . . . courses run from one to three weeks, depending on the student's background in venereal disease control. We find that most students who undertake the training absorb instructions quickly or not at all.

Learning by doing

My earlier remarks about basic concepts in interviewing suggest the content of the training program, which is practical, not theoretical. The courses stress the necessity of establishing and sustaining rapport between interviewer and patient. Students see demonstrated—and later practice—the technique of using seemingly irrelevant questions to lead into crucial facts, and of shifting approaches if they encounter opposition.

Students learn that the men and women who are their patients are, by and large, a promiscuous group with substantially the same pattern of sexual behavior. With this knowledge the interviewer is predisposed to seek multiple contacts.

The student learns to rely upon memory rather than extensive note-taking and to emphasize the confidentiality of the information and its insulation from police measures.

When students understand the problems and frustrations of the man who must seek out contacts, their interest in supplying complete and accurate information quickens. Consequently, they get not only a well-rounded picture of the whole interview-investigation process but also an opportunity to trace the contacts obtained in their interviews.

Thus, the training program is essentially one of learning by doing and seeing. Students observe their instructors and fellow-trainees at work, and they conduct actual interviews. These are usually recorded and subsequently discussed and criticized by both instructors and students.

I would like to turn briefly to the effectiveness of the interview-investigation process as an epidemiologic tool. There is no need to review the necessity for information on incidence and prevalence of venereal disease, on age specific rates, on types of disease and on geographical distribution. All these facts are important in evaluating the problem's extent and location before attempting to control it. They are perhaps even more important in measuring a program's success or failure.

Statistics

Yet within our control program we needed more specialized tools for gauging contact investigation. If we were to lean heavily upon it as a case-finding mechanism, we had to find statistical means for measuring its efficiency. Accordingly, we have developed a group of statistical indices for comparing contact investigation in different areas and for assessing its efficiency in the one area over a certain period. There are four indices:

- Contact index . . . the ratio of the number of contacts obtained to the number of patients diagnosed as having previously untreated primary or secondary syphilis.
- Epidemiologic index . . . the ratio of the number of infected persons identified through contact investigation to the number of patients diagnosed.
- Brought to treatment index . . . the ratio of hitherto unknown cases found through contact investigation to the original patients available for interview.
- Lesion to lesion index . . . the ratio of contacts with primary or secondary syphilis brought to treatment as a result of contact investigation to patients with primary or secondary syphilis.

These indices are easily computed for any area or group of areas for any period. We can use them to compare different areas where contact investigation is employed or to show trends within the same health jurisdiction over a period of time.

The contact index reported early in our program was low . . . reflecting perhaps our failure to appreciate the rather extensive spread of sexual contacts stemming from one promiscuous person. As we became more aware of the extent of this spread, from our own experience and from the Kinsey study, we realized we had to obtain from each patient a number of contacts consistent with our knowledge of the quantitative sexual pattern. The data shows that over the years the contact index has risen. Between 1946 and 1951, the index for 15 areas where contact investigation was in continuous use rose from 1.70 to 3.14.

This improvement reflects the importance of training interviewers. In one study, military interviewers with little training obtained 1.13 contacts per patient for gonorrhea and 1.58 contacts for lesion syphilis. In contrast, from this same group of patients well trained nurse-epidemiologists obtained 1.29 contacts for gonorrhea and 3.46 for syphilis. Not only does the training process increase the interviewer's skill in obtaining contacts and identifying information but, as pointed out earlier, it also stimulates the interviewer to seek a large number of names from each patient.

Furthermore, the contact index provides a measure of the individual interviewer's competence as compared to that of others in the same locality.

The other indices likewise serve to set goals of performance and measure efficiency. Obviously, they are of great value in the management of a venereal disease control program.

So we have sensitive gauges of the effectiveness of our epidemiologic techniques. What then has been the impact of these techniques on our essential problem . . . reducing the amount of venereal disease in our population?

At this time, the answer to this question is hypothetical. I can only pass along to you the opinion that our epidemiologic practices are an essential part of our venereal disease control program, and present evidence to sustain that opinion.

The evidence lies in the pronounced divergence in the trends of syphilis and gonorrhea incidence. While gonorrhea among females is not sufficiently well diagnosed and reported to establish a trend, the gonorrhea rate among males is a fair indication of the trend of its incidence. Since 1947 gonorrhea as reported in the male has declined 37%. Over the same period the estimated minimum incidence of syphilis among males has declined 78%.

(This man does not have VD.)

The interviewer tells why contacts must be located.

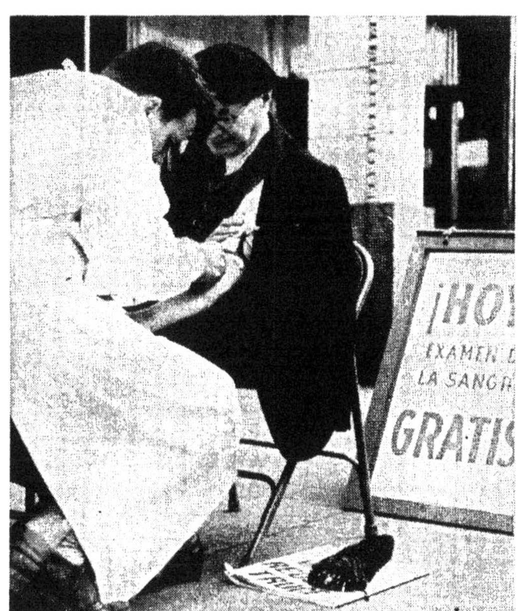

On-the-spot blood tests.

Former emphasis on syphilis

Let me turn back for a moment to the mid-1940's and describe the difference in our approach to the control of syphilis and gonorrhea. At that time, with limited personnel and funds and with a very formidable venereal disease problem before us, we decided to concentrate control efforts primarily upon syphilis, utilizing the interview-investigation program only incidentally for gonorrhea. Three considerations governed this decision:

- Syphilis is a potentially more serious disease than gonorrhea.

- The male patient with gonorrhea, having more uncomfortable symptoms than the patient with syphilis, would be more likely to report for medical care.

- The increasing availability of penicillin and its specificity in small amounts for gonorrhea would tend to treat the disease out of existence without a concerted epidemiologic drive. This consideration anticipated a wide use of penicillin for conditions other than venereal disease that would, it was believed, incidentally bring about the cure of much gonorrhea. It also anticipated that the drug's specificity for gonorrhea, and its low cost, would become well known and thus lead a large number of those infected to volunteer for treatment.

University of Nebraska and Johns Hopkins alumnus. Formerly medical officer of the U. S. Marine Hospital on Ellis Island, and VD control officer for Michigan. Now chief of the VD division, USPHS.

James K. Shafer, M.D.

That gonorrhea has not been treated out of existence is clear from the high rates we continue to see. The factors we expected to aid the control of this disease have not done so to the degree we expected.

Study of our gonorrhea problem has revealed, to some extent, the points at which our expectations went awry. Clinic reports in some areas show a marked unbalance between the number of male and female cases—sometimes reaching the ratio of 10 male cases to one female case. Males with a discharge come in voluntarily, much as we expected, but all too often they return after treatment to the infected female and become reinfected. Many male "repeaters" were returning to the clinic within a short time, reinfected.

Moreover, in the socio-economic group with the highest incidence of gonorrhea, economic considerations and psychological make-up apparently militate against volunteering for medical care. Whether this failure to volunteer is due to lack of motivation to seek treatment, or (in areas where public facilities are limited) is due to a lack of money to pay for treatment, or whether it reflects individual differences in severity of disease is beyond the province of this discussion. The point is that persons with gonorrhea did not volunteer for treatment as we had expected.

As we analyzed our situation, we were convinced that the chief reason for the divergence in syphilis and gonorrhea rates was our organized case-finding attack on the one, its absence in the other. We have felt justified in concluding, on the basis of our experience with syphilis, that interview-investigation is a sound and fruitful epidemiologic process that may be successfully adapted to the particular characteristics of the gonorrhea problem.

Accordingly, we have begun to search actively for contacts of persons known to be infected with gonorrhea. To deal with the characteristics peculiar to gonorrhea, we have developed what we term the "speed zone" concept of epidemiology. I should like to outline briefly the basis and content of this attack.

While the incubation period of experimentally acquired gonorrhea in males has a 31-day range, 85% of infections produce clinical symptoms within six days after exposure. Thus the productive targets for investigation are the contacts of male gonorrhea patients during the period beginning six days before the onset of his clinical symptoms and ending at the time of his appearance at the clinic. This period would encompass in most cases not only the contact from whom he acquired his infection but also those he has exposed during his infectiousness.

I have pointed out the frequency with which, in our experience, the patient treated for gonorrhea becomes reinfected. With this knowledge, it is necessary to locate and treat his known sexual partners before he becomes infected again from one of them. Studies have established that penicillin in aluminum monostearate protects the patient from reinfection for at least 72 hours. Consequently, if we are to break up the pattern of reinfection that we so often meet, we must investigate contacts within the period of penicillin protection . . . 72 hours.

This program operates on detailed working principles. One of the fundamental points is that only certain "zones"—those with high gonorrhea incidence—of selected cities and counties are covered. In the interest of brevity, I shall not describe the complete plan of operation of the "speed zone" concept, but shall mention only five of the principal working premises:

- We interview all symptomatic male gonorrhea patients.
- We send a telegram to all contacts of these patients with identifiable names and addresses within the speed zone on the day of the interview, and request them to report immediately to the venereal disease clinic.
- An investigator seeks out immediately all contacts who do not receive a telegram.
- An investigator personally seeks at once all contacts not responding to the telegram within 24 hours and brings the contacts to the clinic.
- All contacts who come or are brought in for examination receive treatment. Physical examinations are performed and samples taken for diagnostic purposes if considered desirable. We do not wait for confirmation of diagnosis by culture before treating because of the time involved and because we consider the report of contact with an infected individual as presumptive evidence of infection. To require bacteriologic proof of infection before treatment would require greater expenditure of personnel and funds than are available. It would also leave the subject free to expose others, since we have no facilities for hospitalizing contacts pending diagnosis.

The reports from speed zone areas are most encouraging. The gonorrhea contact index is approximately 1.5, and about 70% of the contacts residing within the speed zone are being examined and treated within five working days. Furthermore, the telegram is bringing many contacts to treament within 24 hours. In some areas, the sex ratio is assuming a more proper balance between males and females. Final evaluation of the speed zone process will depend, however, on whether or not the incidence of male gonorrhea cases decreases.

I have presented a fairly full description of the epidemiologic content of our venereal disease control program. As I have indicated, our procedures for discovering new cases were evolved because we recognized that our program would continue to be imperfect unless we could find a means of directly channeling the venereally infected (and infectious) person to treatment while still in the infectious stages. Public health expediency—and nothing else—dictated the specific practices we employ. New techniques or new adaptations of established techniques, new insights into the mind of the venereal disease patient, new wedges into his confidence . . . these are our goals.

It is not my intention to suggest that our methods are universally effective. We believe, however, that for us these methods result in interrupted chains of venereal infection. So long as our public health program of venereal disease control must look to treatment to halt the spread of venereal infection, contact investigation will be a necessary supporting operation. We hope to carry it forward to new levels of performance in the future.

Love graph

THE AGE

BETTER HOMES & GARDENS

Spiritual Health and Development

Third of a series of chapters from Preinduction Health and Human Relations, new curriculum resource for youth leaders by Roy E. Dickerson and Esther E. Sweeney.

(continued from the November issue)

Moral Equality

The American people take pride in the spirit of fair play. There are few things that arouse our antagonism more than unfairness and injustice.

This popular desire to see every person judged by common standards and treated fairly under all circumstances is based on our recognition of the moral equality of all.

Thomas Jefferson emphasized this agreement on moral equality when he spoke in his first inaugural address of "equal and exact justice to all men, of whatever state or persuasion, religious or political."

The whole world was stunned when the Nazis tore legal and political rights from one group of German citizens because of their religious beliefs and subsequently slaughtered millions of them.

Later the Nazis enslaved and murdered millions of Poles, Russians and other non-German peoples on the theory that they should be exterminated because they belonged to "inferior races." Not only was science perverted to create a political philosophy around an absurdity labeled "the master race" but the Nazis carried their denial of the moral equality of man to its greatest extremes and produced the most terrible acts of genocide in history.

Yet in day-to-day living—on a much smaller but no less significant scale—one can be unjust to people unless belief in the moral equality of all men is part and parcel of one's moral and spiritual equipment.

Ideas of social exclusiveness, for example, can cause unfairness and discrimination in relationships with others. It is dangerously easy for a clique of young people to exclude schoolmates from common, pleasurable experiences together.

It's perfectly true that young people with limited spending money cannot always go to expensive places of recreation with friends who have more spending money. But recognition of moral equality and a desire to consider the feelings of others suggest the planning of activities that cost less and can include more of one's friends and classmates.

Using other people is another kind of unfairness, often unthinkingly practiced. Sometimes two or three students are assigned a research task. The one reporting conveys, one way or another, that the major efforts have been his. A boy or girl on a date may "use" each other for emotional or physical satisfactions. A young serviceman, newly assigned to a post, may use his fellow servicemen to help him find his way around and make acquaintances in the community, yet drop his friends once he feels sure of himself and at home in his new situation.

Any form of discrimination or domination over another person or group of persons is exercise of a form of power. Lord Acton wrote, "Power tends to corrupt; absolute power corrupts absolutely." The individual may only momentarily hurt another person by some act of discrimination or injustice, but the harm he does to himself in corrupting his own moral fiber may be grave and lasting.

Youth can close its eyes to unfair, discriminatory practices: the exclusion of certain groups from places of public recreation; unfair generalizations about people of particular races, religions or economic levels; things as seemingly unimportant as class decisions to hold a formal dance which may necessarily exclude those who can't afford the special clothes needed. Or youth can work calmly and consistently, now and continuingly. to help eradicate whatever tends to deny the moral equality of human beings.

The cardinal precept of the moral equality of human beings is found in all the great religions of the world. In common they call for the repudiation of persecution, domination or exploitation of others . . .

Christianity teaches, "Thou shalt love thy neighbor as thyself." Buddhism says, "Minister to friends and families by treating them as one treats himself." Confucianism says, "What you do not like when done to yourself, do not do to others." Hinduism says, "Let no man do to another what would be repugnant to himself." Judaism says, "And what thou thyself hatest, do to no man."

"Do unto others as you would have them do to you"—the Golden Rule—is found in one form or another in practically every language. It is a summation of men's thinking, whether they accept formal religion or not.

Class Discussion

- Why do American courts provide legal services at public expense (when people cannot afford such services) even if they are charged with crimes as grave as arson, murder or larceny?
- How does discrimination show lack of maturity?
- What is the potential danger in the attitude of peace at any price? In making other people the butt of jokes? In assessing one's friends by their clothes, cars, money and ancestry?

Brotherhood

William Penn, the Quaker founder of Pennsylvania, said, "Those people who are not governed by God will be ruled by tyrants." Four explicit references to the spiritual foundations of American life are to be found in the Declaration of Independence, the charter of our freedom: In the first sentence, ". . . to which the Laws of Nature and of Nature's God entitle them. . . ."

In the second sentence, ". . . that all men are created equal, that they are endowed by their Creator with certain unalienable Rights. . . ."

In the next to last sentence, ". . . appealing to the Supreme Judge of the world. . . ."

And in the last sentence, ". . . with a firm reliance on the Protection of Divine Providence. . . ."

In 1858, Abraham Lincoln, in what is referred to as his "lost" speech, spoke these words concerning the Declaration of Independence and the motives of those who wrote it: "This was their lofty and wise and noble understanding of the justice of the Creator to His creatures, to the whole family of men. In their enlightened belief, nothing stamped with the divine image and likeness was sent into the world to be trodden on and degraded, and imbruted by its fellow creatures."

The spiritual value, brotherhood, is not based on easy and pleasant fraternal feelings for the people one can readily like and admire. It springs from the concept of the inherent worth of each human being made in the image of his Creator and from one's consequent moral responsibility to treat one's neighbor with respect and decency, whether or not he is personally likable.

Brotherhood cannot be realized by well-meaning but ineffectual acceptance of the idea of brotherhood without positive, constructive action. Humanitarian sharing of material things demonstrates one's concern for the welfare of others. This is good. But if moral and spiritual values are to imbue the character of each individual and through him contribute to the spiritual growth of the state, one must realize that brotherhood calls for vigorous and dynamic action.

In *Moral and Spiritual Values in the Public Schools*, issued by the Educational Policies Commission of the National Education Association and the American Association of School Administrators, the following statement appears: "We seek to develop a self-reliant and industrious body of citizens, each of whom will earnestly strive to provide through his own efforts for the comfort and well-being of himself and those dependent upon him. Nevertheless, the care of those among us who may be prevented from doing this by a fault not their own—by ignorance, or feebleness, or lack of opportunity, or other misfortune—is an inescapable moral responsibility of all citizens. Whether by individual action, or through voluntary cooperation, or from the public purse, this responsibility must be met. Brotherhood leads to a broad and expanding humanitarianism, a

How does a bank account relate to happiness?

sympathetic concern for the distress of other people. . . . Brotherhood, moreover, implies more than material assistance; it means a willingness not only to share with the needy but also to attack the causes of want and suffering."

Good Will Is Not Enough

To attack the causes of want and suffering—one of the truest exercises of brotherhood—one needs more than good will. One must seriously study many factors and weigh various solutions in the attempt to meet the root causes of human need.

This is a major task of citizens. Inadequate and substandard housing, unemployment, the more or less enforced idleness of older members of the population (many of whose only job disability is age) and many other problems of our fellow citizens will not yield to simple overnight measures. But they must yield to the informed, vigorous, consistent and thoughtful attack of young men and women who accept brotherhood as a spiritual value and who work for its realization in concrete terms.

All over the world underprivileged people look towards the generous, brotherly hearts of Americans for relief from their distress. Sometimes it is said that our demonstrations of brotherhood are taken for granted, and that some countries may become over-dependent upon American generosity. Both are possible and in some instances may be true. It is always important to share with wisdom as well as generosity.

Young people should rightly consider the balance between prudence and generosity. They must weigh the danger of indiscriminate giving that may weaken, not strengthen, the recipient. That is why the Community Chest encourages young people to study their community's philanthropies, to read and study the agencies' annual reports and financial summaries, to visit social agencies on appropriate occasions and ask questions about the why and when and how of giving.

In working to break the chains of ignorance, in working for fair employment opportunities for all, in working to uproot the causes of poverty, loneliness and personal unhappiness, one finds the greatest promise of fulfilling the moral obligation of true and all-inclusive brotherhood.

Class Discussion

- What are some of the everyday things people can do to show brotherhood besides sharing material possessions?
- What do people mean by "It isn't the gift, it's the thought that matters"?
- Employers have moral responsibilities towards employees. Do employees have moral obligations towards employers? How does brotherhood operate in these relationships?
- What steps would be necessary to develop a plan for eradicating slums in any community?
- Cite some instances of the brotherhood shown by American servicemen in occupied countries.
- How does the Marshall Plan demonstrate a prudent yet generous form of brotherhood?

The Pursuit of Happiness

The glorious phrase in the Declaration of Independence—the pursuit of happiness—relates to a vital spiritual value.

America's spiritual heritage recognizes man's right—even his responsibility—to seek happiness.

Each person should have the greatest possible opportunity to pursue happiness, provided that in so doing he does not interfere with the happiness of others. This is an inalienable human right. It relates to the very nature of man, to his possession of reason and judgment, to his capacity for growth and self-expression, to his intellectual, creative, emotional and spiritual endowments.

People's ideas of happiness often differ. This very fact brings about much unhappiness in human experience.

Happiness is, of course, affected to some degree by material factors such as food, clothing, shelter, money. But once these basic needs are met, their importance diminishes.

Wealth and personal possessions are pleasant. But in themselves they cannot supply happiness. Equally, extreme poverty may make the achieving of happiness difficult.

Everyone knows people with many material possessions who—for lack of inner resources, personal stability or ability to handle personal misfortune—have little happiness. On the other hand, everybody knows people with little financial security and few possessions whose every family meal is an occasion for wit, planning, discussions of ideas and world events . . . in short, whose happiness does not depend on material things.

The girl who makes herself a dress for a dance finds great pleasure both in successfully completing her effort and in anticipating the dance itself. If she adds some creative touches to the dress, she also experiences further happiness and the satisfaction of having achieved a concrete form of self-expression. This happiness may be even greater than her anticipation or enjoyment of the dance itself.

The boy who works on an ordinary class assignment—an essay, a piece of research, a poster for an art class—may find real happiness in what perhaps started out as a routine task, even a chore, as he works with ideas and with different ways of presenting his material.

As people mature, relinquish the self-centeredness of childhood and grow genuinely eager to live constructive lives, they recognize that happiness is not just a feeling of exuberance or satisfaction at getting what one wants "when he wants it." They become aware of how happy they feel when they are using themselves and their inner resources to the fullest. Often they find that the happiness all men pursue lies in sacrificing for another person. Or they find it in cheerfully deferring until an appropriate time, place and circumstance something they may want pressingly.

Through Sacrifice

Everyone has experienced the satisfaction that comes from making a personal sacrifice to buy a present for a relative or friend or from contributing pocket-money to a health or welfare program even at the cost perhaps of a few trips to the movies or a new blouse or scarf.

Most people experience happiness in giving a shyer or less popular person a chance to shine.

The mature person recognizes that "man does not live by bread alone." Every realization of one's powers of mind and spirit, of one's creative capacities, contributes to the achievement of happiness.

It is not necessary to have a great intellect to enjoy the experiences of thought. It is not necessary to be a Michelangelo to enjoy creativeness. A skillful cook, an imaginative office worker, a laboratory technician who uses initiative, patience and inventiveness are people in the process of expressing their true selves and thereby achieving happiness.

The inherent spiritual potential of the pursuit of happiness was recognized by the Founding Fathers, who had clear notions of the nature of man. Constitutional guarantees concerning specific human rights—freedom of worship, freedom of speech, freedom of assembly, freedom of the press—could not be complete and assured without a spiritual approach to the true pursuit of happiness.

Class Discussion

- Suppose that an important way of expressing yourself and achieving happiness lies in playing a musical instrument. But your practice periods irritate and annoy other people. What should you do?
- Suppose you have ability and a genuine desire to become a sculptor. At the same time, you have a family that needs your financial help. Devoting your entire time to your art will cause hardship. How might you solve your problem and still pursue your happiness?
- What factors do you consider basic to a truly happy life?

Class Activity

- Have each member of the class contribute orally a two-minute sketch on "The Happiest Person I Know" or on "The Happiest Person I Have Ever Read About."

Spiritual Enrichment

If the basic moral and spiritual value in American life is the inherent worth of every individual, it follows that each person should have every opportunity to enjoy those emotional and spiritual experiences that transcend the materialistic aspects of life. Such experiences are surely as much a right as intellectual experience and the satisfactions of successful physical growth and development.

Many people deny themselves a vast amount of happiness by failing to enrich themselves in the realm of spiritual experience. Sometimes their failure is owing to fear of seeming to be naive and starry-eyed, poetic and fanciful rather than commonsensical.

Yet young people can explore the spiritual aspects of life to the full if they understand first that one does not have to share or display evidence of spiritual experience, that in fact the number of people with whom spiritual experiences can be unselfconsciously and simply shared is usually rather small.

Secondly, young people need to appreciate that everyone in a classroom or in any other group has already had many moments of rich emotional and spiritual experience, although they may not have put the label "spiritual" on those moments.

In a thousand and one ways right now and every day young people are enriching their lives spiritually, aesthetically, creatively and idealistically . . . in religious experience, in the inner satisfactions felt in the presence of natural beauty, in warm feelings of admiration for (possibly even identification with) great men and women, in the sense of achievement in art, music or crafts classes.

Quite often young people fear that the friends with whom they share cokes, play jukeboxes, dance, play tennis and other games will think them odd and unusual if they show interest in the spiritual enrichment of their lives. Yet if any boy or girl makes a list of his friends, decides which one he or she likes best and analyzes the reasons why, it will usually be found that the special friend "has something." Perhaps that something is a personality free enough to enjoy a balanced diet of study, play, ordinary good times plus some food for the heart and spirit.

The Inner Life

The recent report, *Moral and Spiritual Values in the Public Schools,* points out: "Spiritual values, however, take effect mainly in terms of inner emotions and sentiments. The entire outlook of many people is deeply affected by these spiritual feelings. Spiritual values arise from many sources—from the creative artistic expressions of the human spirit, from the noble monuments of architecture, from the impact of great religious pageantry and time-honored ritual, from the memory of heroic men and women who have nobly served

Defender of our spiritual and moral heritage.

humanity, from contemplation of the stars or of a blade of grass, from the simple ceremonies of thankfulness or of grief, from the smile of a well-loved companion, from poetry and music, from sincere religious experience and faith. The well-meaning and high-minded individual who lacks such experience remains an incomplete person. Beyond moral conviction and efficient social action, there is the inner life of the spirit which gives warmth and drive to dispassionate precepts of morality."

The right to live and grow spiritually is peculiarly threatened today. The materialism of totalitarian states is demonstrably at odds with the free development of the spiritual nature of man. While Nazi propaganda spoke glowingly of the spirituality of the German people and while the Nazis included the word church in their *Kinder, Kirche und Kuchen* (Children, Church and Kitchen) slogan for women, they destroyed simultaneously the very core of spirituality . . . freedom.

It is liberty, the heart of the American way of life, that provides the climate for spiritual growth. It was not religious liberty alone that our Founding Fathers guaranteed. It was freedom to be guided by conscience and by the spirit in one's thoughts, beliefs, speech; in one's choice of friends and occupation; in one's movement about the country; in one's marriage and family life; in one's day-by-day efforts to realize the maximum in personal development.

The Army's brochure, *Character Guidance in the Army*, published in 1951, says, "Liberty, or freedom, in the traditional American acceptance of the idea involves the moral integrity of the individual. It is based on the premise that man is a creature of God and enjoys certain rights as well as incurs certain obligations by virtue of this relationship. The exercise of these rights is held in delicate balance by the observance of the obligations, or the keeping of the moral law. Man possesses free will, and therefore he actually can violate the moral law, renounce his obligations. But, to the extent that he does this, he jeopardizes the essential liberty he has from God. Freedom therefore is weighted with a sense of responsibility and the necessity of self-discipline which will promote the cultivation and positive practice of virtues. By the right exercise of liberty, character is developed and strengthened, and conversely, liberty is more surely preserved as the character of man is improved."

Undoubtedly some persons are still able to cultivate their own inner emotional and spiritual lives in countries where liberties have been lost or curtailed. But the external pressures of their world must make the pursuit of spiritual enrichment a difficult one.

The preservation of the freedom to work for one's development spiritually, as well as in other ways, is at the heart of the nation's defense effort.

Young men and women about to enter the Armed Forces have a right to know and a responsibility to learn why they are called upon to serve their country in its military service. Certainly protection of our moral and spiritual heritage is one of the prime factors.

This country and its priceless inheritance can never be secure, however, if the basic human rights of other nations are torn from them.

In his Edwardsville, Ill., speech in 1858 Abraham Lincoln said: "What constitutes the bulwark of our liberty and independence? It is not our frowning battlements, our bristling seacoasts, the guns of our war steamers, the strength of our gallant and disciplined Army. These are not our reliance against the resumption of tyranny. Our reliance is in the love of liberty, which God has planted in our bosoms. Our defense is in the preservation of the spirit which prizes liberty as the heritage of all men, in all lands everywhere. Destroy the spirit and you have planted the seeds of despotism around your own door. Familiarize yourselves with the chains of bondage and you are preparing your own limbs to wear them. Accustomed to trample on the rights of those around you, you have lost the genius of your independence and become the fit subject of the first cunning tyrant who arises."

Class Assignment

- Essay on one of the following topics: Daily Experiences That Can Contribute to Spiritual Growth; The Spiritual Qualities of My Favorite Character in History, Fiction or Biography; Can a Person Possess Spiritual Qualities and Be a Good Sport and a Pleasant Companion?

Class Activity

- Have pupils list (anonymously) the characteristics they desire most in a future husband or wife. After tabulating them, the class should discuss these characteristics in terms of physical, intellectual, emotional-social and spiritual qualities.

Reference

- Character Guidance Discussion Topics, Series I–VI, Department of the Army Pamphlet No. 16-10; Department of the Air Force Pamphlet No. 1-1 to 6, U. S. Government Printing Office, Washington 25, D. C.

  Each of these pamphlets contains excellent bibliographies for both teachers and students.

Safeguards for junior hostesses

by Mrs. William M. Galvin

Pennsylvania native, Vassar graduate, mother of three, grandmother of five, executive secretary of Washington's Armed Services Hospitality Committee

Suppose you have a daughter 20 years old who insisted on coming to Washington to seek her fortune. Suppose she writes you that she and other girls in her rooming house are going to soldier dances every week, riding in an Army bus 20 miles out to the camp and back again at midnight. Suppose that is all you know about these dances. Even though you know you have given your daughter a good education and careful training, you might be worried.

Any mother might say to herself, "I know she has to grow up, and I know she has to have boy friends . . . but that doesn't mean she should be on the loose to that extent, meeting lots of strange men from all over the country and from every kind of household. Does anybody at all pretend to look after these girls as they go to these dances and come home through miles of countryside late at night?"

In Washington we do try to look after the girls.

The War Hospitality Committee (officially appointed by the government of the District of Columbia) had 15,000 junior hostesses enrolled and trained in World War II. Its present successor, the Armed Services Hospitality Committee, has recruited and trained over 3,000 girls since the outbreak of hostilities in Korea. The Volunteer Training Committee, a subcommittee of the Armed Services Hospitality Committee, is responsible for the training course given to all registered hostesses. The 30-odd members of this committee are for the most part professional people working in community recreation. Military representatives insure that the program meets the requirements of the military posts as well as the standards set up by the community members.

The committee is conscious of its responsibility. The safeguards that have been set up are based on 13 years' experience in sending girls to these neighboring military dances. There are military buses and schooled drivers under strict orders. Each agency scheduling girls for the dance sends with each bus a leader who stays through the dance and returns with the girls. She checks the girls on and off the bus. They are not allowed to return to town in private cars.

These leaders are familiar with the standards set up for the junior hostesses, and with our training program. Some of them have worked with us for years. They know that the training course is constantly adapted to changing military situations. Often they point out to us the need for stressing a special angle in the next course.

In the matter of dance floor manners, a leader suggested the following paragraph which was added this spring to the revised edition of our junior hostess training pamphlet *"Mother, may I go out dancing?"* which was copyrighted in 1952 by Recreation Services, Inc., an operating agency for the Armed Services Hospitality Committee, Washington, D. C.

> "Dance Floor Manners—
>
> "When the music stops: What do you do? Dash rapidly across the dance floor to your girl friends—giving everyone the impression you are running away from your partner? Or do you stand where you are for a moment or two—finishing your conversation with your partner or even being quick to say something bright about the dance, the music, the base? Remember — you are a hostess and you cannot afford to dash off as if you were glad that chore is finished. It might make a big difference to a homesick sailor if you handled this more gracefully."

What not to say

In 1944, when the convalescents from the military hospitals began to appear in Washington service clubs, all registered junior hostesses were given the most careful briefing in conversational leads with wearers of the Purple Heart. This training was set up on the advice of the highest military psychiatric specialists because they knew that thoughtless questions could throw back into the hospital a man who had only just got up his nerve to take a trial run downtown in the first place.

The girls were taught that a Purple Heart is not a conversation piece. They were cautioned that if they asked a man where he got a certain campaign ribbon they might be told in words they would never forget.

Commander John Nardini, USN, speaking at the March 1951, training course on this same subject, made some other valuable points. He said:

> "Now just a little about sick and wounded men. Generally speaking, I would say without fail, if pressed to discuss any phase of the subject with wounded men, it would be proper to listen. Never press the subject, because a man's condition is best ignored and you must accept him as if he had no illness or injury. He neither desires nor expects any special favor or consideration. His need of service is not even admitted to himself. He wants to be treated during the course of his illness in a manly way. This, however, is not going to prevent him from bitterness.

> "This will require your patience and I ask you to listen. He will usually have a mixed feeling about combat. Here you can be of some help. Be tolerantly bored.
>
> "The problem of a man wounded, especially one without limbs, is that of being accepted as he is with his injury, and the sooner this approach is made the better. When ~~he is~~ accepted as his usual self, then he begins to be more comfortable and in general tries to be of some degree of help to the medics."

Again in 1951 when the very young draftees began to fill the neighboring camps, the girls were given special training to help them to know how to make friends with a bashful, socially inexperienced boy who sat tongue-tied with his legs around the chair legs. He could never have gotten up the nerve to ask a girl to dance. Our training course at this point included equally bashful new young government workers, mostly brought in by employment scouts from small towns. (An analysis of the registration cards of our 1952 training class showed the majority were from Pennsylvania mining towns and from small southern towns, with very few from metropolitan areas.)

These girls had to be taught not to go onto the dance floor in groups of six or eight, cross the floor in a gang and sit by themselves, like juveniles in a dancing class. They had to be taught to approach in groups of not more than two several servicemen and to say—"I'm Mary. This is Jean. We're both from Pennsylvania. Where are you from? Are you new here?"

We urged them to talk about Ted Williams, and movie actors and actresses, about any common interest. To develop enough poise to do this easily takes time, but it is nevertheless the easiest lesson we give to a new girl.

Extramural dallying

If she makes a hit with that tall Pfc., he might suggest they "beat it out of the service club and take a little hike in the moonlight." He knows he probably can't get away with that, but no harm in trying. She knows, if she has had our training course, that this is the last "on post" dance she is going to get to if she violates our rule—the military hostess rule—that she stay inside the service club for the duration of the dance.

There is no "parking," no opportunity for an unchaperoned private date at this dance.

Our junior hostess also knows why this rule was made, and why she will have to surrender her pass if she breaks the rule. She has been told by an expert on social hygiene that she is the one person who can take care of herself. She has been told that she must surrender this responsibility to nobody else.

She has heard that if she insists, she has, of course, exactly as much right as a man to pick up somebody on the street, but that there are reasons why she is putting herself in more jeopardy than a man. Ray Everett, director of the

She's informed, poised, patriotic.

Social Hygiene Society of the District of Columbia, one of our faculty members, points out in detail the tragic end to a pick-up date here in 1945, which ended in an AWOL marine's murdering a girl in one of the public parks.

Nobody pretends that such a training course will prevent murders . . . but we know that we have given each one of the 3,000 girls on our list a knowledge of the reasons why she has to take care of herself and some knowledge of how to do it.

She has been told that if she goes into lonely parks or goes off in a car with a serviceman she does not really know the situation may involve the use of force, and it has been made clear to her that the odds are very much against her being stronger than a serviceman who has been through basic training.

She has been told that she puts herself in danger if she "pets" or "necks." (The exact use of these words varies with background, we find.) She is told that "a little petting" is not safe. She learns that she cannot necessarily retreat from a man who decides after this little petting that he wants more. She is told there is always the possibility of venereal disease, a serious disease, for which treatment is not invariably 100% effective.

Of course she is informed that she may have an unwanted baby, and that by delivery time the serviceman may be long overseas. Certainly her chances of catching up with him are less than slim, as are her chances of proving paternity and getting the soldier to accept responsibility.

In his speeches, Mr. Everett often says, "Who ever heard of a home for unmarried fathers?"—even the girl with the poorest background can understand that. We use plain English, words of few syllables, no euphemisms, no glossing over, because there is too much at stake. We have prepared a special very simple leaflet for back-country girls near one camp who do not have enough education to read our regular junior hostess pamphlet.

The girls are asked to remember that they must not get too sorry for a man shipping overseas. They must not let him use his imminent departure as a means of breaking down resistance.

On the side of the angels

Recently a captain in the woman's bureau of the Washington police department told us she had never known an instance when one of our registered junior hostesses had shown up as a problem girl. We hope that record holds. We would be happy if we had in the group every lonely girl who is pick-up material.

There are, of course, some less serious aspects of the training program. Expert professional dancers give an exhibition of modern ballroom dance steps. They also point out what good posture can do for a girl on the dance floor.

In our last course the professional dancer gave the girls several rules for success on the dance floor—

- "Dance to please your partner, not to show off," he said.
- "The man is the boss on the dance floor. Don't say, 'John, you did that step wrong.' If he did, you do it wrong too if you want to be a success."
- "The dance floor is no place for a necking party."

Of course we stress suitable costumes, makeup, haircuts. We frown on the unsightly pin-up curls only partly hidden under a scarf, curls that must be combed out in the bus. We discuss tight sweaters and very sheer blouses. We get the big shops to give fashion shows for the class.

"Make up your mind," one of the smart fashion coordinators said in the course last spring. "If you decide to buy a very sheer blouse you are going to have to spend the money to buy the proper underwear or else you'll look a sight." She could have added that improper clothing invites undesirable wolf calls.

An essential of every course is a lecture on military security. The girls are trained by a military officer to recognize a violation of military security on the

The conversational light touch . . . how much better than talk about injuries.

part of a soldier and are told what to do about it. They know they are not on safe ground if they discuss troop movement, weapons, special training. The military adviser takes a positive approach and urges them to keep on subject matter that is their business. During World War II this part of the training was, of course, far more intensive. Elmer Davis, World War II chief of the Office of War Information, said we had the best training in military security for volunteers in the United States.

Over and over again a girl is made to see that to act as a junior hostess at a military dance is an act of patriotism. We urge her to think before she talks, for the sake of morale. Our junior hostess handbook has this to say about thoughtless conversation—

> You will never be so silly as to say: "Oh, but aren't you afraid! Don't you hate going overseas! Isn't the sailor uniform a Little Bit Silly? Do you positively mean they make you button your cuffs? How could you *stand* it? Is the food as bad as they *say*? I bet when you come here you wish you Never Have to Go Back to Camp. Gee — my job is a cinch. I'm glad I'm a girl. I'm lucky."

We say to the girls—

> Who keeps you lucky? If you "sign on" to go to dances at Army camps—and with service personnel—can you remember to say to yourself—"But for these men—where would I be?"

CREDITS

Photo courtesy of British Columbia Government Travel Bureau, Victoria, B. C., p. 395.

Photo courtesy of U. S. Public Health Service, pp. 400, 401.

Photo courtesy of U. S. Department of Defense, p. 412.

Photo courtesy of United Service Organizations, p. 418.

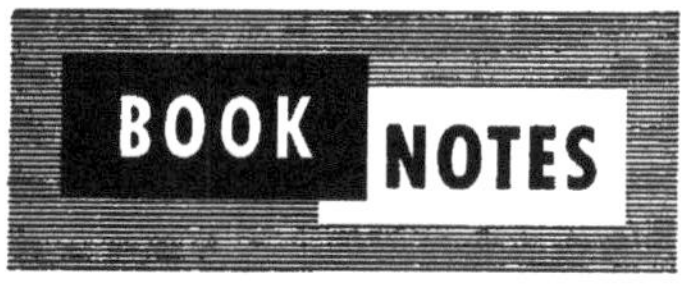

by Elizabeth B. McQuaid

Twenty-five Years of Sex Research, by Sophie D. Aberle and George W. Corner, M.D. Philadelphia, Saunders, 1953. 248p. $4.00.

This is more than a history of the National Research Council's Committee for Research in Problems of Sex during its first 25 years, 1922 to 1947. It is a saga of a long and successful struggle to promote effective research in sexual behavior, despite resistance to such studies by conservatives.

The reader learns about the committee's organizational and planning problems, and its early efforts to define its responsibilities, locate researchers and publish studies. Also of significance were its decisions in regard to promoting basic research, allocating funds properly and controlling grants.

Cited as a successful example of research administration, the committee through its experiences offers assistance to those who plan and organize research in other fields. Much can be learned from this history.

Morey R. Fields, Director
New York City Health Department

Health Principles and Practices, by C. V. Langton and C. L. Anderson. St. Louis, Mosby, 1953. 417p. $4.25.

This book is effectively planned to help college students understand their personal health problems. Emphasis is on basic health principles which make possible a positive approach to these problems, on interrelationships between personal health and community health, on the citizen's responsibility for the health of his community. There is extensive treatment of health organizations and agencies and a description of international, national, state and local health services.

The chapter on sex and reproduction—a frank and objective presentation of facts and problems—helps a young person see sex in relation to other aspects of life, and emphasizes the importance of self-respect and of a sense of responsibility to himself and others. Infections of the genital system are discussed in this chapter and also in the chapter on communicable disease control.

Marjorie Eastabrooks
Washington Department of Public Instruction

The Prostate Gland, by Herbert R. Kenyon, M.D. New York, Random House, 1950. 194p. $2.95.

This volume presents a fairly complete picture of the prostate gland—its location, functional disorders, infectious diseases, the nature, effect and surgical treatment of urinary obstruction, and the challenge of cancer. The author is a specialist in the treatment of genito-urinary disorders, with medical school and hospital affiliations.

A considerable number of men develop enlargement of the prostate gland, and for most surgery is the only method of relief. Many fear and delay surgery, but advances in techniques and the use of antibiotics have largely reduced mortality. For instance, at Bellevue Hospital in New York City the mortality declined from 60% in the early twenties to 2% in 1948.

The author mentions gonorrheal infection of the prostate and the use of sulfonamide drugs, penicillin and other agents which ordinarily control the infection. In some instances the gonorrheal infection is not entirely eradicated.

Well-written, usefully illustrated with line drawings, this volume should clarify many questions and doubts of the sufferer from prostatic disorders.

Dr. Jacob A. Goldberg
New York Tuberculosis and Health Association

Sex and Religion Today, edited by Simon Doniger. New York, Association Press, 1953. 238p. $3.00.

Dr. Simon Doniger, editor of *Pastoral Psychology*, brings together contributions from a well chosen group of experts. A foundation is laid by a comprehensive and well documented historical survey of attitudes toward sex in the Jewish-Christian movement. The extremes of asceticism and license are repudiated, and sex is seen in relation to personality as a whole, to the family and to social well-being. Several of these writers note that facts of the Kinsey report type are inadequate in that they pay scant attention to psychological, social and especially familial aspects of sex.

Understanding of sex in its full meaning is prerequisite to good sex education and counseling. As children begin their sex understanding at home they need open and companionable relationships with understanding parents. Home training is supplemented in school and church. Society has its constant impact. Guardians of morality need to look for the causes of sexual problems rather than try merely to suppress the effects.

Invaluable for teachers and counselors, this book should be helpful also to parents who wish to gain the values of a religious approach that includes biological, psychological and social factors.

Rev. Leland Foster Wood, Ph.D.

Sexual Adjustment in Marriage, by Henry Olsen, M.D. New York, Holt, 1952. 310p. $6.00.

This book is a translation of a publication by the "doctor in charge (since 1937) of sex hygiene instruction at the Continuation School of the Municipality of Copenhagen." Its 667 numbered sections averaging less than half a page deal with a wide range of facts, much folklore and speenlation about sex and many problems of sexual behavior, of which marital adjustment is only a segment. The treatment of so many matters cannot be reviewed briefly.

In general the vocabulary is often too technical for most readers. Masturbation is characterized as "a symptom—of a lack of character." Premarital relations between engaged couples are directly discouraged but indirectly very nearly condoned. It is stated that 43.5% of all first-born children (presumably in Denmark) are conceived before the wedding. Kinsey's statistics are repeatedly and uncritically used.

The book contains much highly interesting, incidental information and stimulating speculation but is baffling for its lack of documentation. In the judgment of this reviewer it is not well suited to the needs and understanding of the general reader.

Roy E. Dickerson
Cincinnati Social Hygiene Society

Parent and Child, by James H. S. Bossard. Philadelphia, University of Pennsylvania, 1953. 308p. $5.00.

This new book is an interesting and detailed extension via report of research studies of the earlier excellent book, *The Sociology of Child Development.*

The author is most impatient with what he calls attempted shortcuts to the understanding of human behavior in general and of family behavior in particular. He emphasizes that real knowledge and understanding must come from detailed and careful examination of the commonplace aspects of human history.

These minutiae include: family size which best insures optimal family integration and development of the child; most effective age to function as a parent; impacts of class and religion as compared to education; effects upon personality integration of childhood pets and visiting.

The book will interest the teacher, clinician, socially sensitive parent and, we hope, researcher who would do well to consider not only the problems suggested for research but also the comments on methods.

Florence Greenhoe Robbins
Ohio State University

INDEX TO VOLUME 39

W

Y

INDEX TO BOOK AND PAMPHLET REVIEWS

By Author and Title

G

H

I

J

K

L

M

N

O

P

Q

R

S

AMERICAN SOCIAL HYGIENE ASSOCIATION

A Platform for Social Hygiene

UDF

★ For every child . . . education in personal and family living.

★ For high school students . . . preparation for satisfying, responsible maturity.

★ Guidance for all in the right use of sex . . . including training for marriage and parenthood.

★ Coordinated social hygiene services in every community.

★ Protection from VD for everybody . . . all over the world.

★ Wholesome communities . . . for servicemen, for you and me.

★ Workable laws against prostitution and VD . . . vigorously enforced.

ASHA is dedicated to this platform. We invite you to join with us in working toward these goals. They hold out to each individual the opportunity to develop his potentialities without exploitation and with full regard for the rights of others.

AMERICAN SOCIAL HYGIENE ASSOCIATION
1790 BROADWAY • NEW YORK 19, N. Y.

Lightning Source UK Ltd.
Milton Keynes UK
UKHW010601110219
337000UK00006B/428/P

9 780483 120686